16 Years 2025-2010

ICSE

CHAPTERWISE TOPICWISE QUESTION BANK

History & Civics

Class 10

Author
Subhasis Swain

arihant
SUCCESS AND NOTHING LESS

arihant
SUCCESS AND NOTHING LESS

ARIHANT PRAKASHAN
(School Division Series)

卐 ADMINISTRATIVE & PRODUCTION OFFICES

Regd. Office
'Ramchhaya' 4577/15, Agarwal Road, Darya Ganj, New Delhi -110002

Tele: 011- 47630600, 43518550

Head Office
Kalindi, TP Nagar, Meerut (UP) - 250002, Tel: 0121-7156203, 7156204

卐 SALES & SUPPORT OFFICES

Agra, Ahmedabad, Bengaluru, Bareilly, Chennai, Delhi, Guwahati, Hyderabad, Jaipur, Jhansi, Kolkata, Lucknow, Nagpur & Pune.

卐 **PO No :** TXT-XX-XXXXXXX-X-XX

Published By Arihant Publications (India) Ltd.

For further information about the books published by Arihant, log on to www.arihantbooks.com or e-mail at info@arihantbooks.com

卐 **PRICE** ₹245.00

Follow us on

Achieving 99+
Marks in Board Exams

Achieving 99+ marks in board exams is definitely an ambitious goal, but with the right approach and these 7 tips from toppers, you can definitely increase your chances of success!

Here are the 7 Topper Tips to ace your board exams:

1. Master the art of consistency

Consistency builds understanding and confidence, both crucial for excelling in exams.

2. Build a winning study strategy

Create a personalised timetable that prioritises subjects based on your strengths and weaknesses.

3. Befriend the syllabus

Focus on high-weightage topics and prioritise mastering core concepts before moving on to advanced ones.

4. Embrace active learning

Explain concepts to yourself or in study groups to solidify understanding.

5. Conquer the past

Solve Past Years' Papers and Sample Papers under timed conditions to practice time management and understand paper pattern.

6. Seek help, when needed!

Don't hesitate to clarify doubts with teachers, tutors, or study groups. Asking questions strengthens your understanding and prevents confusion.

7. Prioritise well-being

Eat nutritious meals, get enough sleep, have exercise and practice stress management techniques like meditation, to stay calm and focused during exams.

These tips are just a starting point, and you can personalise them to fit your learning style and preferences.

Description of

Newly Added Features

01

The Lok Sabha and The Rajya Sabha

TREND ANALYSIS 3 YEARS

TOPIC **01** Lok Sabha & Rajya Sabha

Types of Questions	2023	2020	2019
1 Mark	2	3	2
2/3 Marks	6	–	–
4 Marks	4	–	–
10 Marks	3	–	–

Average No. of Questions Across all Sets

Trend Analysis

At the start of each chapter, Trend Analysis is given to indicate the types of Questions asked from different topics of the chapter. This feature helps students to know the importance of different topics of the given chapter from exam point of view and helps them to prepare accordingly.

2. Discuss the relationship between the two Houses of the Parliament with reference to the following control over Executive. *(ICSE 2013)*

Other Similar Questions

Or Mention four Administrative or Executive powers of the Union Parliament.

Or Mention four ways in which the Lok Sabha exercises control over the Council of Ministers.

Other Similar Questions

Other Similar Questions are given with selected questions that can be asked in different formats but their answers remain same. This feature help students to identify and answer the question correctly.

2. Discuss the relationshi between the two Houses of

Ans. The Parliament exercises control over the Some of them are

(iii) **Adjournment Motion** To bring matters of urgent public importance, the Parliament can bring Adjournment Motion.

(iv) **Censure Motion** It can bring Censure

Various Administrative or Executive Power of the Union Parliament

- Interpellation
- Vote of No-confidence
- Adjournment Motion
- Censure Motion
- Monetary Control

Heading Boxes

Heading Boxes are given in those questions whose answers are divided into different headings. This feature will help students to remember the answer through headings only.

5. How did Tilak bring a new wave in Indian politics that was distinct from the Early Congressmen? *(ICSE 2013)*

HINT *Dear students, this question simply ask you to explain the contribution of Bal Gangadhar Tilak in Indian freedom struggle.*

Ans. (i) Bal Gangadhar Tilak is known as the 'Father of the Assertive Nationalism'. He was a fearless fighter and had no faith in the methods of prayers and petitions.

Hint

Hint provides a clue to the students about what the question is asking to write in the answer. This feature help students to write the answer correctly in sync with the question.

41. An adult Indian citizen holding an office of profit under the State Government wishes to contest for the election of the Lok Sabha. Is he/she eligible? Give a reason to justify your answer.

Ans. No, he/she is not eligible. According to Constitution, a member of Parliament cannot hold any office of profit under Central or State Government.

Additional Info

Qualification for membership of the Lok Sabha are as follows

- He/She should be an Indian citizen.
- He/She should be at least 25 years of age.
- He/She should not be an insolvent and of unsound mind.

Additional Info

Additional Info is given in selected questions with the purpose to give extra information about the concept asked in the question.

Dream, Believe, Achieve

Insights from ICSE Toppers

"Board exams are way easier than you think. It's easy to score if you study regularly for even an hour. Consistency is key,"

ANONDEE SAHA

ICSE Topper (99.6%)

Before the boards, my school had given all students a month to study and I tried my best to study 8-9 hours every day. I relied on revising the syllabus of each subject at least twice during this period and went through past years' question papers and extra questions that my teachers had sent.

DIVYANSH AGARWAL

ICSE Topper (99.40%)

He dedicated time to solving topic-wise papers from the last 10 years, providing valuable practice before his final revision. A planned approach and schedule help to prepare and cover the syllabus better.

For excelling in the boards I would like to advice students to study regularly from DAY 1. They should refer to previous years, Board question papers and should always have a positive attitude and should be confident. But not overconfident

MUSKAN PATHAN

ICSE Topper (99.4%)

"I studied everything independently, which gave me a better understanding of what topics I needed to improve. I studied only 1.5 to 2 hours daily but stayed consistent and regular,"

MIHIKA SANJANWALA

ICSE Topper (99%)

"I had started preparing, chapter by chapter, right from the beginning of the academic session as we had weekly tests on every topic that was covered in class. However, the hard-core preparation started only in late November 2022 which was about three months prior to the board examination."

Previous Years Papers guide me to a great extent as they helped me understand the scope and area of the questions that could be asked. The specimen papers were extremely helpful as we had undergone a change in examination pattern this year.

NILOTMA SINGH

ICSE Topper (99.6%)

"While my primary schooling in Shanghai (China) taught me to be a global citizen, my higher secondary schooling at Greenwood High (Bannerghatta) elevated my inquisitiveness and curiosity on various subjects,"

"Personally, POMODORO technique, a time-management method based on 25-minute stretches of focused work broken by five-minute breaks, helped me immensely not only to organise myself better but also to cover a vast syllabus with the least fatigue,"

SHIVANI NEELAMRAJU

ICSE Topper (99.40%)

Please Note that all the information is collected from different websites.

Contents

Most Important Topics
from each Chapter

On the basis of analysis of last 4 Years' Board Examination Papers, we have identified Important Topics from each chapter.

History

Chapter Name	Important Topics	Weightage in Last 4 Years' Boards			
		2025	2024	2023	2020
The First War of Independence and Growth of Nationalism	First War of Independence	11M	13M	35M	10M
	Growth of Nationalism	11M	3M	5M	–
The Early Nationalists and Assertive Nationalism	Early Nationalists	5M	1M	15M	3M
	Assertive Nationalists	1M	16M	13M	4M
The Partition of Bengal & Formation of Muslim League	Partition of Bengal	–	–	1M	3M
	Formation of Muslim league	2M	–	4M	–
The Lucknow Pact	Lucknow Pact	–	–	1M	–
Mahatma Gandhi and The National Movement	Mahatma Gandhi	–	–	–	–
	Movements of Mahatma Gandhi	10M	4M	27M	13M
The Forward Bloc, The INA, Independence and Partition of India	Forward Bloc and INA	3M	2M	10M	3M
	Independence & Partition	–	10M	14M	–
The First World War and The Rise of Dictatorships	First World War	2M	10M	11M	3M
	Rise of Dictatorships	1M	1M	1M	–
The Second World War	Second World War	10M	3M	11M	9M
	Cold War	–	–	–	–
United Nations Organisation and Major Agencies	United Nations & its Organs	12M	–	20M	3M
	Main Agencies of UN	–	10M	10M	–
Non-Aligned Movement	Non-Aligned Movement	2M	1M	2M	4M

Civics

Chapter Name	Important Topics	Weightage in Last 4 Years' Boards			
		2025	2024	2023	2020
The Lok Sabha and The Rajya Sabha	Lok Sabha & Rajya Sabha	14M	–	66M	3M
	Powers & Functions of Parliament	–	13M	24M	1M
The President and The Vice-President	President of India	8M	1M	46M	3M
	Vice-President of India	3M	–	4M	1M
The Prime Minister and The Council of Ministers	The Prime Minister	2M	–	–	1M
	Council of Ministers	–	10M	2M	1M
The Supreme Court	Supreme Court	3M	10M	12M	11M
The High Courts and The Subordinate Courts	High Court	7M	4M	12M	–
	Subordinate Courts and Lok Adalat	3M	2M	4M	–

Latest Syllabus

History & Civics Class X

SECTION A : CIVICS

1. The Union Legislature

Definition of the federal setup.

(i) Lok Sabha - term, composition, qualifications for membership. Parliamentary procedures: a brief idea of sessions, quorum, question hour, adjournment and no-confidence motion.

Speaker – election and any four functions.

(ii) Rajya Sabha – composition, qualifications for membership, election, term, Presiding Officer.

Powers and functions of Union Parliament – (legislative, financial, amendment of the Constitution, control over executive). Exclusive powers of the two Houses.

2. The Union Executive

(a) **The President:**

Qualifications for election, composition of Electoral College, reason for indirect election, term of office, procedure for impeachment.

Powers : executive, legislative, discretionary and emergency (only the three types of emergencies and circumstances leading to proclamation of these emergencies).

(b) **The Vice-President:**

Qualifications for election, term of office and powers.

(c) **Prime Minister and Council of Ministers:**

Appointment, formation of Council of Ministers, three categories of the Council of Ministers, tenure, functions - policy making, administrative and legislative. Position and powers of the Prime Minister (with reference to the President, the Parliament and role as the Leader of the Nation); Collective and individual responsibility of the members of the Cabinet. Distinction between the Council of Ministers and the Cabinet.

3. The Judiciary

(a) **The Supreme Court:**

Composition, qualifications of judges, appointment, independence of judiciary from the control of executive and legislature; Jurisdiction and functions: Original, Appellate, Advisory, Revisory, Judicial Review and Court of Record. Enforcement of Fundamental Rights and Writs.

(b) **The High Courts:**

Composition, qualifications of judges, appointment; Jurisdiction and functions: Original and Appellate.

(c) **Subordinate Courts:**

Distinction between Court of the District Judge and Sessions Court.

Lok Adalats: meaning and advantages.

SECTION B : HISTORY

1. The Indian National Movement (1857 - 1917)

(a) **The First War of Independence, 1857**

Only the causes (political, socio-religious, economic and military) and consequences (only end of the company's rule and changes introduced in administration). The events, however, need to be mentioned in order to maintain continuity and for a more comprehensive understanding.

(b) Factors leading to the growth of Nationalism

Repressive policies of Lord Lytton and Ilbert Bill Controversy; socio-religious reform movements (any two contributions of Raja Rammohan Roy and Jyotiba Phule) and role of the Press.

Foundation of the Indian National Congress - The year of formation and its founder - the first two sessions and their Presidents should be mentioned. Immediate objectives of the Indian National Congress.

(c) First Phase of the Indian National Movement (1885-1907)

Methods of struggle of the Early Nationalists. Any two contributions of Dadabhai Naoroji, Surendranath Banerjee and Gopal Krishna Gokhale.

Second Phase of the Indian National Movement (1905-1916) - Brief mention of the causes of the Partition of Bengal - Lord Curzon's view and the view of the Nationalists. Objectives and methods of struggle of the Assertive Nationalists. Any two contributions of Bal Gangadhar Tilak, Bipin Chandra Pal and Lala Lajpat Rai. The difference between the objectives and methods of the Assertive and early Nationalists.

The Muslim League : Year of formation, the first session and the name of the President. The objectives of the Muslim League.

Brief mention of the significance of the Lucknow Pact - 1916.

2. Mass Phase of the National Movement (1915-1947)

(a) Mahatma Gandhi - Non-Cooperation Movement : causes (Khilafat Movement, Rowlatt Act, Jallianwala Bagh Tragedy), programme and suspension – Chauri Chaura incident and impact of the Movement; the Civil Disobedience Movement: causes (reaction to the Simon Commission, Declaration of Poorna Swaraj at the Lahore Session of 1929), Dandi March, programme and impact of the Movement, Gandhi-Irwin Pact and the Second Round Table Conference; the Quit India Movement: causes (failure of the Cripps Mission, Japanese threat), Quit India Resolution and the significance of the Movement.

(b) Forward Bloc (objectives) and INA (the name of the founder; objectives and any two achievements; Contribution of Subhas Chandra Bose.

(c) Independence and Partition of India – Mountbatten Plan (clauses and its acceptance); and the Indian Independence Act of 1947 (clauses only).

3. The Contemporary World

(a) The First World War

Causes (Nationalism and Imperialism, division of Europe and Sarajevo crisis) and Results (Treaty of Versailles, objectives of the League of Nations).

(b) Rise of Dictatorships

Causes for the rise of Fascism in Italy and the rise of Nazism in Germany. Similarities between Mussolini's Fascist and Hitler's Nazi ideologies.

(c) The Second World War

Causes (Dissatisfaction with the Treaty of Versailles, Rise of Fascism and Nazism, Japanese invasion of China, Failure of League of Nations and Hitler's invasion of Poland). Consequences (brief mention of defeat of Axis Powers, formation of the United Nations and Cold War between the two power blocs).

(d) United Nations

(i) The objectives of the U.N.
The composition and any four functions of the General Assembly, the Security Council, and the International Court of Justice.

(ii) Major agencies of the United Nations: UNICEF, WHO and UNESCO - any four functions only.

(e) Non-Aligned Movement (NAM)

Brief meaning; objectives; Names of the architects of NAM (Nehru, Nasser and Tito).

Analysis of Pupil Performance: ICSE History & Civics

Topics found difficult/confusing by candidates

The document 'Analysis of Pupils' Performance, 2020' in ICSE Class 10 Examination, is prepared by Research Development and Consultancy Division (RDCD) of the Council for the Indian School Certificate Examination (CISCE).

The purpose of this document is to provide feedback to schools in terms of strengths and weaknesses of the candidates in handling the examination.

TOPICS FOUND DIFFICULT BY STUDENTS

- Session and Quorum.
- Body that decides the major policies of the Government.
- Differences between the Cabinet Ministers and the Council of Ministers.
- Difference between methods adopted by the early nationalists and the aggressive nationalists.
- Objectives of the I.N.A and the Forward Bloc.
- Meaning of imperialism and how it was one of the main causes for the World War I.
- Legislative powers of the Union Parliament.
- Exclusive powers of the Lok Sabha.
- The executive and the legislative powers of the President.
- The power of Judicial Review and the Revisory Power of the Supreme Court.
- Clauses of Mountbatten Plan and the Indian Independence Act 1947.
- Treaty of Versailles as a cause of World War II.

SUGGESTIONS FOR STUDENTS

- Remember History is based on chronology of events and dates.
- Plan your notes in proper chronological order to remember the correct sequence of events to diminish the probability of getting confused.
- Mark and underline the key words and key points in your textbook/s for retention of relevant points and to write the answers specifically to questions.
- Do not miss regular tests and after assessment, take the help of your teacher to resolve your problems.
- Always appear in school assessment tests to improve learning and to be familiar with the pattern of questions.
- Follow the Scope of Syllabus and adjust your learning accordingly.

01

The Lok Sabha and The Rajya Sabha

TREND ANALYSIS 3 YEARS

Topic	Types of Questions	2023	2020	2019
TOPIC 01 Lok Sabha & Rajya Sabha	1 Mark	2	3	2
	2/3 Marks	6	–	–
	4 Marks	4	–	–
	10 Marks	3	–	–
TOPIC 02 Powers & Functions of Parliament	1 Mark	4	1	1
	2/3 Marks	–	–	–
	4 Marks	–	–	–
	10 Marks	2	–	–

Average No. of Questions Across all Sets

The Union Legislature of India comprises the President and the two Houses of Parliament *i.e.,* **the Lok Sabha** (Lower House) and **the Rajya Sabha** (Upper House).

The Lok Sabha is also referred as the House of the People and the Rajya Sabha is called the Council of States. Parliament is the body of people's representatives which has supreme power of governance in a Parliamentary form of democracy.

Federal Set-up in India

In a federal system of government, there is an association of States, in which all the administrative powers are divided between the Central and the State Governments by the Constitution. India has opted for a federal system of government. Both the Centre and the States draw their authority from the same Constitution.

Some important points about the federal set-up are as follows

- India is a large country and it is not possible in the Indian federal system for the any State to break away as a separate unit.
- India is a country of diversity. A federal set-up is of utmost importance if India is to be saved from separatist forces.
- There is a division of legislative and administrative powers between the Union and the State Governments and none of them can violate the limitations imposed by the Constitution.
- The States have been given the right to participate in the functioning of the government.

- The Supreme Court stands at the top of the Judiciary to safeguard the distribution of powers and to prevent any action against the provisions of the Constitution.
- The Constitution of India has made provisions for the distribution of revenues between the Centre and the States.

The Union Legislature in India

Lok Sabha

Election of Members

- The members of the Lok Sabha are directly elected by the people of India. Direct elections are based on **Universal Adult Franchise** as given in the Constitution.
- All adult citizens of India have the right to vote. Earlier, this right was granted at the age of 21. Now, the age limit is 18 (By 61st Amendment Act, 1989).

Term

- The Constitution provides a fixed term of **5 years** for the Lok Sabha. However, it can be dissolved earlier by the President or can be extended for one year at a time during the proclamation of an emergency by the Parliament.
- This extension cannot continue beyond a period of **six months** after the emergency has ceased to operate.

Composition

- The maximum strength of the Lok Sabha is fixed **at 552**. Out of this, 530 members are to be the representatives of the States, 20 members are to be the representatives of the Union Territories and 2 members are to be nominated by the President from the Anglo-Indian community.
- However, the nomination of Anglo-Indian community to Lok Sabha and certain State Assemblies is not extended further as per the 104th Constitutional Amendment Act passed in January 2020.
- At present, the Lok Sabha has 543 members. Of these, 530 members represent the States, 13 members represent the Union Territories.

Qualifications

- The Constitution mentions the qualifications for the membership of the Lok Sabha.

  The conditions for the citizens are that, he/she

  (i) should be an Indian citizen.
  (ii) should be at least 25 years of age.
  (iii) should not hold any office of profit under the government.
  (iv) should not be of unsound mind.
  (v) should have his/her name in the electoral rolls in some part of the country.
  (vi) should not be an insolvent or a proclaimed criminal.
- A person shall be disqualified if, at any point of time, he/she does not fulfil any of the qualifications for being a member of Parliament. Nobody can be a member of both the Houses of Parliament at the same time.

Speaker of the Lok Sabha

The presiding officer of the Lok Sabha is the Speaker. He/She has wide powers to maintain discipline in the House. With respect to the discharge of powers and functions, the Speaker is not answerable to anyone except to the House.

Election of the Speaker

The Speaker of the Lok Sabha is elected from amongst its members soon after the newly elected House meets for the first time.

Role of the Speaker

The main role of the Speaker includes the following duties:

(i) He/She presides over the meetings of the House.
(ii) He/She interprets the rules of procedure of the House.
(iii) He/She signs all the Bills passed by the House before they are sent to the Rajya Sabha or to the President for approval.
(iv) He/She decides whether a Bill is a **Money Bill** or not.
(v) He/She decides the question of disqualification of a member of the Lok Sabha.

Functions of the Speaker

The main functions of the Speaker are as follows :

Administrative Functions

(i) He/She receives all petitions and documents in the House.
(ii) He/She communicates the decisions of the House to the concerned authorities.
(iii) He/She regulates the admission of visitors and press correspondents to the galleries of the House.

Disciplinary Functions

(i) He/She is responsible for maintaining order in the House.
(ii) He/She decides whether there is a case for a matter relating to a breach of privilege or contempt of the House.

(iii) The Speaker is the **ex-officio** Chairperson of some of the committees of the House.

(iv) He/She also appoints the Chairman of all the other committees.

(v) He/She issues directions to the Chairman of these committes about all matters relating to their working and the procedure to be followed.

(vi) He/She presides over the joint sessions of Parliament.

(vii) He/She also nominates personnel for Parliamentary delegations to other countries.

Exclusive or Special Powers of the Lok Sabha

- A Money Bill can be introduced only in the Lok Sabha.
- The **Council of Ministers** is collectively responsible only to the Lok Sabha.
- Only the Lok Sabha can introduce a **motion of no-confidence** against the government.
- Only the Lok Sabha has the power to pass a resolution for the discontinuance of the national emergency.
- The Speaker of the Lok Sabha presides over the joint sitting of the Houses.

Rajya Sabha

Composition

The **maximum strength** of the Rajya Sabha is fixed at 250, out of which, 238 are to be the representatives of the States and Union Territories (elected indirectly) and 12 are nominated by the President.

At present, the Rajya Sabha has 245 members. Of these, 233 members represent the States and Union Territories and 12 members are nominated by the President.

Qualifications

Qualification and disqualification for membership of the Rajya Sabha are same as those for membership of the Lok Sabha except for the minimum age, which is 30 years in the case of Rajya Sabha.

Election of Members

The elected members of the Rajya Sabha are elected indirectly by the members of the State Legislative Assemblies with the system of proportional representation by means of a **Single Transferable Vote.**

Term

The Rajya Sabha is a permanent House. Each member is elected for a period of 6 years and 1/3rd of the total members retire after every 2 years. The Vice-President is the ex-officio Chairman of the Rajya Sabha.

Like the Speaker in the Lok Sabha, the Chairman also cannot vote in the first instance in the Rajya Sabha. He can only cast a vote in case of an equality of votes.

Exclusive Powers of the Rajya Sabha

- Under Article 67 of the Constitution, a resolution seeking the removal of the Vice-President can originate only in the Rajya Sabha. After the Rajya Sabha passes such a resolution by a majority of the members of the House, it goes for approval to the Lok Sabha.
- A resolution seeking to legislate on any subject of the State List can only originate in the Rajya Sabha, if it thinks that it is necessary or expedient in the national interest (Article. 249).
- Any resolution seeking creation of one or more All India Services can only be initiated in the Rajya Sabha. Only after the Rajya Sabha passes a resolution to this effect by a special majority, i.e. two-thirds of the members present and voting, can the Parliament legislate on this.
- Under the Constitution, the President is empowered to declare **national emergency** (Article 352), which normally has to be approved by both Houses.

Presiding Officers

The Constitution stipulates (specify) that the **Vice-President of India** is the ex-officio Chairman of the Rajya Sabha. He presides over its meetings. The Chairman may be removed only if he/she is removed from the office of the Vice-President. Rajya Sabha also has a Deputy Chairman which is elected from its members.

Relationship between the Two Houses

Both the Houses enjoy equal status over matters related to the election of the President and Vice-President. However, the Lok Sabha due to its greater strength, has a greater say in the election. In the impeachment process of either of these incumbents, both the Houses have absolutely equal powers.

Powers and Functions of the Union Parliament

The two Houses of Parliament enjoy equal power and status in all spheres except in financial matters and in terms of the responsibility of the Council of Ministers, which are in the domain of the Lok Sabha. The powers and functions of the Parliament are multidisciplinary *i.e.,* **Legislative, Financial, Executive** and **Constitutional.**

Legislative Powers

- Both the Houses have equal legislative powers in matters pertaining to the **Union List, Concurrent List, Residuary List** as well as ordinance related powers.
- Parliament controls the Council of Ministers in various ways. Some of them are Question Hour, Vote of No-confidence, Adjournment Motion, Censure Motion, etc.
- There are certain matters/subjects, in which the Rajya Sabha enjoys exclusive rights, *e.g.,* under Article 249, the Rajya Sabha, by a resolution adopted by 2/3rd majority, can empower the Parliament to make laws with respect to a matter in the State List.
- Parliament acquires the power to legislate with respect to matters in the State List while a proclamation of national emergency is in operation. When the Lok Sabha is dissolved, the Rajya Sabha becomes the sole **de jure** Parliament.

Financial Powers

- There are certain provisions which are under the exclusive domain of the Lok Sabha. *e.g.,* No-confidence Motion and Money Bill can only be introduced in the Lok Sabha. In case of a deadlock over a Bill other than the Money Bill, the will of Lok Sabha prevails in the joint sitting, because of greater number (*i.e.,* 543 members).
- The Constitution recognises the superiority of Lok Sabha over the Rajya Sabha as the Lok Sabha represents the people directly. On legislative matters pertaining to **Ordinary Bills**, they can originate in either House. In case of a deadlock, a joint sitting is preferred wherein the opinion of the Lok Sabha prevails.
- In case of Money Bills, Rajya Sabha cannot reject or amend them by virtue of its own powers. It must return the Money Bill within a stipulated period of 14 days to the Lok Sabha with its recommendation. It depends upon the Lok Sabha whether to accept or reject the recommendation of the Rajya Sabha.

Executive Power

The Council of Ministers are collectively responsible to the Lok Sabha. The Ministers remain in office as long as they enjoy the confidence of a majority of members of the Lok Sabha. The devices through which Parliament exercises control over the Executive are as follows

(a) **Right of Interpellation** This is a valuable device against the slackness of the government, comprising of the Question Hour. The members can ask questions to the government, which is answerable about its policies and performance.

(b) **Adjournment Motion** It is aimed at censuring the acts of omission and commission of the ministers.

(c) **Monetary Controls** A cut motion may be moved during the budget session. If passed, it ensures that the money is spent in accordance with the decision of Parliament.

Judicial Powers

- Parliament can remove the judges of both the High Courts and the Supreme Court. It can also remove the Election Commissioner (EC), Comptroller and the Auditor-General of India (CAG) etc.
- The Parliament also has the right to remove the President from office through the procedure of impeachment.
- It can also punish a person for obstructing the work of Parliament or for showing any sort of disrespect towards any House.

Electoral Powers

The Parliament along with the State Legislatures elects the President. Parliament by itself elects India's Vice-President as well.

Power to Amend the Constitution

The procedure for amending the Constitution is laid down in Article 368.

A Bill can be introduced in either House of Parliament to amend the Constitution. If passed by an actual 2/3rd majority of both the Houses, the President must give his assent to the Bill. Then the Constitution stands amended.

Parliamentary Procedures

Sessions Generally the Parliament meets thrice a year. The maximum gap between two sessions of Parliament cannot be more than 6 months. The President may call the meeting more often and when required. Normally, there are three Sessions in a year *i.e.,* The **Budget Session, Monsoon Session** and **Winter Session**.

Quorum It means the minimum number of members required to be present in order to enable conduct of the business of the House. It is fixed at **1/10th** of the total membership of each House.

Question Hour The first hour on every working day of the House is the Question Hour, wherein a member of the House may ask questions from the government on matters of public interest. There are three types of questions *i.e.,* Starred, Unstarred and Short Notice questions.

Zero Hour During Zero Hour (From 12 o'clock to lunch), the members raise all types of questions without any permission or prior notice.

A formal proposal made by a member stating that the House should take up some particular matter which is of public importance is called a **Motion.**

Adjournment Motion It is laid to discuss a matter of urgent public importance. Such a motion leads to the interruption of the normal business of the House.

No-confidence Motion It is a proposal expressing lack of confidence in the ministry. The motion is moved by the opposition and admitted when a minimum of 50 members support it. If passed, the government has to resign.

PYQs Previous Years Questions

1 Mark Questions

Multiple Choice Questions

1. An ordinance has be approved by the Parliament within ....weeks. *(ICSE 2023)*

(a) two (b) three
(c) six (d) eight

Ans. (*c*) six

2. A major natural calamity has place and the opposition wants the House to lay aside all other business and take up this matter urgent importance. *(ICSE 2023)*

Which motion should the House move to allow this ?

(a) Adjournment Motion
(b) No-confidence Motion
(c) Confidence Motion
(d) Censure Motion

Ans. (*a*) Adjournment Motion

3. The........ has the power to summon the Houses of Parliament. *(ICSE 2023)*

(a) Speaker (b) President
(c) Vice-President (d) Chief Justice of India

Ans. (*b*) President

4. The interval between two sessions of the Parliament should not be more than .... *(ICSE Specimen 2023)*

(a) two months (b) three months
(c) four months (d) six months

Ans. (*d*) six months

5. The maximum composition of the Lok Sabha is *(ICSE Specimen 2023)*

(a) 530 (b) 540
(c) 550 (d) 556

Ans. (*c*) 550

6.

Lok Sabha member term	5 years
Rajya Sabha member term	?

(ICSE Specimen 2023)

(a) 1 year (b) 2 years (c) 4 years (d) 6 years

Ans. (*d*) 6 years

7. A house has 350 members on a given day, 25 members are present. For which of the following reasons does the Speaker adjourn the session for the day? *(ICSE Specimen 2023)*

(a) Indiscipline in the House
(b) Lack of quorum
(c) Business of the day is over
(d) There are no questions to admit

Ans. (*b*) Lack of quorum

8. The .... is considered to be the leader of the Lok Sabha. *(ICSE Specimen Semester II 2022)*

(a) President (b) Speaker
(c) Vice-President (d) Prime Minister

Ans. (*d*) Prime Minister

9. If the strength of the House is 350 members, the quorum will be .... *(ICSE Specimen Semester I 2021)*

(a) 36 members (b) 40 members
(c) 60 members (d) 35 members

Ans. (*d*) 35 members

10.

Lok Sabha	550
Rajya Sabha	?

(ICSE Specimen Semester I 2021)

(a) 250 (b) 545 (c) 500 (d) 350

Ans. (*a*) 250

11. Residuary power refers to the power to make laws on subjects which are in the .... ***(ICSE Specimen Semester I 2021)***

(a) Union List (b) State List
(c) Concurrent List (d) Not part of these three lists

Ans. (*a*) Union List

12. Who determines the salaries and allowances of MPs and Ministers? ***(ICSE Specimen Semester I 2021)***

(a) The President (b)The Parliament
(c) The Chairman of UPSC (d) The Finance Minister

Ans. (*b*) The Parliament

13. Which of the following procedures authorises the Executive to draw funds from the Consolidated Fund until the Budget is passed by the Parliament? ***(ICSE Specimen Semester I 2021)***

(a) Vote on Account (b) Veto
(c) Prorogation (d) Supplementary Grants

Ans. (*a*) Vote on Account

14. Who elect the members of the Rajya Sabha? ***(ICSE Specimen Semester I 2021)***

(a) The members of the Lok Sabha
(b) The members of the Vidhan Sabha
(c) The members of the Vidhan Parishad
(d) The citizens of India

Ans. (*b*) The members of the Vidhan Sabha

15. Complete the given analogy.
Lok Sabha : Speaker :: Rajya Sabha : ? ***(ICSE Specimen Semester I 2021)***

(a) Vice-President (b) Prime Minister
(c) President (d) Chief Justice of India

Ans. (*a*) Vice-President

16. When can the Parliament not legislate on subjects included in the State List? ***(ICSE Specimen Semester I 2021)***

(a) When the State is ruled by a coalition
(b) During the proclamation of an emergency
(c) When the Rajya Sabha passes a resolution by two-thirds majority
(d) When two or more States are of the opinion the Parliament should legislate on the subject.

Ans. (*c*) When the Rajya Sabha passes a resolution by two-thirds majority

17. Which of these are not exclusive powers of the Lok Sabha? ***(ICSE Specimen Semester I 2021)***

(a) Introduction of a Money Bill
(b) Passing of an Adjournment Motion
(c) Passing of the No-confidence motion
(d) Amendment of the Constitution

Ans. (*d*) Amendment of the Constitution

18. Assuming the powers of the State which is under an emergency, is a .... power of the Parliament. ***(ICSE Specimen Semester I 2021)***

(a) Financial (b) Emergency
(c) Legislative (d) Executive

Ans. (*c*) Legislative

19. Who elect the Speaker of the Lok Sabha? ***(ICSE Specimen Semester I 2021)***

(a) The President
(b) Only the members of the ruling party
(c) The Chairman of the Rajya Sabha
(d) The members of the Lok Sabha

Ans. (*d*) The members of the Lok Sabha

20. The creation of a new All India Services is an exclusive power of the .... ***(ICSE Specimen Semester I 2021)***

(a) President (b) Lok Sabha
(c) Rajya Sabha (d) Supreme Court

Ans. (*c*) Rajya Sabha

21. The Lok Sabha session which is conducted in the months of November and December is the .... ***(ICSE Semester I 2021)***

(a) Summer Session (b) Monsoon Session
(c) Winter Session (d) Budget Session

Ans. (*c*) Winter Session

22. Which of these statements regarding the Speaker is false? ***(ICSE Semester I 2021)***

(a) He/She is the presiding officer of the Lok Sabha.
(b) Elected from among the members of the Lok Sabha.
(c) Elected when the newly elected house meets for the first time.
(d) The members of both the Houses vote to choose the Speaker.

Ans. (*d*) The members of both the Houses vote to choose the Speaker.

23. Which of these does not refer to the control of the Parliament over the Executive? ***(ICSE Semester I 2021)***

(a) No-confidence Motion
(b) Amendment of Constitution
(c) Monetary cuts
(d) Rejection of a Government Bill

Ans. (*b*) Amendment of Constitution

24. Which of the following statements about Ordinances is false? *(ICSE Semester I 2021)*
(a) Promulgated by the President.
(b) Issued when the Parliament is not in session.
(c) Has to be approved within six months from the re-assembly of the Parliament.
(d) Has to be approved by both the Houses of the Parliament.

Ans. (*c*) Has to be approved within six months from the re-assembly of the Parliament.

25. The right of the members to .... is known as interpellation. *(ICSE Semester I 2021)*
(a) ask questions
(b) introduce motions
(c) adjourn the house
(d) interrupt the proceedings

Ans. (*a*) ask questions

26. Which of these is not a qualification required to be a member of the Rajya Sabha? *(ICSE Semester I 2021)*
(a) Should be a citizen of India.
(b) Should not be an insolvent.
(c) Should be at least 30 years of age.
(d) Should be a graduate from any university in India.

Ans. (*d*) Should be a graduate from any university in India.

27. The Rajya Sabha is called a Permanent House because 1/3 members retire every .... *(ICSE Semester I 2021)*
(a) two years (b) one year
(c) three years (d) six years

Ans. (*a*) two years

28. Which of these is considered to be an exclusive power of the Rajya Sabha? *(ICSE Semester I 2021)*
(a) It can approve an Ordinary Bill.
(b) It can make amendments to the Constitution.
(c) It can empower the Parliament to make laws on the State List.
(d) It can make laws on subjects in the Union List.

Ans. (*c*) It can empower the Parliament to make laws on the State List.

29. Complete the given analogy.
Election of Lok Sabha member : Citizens of India
Election of Rajya Sabha member : ? *(ICSE Semester I 2021)*
(a) Members of the Legislative Assembly
(b) Members of the Legislative Council
(c) Members of the Lok Sabha
(d) Members of the Cabinet

Ans. (*a*) Members of the Legislative Assembly

30. The ...... motion allows the house to take up a definite matter of urgent importance. *(ICSE Semester I 2021)*
(a) No-confidence (b) Adjournment
(c) Censure (d) Prorogation

Ans. (*b*) Adjournment

31. What is the quorum of the Indian Parliament?
(a) 1/3 (b) 1/2 *ICSE Semester I 2021)*
(c) 1/10 (d) 1/4

Ans. (*c*) 1/10

32. In case of a conflict between the Centre and the State with reference to a subject in the Concurrent List .... *(ICSE Semester I 2021)*
(a) each follow their own law
(b) the State law will prevail
(c) the President is empowered to decide
(d) the Union law will prevail

Ans. (*d*) the Union law will prevail

33. Under what circumstances may the term of the Lok Sabha be extended by one year at a time?
(a) When the government resigns. *(ICSE Semester I 2021)*
(b) Proclamation of a national emergency.
(c) Economic instability.
(d) Rajya Sabha declares by ¼ majority.

Ans. (*b*) Proclamation of a national emergency.

Very Short Answer Questions

1. Name the two Houses of the Indian Parliament. *(ICSE 2020, 2015)*

Ans. The two Houses of the Indian Parliament are
(i) The Lok Sabha (ii) The Rajya Sabha

2. What is meant by the term 'Session'? *(ICSE 2020)*

Ans. A session simply means that the Parliament is sitting and it is functioning and transacting its business.

3. How is the Speaker of the Lok Sabha elected? *(ICSE 2020, ICSE Specimen 2018, 2013, 2000)*

Ans. The Speaker of the Lok Sabha is elected from its own members.

4. What is the term of office of a Rajya Sabha member? *(ICSE 2020)*

Ans. The term of office of a Rajya Sabha member is 6 years.

5. What is the normal term of office of the Lok Sabha? *(ICSE 2019, 2016, 2000)*

Ans. The Constitution provides a fixed and normal term of 5 years for the office of Lok Sabha.

6. State the meaning of the term Question Hour. *(ICSE 2019, 2007)*

Ans. In the context of Parliamentary procedures in India, Question Hour represents the first hour of every working day of the House in which the members can ask questions from the government on matters of public interest.

7. Name the presiding officer of the Lok Sabha. *(ICSE 2019)*

Ans. The presiding officer of the Lok Sabha is the Speaker. He/She has wide powers to maintain discipline in the House. With respect to the discharge of powers and functions, the Speaker is not answerable to anyone except to the House.

8. Name the two types of authority in a federal set-up in India. *(ICSE Specimen 2018, 2013)*

Ans. Two types of authority in a federal set-up in India are-Union at the centre and the States at the periphery.

9. What is the term of the 'Lok Sabha'? *(ICSE Specimen 2018)*

Ans. The normal term of the Lok Sabha is 5 years, but it may be dissolved earlier by the President.

10. Who presides over the sessions of the Rajya Sabha in the absence of its Chairman? *(ICSE Specimen 2018)*

Ans. The Deputy Chairman, who is elected from amongst the House's members, takes care of the day-to-day matters of the House in the absence of the Chairman.

11. Name the Bill that cannot originate in the Rajya Sabha. *(ICSE 2018, 2012, 2006)*

Ans. A Money Bill which deals with the imposition or abolition of tax or borrowing of money by the Government of India cannot originate in the Rajya Sabha. It can only be introduced in the Lok Sabha.

12. What is meant by the term 'quorum'? *(ICSE 2018, 2009, 2005)*

Ans. Quorum refers to the required number of members needed to be present in either of the Houses of Parliament for passing a Bill. At present, the quorum is 10% of the total membership of each House.

13. What is the maximum gap allowed between the two Parliamentary sessions? *(ICSE 2018, 2007)*

Ans. The maximum gap allowed between the two Parliamentary sessions should not be more than six months.

14. How are members to the Lok Sabha elected? *(ICSE Specimen 2017)*

Ans. The members to the Lok Sabha are elected directly by the people of India.

15. Mention any two electoral functions of the Union Parliament. *(ICSE Specimen 2017)*

Ans. Two electoral functions of the Union Parliament are as follow

(a) It, along with the State Legislatures, elects the President of India.

(b) The Vice-President of India is also elected by them.

16. Mention two provisions of the Constitution, which clearly establish the supremacy of the Lok Sabha with regard to the Money Bill. *(ICSE Specimen 2017)*

Ans. Two provisions of the Constitution are as follow

(a) The Rajya Sabha does not have the power to reject the Money Bill, nor can it amend the same.

(b) The ultimate authority to either pass or reject it, lies with the Lok Sabha.

17. State any one federal feature of the Indian Constitution. *(ICSE 2017)*

Ans. The Constitution of India has made provisions for the distribution of revenues between the Centre and the States. It is one of the federal features of the Indian Constitution.

18. How are the Rajya Sabha members elected? *(ICSE 2017)*

Ans. The members of the Rajya Sabha are elected by the Members of Legislative Assemblies on the basis of proportional representation with a 'Single Transferable Vote'.

19. Who presides over the joint session of the two Houses of Parliament? *(ICSE 2017)*

Ans. The Speaker of the Lok Sabha presides over the joint session of Parliament.

20. When can the Speaker of the Lok Sabha cast his vote? *(ICSE 2017)*

Ans. The Speaker of the Lok Sabha does not cast his vote in the House except when there are equal votes on both sides, i.e., the treasury benches and the opposition.

21. How long can the Rajya Sabha retain the Money Bill sent by the Lok Sabha? *(ICSE 2017)*

Ans. The Rajya Sabha can retain the Money Bill sent by the Lok Sabha only for 14 days.

22. What is meant by 'Residuary Powers' of the Parliament? *(ICSE 2016)*

Ans. 'Residuary Powers' of Parliament are exclusive powers to make any law with respect to any matter which is not enumerated in the Concurrent list or State List.

23. State any one subject wherein the Lok Sabha and the Rajya Sabha enjoy co-equal powers in legislation of laws. *(ICSE 2016)*

Ans. Introduction and passage of a Constitutional Amendment Bill is the subject wherein the Lok Sabha and the Rajya Sabha enjoy co-equal powers in legislation of laws.

24. What is the required quorum to hold the meetings of the Lok Sabha? *(ICSE 2015)*

Ans. The required quorum to hold the meetings of the Lok Sabha is one-tenth of the total members.

25. Mention one provision of the Constitution which clearly establishes the supremacy of the Lok Sabha with regard to Money Bills. *(ICSE 2015)*

Ans. Money Bill can be introduced only in the Lok Sabha and not in the Rajya Sabha.

26. Why is the Rajya Sabha called a 'Permanent House'? *(ICSE 2014)*

Ans. Rajya Sabha is called a 'Permanent House' because it is not subject to dissolution, 1/3 rd of its members retire every two years and are replaced by new members.

27. State the minimum number of times the Lok Sabha must meet in a year. *(ICSE 2014)*

Ans. The Lok Sabha should meet at least twice a year. According to Constitutional Provisions, the interval between two consecutive sessions cannot be more than 6 months.

28. Who is the Chairman of the Rajya Sabha? *(ICSE 2014)*

Or Who is the ex-officio Chairperson of the Rajya Sabha? *(ICSE 2006)*

Ans. Vice-President of India is the ex-officio Chairman of the Rajya Sabha.

29. What is meant by the term Universal Adult Franchise? *(ICSE 2013, 2008)*

Ans. Universal Adult Franchise means that, every person above the age of 18 years is entitled to vote and is not to be disqualified on the basis of caste, creed, religion or sex and gender.

30. When can the Vice-President cast a vote in the Rajya Sabha? *(ICSE 2013)*

Ans. The Vice-President has the right to vote only in the case of equality of votes *i.e.,* tie or deadlock. The vote of the Vice-President is a tie-breaking vote.

31. Name the law-making body of the Union Government. *(ICSE 2012)*

Ans. The Parliament is the authorised law-making body of the Union Government.

32. What is the difference in the term of office between the Lok Sabha and the Rajya Sabha? *(ICSE 2012)*

Ans. The term of office of the Lok Sabha is 5 years, whereas that of the Rajya Sabha is 6 years.

Note However, the term of Lok Sabha can be extended by 1 year during National Emergency by the Parliament.

33. Name the main constituents of the Indian Parliament. *(ICSE 2012)*

Ans. There are three main constituents of the Indian Parliament are

(i) The President of India

(ii) The Lok Sabha

(iii) The Rajya Sabha

34. A Legislative Assembly has 230 members. How many members need to be present in order to enable the House to transact its business? *(ICSE 2011)*

Ans. The minimum number of members required to be present in order to enable the House to transact its business is termed as 'Quorum', which is 1/10th of the total strength. In the case of an Assembly having the above strength, 23 members would need to be present.

35. Mention any one situation when both the Houses of Parliament meet for joint sessions. *(ICSE 2010)*

Ans. Whenever the two Houses differ on an issue (Bill) other than those related to financial matters, the President calls for a joint sitting of both the Houses to discuss and resolve the deadlock.

36. Mr Gurudev was nominated by the President to the Rajya Sabha. Mention any one criterion on which the President would have nominated him. *(ICSE 2010)*

Ans. The President nominates 12 members to the Rajya Sabha from among persons having special knowledge or practical experience in matters such as literature, science, art and social science. Mr Gurudev must have been selected on the above criterion.

37. What happens to the ruling government when a Vote of No-confidence is passed against it? ***(ICSE 2010)***

Ans. The passage of No-confidence means that the Parliament has lost its faith on the government and the government has to resign as a result.

38. Mention one advantage of the Lok Sabha. ***(ICSE 2009)***

Ans. The main advantage of Lok Sabha is that its members are elected directly by the people and therefore, can better address the concerns of the common people.

39. What is meant by a Constituency? ***(ICSE 2008)***

Ans. Constituency is a territorial area which elects its representative either to the Lok Sabha or to the Legislative Assembly.

40. Name the body which elects the members of the Rajya Sabha. ***(ICSE 2007)***

Ans. The members of the Rajya Sabha are elected by the members of State Legislative Assembly.

41. An adult Indian citizen holding an office of profit under the State Government wishes to contest for the election of the Lok Sabha. Is he/she eligible? Give a reason to justify your answer. ***(ICSE 2006)***

Ans. No, he/she is not eligible. According to Constitution, a member of Parliament cannot hold any office of profit under Central or State Government.

Additional Info

Qualification for membership of the Lok Sabha are as follows
- He/She should be an Indian citizen.
- He/She should be at least 25 years of age.
- He/She should not be an insolvent and of unsound mind.

42. Mention one priviledge of a Member of Parliament. ***(ICSE 2005)***

Ans. The Right to Freedom of Speech is applied to a broader view to the MPs. They cannot be questioned in a Court of Law in regard to the speech made by them in the Parliament.

43. What is the procedure adopted for resolving a deadlock between the two Houses of Parliament with regard to an Ordinary Bill? ***(ICSE 2000)***

Ans. The procedure so adopted, is the call for a joint sitting by the President to resolve the deadlock.

2/3 Marks Questions

1. Explain the tenure of the members of the Lok Sabha and the Rajya Sabha. ***(ICSE 2014)***

Ans. **Lok Sabha** The Constitution provides for a fixed term of 5 years for the Lok Sabha.

However, it can be dissolved earlier by the President or can be extended for one year at a time of proclamation of an emergency by the Parliament.

Rajya Sabha The tenure of the Rajya Sabha is 1 year more than the Lok Sabha *i.e.,* 6 years. Besides it, 1/3 rd of the total members retire after every 2 years.

2. Mr Koushal is 26 yrs of age, which House of Parliament can he be a member of? Why? ***(ICSE Specimen 2013)***

Ans. Mr Koushal can be a member of Lok Sabha because for the membership of Lok Sabha, a person must not be less than 25 years of age.

3. Discuss the relationship between the two Houses of the Parliament with reference to the Money Bill. ***(ICSE 2013)***

Ans. A Money Bill can originate in the Lok Sabha only. After the Bill gets passed by the Lok Sabha, it is then sent to Rajya Sabha for recommendations, which it must send back within 14 days. The Bill then comes to the Lok Sabha again, which is upon them to either accept or reject any of the recommendations. In financial matters, the Rajya Sabha has only an advisory role.

4. Discuss the relationship between the two Houses of the Parliament with reference of a Non-money Bill. ***(ICSE 2013)***

Ans. A Non-money Bill may originate in either House. On disagreement between the two Houses, the Bill is referred to a joint sitting of both the Houses. In such cases, both the Houses are placed on an equal footing, however due to larger strength, the will of the Lok Sabha prevails in the joint sitting.

5. With reference to the Union Parliament, answer the following questions.

The two Houses of the Parliament enjoy co-equal powers in many spheres. Explain it by giving three examples. ***(ICSE 2012)***

Or Mention three powers which are common to both the Houses of the Parliament. ***(ICSE 2008)***

Ans. The two Houses of Parliament enjoy co-equal powers in the following subjects

(i) Emergencies proclaimed by the President, have to be approved by both the Houses of Parliament.

(ii) Impeachment of the President.

(iii) Constitutional Amendments.

6. Mention three Legislative powers of Union Parliament. *(ICSE 2011)*

Ans. The Legislative powers of the Parliament are exclusive in following subjects

(i) Matters in the Union List

(ii) Matters in the Residuary List

(iii) Ordinance power of the President must be approved by the Parliament

(a) In matters of the Concurrent List, if both the Parliament and State Legislature make law on a subject, the Parliament law will ultimately prevail.

(b) The Union Parliament can legislate in subjects of the State List during proclamation of an emergency.

7. Mention three Financial powers of the Union Parliament. *(ICSE 2011, 2006)*

Ans. The financial powers of the Union Parliament are as follows

(i) The Budget of the Union is passed by the Parliament.

(ii) The salaries and allowances of MPs and Ministers are determined by the Parliament.

(iii) No taxes can be imposed unless approved by the Parliament.

8. Mention two ways in which the Lok Sabha can control the Executive. *(ICSE 2010)*

Ans. The Lok Sabha can control the Executive *via* Interpellation and can also pass a resolution in matters of public interest. Other methods to control the Executive is through the vote of No-confidence, Adjournment Motion or *via* Monetary Control.

9. Explain three reasons to justify why the Lok Sabha is considered to be more powerful than the Rajya Sabha. *(ICSE 2009)*

Or Which House is considered to be more powerful the Lok Sabha or the Rajya Sabha? State two reasons to justify your answer. *(ICSE 2005)*

Ans. The members of the Lok Sabha are elected directly by the people. It enjoys superiority over Rajya Sabha in the following matters

(i) Motions of No- confidence can only be introduced and passed in the Lok Sabha.

(ii) Money Bills can only be introduced in the Lok Sabha and they enjoy superior position, in financial matter.

(iii) In case of a deadlock, the will of the Lok Sabha prevails due to its larger strength.

10. Mention three functions of the Speaker of the Lok Sabha. *(ICSE 2009)*

Ans. The three functions of the Speaker of the Lok Sabha are as follows

(i) The Speaker decides whether a Bill is a Money Bill or not.

(ii) He/She appoints Chairman of all the Parliamentary Committees.

(iii) He/She after consulting the Chairman of the Rajya Sabha, nominates the personnel for Parliamentary delegations to various countries.

(iv) The Speaker presides over a joint sitting of the two Houses of Parliament.

11. Mention the Judicial powers of the Parliament. *(ICSE 2008)*

Ans. Judicial powers of the Parliament are as follows

(i) The Parliament can remove the judges of the Supreme Court and the High Courts.

(ii) The Parliament can punish a person for its contempt of or for obstructing the work of the Parliament.

(iii) The Parliament has the right to remove the President through impeachment process and also has the right to remove the Vice-President. (President can be impeached only for violation of Constitution).

12. Mention three instances when the Parliament can make laws on the subject entered in the State List. *(ICSE 2006)*

Ans. The instances when the Parliament can make laws on the subject entered in the State List are

(i) Rajya Sabha, under Article 249, may pass a resolution which authorises the Parliament to make law on a subject mentioned in the State List which it considers of national importance.

(ii) The Parliament can legislate on matters of State List, during proclamation of a National Emergency.

(iii) When two or more states by resolution request the Parliament to legislate on a subject given on State List. The act made by the Parliament would be applicable to consenting states only.

13. How is the Speaker of the Lok Sabha elected? Mention two functions of the Speaker during the session of the Parliament. *(ICSE 2005)*

Or The Speaker is elected soon after the first meeting of the newly elected Lok Sabha. In this context, answer the following question. How is the Speaker elected? *(Modified 2001)*

Ans. The Speaker of the Lok Sabha is elected soon after the first meeting of the newly elected Lok Sabha from among its own members.

For functions, refer to Q. 10 of 2/3 marks questions.

4 Marks Questions

1. With reference to the Indian Parliament, explain the following powers to make laws on the subject mentioned in the *(ICSE 2014, 2006)*

(i) Union List (ii) Concurrent List

Ans. (i) **Union List** The Parliament has exclusive powers to make laws with respect to matters mentioned in the Union List. If emergency is proclaimed throughout the country or in any State, then all the lists will come under the Centre and Parliament will make laws on all the subject lists.

(ii) **Concurrent List** On subjects mentioned in Concurrent List, both the Parliament and the State Legislature can legislate. If a conflict occurs between State and Centre, then Centre will be overruled on the State law.

2. Discuss the relationship between the two Houses of the Parliament with reference to the following control over Executive. *(ICSE 2013)*

Other Similar Questions

Or Mention four Administrative or Executive powers of the Union Parliament.

Or Mention four ways in which the Lok Sabha exercises control over the Council of Ministers.

Ans. The Parliament exercises control over the Executive using various instruments/controls. Some of them are

(i) **Interpellation** The Parliament can ask questions to the governments about its policies and performance.

(ii) **Vote of No-confidence** If a government does not follow the provisions of Constitution, the Parliament can show No-confidence to the government.

(iii) **Adjournment Motion** To bring matters of urgent public importance, the Parliament can bring Adjournment Motion.

(iv) **Censure Motion** It can bring Censure Motion over the policies of the government.

(v) **Monetary Control** The Parliament can bring cut motion during the budget session to disapprove any monetary policy of the government. It also examines the report of Comptroller and Auditor-General (CAG).

Various Administrative or Executive Power of the Union Parliament
- Interpellation
- Vote of No-confidence
- Adjournment Motion
- Censure Motion
- Monetary Control

3. Explain any three of the Rajya Sabha's power in India's federal set-up. *(ICSE 2012)*

Or Mention four special powers of the Rajya Sabha. *(ICSE 2010)*

Ans. The powers of Rajya Sabha are as follows

(i) Rajya Sabha can authorise the Parliament to make law on subject mentioned in State List by passing a resolution with 2/3rd majority.

(ii) The Rajya Sabha may declare that the creation of new All India Services be made in the national interest.

(iii) If the Lok Sabha is dissolved before or after an emergency proclamation, the Rajya Sabha takes over the functions of Parliament.

(iv) Under Article 67, a resolution seeking the removal of the Vice-President can originate only in the Rajya Sabha.

4. State the procedure to be followed by the Union Parliament for passing a Money Bill. *(ICSE 2009)*

Ans. A Money Bill can only originate in the Lok Sabha. The procedure is as follows

(i) After its introduction in the Lok Sabha, the Bill is discussed, debated and voted in the House.

(ii) After being passed by the Lok Sabha, the Bill is then sent to the Rajya Sabha for recommendations.

(iii) The Rajya Sabha must return the Bill within 14 days with or without recommendations.

(iv) The Bill then comes to the Lok Sabha, which may accept or reject any or all of the recommendations of the Rajya Sabha.

(v) After 14 days, if the Bill is not returned, it is deemed to have been passed by both the Houses.

5. What are the qualifications necessary to become a member of the Rajya Sabha? ***(ICSE 2000)***

Ans. The qualifications for membership of the Rajya Sabha are as follows

(i) He/She should be an Indian citizen.

(ii) He/She should be at least 30 years of age.

(iii) He/She should have his/her name in the electoral roll in some part of the country.

(iv) He/She should not be an insolvent.

(v) He/She should not hold any office of profit under the Central or State Government.

(vi) He/She should not be a proclaimed criminal.

(vii) He/She should be of a sound mind.

6/7 Marks Question

1. What are the functions of the Lok Sabha's Speaker? ***(ICSE 2001)***

Ans. The role of Speaker may be categorised under following heads

(a) **Conducting the Business of the House**

(i) The Speaker presides over the meeting of the House.

(ii) All Bills passed by the House must be signed by the Speaker before being sent to the Rajya Sabha or President.

(iii) He decides on the disqualifications of the motions, resolutions and questions.

(iv) Speaker is the sole authority to decide whether a Bill is Money Bill or not.

(b) **Administrative Functions**

(i) He receives all the petitions, documents in the House and communicates the decisions to concerned authority.

(ii) He regulates the admission of visitors and press correspondents to the galleries of the House.

(c) **Disciplinary Functions**

(i) The responsibility to maintain order in the House lies with the Speaker and he may take actions against members who become unruly.

(ii) The case related to contempt or breach of privileges are decided by the Speaker.

(iii) In matters relating to defection, the Constitution says that the Speaker's decision shall be final and in this regard, he is not answerable to any Court of Law.

(d) **Parliamentary Committees**

(i) He is the ex-officio Chairman to many of the Committees.

(ii) He appoints the Chairman of all the Committees and directs the rules and procedures to be followed.

The functions of the Lok Sabha's Speaker
- Conducting the Business of the House
- Administrative Functions
- Disciplinary Functions
- Parliamentary Committees
- Miscellaneous Functions

(e) **Miscellaneous Functions**

(i) He presides over the joint sitting of the Parliament.

(ii) He nominates personnel for Parliamentary delegations to various countries, after consultation with the Chairman of the Rajya Sabha.

2. Describe the Legislative and Financial powers of the Rajya Sabha. ***(ICSE 2000)***

Ans. Legislative powers of the Rajya Sabha are as follows

(i) The Parliament enjoys exclusive right to make laws on subjects enumerated in the Union List and Residuary List. The Rajya Sabha by passing a resolution can authorise the Parliament to legislate on subjects mentioned in the State List.

(ii) All ordinances must be approved by both the Houses of the Parliament.

(iii) If the Lok Sabha is in a dissolved state, the Rajya Sabha takes over the functions of the Parliament during the emergency proclamation. Financial powers of the Rajya Sabha are as follows:

Rajya Sabha enjoys only an advisory role in financial matters.

- A Money Bill after being passed from the Lok Sabha comes to the Rajya Sabha which they have to return within 14 days with or without recommendations.
- It is upto the Lok Sabha to accept or reject all or any of the recommendations.

10 Marks Questions

1. The Union Legislature comprises the President and the two Houses of the Parliament. With reference to the Parliament, answer the following questions.

(a) Mr Raj wants to be a member of the Lok Sabha. Mention any three qualifications required to contest elections for the Lok Sabha. ***(ICSE 2023)***

(b) Mention any three Legislative powers of the Union Parliament.

(c) The Parliament controls the Executive. Mention any four ways in which it exercises its control.

Ans. (a) The Constitution mentions the following qualifications for the membership of the Lok Sabha

(i) Should be an Indian citizen.

(ii) Should be at least 25 years of age.

(iiii) Should not be of unsound mind.

(b) Three Legislative powers of the Union Parliament are as follows

(i) Both the Houses have equal legislative powers in matters pertaining to the Union List, Concurrent List, Residuary List as well as ordinance related powers.

(ii) Parliament controls the Council of Ministers in various ways. Some of them are Question Hour, Vote of No-confidence, Adjournment Motion, Censure Motion, etc.

(iii) There are certain matters/subjects, in which the Rajya Sabha enjoys exclusive rights, *e.g.*, under Article 249, the Rajya Sabha, by a resolution adopted by 2/3rd majority, can empower the Parliament to make laws with respect to a matter in the State List.

(c) The ways by which Parliament controls the Execultive are

(i) The Lok Sabha can control the Executive *via* Interpellation and can also pass a resolution in matters of public interest.

(ii) Other methods to control the Executive is through the vote of No-confidence, Adjournment Motion or via Monetary Control.

(iii) The Parliament exercises control over the Executive through question-hour, zero hour, half-an-hour discussion, short duration discussion, calling attention motion, Adjournment Motion, No-confidence Motion, Censure Motion and other discussions.

(iv) It also supervises with the help of its committees.

2. With reference to the Union Legislature, answer the following questions. ***(ICSE 2020)***

(a) Explain any three Legislative powers of the Union Parliament.

(b) State any three exclusive powers of the Lok Sabha that is not enjoyed by the other House.

(c) List any four functions of the Speaker of the Lok Sabha.

Ans. (a) Refer to Q. 1 (b) of 10 marks questions.

(b) Following are the three exclusive powers of the Lok Sabha that are not enjoyed by the other House

(i) Money Bill can be introduced only in the Lok Sabha and not in the Rajya Sabha. The Rajya Sabha cannot amend or reject the Money Bill, it should return the Bill to the Lok Sabha within the period of 14 days. The final power to decide whether a Bill is Money Bill or not is also vested with the Presiding officer of the Lok Sabha i.e. Speaker.

(ii) Rajya Sabha can only discuss the budget but cannot vote on the demand for grants.

(iii) The resolution for the discontinuance of the National Emergency can be passed only by the Lok Sabha and not by the Rajya Sabha.

(c) Functions of the Speaker of Lok Sabha are

(i) The Speaker presides over the meetings of the House, except when a resolution for his/her removal is being considered.

(ii) The Speaker has the final power to maintain order in the House and to interpret its rules of procedure.

(iii) He/She can ask a member to withdraw from the House for disorderly behaviour or may even suspend a member from the service of the House on a motion for gross disorderly behaviour.

(iv) He/She decides whether a Bill is a Money Bill or not.

Examiner's Comment

- Most candidates wrote the three Legislative powers of the Union Parliament correctly. However, a few confused Legislative powers with Executive powers.
- Majority of the candidates wrote the correct answer. A few candidates wrote about the general powers and got confused between the powers of the Lok Sabha and the Rajya Sabha. A few could not understand the word 'exclusive'.

Suggestions for Students

- Clarify the word 'exclusive' and explain the exclusive powers of both the Lok Sabha and the Rajya Sabha thoroughly to the students, giving reasons.
- Learn the general powers of the Speaker.

3. The Parliament is the body of people's representatives who have supreme power in a democracy. With reference to the Union Legislature answer the following. *(ICSE 2019)*

(a) How are the members of the Rajya Sabha elected?

(b) Why is it called a Permanent House ?

(c) State any two Financial and any two Legislative powers of the Indian Parliament.

Ans. (a) Refer to Q. 18 of very short answer questions.

(b) Refer to Q. 26 of very short answer questions.

(c) Refer to Q. 6 and Q. 7 of 2/3 marks questions.

Examiner's Comment

- Some candidates, instead of writing the manner of the election of the members of the Rajya Sabha, wrote about its composition.
- Majority of the candidates answered this question very well by writing the required points.
- Some candidates could not distinguish between the Financial and Legislative powers of the Indian Parliament and mixed up the points in their answers.

Suggestions for Students

- Explain the direct and indirect method of elections.
- Remember that the Rajya Sabha is a permanent house as it cannot be dissolved by the President. One-third of its members retire every second year and new members are elected but the house is never dissolved.
- Explain the meaning of financial and legislative powers of the Indian Parliament.

4. With reference to the Union Parliament, answer the following questions.

(a) Give three reasons as to why the Lok Sabha is considered more powerful than the Rajya Sabha. *(ICSE Specimen 2018)*

(b) State three exclusive powers of the Rajya Sabha.

(c) Mention any four functions of the Speaker of the Lok Sabha.

Ans. (a) Refer to Q. 9 of 2/3 marks questions.

(b) Three exclusive powers of the Rajya Sabha are

(i) Parliament can assume temporary power to legislate on State List subjects. It is done only if Rajya Sabha passes a resolution, which is supported by 2/3rd majority of its members present and voting.

(ii) The establishment of All-India Services also depends on the Rajya Sabha. The House will pass a resolution which is supported by 2/3rd majority of its members, present and voting.

(iii) During the emergency, if the Lok Sabha is dissolved then Rajya Sabha becomes the de-facto (effective) and de-jure (legal) because Rajya Sabha is a permanent body.

(c) Refer to Q. 10 of 2/3 marks questions.

5. Compare the powers of the two Houses of the Union Parliament with reference to the following

(i) Legislative Powers. *(ICSE Specimen 2017)*

(ii) Financial Powers.

(iii) Control over the Executive.

Ans. (i) **Legislative Powers** In the case of Ordinary Bills, though they may originate in any House, but in the event of a deadlock on the Bill, where a joint sitting of both the Houses prevail, the Rajya Sabha is always in a weaker position, due to its total membership being less than that of the Lok Sabha.

In the case of a Money Bill, the ultimate authority to either reject or pass it lies only with the Lok Sabha. Moreover, Money Bills can only be introduced in the Lok Sabha.

(ii) **Financial Powers** In matters of finance, the Lok Sabha always has an upper hand. Money Bills can only be introduced in the Lok Sabha, with the Rajya Sabha not having the power to pass/reject, or even amend them.

The Rajya Sabha, in the event of receiving a Money Bill, has to send it back to the Lok Sabha within a time of 14 days. Its recommendation can/cannot be accepted by the Lok Sabha.

(iii) **Control over the Executive** Though the members of both the Houses can put questions to the ministers about the work of their departments, but even in this context, the power of the Lok Sabha is more. Rajya Sabha cannot pass a No-confidence Motion against the Council of Ministers. Even the Adjournment Motion indicating a strong disapproval of the policy of government is moved only in the Lok Sabha.

6. With reference to the Union Legislature, answer the following questions. *(ICSE 2016)*

(a) How is the Speaker of the Lok Sabha elected ? State two disciplinary functions of the Speaker.

(b) Explain two conditions under which a member of Parliament can be disqualified under the Anti - Defection Law.

(c) Give reasons to justify why the Lok Sabha is considered to be more powerful than the Rajya Sabha.

Ans. (a) The Speaker of the Lok Sabha is elected from its own members soon after the newly elected House meets for the first time.

Two disciplinary functions of the speaker are as follows

(i) He maintains order and decorum in the Lok Sabha for conducting its business and regulating its proceedings.

(ii) The Speaker decides whether there is a case for a matter relating to a breach of privilege or contempt of the House.

(b) Two important conditions under which a member of Parliament can be disqualified under the 10th Schedule are as follows

(i) A member of a Parliament belonging to any political party becomes disqualified for being a member of the Parliament, if he has voluntarily given up his membership of such political party.

(ii) If he votes or abstains from voting in such house contrary to any direction issued by the political party to which he belongs.

(c) Refer to Q. 9 of 2/3 marks questions.

7. The Rajya Sabha is the second chamber of the Indian Parliament and represents the interest of the States. In this context explain the following ***(ICSE 2015)***

(a) Its composition.

(b) Qualifications for membership.

(c) Term of the House and any two of its legislative powers.

Ans. (a) The maximum strength of the Rajya Sabha is fixed at 250 members, out of which, 238 members are to be the representatives of the States and Union Territories and 12 members are nominated by the President.

At present, the Rajya Sabha has 245 members; out of these, 233 members represent the States and the Union Territories and 12 members are nominated by the President.

(b) The Constitution lays down the following qualifications for a person to be chosen a member of the Rajya Sabha

- He/She must be a citizen of India.
- He/She should be of minimum 30 years of age.
- He/She should not be a proclaimed offender.
- He/She should not be holding any office of profit.
- He/She should have his/her name on the electoral roll.

(c) The Rajya Sabha is a continuing body, i.e. it is a permanent body and not subject to dissolution. Term of office of a member of the Rajya Sabha shall be six years. One-third of its members retire every second year.

Legislative Powers of Rajya Sabha are as follows

- It can authorise the Parliament to make a law on a subject enumerated in the State List.
- Rajya Sabha has equal power with Lok Sabha in case of introduction and passage of Constitutional Amendment Bills.

CHAPTER TEST

01 Mark Questions (MCQ)

1 Who among the following is the ex-officio chairman of the Rajya Sabha?
(a) Prime Minister (b) President
(c) Vice-President (d) Speaker

2 The maximum composition of the Rajya Sabha is
(a) 238 (b) 250 (c) 240 (d) 245

3

Lok Sabha	House of the People
Rajya Sabha	?

(a) Lower House (b) Upper House
(c) Council of State (d) Both (b) and (c)

4 To be chosen as a member of the Lok Sabha, a person must be a citizen of India and not less than .... years of age.
(a) 25 (b) 30 (c) 35 (d) 18

5 A Money Bill can be introduced only in the ....
(a) Rajya Sabha (b) Lok Sabha
(c) Both (a) and (b) (d) None of these

Answers

1. (c) | 2. (b) | 3. (d) | 4. (a) | 5. (b)

02 Marks Questions

6 Mention any two electoral functions of the Union Parliament.

7 Mention any three circumstance under which the Union Parliament may make laws on subjects in the State List.

8 What are the two Judicial functions of the Union Parliament?

9 What is an Adjournment Motion?

10 Marks Question

10 With reference to the composition of the Lok Sabha, answer the following questions.
(i) What is the maximum strength fixed by the Constitution? What is the term of the House? By whom and on whose advice can the Lok Sabha be dissolved?
(ii) State any three qualifications needed to contest for the Lok Sabha seat.
(iii) Give two reasons to justify how the Lok Sabha is more powerful than the Rajya Sabha.

02

The President and The Vice-President

TREND ANALYSIS 3 YEARS

Average No. of Questions Across all Sets

Topic	Types of Questions	2023	2020	2019
TOPIC 01 President of India	1 Mark	2	3	2
	2/3 Marks	6	—	—
	4 Marks	4	—	—
	10 Marks	1	—	—
TOPIC 02 Vice President of India	1 Mark	4	1	1
	2/3 Marks	—	—	—
	4 Marks	—	—	—
	10 Marks	—	—	—

The President of India

The President is the **Executive head** of the Union of India. He/She is the head of the State but, according to our Constitution, he/she is bound to follow the advice given by the Prime Minister and the Council of Ministers. The Constitution makes it necessary on the part of the President to exercise his/her functions in accordance with the advice of the Council of Ministers.

Qualifications

A person shall be eligible for election as a President, if he/she

(i) is a citizen of India.

(ii) has completed the age of 35 years.

(iii) is qualified for election as a member of the Lok Sabha.

(iv) does not hold any office of profit under the Government of India or Government of any State or any other public authority.

Note A candidate can be elected as a President more than once and a sitting President, Vice-President, Governor or Minister of the Union or any State is not deemed to hold any office of profit, hence is qualified as a presidential candidate.

The election of the President is held in accordance with the system of proportional representation by means of 'Single Transferable Vote.' The voting is done by a secret ballot. All the disputes regarding the election of the President shall be decided by the Supreme Court of India.

Composition of the Electoral College

The President is elected indirectly by the members of an Electoral College consisting of

(i) the elected members of both Houses of Parliament.

(ii) the elected members of the Legislative Assemblies of the States and those of the National Capital Territory of Delhi and the Union Territory of Puducherry.

Thus, the nominated members of both the Houses of Parliament, the nominated members of the State Legislative Assemblies, the members (both elected and nominated) of the state legislative councils, and the nominated members of the **Legislative Assemblies of Delhi** and **Puducherry** do not participate in the election of the President.

Procedure of Election

The President is indirectly elected by the elected members of the Vidhan Sabha, the elected members of the Lok Sabha and the Rajya Sabha, according to proportional representation by means of a 'Single Transferable Vote.'

(i) Value of the Vote of an MLA

$$= \frac{\text{Total Population of State}}{\text{Total Number of Elected Members in State Legislative Assembly}} \times \frac{1}{1000}$$

(ii) Value of vote of an MP

$$= \frac{\text{Total Number of Votes of all the MLAs of all States}}{\text{Total Number of Elected MPs}}$$

Reasons for Indirect Election

The President is indirectly elected because

(i) if elected directly, he could become a rival centre of power to the Council of Ministers.

(ii) an indirect election protects the President from becoming a nominee of the Ruling Party at the Centre.

(iii) the inclusion of members of State Legislative Assembly in the Electoral College makes the President the elected representative of the whole nation. Thus, by this method, clear voice would be given to the States as well.

Oath of Office

Before entering office, the President takes on oath in the presence of the Chief Justice of India (or in his absence the seniormost Judge of the Supreme Court) to

(i) discharge the functions of the President of India,

(ii) preserve, protect and defend the Constitution and the law, and

(iii) devote himself/herself to the service and well-being of the people of India.

Term of Office

- The President holds office for a term of 5 years from the date on which he/she enters office.
- The President may resign before the completion of his/her term. In that case, he/she can submit his resignation to the Vice-President of India. The vacant seat of the President must be filled within 6 months.

Procedure for Impeachment

- The President can be expelled from office in case of the violation of the Constitution by the process of impeachment. Either House can initiate the procedure by mentioning the charge for violation of the Constitution. A 14 days notice should be given to the President in writing signed by at least 1/4 th of the total members of the House that framed the charges.
- After the lapse of 14 days, a resolution is moved which is to be passed by a majority of not less than 2/3 rd of the total strength of the House.
- The resolution then moves to the other House, which should investigate the charges. During the process, the President has the right to appear and to represent himself in such investigation. If the resolution after investigation is passed by the second House by a majority of not less than 2/3 rd of the total Membership of the House investigating, the President will stand impeached.

Powers of the President of India

The President has many powers, but the Constitution has clearly stated that the President shall act in accordance with the advice given by the Prime Minister and the Council of Ministers.

Executive Powers

- He/She is the **head of Union Administration** and all Executive orders are issued in his/her name.
- He/She makes appointments to key posts to run the Government's administration. He/She appoints the Prime Minister and the Council of Ministers (CoM) on Prime Minister's advice. He/She also appoints the Chief Justice and the Judges of the Supreme Court and the High Courts, the Governors of the States, Lt. Governors and various other constitutional heads.
- He/She can appoint an inter-state council to promote centre state and inter-state cooperation.
- Union Territories and the Border Areas Administration is the responsibility of the President.

Legislative Powers

- He/She usually addresses a Joint Session of both the Houses of Parliament at the beginning of the first session (usually the Budget Session) of the year and after each general election to the Lok Sabha.
- The President can send message to either House of the Parliament, at any point with regard to any matter of importance.
- The President has the power to summon and prorogue the Houses and to dissolve the Lok Sabha. The President nominates 14 members to Parliament (12 to the Rajya Sabha and 2 to the Lok Sabha), on the advice of Prime Minister and the Council of Ministers.
- Any Bill cannot become an act until it is approved by the President. He/She may send it back with some recommendations, but the second time he/she has to give his/her assent.
- A Bill with regard to **formation of a new State** can only move in the Parliament after the assent of the President.
- The Governor of the State may reserve some Bills passed by the State Legislature for the consideration of the President.
- The President can promulgate an ordinance under Article 123, which is a short-term law made on the recommendation of the Union Cabinet when Parliament is not in session.

  The ordinance is subject to conditions like

  (i) The President must feel the urge to take immediate action in the given circumstances.

  (ii) The ordinance can only be promulgated when both Houses of the Parliament are not in session.

  (iii) It has to be laid before both the Houses when they reassemble.

  (iv) It lapses, if it is replaced by an Act of Parliament.

When an Ordinary Bill is sent to the President after it has been passed by the Parliament, he can

(i) give his assent to the Bill, or

(ii) withhold his assent to the Bill, or

(iii) return the Bill. However, if the Bill is passed again by the Parliament; with or without amendments, the President has to give his assent to the Bill.

Financial Powers

- It is the responsibility of the President to introduce the Annual Budget every year in the Parliament. Under constitutional provision, it is the duty of the President to appoint a Finance Commission after every 5 years to recommend the distribution of revenues between the Centre and the States.
- He/She is authorised to withdraw money from **Contingency Fund of India** to meet certain emergency requirement.
- A Money Bill can only be introduced after the President's recommendation.
- No demand for grant can be made except on his recommendation.

Judicial Powers

- He/She appoints the Chief Justice and the Judges of the Supreme Court and High Courts.
- He/She has the power to grant pardons, respites, reprieves or remissions to remit or commute the sentence of any person convicted for an offence.
- No criminal suit can be initiated against the President during his/her tenure of office and he/she is not answerable before any Court of Law for exercising his/her powers and the duties of his/her office.

Discretionary Powers

- When no party gains majority of the Lok Sabha, the President using his/her discretionary power to appoint the Prime Minister.
- After a vote of no-confidence is passed against the prevailing government, the President may dissolve the Parliament or ask the leader of another party to prove its majority on the floor of the House.
- He/She can also dismiss the Council of Ministers in case, the Council of Ministers loses the confidence of the House but refuses to resign.

Emergency Powers

The President can proclaim a state of emergency in the following cases

(i) National Emergency (Article 352)

- The President, if satisfied that the security of the nation is threatened by war or external aggression or an armed rebellion, he/she can issue the proclamation of National Emergency.
- Every such proclamation must be approved by the Parliament within 1 month by a special majority. Once passed, it remains operational for 6 months. Beyond that it has to be passed again by the Parliament.
- During the proclamation, Fundamental Rights are suspended (Except those under Article 20 and 21). The Constitution assumes a unitary role and grants Parliament the power to make laws on 66 subjects of State List. Many of the powers of the States are curtailed.
- The country has to lose its federal spirit, as the States, under an emergency, are obliged to carry out the instructions of the Centre.

- The financial provisions of the Constitution are also suspended.
- The Lok Sabha, under such circumstances, can be extended for a period of up to one year.

(ii) President's Rule (Article 356)

- On receipt of a report from the Governor, if the President is satisfied that there is a breakdown of constitutional machinery in any State, he may declare President's rule in the State, assuming all or any functions of the State to himself.
- Once proclaimed, it must be ratified by the Parliament within 2 months, after which, it remains operational for 6 months.

  To extend it beyond a year, it must fulfil two conditions
  - (i) If the proclamation of National Emergency is in operation in the nation or in any **part of the country**.
  - (ii) The **Election Commission** must certify that holding elections to the Legislative Assembly of the State (concerned) is difficult or not possible.

  Effects of such State emergencies include
  - (i) State administration is directly placed under the President with the **Governor** acting in accordance with the instructions issued by the Union Government.
  - (ii) The President may either dissolve the Vidhan Sabha and dismiss the Council of Ministers or keep them in suspended animation.
  - (iii) The President may authorise expenditure from the State Consolidated Fund, when the Lok Sabha is not in session. He may also suspend the provision of the Constitution relating to the authority of the State.

(iii) Financial Emergency (Article 360)

- If a situation has arisen whereby the financial stability or credit of the nation is threatened, the President can declare Financial Emergency.
- The President may appoint a **Finance Commission** to suggest methods to get out of the financial crisis, he may reduce salaries and allowances of all or any class of persons including those of the Supreme Court or High Court Judges.
- He can also issue instructions to the States in regard to the utilisation of funds in the manner he may deem fit and may order the state to submit Money Bills to him for his/her assent.

Position of the President in the Constitution

- The President is required to exercise his/her powers on the aid and advice of the Council of Ministers. The 42nd Amendment Act makes it binding on the President to accept such advice.
- The **44th Constitutional Amendment Act** of 1978 authorised the President to ask the Council of Ministers to reconsider such advice, if necessary.
- Without any ratification from Parliament, the emergency proclamation ceases to operate after a fixed time.
- Though the President is only a Constitutional Head of State and has little effective power at his/her disposal, the office of the President is one of great honour, prestige and dignity.

Vice-President of India

The Vice-President of India is elected by the member of the Electoral College, according to a system of proportional representation by a single transferable vote.

Qualification for Election

A person shall be eligible for the election of the Vice-President, if he/she

- (i) is a citizen of India.
- (ii) has completed the age of 35 years.
- (iii) is qualified for election as a member of the Rajya Sabha.
- (iv) should not hold any office of profit under the Union Government or any State Government or any local or other authority or any public authority.

Composition of the Electoral College

The Electoral College for the election of the Vice-President consists of members of both Houses of the Parliament. The nomination should be proposed by at least 20 electors and another 20 electors as seconders. The President of India administers the oath of office of the Vice-President.

Term of Office and Power

- The Vice-President shall hold office for a term of 5 years from the date he/she enters his/her office.
- He/She may resign from his/her post by writing to the President or he/she may be removed from his/her office for the violation of the Constitution by the Parliament.
- The Vice-President is the ex-officio Chairman of the Rajya Sabha. He/She mainly performs his/her duties with regard to the Chairman of the Rajya Sabha. His/Her salary is also paid in this capacity.
- The Vice-President takes over the office of the President, if the President is unable to discharge his/her duties or the office of the President becomes vacant.
- In the above event, the Vice-President draws all the emoluments and salary of the President.

PYQs Previous Years' Questions

1 Mark Questions

Multiple Choice Questions

1. The procedure to remove the President is called .... *(ICSE Specimen Semester II 2022)*

(a) Impeachment (b) Interpellation
(c) Resolution (d) Prorogation

Ans. (*a*) Impeachment

2. The President's address is prepared by the .... *(ICSE Specimen Semester II 2022)*

(a) Vice-President (b) Rajya Sabha
(c) Cabinet (d) Parliament

Ans. (*c*) Cabinet

3. A person should have completed the age of .... to be eligible for election as Vice-President. *(ICSE Semester II 2022)*

(a) 21 years (b) 30 years
(c) 35 years (d) 25 years

Ans. (*c*) 35 years

4. The President can declare a National/General Emergency when .... *(ICSE Semester-II 2022)*

(a) there is a threat to the security of the country
(b) there is financial instability in the country
(c) the Governor gives a report recommending Emergency
(d) the Election Commission recommends its proclamation

Ans. (*a*) there is a threat to the security of the country

5. Who is empowered to promulgate an Ordinance when the Parliament is not in session? *(ICSE Specimen Semester 2021)*

(a) The Vice-President
(b) The President
(c) The Prime Minister
(d) The Attorney General of India

Ans. (*b*) The President

Very Short Answer Questions

1. Who is the Supreme Commander of the Armed Forces of India? *(ICSE 2020)*

Ans. The President of India is the Supreme Commander of the Armed Forces of India.

2. What is the normal term of office of the Vice-President of India? *(ICSE 2020)*

Ans. The normal term of office of the Vice-President of India is 5 years.

3. Write any one circumstance when the President can declare a National Emergency. *(ICSE 2019)*

Ans. Under Article 352, the President can proclaim a National Emergency, only if he is satisfied that the security of the nation is threatened due to war or external aggression or due to armed rebellion.

4. State any one condition when the Parliament can legislate on subjects in the State List. *(ICSE 2019, 2011)*

Ans. The Parliament can legislate on subjects included in the State List, during the proclamation of a National Emergency.

5. Name the procedure for the removal of the President of India. *(ICSE Specimen 2018)*

Or Name the official procedure by which the President can be removed. *(ICSE 2016)*

Or When and how can the President of India be removed from office?

Ans. The President can be removed from his office through the impeachment process. The impeachment process against the President can be initiated only on the grounds of violation of the provisions of Constitution.

6. Mention one important function of the Vice-President of India. *(ICSE Specimen 2018, 2017)*

Ans. One important function of the Vice-President is that, if the President is not able to perform his functions due to absence or illness, etc, then the Vice-President shall perform the functions of President until the President resumes his duty.

7. Who administers the oath of office to the Council of Ministers? *(ICSE 2018)*

Ans. The President of India administers the oath of office to the Council of Ministers.

8. What is an ordinance? *(ICSE 2018)*

Or What is an 'Ordinance'? When can it be passed? *(ICSE 2014, 2007)*

Or When can ordinances be issued by the President? *(ICSE 2009, 2000)*

Ans. Ordinances are short-term laws that are promulgated by the President of India on the recommendation of the Union Cabinet when the Parliament is not in session.

9. State any one reason why the President is elected indirectly. **(ICSE 2018)**

Or State one reason why the President is elected indirectly. **(ICSE 2013)**

Ans. Indirect election of the President is in harmony with the Parliamentary system of government envisaged in the Constitution. Thus, the President is elected indirectly.

10. When can the President use his discretionary power to appoint the Prime Minister? **(ICSE 2017)**

Or Mention one circumstance when the President can appoint the Prime Minister using his/her discretionary power. **(ICSE 2011, 2006)**

Ans. The President of India uses his discretionary power to appoint the Prime Minister in a situation where no single party commands the clear support of the majority of the Lok Sabha Members and there is a hung Parliament.

11. What is meant by the discretionary power of the President? **(ICSE Specimen 2017)**

Ans. Discretionary powers refer to those powers, which are applicable in the situations where the President may have to use his/her wisdom and judgement.

For example, in the case of appointment of the Prime Minister and in case where no single party has a major support. **(ICSE 2006)**

12. Mention any one important occasion when the President addresses a Joint Session of Parliament. **(ICSE 2016)**

Ans. At the beginning of the first session of each year, normally the Budget session,the President addresses a Joint Session (sitting) of Parliament.

13. Who has the power to promulgate an Ordinance at the Centre? When can it be promulgated? **(ICSE 2014)**

Ans. The President of India has the power to promulgate an Ordinance at the Centre. He can promulgate ordinances when the Parliament is not in session.

14. State any one qualification necessary for the election of the President of India. **(ICSE 2014)**

Ans. One qualification necessary for the election of the President of India is that he/she should be qualified for election as a member of the Lok Sabha.

15. State the composition of the Electoral College in the election of the President of India. **(ICSE Specimen 2017, 2014)**

Ans. Electoral College comprises of

(i) elected members of the Parliament.

(ii) elected members of the Legislative Assemblies of all States and the UTs of Delhi and Puduchery.

16. Who is the Executive head of the nation? **(ICSE 2013)**

Ans. The President is the Executive head of the nation.

17. Mr Konar was not found eligible for the election as the Vice-President of India even though he had the qualifications of being a citizen of India and not being a member of the Parliament and the State Legislature. On what grounds was he disqualified? Give one reason. **(ICSE 2009)**

Ans. To become the Vice-President of India, a person should be qualified as a member of the Council of States. Mr Konar was disqualified on that ground.

18. Mention two Military Powers of the President of India. **(ICSE 2007)**

Ans. Being the Supreme Commander of the Armed Forces, the President

(i) has the power to declare War or conclude Peace.

(ii) appoints the Chiefs of the three wings of the Defence Forces, (*i.e.*, Army, Navy and the Air Force).

19. Mention one difference in the election of the Vice-President and that of the President of India, as far as the electorate is concerned. **(ICSE 2005)**

Ans. The electoral college of the President comprises the elected members of the Parliament and the elected members of Legislative Assemblies of all States and UTs of Delhi and Puducherry. The electoral college of the Vice-President comprises only the elected members of the Parliament.

20. Mention any two financial powers of the President of India. **(ICSE 2001)**

Ans. Financial powers of the President include

(i) The President appoints a Finance Commission after every 5 years to recommend on financial matters.

(ii) Money Bill can only be introduced in the Lok Sabha with prior recommendation of the President.

2/3 Marks Questions

1. Besides being a citizen of India, state three other qualifications required by a person to be eligible to be the President of India. *(ICSE 2012)*

Or Mention the qualifications required to be eligible to become the President of India. *(ICSE 2007)*

Ans. Other qualifications required to be eligible to be the President of India are as follows

(i) He/She must have completed the age of 35 years.

(ii) He/She should be qualified for election as a member of the Lok Sabha.

(iii) He/She should not hold any office of profit under the Government of India or Government of any State or under any local authority.

2. Under what circumstances can the President of India declare an emergency in the country? *(ICSE 2012)*

Or Describe the circumstances under which the President can declare an emergency in the country. *(ICSE 2005)*

Ans. The President of India can declare an emergency under the following circumstances

(i) **National Emergency** When the President is satisfied that the security of the nation is threatened by the war or external aggression or armed rebellion.

(ii) **State Emergency** If the Governor of a State reports the President of the breaking of constitutional machinery in the State and if the President is satisfied with the report so given, he can declare a State Emergency.

(iii) **Financial Emergency** When the financial stability or credit of the nation is threatened, the President can declare the Financial Emergency.

3. The President is the constitutional head of the nation. In this context, explain the manner of election and term of his office. *(ICSE 2011)*

Ans. The President is elected indirectly by the Electoral College which comprises the elected members of the Parliament and elected members of the Legislative Assembly of all States and the UTs of Delhi and Puducherry. The term of office of the President is 5 years.

4. Why is the President of India referred to as a nominal head of the State? State two examples of his legislative powers that suggest his nominal status. *(ICSE 2010)*

Or Discuss the reasons as to why President is referred to as nominal head of the state.

Ans. According to constitutional provisions, the President exercises his powers on the advice of the Prime Minister and the Council of Ministers.

For two legislative power of the President, refer to page no. 22.

5. Mention the circumstances when the President can declare National Emergency. *(ICSE 2010)*

Or On which grounds can the President declare National Emergency.

Ans. Under Article 352, the President can proclaim a National Emergency, only if he is satisfied that the security of the nation is threatened due to war or external aggression or due to armed rebellion.

6. With reference to the powers of the President, write down the reasons for adopting the indirect method of election for the Presidential Election. *(ICSE 2009)*

Ans. The reason behind the indirect election of the President are as follows

(i) Since the Membership of Parliament is dominated by a party, this will turn the President as a mere nominee.

(ii) The inclusion of State Legislative Assembly's elected members provides the President a clear voice and support of the States as well.

(iii) If elected directly, it could develop into a rival Centre of power for the Council of Ministers.

7. With reference to the powers of the President, write down the options open to the President when an Ordinary Bill is sent to him for his assent. *(ICSE 2009)*

Ans. A Bill when passed by both the Houses, is sent to the President for his approval. The President may give his assent or withhold the Bill or send it back to the House with recommendation, however, if the same Bill comes again, the President is bound to give his assent.

8. Mention the three Executive powers of the President. *(ICSE 2008)*

Ans. The Executive powers of the President are as follows

(i) As a head of the Union Administration, all Executive orders are issued in the name of the President.

(ii) He makes appointment to the key posts to run the Government's Administration.

(iii) The Administration of the Union Territories (UTs) and the Border Areas is the responsibility of the President.

(iv) He makes rules for more convenient transaction of business of the Union Government.

9. Mention the three financial powers of the President.

Ans. The Financial powers enjoyed by the President are as follows

(i) Without his recommendation, a Money Bill cannot be introduced in the Lok Sabha.

(ii) The President is responsible for laying the Annual Budget of the government.

(iii) The President appoints Finance Commission after every 5 years which gives its recommendations on financial matters.

10. The President of India is the head of the Indian Republic. In this context, answer the following questions. ***(ICSE Modified 2005)***

(i) Besides being a citizen of India, state three other qualifications required by a person to be eligible to be the President of India.

(ii) Justify the need for 'Indirect Election' of the President.

Ans. (i) Refer to Q. 1 of 2/3 marks questions.

(ii) Refer to Q. 6 of 2/3 marks questions.

4 Marks Questions

1. The President is the constitutional head of nation. In this context, explain the Executive powers of the President with reference to ***(ICSE 2011)***

(i) Appointments

(ii) Right to be informed

Ans. (i) **Appointments** The President makes appointments to key posts to run the Administration of the Union as well as the State. He appoints

(a) the Prime Minister and Council of Ministers

(b) the Chief Justice and Judges of Supreme Court and High Courts

(c) the Governors of the States

(d) the Attorney General of India

(e) the Comptroller and Auditor General of India

(f) chief of three Wings of the Armed Forces, etc.

(ii) **Right to be Informed** According to constitutional provisions, it is the responsibility of the Prime Minister to inform the President regarding the policy matters and international treaties on day-to-day basis.

2. Explain two discretionary powers of the President. ***(ICSE 2010)***

Ans. Two discretionary powers of the President are as follows

(i) The President appoints the Prime Minister in a situation where no single party secures the majority of the Lok Sabha.

(ii) The President can dismiss the ministers in case the Parliament loses confidence of the house and refuses to resign.

3. Write down any two Judicial powers and two Discretionary powers of the President. ***(ICSE 2009)***

Ans. Judicial Powers of the President are as follows

(i) The President has the power to grant pardons, reprieves, respites or remissions of the punishment or to suspend, remit or commute the sentence of any person convicted for an offence.

(ii) The President is not answerable before any Court of Law for exercising the powers and duties of his office.

Discretionary powers of the President are as follows

(i) When no party gains majority of the Lok Sabha, the President using his/her discretionary power to appoint the Prime Minister.

(ii) After a vote of no-confidence is passed against the prevailing government, the President may dissolve the Parliament or ask the leader of another party to prove its majority on the floor of the House.

10 Marks Questions

1. The President of India is the nominal head of the Union Administration. With reference to the President, answer the following questions. ***(ICSE Specimen 2023)***

(a) What is the term of the President? Give two reasons for the indirect election of the President.

(b) Name the three kinds of emergencies which the President can declare.

(c) State any four legislative powers of the President.

Ans. (a) The President's term of office is 5 years from the date on which he/she enters upon the office.

Two reasons for the indirect election of the President are

(i) An indirect election protects the President to become a nominee of the Ruling Party at the centre.

(ii) The inclusion of members of State Legislative Assembly in the Electoral College makes the President the elected representative of the whole nation. A clear voice would be given to the states as well by this process.

(b) The three kinds of emergencies which the President can declare are as follows

(i) **National Emergency** As per **Article 352**, the President has the power to make a 'Proclamation of Emergency' on the ground of threat to the security of India or any part thereof by war, external aggression or armed rebellion. The President can declare such an emergency only on the basis of a written request by the Cabinet of Ministers headed by the Prime Minister.

President can declare three kinds of Emergencies
- National Emergency
- State Emergency
- Financial Emergency

(ii) **President's Rule** Article 356 of the Constitution authorise the President to make a proclamation of Emergency in the following two situations
- If he/she is satisfied that the government of a State cannot be carried on in accordance with the provisions of the Constitution.
- If the State fails to comply with or give effect to any of the directions given by the Centre in the exercise of its Executive power. It is also called State Emergency or Constitutional Emergency.

(iii) **Financial Emergency** Article 360 of the Constitution of India deals with Financial Emergency. The President can declare this Emergency if he/she
- is satisfied that a situation has arisen whereby the financial stability of the country is threatened.
- is satisfied that credit of India or of any part of its territory is threatened.

(c) Four Legislative powers of the President are as follows
- **Summon or Prorogue the Parliament** The President can summon or prorogue the Parliament and dissolve the Lok Sabha. He/she can also summon a joint sitting of both the Houses of the Parliament.
- **Address to the Parliament** The President can address both Houses of the Parliament at the commencement of the first session after each general election and the first session of each year, i.e. the budget session.
- **Send Message to the Houses** The President can send messages to the Houses of the Parliament, whether with respect to a Bill pending in the Parliament or otherwise.
- **Prior Recommendation** The President's prior recommendation or permission is needed to introduce certain types of bills in the Parliament.

2. The President is the head of the State and exercises his /her power on the advice of the Prime Minister and Council of Ministers. With reference to this, answer the following questions. ***(ICSE 2023)***

(a) What are the three types of emergencies that can be proclaimed by the President ?

(b) Mention any three Legislative powers of the President.

(c) Give any two reason to justify the need for indirect election of the President. What is the composition of the Electoral College which elects the President ?

Ans. (a) Refer to Q. 2 of 2/3 marks questions.

(b) Refer to Q. 1 (c) of 10 marks questions.

(c) The reasons that were given for adopting the method of Indirect Election for Presidential election

(i) The power resided in the Council of Ministers, headed by the Prime Minister and the Union Parliament and not in the President as such. Therefore, it would be not be appropriate if the President is to be elected directly by the people and is not given any real power.

(ii) Tremendous loss of time, energy and money would be involved in a direct Presidential election.

For composition of Electoral College, refer to Q. 15 of 1 mark questions.

3. The Executive power of the Indian Union is vested in the President of India. In this context, answer the following questions. ***(ICSE Specimen Semester II 2022)***

(a) Give any two reasons for the indirect election of the President.

(b) Mention any two financial powers of the President.

(c) Mention any three Legislative powers of the President.

(d) Name the three kinds of emergencies that can be proclaimed by the President.

Ans. (a) For answer, refer to Q. 1 (a) of 10 marks questions.

(b) For answer, refer to Q. 9 of 2/3 marks questions.

(c) For answer, refer to Q. 1 (c) of 10 marks questions.

(d) For answer, refer to Q. 2 (a) of 10 marks questions.

4. The Executive power of the Indian Union is vested in the President. In this context, answer the following. ***(ICSE 2020)***

(a) How is the President of India elected? State the composition of the Electrol College that elects him.

(b) Explain any three discretionary powers of the President.

(c) Mention any four Executive powers of the President.

Ans. (a) The manner and procedure of election of the President of India is mentioned in Article 55 of the Indian Constitution. The President's election is held in accordance with the system of proportional representation by means of the single transferable vote and the voting is done by secret ballot.

For answer, refer to Q. 14 of very short answer questions.

(b) The three discretionary powers of the President are

- When no party gains majority of the Lok Sabha, the President using his/her discretionary power, appoints the Prime Minister.
- After a vote of no-confidence is passed against the prevailing government, the President may dissolve the Parliament or ask the leader of another party to prove its majority on the floor of the House.
- He/She can also dismiss the Council of Ministers in case, the Council of Ministers loses the confidence of the House but refuses to resign.

(c) For answer, refer to Q. 8 of 2/3 marks questions.

Examiner's Comment

- This subpart was attempted well by most candidates. Some wrote that the President of India is elected by Direct elections. Some candidates did not give the composition of the Electoral College correctly.
- Many candidates did not write the Discretionary Powers of the President correctly.
- A large number of candidates answered this part correctly. However, some candidates mixed up the Legislative and the Executive powers.

Suggestions for Students

- Identify technical terms such as Electoral College, etc. to be used in Civics and explain the meaning of these terms to the students in detail.
- Learn the discretionary powers of the President with instances.
- Clarify the distinction between the Executive powers and Legislative powers of the President.

5. The President and the Vice-President are part of the Union Executive. In this context, answer the following questions. ***(ICSE 2018)***

(a) State any three qualifications required for a candidate to be elected as the Vice-President of India.

(b) State the three functions of the Vice-President.

(c) Explain briefly any two Legislative and any two Executive powers of the President.

Ans. (a) Three qualifications required for a candidate to be elected as the Vice-President of India are the following

(i) He/she must be a citizen of India.

(ii) He/she should have completed 35 years of age.

(iii) He/she should be qualified for the election as a member of the Rajya Sabha.

(b) Three functions of the Vice-President are the following

(i) The Vice-President acts as an ex-officio Chairman of the Rajya Sabha.

(ii) The Vice-President acts as the President when a vacancy occurs in the office of the President due to his/her removal or his/her death or otherwise.

(iii) When the sitting President is unable to discharge his/her functions, the Vice-President acts as the President until the President resumes his/her office.

(c) For Executive powers of the President, refer to Q. 8 of 2/3 marks questions.

For Legislative powers of the President, refer to Q. 1 (c) of 10 marks questions.

Examiner's Comment

- Most of the candidates answered the question correctly. However, a few candidates, instead of writing the qualifications of the Vice-President wrote the qualifications required for membership of the Lok Sabha.
- Most candidates wrote the three functions of the Vice-President correctly.

Suggestions for Students

- Explain the qualifications for the election of the Vice-President of India, his term of the office, functions.
- Draw a flow chart to explain the Executive powers and Legislative powers of the President.

7. With reference to the President of India, briefly explain the following. ***(ICSE Specimen 2017)***

(a) Reasons for the indirect election.

(b) Emergency powers.

(c) Procedure for removal.

Ans. (a) Following are the main reasons for the indirect election of the President

(i) Electing the President directly would make him a rival centre of power to the Council of Ministers, which would be against the Parliamentary system.

(ii) Since, the membership in both the Houses of the Parliament is likely to be dominated by one party, election of the President directly would make him a nominee of the ruling party.

(iii) The electoral college, consisting of the elected members of both the Houses, along with those of the Legislative Assemblies, is a better composition to elect him, which would lend a voice to the entire nation.

(b) The President can declare an Emergency in the following cases

(i) When the security of India or a part of it is threatened by war or external aggression or armed rebellian (Article 352).

(ii) In the event of the breakdown of the constitutional machinery or a deadlock because of political uncertainty or otherwise (Article 356).

(iii) In the case of a setback to the financial stability or credit feasibility of the country.

(c) The procedure to impeach the President can be initiated in either House of the Parliament as follow

(i) A resolution is moved after at least 14 days, notice in writing is signed by not less than 1/4th of the total number of members of the House.

(ii) The resolution is to be passed by a majority of not less than 2/3rd of the total membership of the House.

(iii) The other House has to then investigate the charges so levelled, with the President having the right to appear and be represented at such investigations.

(iv) If as a result of the investigations, a resolution is passed by a majority of not less than 2/3rd of the total membership of the House, declaring that the charge has been sustained, such a resolution will have the effect of removing the President from his office.

8. The President of India is the Constitutional Head of the Indian Republic. In this context answer the following questions. ***(ICSE 2016)***

(a) How is the President elected ?

(b) Mention three types of emergencies that the President is empowered to proclaim.

(c) Explain briefly any four 'Executive Powers' of the President.

Ans. (a) For answer, refer to Q. 4 (a) of 10 marks questions.

(b) For answer, refer to Q. 2 of 2/3 marks questions.

(c) For answer, refer to Q. 8 of 2/3 marks questions.

CHAPTER TEST

01 Mark Questions

1 The Vice-President of India is elected for a period of ………… years.

(a) 6 (b) 5 (c) 2 (d) 3

2 To be eligible for election as President of India, a person must have completed the age of ………… .

(a) 25 years (b) 30 years
(c) 35 years (d) 40 years

3 All the Executive power in Indian Constitution are vested with which among the following?

(a) President (b) Prime Minister
(c) Parliament (d) Council of Ministers

4

President	Member of the Lok Sabha
Vice-President	?

(a) Member of the Lok Sabha
(b) Member of the Rajya Sabha
(c) Member of the State Legislative Assembly
(d) Member of the State Legislative Council

5 What is the maximum age limit prescribed for the post of the President of India?

(a) 58 years (b) 60 years
(c) 62 years (d) There is no maximum age limit

Answers

1. (b) 2. (c) 3. (a) 4. (b) 5. (d)

02 Mark Questions

6 Mention any two Legislative power of the President of India.

7 What are the qualification should a person in order to be elected as Vice-President?

8 Mention any two discretionary powers of the President.

9 Mention the circumstances when the President can declare a National Emergency.

10 Marks Questions

10 With reference to Emergency in the event of failure of constitutional machinery in a State, answer the following questions.

(a) When is such an Emergency proclaimed?
(b) What is the duration of the Emergency?
(c) What are the effects of the imposition of the President's Rule?

03

The Prime Minister and The Council of Ministers

TREND ANALYSIS 3 YEARS

		Average No. of Questions Across all Sets		
	Types of Questions	2023	2020	2019
TOPIC 01 The Prime Minister	1 Mark	—	1	—
	2/3 Marks	—	—	—
	4 Marks	—	—	—
	10 Marks	—	—	1
TOPIC 02 Council of Ministers	1 Mark	2	1	2
	2/3 Marks	—	—	—
	4 Marks	—	—	—
	10 Marks	—	—	—

The Constitution of India provides for a **Council of Ministers** with the **Prime Minister** as its head. The President of India exercises his authority on the advice of the Council of Ministers. In the Parliamentary form of Government, the President is the nominal head of State and the Council of Ministers (CoM) headed by the Prime Minister is the real Executive head of the State.

The Prime Minister

Appointment

The Prime Minister (PM) is appointed by the **President**, who according to convention, invites the leader of the majority party or group in the Lok Sabha to form the government.

The members of the majority group/party elect their leader in the Lok Sabha to be appointed as the Prime Minister.

The President may use his discretionary power to appoint the Prime Minister when no single party or group secures the majority in the House, but has to appoint the person who can prove his majority in the House with the support of some smaller groups or parties.

Term of Office

The term of office of the Prime Minister is 5 years. However, the President may dismiss him/her before time if he loses the majority support in the Lok Sabha.

Position and Powers of the Prime Minister

The Prime Minister, with the backing of the majority party or groups in the Parliament, is the real Executive head of the nation (*i.e.,* de-facto head).

Relationship of the Prime Minister with the President

- The Prime Minister is the **principal advisor** to the President. The Prime Minister chooses the ministers and on his advice the President appoints them. He acts as a link between the President and the Council of Ministers.
- According to the Constitution, it is the duty of the Prime Minister to communicate to the President all the decisions of the Council of Ministers relating to the administration of the Union and the proposals for legislation. He advises the President with regard to the appointment of important officials like the Attorney General of India, Comptroller and Auditor-General of India, Chairman and members of the UPSC, Election Commissioners etc.
- The President may call for information regarding the affairs of the Union. Then the Prime Minister has to furnish this information.

Prime Minister and the Cabinet

- The Prime Minister is the head of the Union Council of Ministers. He recommends persons who can be appointed as ministers and to allocate them portfolios, by the President. It is binding for the President to do so. He can re-shuffle his Council of Ministers whenever he needs to do so.
- The Prime Minister is the chief coordinator between various ministries on policy issues. He can ask a minister to resign or advise the President to dismiss him in case of difference of opinion. The resignation of the Prime Minister implies the resignation of the whole Cabinet.

Prime Minister Inside Parliament

The Prime Minister is the **leader of the Lower House** in Parliament and the chief spokesperson of the government in Parliament. Whenever an unwanted situation arises in Parliament, the matter generally ends with the intervention of the Prime Minister.

Prime Minister as the Leader of the Nation

The Prime Minister represents the nation. He decides the kind of relations India should have with other countries. He tries to protect the interests of the country in international forums. He is the **ex-officio** Chairman of the **NITI (National Institution for Transforming India) Aayog** that replaced Planning Commission of India. He is also the Chairman of the **Atomic Energy Commission.**

Check on the Authority of the Prime Minister

Though the Prime Minister is the leader of the majority party, he has to ensure the support of his party as well as the ministers. Parliament keeps an effective check on the power of the Prime Minister. Parliament exercises control over the Prime Minister through question-hour, calling attention motion, No-Confidence motion and other discussions.

PM relationship with individual Ministers-only some minister's designation is shown for representation purposes

Council of Ministers

Appointment

Article 75(1) states that, "The Prime Minister shall be appointed by the President and other ministers shall be appointed by the President on the advice of the Prime Minister". Only members of Parliament are usually appointed as Ministers. However, if a non-member is appointed, he must become a member of Parliament within six months. Failing this, he will have to resign from the post.

Formation

The Constitution originally did not specify the number of ministers in the Council of Ministers. However, the Constitution (91st Amendment Act, 2003) put a ceiling on the size of the Council of Ministers to **15%** of the strength of the Lok Sabha or the State Legislatures. The Constitution does not classify the members of the Council of Ministers into different ranks.

Composition

The Council of Ministers consists of all the three categories of Ministers i.e. Cabinet Ministers, Ministers of State and Deputy Ministers.

Cabinet Ministers

The Cabinet is composed of a small but important body of senior leaders of the government. They hold important **portfolios** like home, defence, finance, external affairs, railways, etc. The Cabinet decides major programmes and policies of the government.

Ministers of State

Ministers of State are the second category of ministers. They may or may not hold charge of independent ministries. They are sometimes invited to the Cabinet meetings to discuss matters related to their departments.

Deputy Ministers

The third category of ministers are the Deputy Ministers who are responsible to assist the Cabinet Ministers and the Council of Ministers. They are junior ministers and are placed under senior ministers. They do not take part in Cabinet deliberations.

Powers and Functions of the Council of Ministers

The main powers of Council of Ministers are as follows

Administrative Powers

The Council of Ministers formulates both external and domestic **policies of the government** on important matters such as defence, economic policy, security needs, important reforms etc. Once decided, the policy is conveyed to the Ministers of State and Deputy Ministers, and details are worked out and passed to civil servants under the ministry to implement the decisions.

The Council of Ministers coordinates the working of various departments for the smooth implementation of government policies. All major appointments are decided by the Council of Ministers and appointed by the President.

Legislative Powers

Almost 95% of the Bills initiated in the legislature are finalised by the Cabinet. These are called **Official Bills**. These are given priority and preference over Private Bills. The ministers along with the secretaries of the concerned departments answer the questions put to them by the members of Parliament regarding these Bills.

The Cabinet is instrumental in planning and moving the Amendments to the Constitution. Although the House is summoned by the President, initiative is taken by the concerned ministry. The President's address to both Houses is prepared by the Cabinet.

Financial Powers

The Finance Minister prepares the annual budget containing estimates of income and expenditure for the ensuing year. The Cabinet is responsible for the expenditure of the government, for presenting the demand for grants and also for raising necessary income by various means.

Emergency Powers

The President can declare a proclamation of National Emergency under **Article 352**. However, after the 44th Amendment Act, such proclamation can only be made after the written recommendation of the Cabinet to the President.

Collective Responsibility and Individual Responsibility of the Members of the Cabinet

- **Article 75(3)** of the Constitution states that, "The Council of Ministers shall be collectively responsible to the House of the People" (or Lok Sabha).
- This means that, if the ministry loses the confidence of the Lok Sabha, all ministers including those, who are from the Rajya Sabha have to go. The entire ministry is obliged to resign.
- This means that ministers fall and stand together. This is called **Rule of Collective Responsibility**. However, 'individual responsibility' means that individual ministers hold office during the pleasure of the President. It means that this is a 'powerful tool of the President in the hands of the Prime Minister. Losing confidence of the Prime Minister leads to dismissal by the President of the concerned minister.

Relationship with the President

- The relationship between the President and the Council of Ministers has been emphasised by various Constitutional Amendments. According to the 42nd Amendment to the Constitution, the President shall act in accordance with the advice rendered by the Council of Ministers expressed through the Prime Minister. Thus, the advice of the Council of Ministers to the President is legally binding on him.
- The 44th Amendment Act provides that the President shall not issue a proclamation of National Emergency unless the decision of the Union Cabinet has been communicated to him in writing.

Term of Office

- The ministers hold office during the pleasure of the President. But the President has little power in this regard because the Prime Minister and the Council of Ministers are directly responsible to the Lok Sabha.
- The Council of Ministers is collectively responsible to the Lok Sabha. If the Lok Sabha passes a vote of No-confidence against the Council of Ministers, they have to resign collectively.

The President administers the oath of office and secrecy to the Prime Minister and the Council of Ministers. The salaries and allowances of Ministers are determined by Parliament from time to time. Each minister gets a sumptuary allowance at a varying scale according to his rank, as well as free accommodation and other benefits.

Distinction between the Cabinet and the Council of Ministers

Cabinet	Council of Ministers
• The Cabinet is a smaller group consisting of senior ministers holding important portfolios. The Cabinet meets as a body, periodically, to shape national policies and programmes of the Government.	The Council of Ministers consists of all three categories of Ministers–Cabinet Ministers, Ministers of State and Deputy Ministers.
• The Prime Minister consults the Cabinet before taking an important decision.	The Prime Minister may or may not consult the other ministers below the rank of Cabinet Ministers.
• The Cabinet takes over the functions assigned by the Constitution to the Council of Ministers. The Cabinet advises the President through the Prime Minister.	The Council of Ministers does not have this authority.

Note The Cabinet has now become an institution with its own organisation. There is a separate Cabinet Secretariat which maintains records of the decision taken by the Cabinet and prepares reports in regard to the follow-up actions.

PYQs Previous Years' Questions

1 Mark Questions

Multiple Choice Questions

1. The junior category of ministers who assist senior ministers *(ICSE 2023)*
   (a) Cabinet Ministers (b) Ministers of State
   (c) Deputy Ministers (d) Council of Ministers

Ans. (c) Deputy Ministers

2. The Council of Ministers is collectively responsible to the .... *(ICSE Specimen 2023)*
   (a) Lok Sabha (b) Rajya Sabha
   (c) Prime Minister (d) President

Ans. (a) Lok Sabha

Very Short Answer Questions

1. State any two Legislative powers of the Cabinet. *(ICSE 2023)*

Ans. The two Legislative powers of the Cabinet are as follows
   (i) All major policies, decisions or amendments are moved by the Cabinet in the Parliament. These Legislative proposals are called Official Bills.
   (ii) The ministers along with the secretaries of the concerned departments answer the questions of the members of the Parliament.

2. Who appoints the Prime Minister of India? *(ICSE 2020)*

Ans. The President appoints the Prime Minister of India.

3. State the body that decides the major policies of the government. *(ICSE 2020)*

Ans. The body that decides the major policies of government are the Council of Ministers.

4. On whose advice can the President appoint the Council of Ministers? *(ICSE 2019)*

Or By whom and on whose advice are the Council of Ministers appointed? *(ICSE Specimen 2018, 2016, 2009, 2000)*

Ans. The Council of Ministers are appointed by the President on the advice of the Prime Minister.

5. What happens when a motion of No-confidence is passed against a minister? *(ICSE 2019)*

Or What happens if a vote of No-confidecne is passed against a minister in the Lok Sabha? *(ICSE 2015)*

Ans. If a motion of No-confidence is passed against a minister in the Lok Sabha, then he/she is removed from the ministery.

6. Mention one Legislative function of the Council of Ministers. *(ICSE Specimen 2018)*

Ans. The Council of Ministers advises the President to issue an ordinance when the Parliament is not in session.

7. State any one administrative function of the Cabinet. *(ICSE 2018)*

Ans. The Cabinet takes decisions on important matters such as defence, finances, foreign affairs, etc. It also formulates and decides the domestic and international policies of the government.

8. Mention one difference between the Council of Ministers and the Cabinet Ministers. *(ICSE Specimen 2017)*

Ans. Prime Minister may or may not consult the Council of Ministers, whereas the Cabinet Ministers form the most trusted colleagues of the Prime Minister.

9. Mention one important function of the Prime Minister in relation to the Council of Ministers. *(ICSE Specimen 2017)*

Ans. The Prime Minister acts as the Chairman of the Council of Ministers and hence, exercises a casting vote.

10. Under what condition can a non-member of Parliament be made a minister? *(ICSE 2017)*

Ans. If a political party gets majority in Lok Sabha election and forms the government, it can appoint any one from its party who is not a member of Parliament as a minister. But within six months he/she has to be elected from any of the Houses.

11. What is meant by 'collective responsibility' of the Cabinet? *(ICSE 2017, 2013)*

Or What does the term 'collective responsibility of the Council of Ministers' imply? *(ICSE 2009, 2001)*

Or To whom is the Council of Minister responsible? *(ICSE 2007)*

Ans. Under Article 75 (3) of the Constitution, "the Council of Ministers shall be collectively responsible to the House of the people". It implies that the Council of Ministers remains in office till it enjoys the support of a majority of members in the Lok Sabha.

12. What is understood by the term 'individual responsibility' in a Parliamentary democracy? ***(ICSE 2014)***

Or The Cabinet holds a pivotal position in the working of the Indian Parliamentary Government. In this context discuss the following. The formation of the Cabinet. ***(ICSE 2014)***

Ans. Individually the ministers are responsible to the President of India. They hold office on the pleasure of the President, who can dismiss them on advice of the Prime Minister.

Or The Cabinet is composed of a small but important body of senior leaders of the Government, who are included in the Council of Ministers. They hold important portfolios like home, defence, finance, external affairs, railways, etc and decide major policies of the Government.

13. Who presides over the meeting of the Cabinet? ***(ICSE 2012)***

Ans. The Prime Minister of India presides over the meeting of the Cabinet.

14. State one point of difference between the Cabinet and the Council of Ministers with reference to their responsibilities in the government. ***(ICSE 2010)***

Ans. The Cabinet is a group of seniormost ministers which mainly formulates the policy while the Council of Ministers is a large group responsible for the implementation of the policies.

15. Under what provision can a non-member of the Union Legislature be appointed as a minister? ***(ICSE 2009, 2001)***

Ans. If a non-member of Parliament is appointed as a minister, he must become a member within a period of 6 months from the date of his appointment, if failed he has to resign.

16. What is the term of office of the Prime Minister? ***(ICSE 2006)***

Ans. The term of office of the Prime Minister is 5 years. However, the President may dismiss him before, if the Prime Minister loses the majority support of the Lok Sabha.

17. What is meant by the term 'Cabinet'? ***(ICSE 2005)***

Ans. The Cabinet is a small cohesive group of seniormost ministers who determine the policy and programmes of the government.

2/3 Marks Questions

1. As the head of the Council of Ministers in the country is the Prime Minister, who is the real Executive head of the government. In this context, explain the following questions. ***(ICSE 2013)***

(i) The appointment of the Prime Minister.

(ii) His relationship with the Council of Ministers.

Ans. (i) The Prime Minister is appointed by the President. According to the convention, the President invites the leader of the majority party or group in the Lok Sabha to form the government. The members of the majority party elect their leader to be appointed as the Prime Minister.

(ii) The Prime Minister enjoys superior position among the Council of Ministers. He is the leader of the Cabinet and allocate portfolios and can reshuffle the council. He has power to recommends persons who can be appointed as ministers by the President. He can ask a minister to resign. The Prime Minister coordinates between various ministers and his resignation implies the resignation of whole Cabinet.

2. Explain three functions of the Prime Minister in relation to the President. ***(ICSE 2009)***

Ans. Three functions of the Prime Minister in relation to the President are as follows

(i) He communicate all decisions of the Council of Ministers to the President. He is the Chief Advisor of the President.

(ii) The President summons and prorogues the Parliament and dissolves the Lok Sabha on the advice of the Prime Minister.

(iii) The Council of Ministers is appointed by the President, but these ministers are chosen by the Prime Minister.

Additional Info

Other functions of the Prime Minister are

- Prime Minister acts as the link between President and Council of Ministers.
- He advises President regarding the appointment of various officials such as Attorney General of India, Chairman and members of UPSC, etc.

3. Explain three important functions of the Prime Minister. *(ICSE 2007)*

Ans. The three functions of the Prime Minister are as follows

(i) He is the leader of the Lok Sabha and Chief Spokesperson of the government.

(ii) The Prime Minister represents the nation. He plays a significant role in shaping the foreign policy of the country.

(iii) He advices the President on various appointments to important posts such as judges of Supreme Court, the Governors and Ambassadors.

4. What is the difference between the Council of Ministers and the Cabinet in the Central Executive? *(ICSE 2007)*

Ans. The differences between the Council of Ministers and the Cabinet in the Central Executive are as follows

(i) The Cabinet is a small group consisting of senior ministers holding important portfolios whereas Council of Ministers is a large body consisting of all categories of ministers such as Cabinet Ministers, Ministers of State and Deputy Ministers.

(ii) Cabinet Ministers are the most trusted colleagues of the Prime Minister and he always consults them. But like this Prime Minister may or may not consult the other ministers.

(iii) Cabinet is the group of senior ministers who meet frequently to determine policy and programmes of the government whereas in day-to-day working Council of Ministers rarely meet.

(iv) According to Constitution, the President acts on the advice of the Council of Ministers but in reality, it is the Cabinet who advices the President on various issues.

5. How is Council of Ministers collectively responsible to the Lok Sabha? What procedure is followed when a government is defeated in a No-confidence motion? *(ICSE 2006)*

Ans. The Council of Ministers is collectively responsible to the Lok Sabha, this means that all the ministers own joint responsibility to the Lok Sabha for all their acts of ommission and commission. When a vote of No-confidence is passed in the Union Legislature, the whole Council of Ministers has to resign.

4 Marks Questions

1. Explain any two administrative powers of the Cabinet. *(ICSE 2014)*

Ans. The two administrative powers of the Cabinet are as follows

(i) All major appointments to various key posts which are made by the President are advised by the Cabinet.

(ii) The Cabinet being the senior leaders'/ministers' group co-ordinates the functioning of various ministries for smooth implementation of government policies.

2. Explain any two legislative powers of the Cabinet. *(ICSE 2014)*

Ans. The two Legislative powers of the Cabinet are as follows

(i) All major policies, decisions or amendments are moved by the Cabinet in the Parliament. These Legislative proposals are called Official Bills.

(ii) The ministers along with the secretaries of the concerned departments answer the questions of the members of the Parliament.

3. Explain Prime Minister's relations with the President. *(ICSE 2013)*

Ans. Refer to Q. 2 of 2/3 marks questions.

4. Explain any four functions of the Prime Minister in relation to the Union legislature. *(ICSE 2009)*

Or Mention any four functions of the Prime Minister in relation to the Council of Ministers. *(ICSE 2006)*

Ans. The four functions of the Prime Minister in relation to the Union legislature are as follows

(i) He communicates to the President all decisions of Council of Ministers.

(ii) He is the Chief Spokesperson of the government in the Parliament.

(iii) The Prime Minister defends the government in the Parliament.

(iv) Whenever an unwanted situation arises in the Parliament, the Prime Minister intervenes in the matter to control the situation.

5. How is the Prime Minister appointed at the Centre? *(ICSE 2007)*

Ans. After each general election, the party who wins the majority seats in the Lok Sabha elects their leader in the House to be elected as the Prime Minister. The President invites the leader to form the government and appoints him as the Prime Minister. When no party gains majority seats in the Lok Sabha then the President uses his discretionary power to appoint the Prime Minister.

10 Marks Questions

1. The Prime Minister and his Council of Ministers formulate and implement the policies which govern the country. In this context, answer the following questions. *(ICSE Semester II 2022)*
   (a) Under what circumstances can the President use his discretion to appoint the Prime Minister? On whose advice does he appoint the Council of Ministers?
   (b) What is meant by the term Collective Responsibility of Ministers?
   (c) Name the three categories of the Council of Ministers.
   (d) Mention any three powers of the Prime Minister with reference to the President.

Ans. (a) Due to the sudden death of the Prime Minister, the President use his discretion to appoint the Prime Minister.

Council of Ministers are appointed by the President on the advice of Prime Minister.

(b) Refer to Q. 11 of 1 mark questions.

(c) The three categories of ministers are as follows:

(i) **Cabinet Ministers**
These are the first and most important members of the Council of Ministers. They hold important portfolios.

Three Categories of Ministers
- Cabinet Ministers
- Ministers of State
- Deputy Ministers

(ii) **Ministers of State** These are second category ministers, which may or may not hold any independent portfolios. They are sometimes invited to attend Cabinet meetings to discuss the matters relating to their departments.

(iii) **Deputy Ministers** These are third category of ministers, who assist the remaining two categories of ministers. They never take part in Cabinet deliberations.

(d) For answer, refer to under heading 'Relationship of the Prime Minister with the President' on pg. 33.

2. The Council of Ministers headed by the Prime Minister, is the most powerful institution in the Indian Polity. In this context, answer the following. *(ICSE 2019)*
   (a) State briefly the position of the Prime Minister in the Parliamentary system of Government. State any two powers the Prime Minister has as a leader of the nation.
   (b) Distinguish between the Council of Ministers and the Cabinet.
   (c) Write any four functions of the Cabinet.

Ans. (a) The Prime Minister, with the backing of the majority party or groups in the Parliament, is the real Executive head of the nation (i.e. de-facto head).

The Prime Minister represents the nation. He decides the kind of relations India should have with other countries. He tries to protect the interests of the country in international forums. He is the ex-officio Chairman of the NITI (National Institution for Transforming India) Aayog that replaced Planning Commission of India. He is also the Chairman of the Atomic Energy Commission.

(b) For answer, refer to under heading 'Distinction between the Cabinet and the Council of Ministers' on pg 35.

(c) The functions of the Cabinet are as follows

(i) All major appointments to various key posts which are made by the President are advised by the Cabinet.

(ii) The Cabinet being the senior leaders'/ministers' group co-ordinates the functioning of various ministries for smooth implementation of government policies.

(iii) All major policies, decisions or amendments are moved by the Cabinet in the Parliament. These Legislative proposals are called official bills.

(iv) The ministers along with the secretaries of the concerned departments answer the questions of the members of the Parliament.

Examiner's Comment
- Most of the candidates were able to write the correct answer. However, some candidates were not clear regarding the powers of the Prime Minister as a leader of the Nation. A few candidates mentioned his functions in relation with the Council of Ministers and the President.
- A few candidates could not distinguish between the Cabinet and the Council of Ministers and explained the three categories of ministers.

Suggestions for Students
- Clearly explain the power, position and functions of the Prime Minister.
- Learn the difference between the functions of the Cabinet and its features.

3. The Union Executive which consists of the President, Prime Minister and the Council of Ministers is a powerful body in a Parliamentary democracy. In this context, answer the following questions. *(ICSE 2017)*

(a) State the position of the Prime Minister and state any two of his powers in relation to the President.

(b) Mention the three categories of minister in order of their rank and status.

(c) Mention any four Legislative powers of the Cabinet.

Ans. (a) The Prime Minister with the backing of the majority party or groups in the Parliament is the real Executive head of the nation.

Two of his powers in relation to the President are

(i) The President summons and prorogues the Parliament on the advice of the Prime Minister.

(ii) The President appoints the Council of Ministers on the advice of the Prime Minister.

(b) Refer to Q. 1 (c) of 10 marks questions.

(c) Four legislative powers of the Cabinet are as follows

(i) Almost 95% of the Bills initiated in the legislature are done by the Cabinet. These are called Official Bills. These are given priority and preference over private bills.

(ii) The ministers, along with the secretaries of the concerned department, answer the questions put to them by the members of Parliament.

(iii) The Cabinet is instrumental in planning and moving the amendments to the Constitution.

(iv) When Parliament is not in session, the Cabinet recommends to the President the promulgation of ordinances whenever necessary.

4. The makers of our Constitution adopted the Parliamentary and the Cabinet form of government. With reference to this, answer the following questions. *(ICSE 2015)*

(a) (i) Who is the Constitutional Head of the Union Government?

(ii) What is meant by the Collective and Individual Responsibility of the members of the Cabinet?

(b) Explain briefly the position and powers of the Prime Minister in relation to the Cabinet.

(c) Distinguish between the Cabinet and the Council of Ministers.

Ans. (a) (i) The President is the Constitutional Head of the Union Government.

(ii) **Collectively Responsibility** It lies in the hands of the members of Cabinet. This means that all the ministers own joint responsibility to the Lok Sabha for all their acts of legislation and execution.

Individual Responsibility If a minister has taken a departmental decision independently in the best interest of the department, then he is individually responsible to the President. However, the President acts on the advice of the minister in these matters.

(b) The Prime Minister is the head of the Cabinet. He has the real power to recommend persons who can be appointed as minister by the President. The Prime Minister also allocates and reshuffles various portfolios among the ministers.
He can ask a minister to resign or advise the President to dismiss him in case of differences with him. The Prime Minister is the Chief Coordinator between various ministeries on policy issues. He can bring about the collapse of the Cabinet by resigning from office.

(c) Refer to Q. 4 of 2/3 marks questions.

CHAPTER TEST

01 Mark Questions

1

Nominal Executive Head	President
Real Executive Head	?

(a) Governor (b) Prime Minister
(c) Vice-President (d) President

2 Who among the following is head of the Union Council of Ministers?
(a) Prime Minister (b) Home Minister
(c) President (d) Vice-President

3 The term of the office of the Prime Ministers is .... years.
(a) 6 (b) 5
(c) 4 (d) 3

4 .... is collectively responsible to the House of the people.
(a) Council of Ministers (b) Minister of State
(c) Deputy Ministers (d) President

5 Who among the following is the ex-officio Chairman of the NITI (National Institution for Transforming India) Aayog?
(a) Home Minister (b) Prime Minister
(c) President (d) Defence Minister

Answers

1. (b) | 2. (a) | 3. (b) | 4. (a) | 5. (b)

02 Marks Questions

6 What do you understand by individual responsibility?

7 Mention any two administrative power of the Cabinet.

8 State any two financial power of the Cabinet.

9 What are the role of Prime Minister inside Parliament?

10 Marks Questions

10 The Prime Minister is the real head of the Union Administration. With reference to the Prime Minister, answer the following questions.
(a) How can we say that the Prime Minister occupies a unique position in the Parliament?
(b) State any three powers of the Prime Minister as a chairperson of the Cabinet.
(c) Mention three ways in which the Constitution ensures the pre-eminent position of the Prime Minister in relation to the Union Council of Minister.

04

The Supreme Court

TREND ANALYSIS 3 YEARS

TOPIC 01 Supreme Court

Average No. of Questions Across all Sets

Types of Questions	2023	2020	2019
1 Mark	2	1	1
2/3 Marks	–	–	–
4 Marks	–	–	–
10 Marks	1	1	–

The Constitution of India provides a **single integrated system** of courts for the Union and the States. A single integrated Judiciary system implies that the Supreme Court is the head of the Judiciary. It supervises and exercises control over the functioning of other courts. There is a single civil as well as criminal system that operates throughout the country. All cases coming from the Lower Courts can be taken to the next Higher Court by way of appeal.

Composition of Supreme Court

The Supreme Court of India consists of a Chief Justice of India and not more than 30 other judges, until Parliament by law prescribes a larger number of judges. Originally the strength was fixed at 8 (one Chief Justice and seven other judges).

Qualification of Judges

A person is eligible to be appointed as a Judge of the Supreme Court if

(i) He/she is a citizen of India.

(ii) He/she has been a Judge of a High Court for at least five years or of two or more such courts in succession, or has been an advocate of a High Court for at least 10 years or two or more such courts in succession.

Or He/she should be a distinguished jurist in the opinion of the President.

Appointment of Judges

- The Chief Justice of India is appointed by the President of India after consulting Judges of the Supreme Court and of the High Courts, as he deems fit.
- In the case of appointing other Judges in the Supreme Court, the President does so after consultation with the Chief Justice and such other Judges of the Supreme Court and the High Courts as he deems necessary.
- Usually the seniormost Judge of the Supreme Court is appointed as the Chief Justice of India. If the Chief Justice is unable to perform the duties of his office, the President may appoint another Judge of the Supreme Court as acting Chief Justice of India.

- The Chief Justice may appoint a Judge of the High Court as an **ad hoc** (Temporary) Judge of the Supreme Court for a period as may be necessary.

Term of Office

- A Judge of the Supreme Court holds office until he attains the age of 65 years or by submitting his resignation letter to the President.
- A Judge of the Supreme Court can be removed from his office on the ground of proved misbehaviour or incapacity by the President. The President can pass such an order only after the passage of a resolution by Parliament with a special majority of not less than 2/3 rd of the members of each house.

Independence of the Judiciary from the Control of Executive and Legislature

The independence of the Judiciary is ensured through the following

(i) Every Judge of the Supreme Court is appointed by the President after consulting the Chief Justice and the other Judges of the Supreme Court and the High Courts.

(ii) The salaries and other emoluments of the Judges cannot be changed to their disadvantage during their term of office, except in case of financial emergency.

(iii) The Judges have complete freedom to announce their decisions and discuss in the court chambers.

(iv) The Supreme Court can punish for contempt of court, any person/authority making an attempt to lower its authority and dignity.

(v) The court is free to decide its own procedure of work. The Constitution declares Delhi as the seat of Supreme Court. But it also authorises the Chief Justice of India to appoint other places as the seat of the Supreme Court.

Need for an Independent Judiciary

- India opted for a federal system of administration. To protect the constitutional division of powers, an independent and supreme Judiciary is an essential requirement. It is an essential requisite for ensuring human rights and protecting democracy.
- In a representative democracy, administration of justice assumes special significance in view of the rights of individuals which need protection against Executive or Legislative interference. This type of right makes the Judiciary free from the organs of the government.

Jurisdiction and Powers of the Supreme Court

Jurisdiction is the power that a court of law exercises to carry out judgements and enforce laws. The Supreme Court is the protector and **final interpreter of the Constitution**.

Original Jurisdiction

It refers to the power to hear and determine a dispute in the first instance. It happens in the cases which cannot be moved in any court other than the Supreme Court. These include

(i) Disputes between two States or between the Government of India and one or more States.

(ii) The Centre and any State or States on one side and one or more States on the other side.

Writ Jurisdiction/Enforcement of Fundamental Rights

The Constitution has constituted the Supreme Court as the guarantor and defender of the Fundamental Rights of the citizen.

The Supreme Court and High Courts are empowered to issue writs for the enforcement of the Fundamental Rights. These writs fall in the following categories

(i) Habeas Corpus
(ii) Mandamus
(iii) Writ of Prohibition
(iv) Quo-warranto
(v) Writ of Certiorari

Appellate Jurisdiction

The appellate jurisdiction of the Supreme Court extends to constitutional, civil and criminal cases. Any matter that involves important points of law and needs interpretation of the Constitution can be brought before the Supreme Court. Some types of cases which can be appealed in the Supreme Court are as follows

(i) **Civil Cases** Appeals in civil matters can be filed in the Supreme Court if the High Court certifies either that the case involves a substantial question of law of general importance or that the question needs to be decided by the Supreme Court.

(ii) **Criminal Cases** Two appeals in criminal cases can be filed in the Supreme Court.

These are as follows

(a) Cases without the certificate of the High Court.

(b) Cases with the certificate of the High Court.

(iii) **Constitutional Cases** An appeal can be filed in the Supreme Court against the decision of the High Court if the latter certifies that the case involves an interpretation of the Constitution. If the High Court refuses to give such a certificate, the Supreme Court may grant special leave of appeal.

Advisory Jurisdiction

(i) **Article 143** of the Indian Constitution confers upon the Supreme Court advisory jurisdiction. The President may ask for the advice of the Court in any matters relating to public importance or on any question of law. Such opinion of the court is not binding on the President. However, the Supreme Court is not bounded to render advice.

(ii) Disputes related to Pre-Constitution treaties and agreements are excluded from original jurisdiction by **Article 131**.

(iii) Any person can file a Public Interest Litigation (PIL) in the Supreme Court under some special grievance of women, children and other weaker sections by even writing them on a postcard.

Revisory Jurisdiction

The Supreme Court has power to review its own judgement or order with a view to remove any mistake or error that might have crept (occur) in the judgement or orders. But it is not bound by its previous decisions.

Judicial Review

The Supreme Court is the sole interpreter of the Constitution. It has the power to review any laws passed by the Union or State Legislature. If any law passed by the Legislature is against the spirit of the Constitution or contravenes any provision of the Constitution, the Supreme Court can declare such law as null and void.

Need for Judicial Review

- The Constitution has provided for a **balance of powers** between the Centre and the States. The power of review is essential to prevent any encroachment on each other's executive domains.
- The Legislature may not possess the wisdom, experience and impartiality which are needed to explain what the law means. This function can be best performed by the Supreme Court.
- Judicial Review is required to uphold the principle of the supremacy of the Constitution and to protect the Fundamental Rights of the citizens.

Court of Record

- A 'court of record' is a court whose judgements are recorded for evidence and testimony. The judgements are in the nature of precedents i.e., the High Courts and other courts are bound to give a similar decision in a similar case.
- According to the Constitution, the Supreme Court and the High Courts are the 'Courts of Record' and shall have all the powers including the power to punish anyone for contempt of court.

Other Powers

The Supreme Court, under Article 137, can revise any judgement made by it with a view of removing any error, or correct the same after any new evidence/question comes up. This is important, as the Supreme Court is a court of record, its decisions being of value as evidence.

Administrative and Supervisory Functions

The administrative and supervisory functions of Supreme Court are as follows

(i) Appointment of officers and staff of the Supreme Court is made by the Chief Justice of India.

(ii) The court makes rules regarding the conduct of advocates and other persons appearing before it.

(iii) The recommendations of the Chief Justice of India to transfer Judges of the High Courts are binding on the government, if they were made after consulting at least four seniormost Judges of the Supreme Court.

PYQs Previous Years' Questions

1 Mark Questions (MCQ)

Multiple Choice Questions

1. When the Supreme Court reviews any judgement made by it to remove an error, it falls under .... jurisdiction. *(ICSE 2023)*
   (a) advisory (b) revisory
   (c) original (d) appellate

Ans. (*b*) revisory

2. The composition of the Supreme Court is .... *(ICSE Specimen Semester II 2022)*
   (a) 31 judges and 1 Chief Justice
   (b) 30 judges and 1 Chief Justice
   (c) 20 judges and 1 Chief Justice
   (d) 22 judges and 1 Chief Justice

Ans. (*b*) 30 judges and 1 Chief Justice

Very Short Answer Questions

1. Mention any two ways in which the Constitution ensures the independence of the Judiciary from the Executive. *(ICSE 2023)*

Ans. The ways by which the Constitution ensures the independence of Judiciary from the Executive are

(i) Every Judge of the Supreme Court is appointed by the President after consulting the Chief Justice and the other Judges of the Supreme Court and the High Courts.

(ii) The salaries and other emoluments of the Judges cannot be changed to their disadvantage during their term of office, except in case of financial emergency.

2. Name the courts that are empowered to issue writs for the enforcement of Fundamental Rights. *(ICSE 2020, 2013)*

Ans. The Supreme Court and the High Court are empowered to issue writs for the enforcement of Fundamental Rights.

3. What is meant by appellate jurisdiction of the Supreme Court? *(ICSE 2019)*

Ans. The Supreme Court has the power of appellate jurisdiction by which it hear the cases that are against the order of a High Court or a Tribunal Court.

4. On what grounds can a Judge of the Supreme Court be removed? *(ICSE Specimen 2018)*

Ans. A Judge of the Supreme Court can be removed on the grounds of 'proved misbehaviour and incapacity'.

5. Mention two ways in which the Constitution ensures the independence and impartiality of the Judges of the Supreme Court. *(ICSE Specimen 2017)*

Ans. Two ways in which the Constitution does it are as follow

(i) The salaries of the judges are secured and cannot be reduced, except during a financial emergency.

(ii) There is no discussion in the Legislature on the conduct of judges.

6. Name any two writs issued by the Supreme Court. *(ICSE 2014)*

Ans. Two writs issued by the Supreme Court are Certiorari and Quo-warranto.

7. What is meant by a Single Integrated Judicial System as provided in the Indian Constitution? *(ICSE 2014)*

Ans. Single Integrated Judicial System implies a single uniform civil as well as criminal law applicable throughout the country with the Supreme Court at the top and the High Courts and Lower Courts as subordinates to it.

8. What is the tenure of a Judge of the Supreme Court? *(ICSE 2012)*

Ans. A Judge of Supreme Court can remain in office till he attains the age of 65 years.

9. Who can increase the number of Judges of the Supreme Court? *(ICSE 2011)*

Ans. The Parliament by passing an Amendment Bill can increase the number of Judges of the Supreme Court.

10. What is meant by Judicial Review? *(ICSE 2010)*

Ans. Being the chief interpreter of the Constitution, the Supreme Court has the power of Judicial Review wherein it checks the validity of a law made by the legislature. If any such law contravenes the provisions of the Constitution, the Supreme Court declares it null and void.

11. Why is the Supreme Court said to be the Guardian of the Constitution? ***(ICSE 2010)***

Ans. The Supreme Court issues writs if the Fundamental Rights of any individual are violated and also it can declare any law null and void if it contravenes the provisions of the Constitution. The above two powers of Supreme Court make it the Guardian of the Constitution.

12. Who appoints the Chief Justice of the Supreme Court? ***(ICSE 2009, 2001)***

Ans. The Chief Justice of the Supreme Court is appointed by the President after consultation with the Judges of Supreme Court and the High Court as he deems fit.

13. Under what circumstances can the salaries and allowances of the Supreme Court be reduced? ***(ICSE 2008)***

Ans. The President has the power to reduce the salaries of the Judges of the Supreme Court at the time of financial emergency.

14. If the President of India considers that a question of law may be referred to the Supreme Court, under which jurisdiction will the Supreme Court express its opinion on the matter? ***(ICSE 2007)***

Ans. Under advisory jurisdiction, the President can ask for the opinion of the Supreme Court on an important question of law.

15. Which body has the final authority to interpret the Constitution of India? ***(ICSE 2006)***

Ans. The Supreme Court of India has the final authority to interpret the Constitution.

2/3 Marks Questions

1. What are the qualifications required for the appointment of Judges of the Supreme Court? ***(ICSE Specimen 2018)***

Ans. For the appointment of the Judges of the Supreme Court following qualifications are required, such as

(i) She/he must be a citizen of India.

(ii) She/he should have been the Judge of a High Court or of two or more such courts in succession for at least five years.

2. With reference to the Supreme Court, explain its function as stated below. ***(ICSE 2014)***

(i) Explain original jurisdiction of Supreme Court.

(ii) Explain advisory functions of the Supreme Court.

Ans. (i) Original jurisdiction means the power to hear and determine a dispute in the first instance. It has following terms

(a) The Supreme Court enjoys original jurisdiction over matters related to dispute between Government of India and one or more States.

(b) Dispute between any Union Territory and State.

(c) Dispute between two or more States.

(ii) The advisory function of the Supreme Court is that the President can ask its advice on any important matter or on questions relating to the Constitution. The advice of Supreme Court is not binding on the President. The court is also not bound to render such advice.

3. The country's Judicial System has the Supreme Court at its apex. In this context discuss the following. ***(ICSE 2013)***

Explain manner of appointment of the judges.

Ans. The President appoints the Chief Justice of the Supreme Court after consulting the Judges of the Supreme Court or the High Courts as he deems fit. While appointing other judges, the President shall consult the Chief Justice of the Supreme Court.

4. The Supreme Court is the apex Court of our country. In this context. ***(ICSE 2011)***

Explain the composition of the Supreme Court of India.

Ans. The Supreme Court of India comprises of one Chief Justice, who is called Chief Justice of India and 30 other judges. Parliament by laws can increase the number of Judges of Supreme Court.

5. Explain the meaning of an Independent Judiciary and the need to do so.

Ans. India has opted for single integrated judicial system which is independent of the remaining two organs of the government i.e., of the Executive and Legislature.

The need for an Independent Judiciary is as follows

(i) In a representative democracy, administration of justice assumes special significance in view of rights of people. The independence of Judiciary is essential to protect any violation of the rights of people.

(ii) In a federal set-up, there is a constitutional division of powers between the Executive, Legislature and Judiciary. An independent and impartial Judiciary is essential for a federal governance.

6. The Supreme Court is the apex court in the entire judicial set-up in India. In this context, answer the following question. ***(ICSE 2010)***

What is meant by the term Single Integrated Judicial System?

Ans. The Constitution provides for a Single Integrated Judicial System with the Supreme Court at its apex. By the system we mean

(i) The entire system of Judiciary is headed by the Supreme Court which not only supervises the system, but also exercises its control over the functioning.

(ii) A uniform set of laws both civil and criminal is followed throughout the country.

(iii) All cases are taken according to a fixed procedure and can be heard in the Supreme Court after been taken first in the Lower Courts and then in the High Court.

7. With reference to the powers and functions of the Supreme Court, answer the following.

(i) What is meant by Judicial Review and original jurisdiction? ***(ICSE 2007)***

(ii) What is appellate jurisdiction? Mention any two types of cases over which the Supreme Court has appellate jurisdiction.

Ans. (i) For Judicial Review, refer to Q. 10 of 1 mark questions.

For Original Jurisdiction, refer to Q. 2 of 2/3 marks questions.

(ii) The Supreme Court hears the cases on appeal made against the order of a High Court or a Tribunal.

The Supreme Court has appellate jurisdiction regarding all types of cases, *i.e.* constitutional, civil and criminal. These are as follows

Constitutional Cases If the High Court certifies that the case involves a substantial question of law and needs to be heard in the Supreme Court.

Civil Cases Any such case which the High Court certifies, that the case involves a substantial question of law and needs to be decided by the Supreme Court.

Criminal Cases When the Lower Court acquits the accused and on appeal, the High Court reverses the decision and gives death penalty.

8. The Supreme Court is the apex judicial body in the country. With reference to this, answer the following questions.

(i) State the composition of the Supreme Court. Mention the qualifications required to become a Supreme Court Judge. ***(ICSE 2005)***

(ii) Describe the Supreme Court's power of Judicial Review. What is meant by a court of record?

Ans. (i) For composition of Supreme Court, refer to Q. 4 of 2/3 marks questions.

For qualifications required to become a Supreme Court Judge, refer to Q. 1 of 2/3 marks questions.

(ii) For explanation of Judicial Review, refer to Q. 10 of 1 mark questions.

Court of Record A court whose judgements are recorded for evidence and testimony, is known as the court of record. These judgements are in the nature of precedents, *i.e.* the High Courts and other courts are bound to give a similar decision in a similar case.
A court of record has the power to punish for contempt of court.

4/5 Marks Questions

1. With reference to the Supreme Court, explain the questions stated below.

(i) As a guardian of Fundamental Rights. ***(ICSE 2014)***

(ii) Its power of Judicial Review.

Ans. (i) Any citizen whose Fundamental Rights are violated may move to the Supreme Court for the enforcement of the rights. The Constitution provides the Supreme Court with a power to issue writs or orders in the nature of habeas corpus, mandamus, writ of prohibition, quo-warranto and writ of certiorari for the enforcement of any of the Fundamental Rights. Any such law which takes away or abridges the Fundamental Rights of the people, shall be declared null and void by the Supreme Court.

(ii) Refer to Q. 10 of 1 mark questions.

2. Explain the manner in which the Constitution seeks to maintain the independence of the Judiciary. *(ICSE 2011)*

Ans. Independence of Judiciary is ensured by the following devices

(i) Every Judge of the Supreme Court is appointed by the President after consulting judges of the Supreme Court and High Court.

(ii) A judge can remain in office till he attains the age of 65 years.

(iii) The salaries and allowances of the judges cannot be altered to their disadvantage during their term in office.

(iv) The judges are free to announce their decisions and discuss in the court chamber

Additional Info

Other ways by which Constitution seeks to maintain the independence of Judiciary are

- The court can punish any authority or person for its contempt.
- No decision of the court can be discussed in the Legislature.
- The court is free to decide its own procedures of work as well as establishment.
- The judges are prohibited to practice after their retirement.

3. In the extensive jurisdiction of the Supreme Court, state the difference between original jurisdiction and appellate jurisdiction. Mention two functions that come under original jurisdiction. *(ICSE 2010)*

Ans. The original jurisdiction refers to the matters which the Supreme Court hears and decides in first instances, *i.e.* in such cases, the person directly approaches Supreme Court whereas the appellate jurisdiction of the court includes all the cases which are already heard in Lower Courts and High Courts. These cases are brought before the Supreme Court only through an appeal.

For functions which come under Original Jurisdiction, refer to Q. 2 of 2/3 marks questions.

4. With reference to the powers and functions of the Supreme Court, answer the following.

(i) Why is the Judiciary kept independent from the control of the Executive and Legislature? *(ICSE 2007)*

(ii) Explain how the independence of the Judges of the Supreme Court is ensured by the Constitution.

Ans. (i) For answer, refer to Q. 5 of 2/3 marks questions.

(ii) For answer, refer to Q. 2 of 4 marks questions.

5. With reference to the Judiciary, write short notes on the following *(ICSE 2001)*

(i) Original jurisdiction of the Supreme Court.

(ii) The Supreme Court as a Court of Record.

Ans. (i) For answer, refer to Q. 2 of 2/3 marks questions.

(ii) A court of record is one whose judgements are recorded for evidence and testimony. These judgements are in nature of precedents, *i.e.* the Lower Courts and the other courts are bound to give a similar decision in a similar case. However, such a boundation is not applicable on the Supreme Court.

A Court of Record has two implications, which are

(i) All the orders and judgements are preserved as a record.

(ii) If a person commits a contempt of court, the court has the authority to punish him.

10 Marks Questions

1. An Independent Judiciary is a feature of federal governance. With reference to the Supreme Court, answer the following questions. *(ICSE Specimen 2023)*

(a) Who appoints the judges of the Supreme Court? What is the composition of the Supreme Court?

(b) Mention the three kinds of cases which come under the appellate jurisdiction of the Supreme Court.

(c) Explain the terms

(i) Revisory Jurisdiction (ii) Advisory Jurisdiction

Ans. (a) The President of India appoints the Judges of the Supreme Court through the following procedure

- When the President appoints the Chief Justice he/she may consult with Judges of the Supreme Court and the High Court.
- When the President appoints other Judges of the Supreme Court, he/she consults with the Chief Justice of India. Usually, the seniormost Judge of the Supreme Court is appointed as the Chief Justice of India.

At present, the Supreme Court is composed of 31 judges in which there is one Chief Justice and 30 other judges. Originally, the strength was fixed at 8 (One Chief Justice and 7 other judges).

(b) The appellate jurisdiction of the Supreme Court extends to constitutional, civil and criminal cases. These are discussed below

- **Constitutional Cases** In the Constitutional cases, an appeal can be made to the Supreme Court against the judgement of the High Court, if the High Court certifies that the case involves substantial questions of law that requires the interpretation of the Constitution. Based on the certificate, the party in the case can appeal to the Supreme Court on the ground that the question has been wrongly decided.

- **Civil Cases** In this case, an appeal lies to the Supreme Court if the High Court certifies
  - (i) that the case involves a substantial question of law of general importance.
  - (ii) that the question needs to be decided by the Supreme Court.

The Three Appellate Jurisdiction of the Supreme Court
- Constitutional cases
- Civil cases
- Criminal cases

- **Criminal Cases** The Supreme Court hear appeals against the judgement in a criminal proceedings of a High Court, if the High Court
  - (i) has an appeal reversed an order of acquittal of an accused person and sentenced him/her to death.
  - (ii) has taken before itself any case from any subordinate court and convicted the accused person and sentenced him/her to death.
  - (iii) satisfies that the case is a fit one for appeal to the Supreme Court.

(c) (i) **Revisory Jurisdiction** The Supreme Court has power to review its own judgement or order with a view to remove any mistake or error that might have crept (occur) in the judgement or orders. But it is not bound by its previous decisions. This is known as the revisory Jurisdiction.

(ii) **Advisory Jurisdiction** Under Article 143, the Constitution of India authorises the President to seek the opinion of the Supreme Court on two categories of matters. This is generally known as advisory jurisdiction. These are
- On any question of law or fact of public importance which has arisen or which is likely to arise. The advice is not binding on the President who may or may not accept it.
- On any dispute arising out of any pre-Constitution treaty, agreement, (contract), engagement or other similar instruments.

2. The Supreme Court is the head of the entire system of Judiciary. In this context, answer the following questions. *(ICSE Specimen Semester II 2022)*

(a) Mention any two qualifications required by a person to be the Judge of the Supreme Court.

(b) Who appoints the Judges of the Supreme Court? What is their term of office?

(c) Mention any three cases which come under the original jurisdiction of the Supreme Court.

(d) Why is the Supreme Court called the court of record?

Ans. (a) For answer, refer to Q. 1 of 2/3 marks questions.

(b) The President of India appoints the Judges of the Supreme Court.

The Constitution of India has not provided the fixed term for the Judges of the Supreme Court. However, it makes the following provisions in this respect

(i) He/she holds office until the age of 65 years.

(ii) He/she can resign from his/her office by writing to the President.

(iii) He/she can be removed from the office by the President on the recommendation of the Parliament.

(c) Three cases that come under the original jurisdiction of the Supreme Court are

(i) Interpretation of the Constitution in case of a dispute between the Union Government and one or more States.

(ii) Interpretation of the Constitution in case of dispute between two or more states, interests, relating to some justiciable right.

(iii) The Supreme Court has the exclusive jurisdiction to determine the constitutional validity of the Union laws. Such cases are debated by a majority of the full Constitutional Bench of 7 judges.

(d) The Supreme Court is called the court of record due to the following powers
- The judgements, proceedings and acts of the Supreme Court are recorded for perpetual memory and testimony. These records cannot be questioned when produced before any court. The judgements are in nature of precedents i.e., the High Court and other courts are bound to give a similar decision in a similar case.

- It has power to punish for the contempt of court (which are of two types i.e. Civil contempt and Criminal contempt) either with simple imprisonment for a term of 6 months of fine up to ₹ 2000 or with both.

3. The Supreme Court is at the apex of the entire system of Judiciary, In this context, answer the following questions. ***(ICSE Semester II 2022)***

(a) What is meant by Judicial Review?

(b) Explain the term original jurisdiction of the Supreme Court. Mention any two kinds of cases which come under this jurisdiction.

(c) Name any three writs which can be issued by the Supreme Court.

Ans. (a) For answer, refer to Q. 10 of 1 mark questions.

(b) For answer, refer to Q. 2 of 2/3 marks questions.

(c) Three writs which can be issued by the Supreme Court are

(i) Habeas Corpus (ii) Mandamus

(iii) Prohibition

4. With reference to the Supreme Court as the Apex Court in our Indian Judiciary, explain the following. ***(ICSE 2020)***

(a) Any three cases that come under the original jurisdiction of the Supreme Court.

(b) Power of Judicial Review.

(c) Supreme Court as a court of record.

Ans. (a) For answer, refer to Q. 2 of 2/3 marks questions.

(b) For answer, refer to Q. 10 of 1 mark questions.

(c) For answer, refer to Q. 2 (d) of 10 marks questions.

Examiner's Comment

- Most candidates attempted this part of the question well. However, a few got confused with the Appellate and other jurisdictions.
- Many candidates confused Judicial Review with Revisory Jurisdiction and hence could not explain the 'Power of the Judicial Review'.
- This was a well attempted question.

Suggestions for Students

- Teach students the meaning of the Original Jurisdiction of the Supreme court.
- Spell out the meaning of the term 'Judicial Review' and explain how this power of the Judiciary can invalidate both the Executive and the Legislature when they go against the Constitution.
- While explaining Supreme Court as a Court of Record, lay stress on the keywords as 'records' and 'future reference'.

5. Our Judicial system has a Supreme Court at its apex, followed by the High Court and other Subordinate Courts. In the light of this statement, explain the following. ***(ICSE 2018)***

(a) Any three types of cases in which the Supreme Court exercises its original jurisdiction.

(b) Any three ways by which the Constitution ensures the independence of the Judiciary.

(c) 'Advisory' and 'Revisory' Jurisdiction of the Supreme Court.

Ans. (a) For answer, refer to Q. 2 of 2/3 marks questions.

(b) For answer, refer to Q. 2 of 4 marks questions.

(c) For answer, refer to Q. 1 (c) of 10 marks questions.

Examiner's Comment

- Most of the candidates answered this question correctly. However, a few candidates, instead of writing on the cases in which the Supreme Court exercises its Original Jurisdiction, wrote on cases which come under other jurisdictions of the Supreme Court.
- Most of the candidates answered three ways by which the Constitution ensures the Independence of the Judiciary correctly.
- Some candidates got confused between the Advisory and Revisory Jurisdiction of the Supreme Court.

Suggestions for Students

- Stress on the word original while explaining Original Jurisdiction of the Supreme Court so that students are clear on the type of cases under it.
- Explain to the students how and why the independence of Supreme Court is essential for the functioning of democracy.
- Clarify to the students, the difference between the terms Revise and Review with reference to the powers of the Supreme Court.

6. With reference to the jurisdiction and functions of the Supreme Court, explain the following

(a) Advisory Jurisdiction. ***(ICSE Specimen 2017)***

(b) Custodian of Fundamental Rights.

(c) Judicial Review.

Ans. (a) **Advisory Jurisdiction**

(i) The Supreme Court has advisory jurisdiction on any question of law or fact of public importance as may be referred to it for consideration by the President.

(ii) Any question of law may be referred to it; if the President considers the question to be of public importance, though any opinions of the Supreme Court on the same is not binding on the government.

(iii) Any disputes arising out of pre-Constitution treaties and agreements or excluded from original jurisdiction are also referred to the Supreme Court.

(b) The Supreme Court issues orders or writs, in the event of encroachment of anyone's Fundamental Rights. It also has the power to declare, any such law abridging the Fundamental Rights, null and **void**. The writs that it issues are as follow

(i) **Habeas Corpus**

Enabling to get the body of any person released if unlawfully, detained by another person / a group of persons /by the State.

(ii) **Mandamus** An order to the Lower Court to perform a certain duty.

(iii) **Prohibition** For a Lower Court to stop any further proceedings.

(iv) **Certiorari** Issued with a desire to be informed about the proceedings so happening in the Lower Court.

(v) **Quo-Warranto** Issued, when a person has usurped any office, it means 'by what authority or warrant'.

(iii) **Power of Judicial Review**

The Supreme Court also stands as the final interpreter of the Constitution and of any such decisions regarding it. It has the power to review any laws passed by the Union or State Legislatures and can declare any law, against the letter and spirit of the Constitution, null and void. It also has the power to review all the national and state laws and executive order and declare them null and void.

7. The Supreme Court has an extensive jurisdiction. In the light of this statement, answer the following questions. *(ICSE 2016)*

(a) What are the qualifications of the Judges of the Supreme Court?

(b) (i) Explain the composition of the Supreme Court.

(ii) How are the Judges of the Supreme Court appointed?

(c) Explain the cases in which the Supreme Court enjoys original jurisdiction.

Ans. (a) For answer, refer to Q. 1 of 2/3 marks questions.

(b) (i) **Composition of the Supreme Court** The Supreme Court of India consists of a Chief Justice of India and not more than 30 other judges, until the Parliament by law prescribes a larger number of judges. Originally the strength was fixed at eight (one Chief Justice and seven other judges).

(ii) **Appointment of Judges in Supreme Court** Each Judge of the Supreme Court is appointed by the President of India after consultation with the other Judges of the Supreme Court and of the High Courts as he deems necessary. In case of appointing a judge other than the Chief Justice, the Chief Justice of India shall be consulted. The seniormost Judge of the Supreme Court is normally appointed as the Chief Justice of India by the President.

(c) For answer, refer to Q. 2 of 2/3 marks questions.

CHAPTER TEST

01 Mark Questions

1 The power of the Supreme Court of India to decide disputes between the Centre and States fall under ……………. jurisdiction.

(a) advisory (b) appellate
(c) revisory (d) original

2 ………is the final authority to interpret the Constitution.

(a) The Supreme Court (b) The President
(c) The Parliament (d) The Lok Sabha

3 The salaries of the Judge of the Supreme Court are determined by

(a) Law Commission (b) President
(c) Parliament (d) Prime Minister

4 The Chief Justice of the Supreme Court is appointed by …………… .

(a) the President alone
(b) the President on the recommendation of the Prime Minister
(c) the President in consultation with the Judges of the Supreme Court and High Court
(d) the President on the recommendation of law commission

5 Complete the given analogy.

Composition of Supreme Court	Number of Judge
Original	8
Currently	?

(a) 30 (b) 32 (c) 31 (d) 34

Answers

1. (d) | 2. (a) | 3. (c) | 4. (c) | 5. (d)

02 Marks Questions

6 What are the qualifications to become a Judge of the Supreme Court?

7 Mention the type of writ jurisdiction of the Supreme Court.

8 What do you understand by the term 'Judicial Review'?

9 Mention the functions that come under revisory jurisdiction of the Supreme Court.

10 Marks Question

10 An Independent Judiciary is a feature of federal governance. With reference to the Supreme Court, answer the following questions.

(i) Mention the three kinds of cases which come under the appellate jurisdiction of the Supreme Court.

(ii) What is meant by the statement that the Supreme Court is a court of record?

(iii) Explain the terms

(a) Single Integrated Judicial system
(b) Advisory Jurisdiction

05

The High Courts and the Subordinate Courts

TREND ANALYSIS 3 YEARS

Average No. of Questions Across all Sets

	Types of Questions	2023	2020	2019
TOPIC 01 High Court	1 Mark	2	–	–
	2/3 Marks	–	–	–
	4 Marks	–	–	–
	10 Marks	1	–	–
TOPIC 02 Subordinate Courts and Lok Adalat	1 Mark	1	–	1
	2/3 Marks	1	–	–
	4 Marks	–	–	–
	10 Marks	–	–	–

The High Court

- The Constitution of India provides a High Court for each State. At present, there are 25 High Courts in our country. Parliament may however, establish a common High Court for two or more States/Union Territories, according to 7th Amendment Act of 1956. This depends on the area and the population to which a High Court has to serve and the amount of work it has to handle.
- The **only Union Territory having a High Court** is Delhi. There are some High Courts which have jurisdiction over more than one State i.e. Guwahati High Court, Punjab and Haryana High Court, etc. Other Union Territories come under the jurisdiction of different High Courts.

Composition of a High Court

- Each High Court consists of a Chief Justice and other judges as appointed by the President from time to time. Besides this, the President can appoint additional judges in consultation with the Chief Justice of India for a period of not more than 2 years at a time.
- The President can appoint any Judge of the High Court as the acting Chief Justice of the High Court when the Chief Justice is unable to perform his duties.

Qualifications of Judges

According to the provisions of the Constitution, a person shall possess the following qualifications to be appointed as a Judge of a High Court

(i) He/She should be a citizen of India.

(ii) He/She should not be above 62 years of age.

(iii) He/She has held a judicial office within Indian Territory for at least 10 years.

Or He/She has been an advocate of a High Court (or High Courts in succession) for at least 10 years.

Appointment of Judges

The Chief Justice of a High Court is appointed by the President in consultation with the Chief Justice of India and the Governor of the concerned State. While appointing other judges, the President consults the Chief Justice of India, Governor of the concerned State and Chief Justice of that High Court.

Conditions of Service

- All High Court Judges are given service conditions so that they can carry out work independently without interference from other organs of the government.
- A Judge of a High Court enjoys security of tenure and can remain in office till he has attained the age of 62 years. Before this age, he can only be removed from office on **proved misbehaviour or incapacity**. The procedure of removal of a High Court Judge is the same as that of a Supreme Court Judge. He/She can be removed from office by the President on the recommendation of Parliament.
- The President can transfer a Judge of a High Court after the fulfilment of the following conditions
  (i) Orders can be issued only after consulting the Chief Justice of India.
  (ii) The Chief Justice of India must make recommendation only after consulting four seniormost Judges of the Supreme Court and the Chief Justice of two High Courts (one from which the judge is being transferred and the other to which he is being transferred).
  (iii) When a judge has been transferred, he/she shall be entitled to compensatory allowance in addition to his/her salary.
- The Chief Justice of a High Court and other Judges of the High Court are paid a monthly salary as decided by Parliament. They are entitled to free accommodation and other allowances. After retirement, they get a pension.
- The salaries and allowances of the Judges of a High Court are charged to the **Consolidated Fund of the State** and cannot be changed to their disadvantage during the course of their service.
- A Judge of the High Court after retirement can only practice in the Supreme Court or the other High Courts where he has not served as a judge. This ensures that they do not favour anyone in the hope of future favour.

Powers and Jurisdiction

The Jurisdiction of a High Court extends to the territorial limits of the State.

The powers and jurisdictions of High Court are as follows

Original Jurisdiction

It means the power of a High Court to hear disputes in the first instance, not by way of appeal. These include the following

- Will, divorce, marriage, company law, contempt of court.
- Matters of admirality.
- State revenue and its collection.
- Enforcement of Fundamental Rights of citizens.

Appellate Jurisdiction

- The High Court's appellate jurisdiction is over the decision of the Subordinate Court and also over the decision of a single judge bench of the High Court.
- The appellate jurisdiction of High Courts extends to both civil and criminal cases as well as to cases tried by courts of Munsifs and district judges. In criminal cases, it extends to cases decided by session and additional session judges. Thus, the jurisdiction of the High Courts extends to all cases under the state or federal laws.
- It also extends to those cases in which the sentence of imprisonment exceeds 7 years or the cases in which a death sentence has been awarded.

Revisory Jurisdiction

A High Court has the power of superintendence over all courts and tribunals functioning in its territorial jurisdiction except military courts.

The High Court can call for the record of any court to satisfy itself about the correctness of the legality of the orders passed. Thus, it can

(i) call for returns from such courts.

(ii) issue general rules and prescribe forms for regulating the practice and proceedings of such courts.

(iii) prescribe forms in which books of account are being kept by the officers of any lower court.

Advisory Jurisdiction

The High Court can advise any government department, Legislature or the Governor, if they seek such advice on constitutional as well as on other matter of law.

Judicial Review

The High Court has the power of Judicial Review. The power of the High Court includes examining the constitutionality of legislative enactments and executive orders. If any law contravenes the provision of the Constitution, the High Court can declare it null and void.

Court of Record

Like the Supreme Court, the High Court is a court of record. The implications, functions and powers of the High Court as a court of record are the same as that of the Supreme Court.

Enforcement of Fundamental Rights

- All the High Courts are empowered to issue writs in cases related to enforcement of Fundamental Rights.
- A writ is an order from a judicial authority asking a person to perform some act or refrain from performing an act. The writs that are issued are Habeas Corpus, Mandamus, Prohibition, Quo-Warranto and Certiorari.
- The writ jurisdiction of a High Court is much wider than the Supreme Court. The High Court can issue writs only for enforcing Fundamental Rights.

Subordinate Courts

- In every State, besides the High Court there are number of judicial courts to administer justice. These courts function under the complete control and supervision of the High Court.
- A State has got exclusive legislative competence to determine the constituent organisation and territorial jurisdiction of all courts subordinate to the High Court. However, the organisation of subordinate courts throughout the country is generally uniform.

Structure and Compositions

For judicial administration purpose, every State is divided into a number of districts, with each under the jurisdiction of a **District Judge**. Every district has Civil Courts, Criminal Courts and Courts of Revenue.

Civil Courts

Civil Courts exercise jurisdiction in cases related to land, property and money transactions, arbitration, guardianship, marriage, divorce, cases involving a will, etc.

Court of District Judge decides both civil and criminal cases and is the highest court of the District. When a judge decides civil cases, he is called as District Judge and when he decides criminal cases, he is called **Session Judge.**

He supervises all the civil courts in the district. In his judicial capacity, he takes up cases involving a sum of above ₹ 5,000. He also takes up appeals in civil cases against the decisions of the lower courts in the district.

The sub-judges, under various categories, deal with cases involving not more than a sum of ₹ 5,000. The **Munsif's courts** are below the sub-judge's courts and deal with cases involving not more than a sum of ₹ 2,000. The small courts are the lowest level of courts and deal with cases of nominal value. There is no appeal against their decisions.

Term of Office

The District Judges are appointed by the Governor in consultation with the Judges of the High Court of the concerned State. All other judges are appointed through **competitive examinations** held by the State Public Service Commission.

The District Judges exercise administrative control over all civil courts in the district.

Criminal Courts

These courts exercise jurisdiction in cases related to murder, robbery, theft, assault etc. Criminal courts are broadly classified as

- **Sessions Court** It is the **highest criminal court of the district**. It deals with cases concerning robbery, dacoity and murder. It can award sentence up to life imprisonment or death sentence. But it is mandatory that a death sentence must be confirmed by the High Court before its execution irrespective of whether an appeal is made to the High Court or not.
- **Court of Chief Metropolitan Magistrate** deals with less serious offences and can award fine of ₹ 5,000 and a sentence of up to 7 years imprisonment.

- **Court of First Class Magistrate** can award a sentence of up to 3 years imprisonment or fine of ₹5,000 or both.
- **Court of Second Class Magistrate** can award a sentence of not more than 2 years or impose a fine of ₹1,000 or both.
- **Court of Third Class Magistrate** can award sentence of up to 1 month of simple imprisonment or a fine of up to ₹5,000 or both. It deals with criminal cases involving simple individual quarrels or rioting.

Courts of Revenue

These courts deal with cases relating to the maintenance of land records and assessment and collection of Land Revenue. Some revenue courts are as follows

(i) Board of Revenue
(ii) Commissioner's Court
(iii) Collector's Court
(iv) Tehsildar's Court
(v) Naib Tehsildar's Court

Distinction between Court of the District Judge and Sessions Court

(i) The court of District Judge is the **highest civil court of the district**, whereas sessions court is the highest criminal court of the district.

(ii) The presiding officer in the civil court is called as District Judge, while the sessions court is presided over by a Sessions Judge.

(iii) The District Judge acts as a Deputy Commissioner and in this capacity he maintains law and order and supervises the collection of revenue and taxes in the district, whereas the Sessions Judge does not perform any administrative functions.

Lok Adalat : Meaning

Lok Adalat is the people's court set up on the recommendation of **Justice PN Bhagwati** under Legal Services Authorities Act, 1987. It is a legal forum to provide aid and justice to those who are not in a position to engage lawyers or bear expenses of legal proceedings.

Disputes in these courts are settled in a spirit of harmony and compromise. The cases are settled informally and cordially with the involvement of the conflicting parties. Lok Adalats solve cases which are yet to go to any court.

Working of Lok Adalat

- The judges of these courts are actually counsellors. These adalats are assisted by **Legal Aid Committee** and **Social Action Groups** which advise the people about legal matters and help them to solve the cases through mutual participation.
- The Legal Services Authorities Act, 1987 provides that every State and District authority shall organise Lok Adalats from time to time. All decisions given by the Lok Adalats shall be deemed to be decrees of a Civil Court and shall be binding on the parties.

Advantages of Lok Adalat

The advantages of Lok Adalat are as follows

(i) These adalats work in the spirit of compromise and understanding, which result into satisfaction of both the parties.

(ii) These courts deliver **fast** and **inexpensive justice**. Any person can move the Lok Adalat by an application on a plain paper in a prescribed format.

(iii) Lok Adalats reduce workload of other courts, enabling them to deal with more serious matters.

Scope of Lok Adalats

The system of Lok Adalats has now become so popular that various government departments began to hold Lok Adalats.

This court plays a significant role in the settlement of disputes between families and friends, neighbours and minor cases of assault and injury. Weaker sections of society cannot afford the delay or the cost involved in normal court procedures.

Family Courts

- The Family Courts Act, 1984, was enacted to secure speedy settlement of disputes relating to marriage and family affairs. The act provides for setting up of family courts in cities having population of over 10 Lakhs.
- On a recommendation made by the Parliamentary Committee on Empowerment of Women, all State Governments/Union Territory Administrations have been asked to establish one family court in each district of the country.

PYQs Previous Years' Questions

1 Mark Questions

Multiple Choice Questions

1. Complete the given analogy.
Court of District Judge : Civil Cases : : Sessions Court : ? Cases. *(ICSE 2023)*
(a) Advisory
(b) Criminal
(c) Constitutional
(d) Appellate

Ans. (*b*) Criminal

2. When a case comes from a Subordinate Court, the High Court deals with it under .... *(ICSE Specimen 2023)*
(a) revisory jurisdiction
(b) advisory jurisdiction
(c) original jurisdiction
(d) appellate jurisdiction

Ans. (*d*) appellate jurisdiction

3. Under the .... powers, the High Court will check the judgement of the Subordinate Court. *(ICSE Specimen Semester II 2022)*
(a) advisory (b) revisory
(c) judicial Review (d) original

Ans. (*b*) revisory

4. The High Court Judge can remain in office till he/she attains the age of .... *(ICSE Semester II 2022)*
(a) 60 years (b) 65 years
(c) 62 years (d) 55 years

Ans. (*c*) 62 years

5. The Sessions Court deals with .... case. *(ICSE Semester II 2022)*
(a) civil
(b) criminal
(c) constitutional
(d) revenue

Ans. (*b*) criminal

6. Which of the following statements does not apply to the Lok Adalat? *(ICSE Semester II 2022)*
(a) It reduces the burden on High Courts
(b) Works on the spirit of compromise
(c) The cases take a long time to get resolved
(d) It involves very less expenses

Ans. (*c*) The cases take a long time to get resolved

Very Short Answer Questions

1. Mention any one advantage of the Lok Adalat. *(ICSE 2020, 2015)*

Ans. An advantage of the Lok Adalat is that is encourages the settlement of disputes through compromise between two parties.

2. State one point of distinction between a District Judge and a Sessions Judge. *(ICSE 2019, 2014)*

Ans. A District Judge hear cases related to civil matter wherease a Sessions Judge decide cases related to criminal matters.

3. Which is the highest criminal court in a district? Who presides over it? *(ICSE Specimen 2018)*

Other Similar Questions

Or Name the highest criminal court in a district.

Or Which is the highest Criminal Court in the district?

Ans. The Sessions Court is the highest criminal court in a district. District Judge presides over it.

4. What is meant by Lok Adalat? *(ICSE 2018, 2012, 2016, 2006)*

Ans. Lok Adalat is the people's court to provide aid and justice to those who are not in a position to engage lawyers or bear expenses of legal proceedings.

5. What is meant by High Court being a court of record? *(ICSE Specimen 2017)*

Ans. It means that the judgements passed in the High Court will be recorded and referred to later, in the event of similar cases.

6. State one other qualification required to become a Judge of the High Court, apart from Indian citizenship. *(ICSE 2017)*

Ans. A Judge of the High Court has been an advocate of a High Court for at least 10 years.

7. Mention one reason to state that the Lok Adalat has its own advantage. ***(ICSE 2017)***

Or Mention one reason why the system of Lok Adalat has become popular. ***(ICSE 2011)***

Ans. Lok Adalat has its own advantage because it delivers fast and inexpensive justice. Any person can move a Lok Adalat by an application on a plain paper in a prescribed format.

8. Name the highest Civil Court in a district. ***(ICSE 2016)***

Or Name the highest court dealing with civil cases at the District level. ***(ICSE 2007)***

Ans. The District Judge Court is the highest Civil Court in a district.

9. How does the High Court protect the Fundamental Rights of individuals? ***(ICSE 2012)***

Ans. High Court can protect the Fundamental Rights of individuals by issuing writs against the authority violating it.

10. What is the appellate jurisdiction of the High Court? ***(ICSE 2014)***

Ans. Appellate jurisdiction of the High Court is related to cases whose appeal is over the decision of the Subordinate Courts. The High Court also hears cases of appeal on tribunal decisions.

11. What is meant by the term 'Judicial Review' of the High Court ? ***(ICSE 2016)***

Ans. Judicial Review is the power of the High Court to examine the constitutionality of legislative enactments and executive orders of both the Central and State Government.

12. What is meant by original jurisdiction of the High Court? ***(ICSE 2011, 2005)***

Ans. Original jurisdiction of High Court extends to cases relating to will, marriage admirality.
These type of cases can be taken to High Court at first instance.

13. Who administers the oath of office to the High Court Judges? ***(ICSE 2011)***

Ans. The Governor of State administers the oath of office to the Judges of the High Court.

14. Mention three types of courts that a district usually has. ***(ICSE 2010)***

Ans. A district has three types of courts. These are
(i) Civil Courts (ii) Criminal Courts
(iii) Courts of Revenue

15. What is understood by the revisory jurisdiction of the High Court? ***(ICSE 2009)***

Ans. The High Court can call for the records of a case which has been decided by a Subordinate Court. This is done, if the High Court feels that the Subordinate Court has not followed proper procedure.

16. Name the writ issued by the High Court which provides a remedy for a person, who has been unlawfully detained in prison. ***(ICSE 2008)***

Ans. In such a case the High Court can issue the writ of Habeas Corpus against the authority/ person who violated the Fundamental Rights of the person.

2/3 Marks Questions

1. Ms Anita wants to approach the Lok Adalat regarding a case. Mention any two advantages she will have by taking her case to the Lok Adalat. ***(ICSE Specimen 2023)***

Ans. Two advantages Ms Anita would have by taking her case to the Lok Adalat are
(i) It reduces the workload of other courts enabling them to deal with more serious matters. It promotes social justice by providing legal aid to weaker sections of the society.
(ii) It delivers fast and inexpensive justice.

2. Explain the term 'Judicial Review' of the High Court. ***(ICSE Specimen 2018)***

Ans. Under the 'Judicial Review' the High Court examines the constitutionality of Legislative enactment and executive orders of both the Centre and the State Governments. If the enactments and orders are found to be violative of the contitution, they can be declared as illegal, unconstitutional and invalid (null and void) by the High Court.

3. Why is the High Court also known as court of record? ***(ICSE 2012)***

Ans. The judgements and orders of the High Courts are preserved as a record for future reference. These records are admitted before any Subordinate Court. As a court of record, if a person commits the contempt of the court, the court has the power to punish him.

4. State the composition of the High Court. State the qualifications required to become a High Court Judge. *(ICSE 2012)*

Ans. Each High Court consists of a Chief Justice appointed by the President and other judges appointed by the President from time to time.

The qualifications required for appointment of a Judge of High Court are as follows

(i) He/She should be a citizen of India.

(ii) He/She has held a judicial office in the Territory of India for at least 10 years.

5. State any three advantages of the Lok Adalat. *(ICSE 2012, 2008)*

Ans. Three advantages of Lok Adalats are as follows

(i) Lok Adalats work on the spirit of compromise and understanding. As a result both the parties feel satisfied.

(ii) Lok Adalats deliver fast and inexpensive justice.

(iii) Lok Adalats reduce the workload of other courts.

6. Mention the three cases, in which the High Court enjoys original jurisdiction. *(ICSE 2008)*

Ans. Cases in which the High Court has the authority to hear and decide at first instance comes under the original jurisdiction of the High Court. These are as follows

(i) Settle disputes relating to State revenue and its collection.

(ii) Cases regarding wills, divorce, marriage, company law and contempt of court to interpret the Constitution.

(iii) Enjoys original jurisdiction for the enforcement of the Fundamental Rights.

7. Under which jurisdiction can High Court accept an appeal against the decisions of the District courts? *(ICSE 2008)*

Ans. Under appellate jurisdiction, High Court can accept an appeal against the decisions of the Subordinate Courts in both the civil and criminal cases. Its jurisdiction extends to case tried by courts of munsif's and district judges.

4 Marks Questions

1. What do you mean by 'Lok Adalat'? State any three advantages of the Lok Adalat. *(ICSE Specimen 2018)*

Ans. Lok Adalat is a system of alternative dispute resolution developed in India. It roughly means 'People's Court'.

For advantages of Lok Adalat, refer to Q. 5 of 2/3 marks questions.

2. Name the three types of courts at the District level. Explain the different categories of cases that fall under the jurisdiction of each. *(ICSE 2006)*

Ans. Every district has three types of courts which are

(i) **Civil Courts** These courts exercise jurisdiction in the cases related to land, property and money transactions, arbitration, marriage and cases involving a will.

Three types of Courts at District level
- Civil Courts
- Criminal Courts
- Courts of Revenue

(ii) **Criminal Courts** These courts exercise jurisdiction in cases related to theft, robbery, assault, murder, etc.

(iii) **Courts of Revenue** These courts deal with cases relating to the maintenance of land records and the assessment and collection of land revenue.

10 Marks Questions

1. The Constitution of India provides for a High Court for each State. With reference to the High Courts and Subordinate Courts, answer the following questions. *(ICSE 2023)*

(a) Who appoints the Judges of the High Court ? Mention any two qualifications required for a person to be appointed as a Judge of a High Court.

(b) Mention any three cases that come under the original jurisdicition of the High Court.

(c) What are Lok Adalats? Mention any three advantage of the Lok Adalats.

Ans. (a) The Chief Justice of a High Court is appointed by the President in consultation with the Chief Justice of India and the Governor of the concerned State.

For qualification required for a person to be appoint as a judge of High Court.

Refer to Q. 4 of 2/3 marks questions.

(b) For answer, refer to Q. 6 of 2/3 marks questions.

(c) For answer, refer to Q. 1 of 4 marks questions.

2. With reference to the powers and functions of the High Court, explain briefly the meaning and scope of the following ***(ICSE 2017)***

(a) Its appellate jurisdiction

(b) The High Court as a court of record

(c) Judicial review

Ans. (a) **Appellate Jurisdiction of the High Court**

The High Court's appellate jurisdiction is over the decision of the subordinate courts under its supervision and also over the decision of single judge bench of the High Court.

The appellate jurisdiction of High Courts extends to both civil and criminal cases. The jurisdiction also extends to cases tried by courts of munsifs and district sub-judges.

In criminal cases, it extends to cases decided by Session and Additional Session Judges. Thus, the jurisdiction of the High Courts extends to all cases under the state or federal laws in which the sentence of imprisonment exceeds 7 years or the death sentence.

(b) The High Court is a court of record. This implies

(i) Its judgements are kept as a record and are used as a precedent. It is binding on all subordinate courts in the state.

(ii) If a person commits contempt of a High Court, it has the authority to punish him. The Supreme Court or the Parliament cannot deprive the High Court of this power.

(c) Judicial review is the special power vested in the Judiciary by which it examines the constitutionality of the laws passed by the legislature and the acts of the government. If, in view of the court, any executive order or any law passed by the legislature violates any provision of the Constitution, it declares it unconstitutional.

CHAPTER TEST

01 Mark Questions (MCQ)

1 Each High Court consists of a .... and other judges as appointed by the President from time to time.

(a) Adhoc Judge (b) Chief Justice of State
(c) District Judge (d) Chief Justice of India

2 A Judge of the High Court shall hold office Until he/she attains the age of ....

(a) 60 years (b) 65 years
(c) 62 years (d) 63 years

3

High Court Judge appointed by	President
District Court Judge appointed by	?

(a) Governor (b) Chief Minister
(c) Chief Secretary (d) President

4 The Lok Adalat is the people's court set up on the recommendation of ....

(a) PN Bhagwati (b) CM Singhvi
(c) PK Mishra (d) SN Bhagwati

5

District Court	Civil Cases/matter
Session Court	?

(a) Criminal Cases (b) Revenue Case
(c) Marriage Case (d) Divorce Case

6 Which of the following is considered as the people's court?

(a) Lok Adalat (b) High Court
(c) District Court (d) Taluk Court

7 The Constitution of India provides a High Court for each State. At present, there are .... High Courts in our country.

(a) 24 (b) 25
(c) 28 (d) 29

Answers

1. (b)	2. (c)	3. (a)	4. (a)	5. (a)	6. (a)	7. (b)

02 Marks Questions

8 What is the composition of a High Court?

9 Mention any two types of cases in which the High Court exercises original jurisdiction.

10 State any two advantages of Lok Adalat.

11 What are the qualifications to become a Judge of the High Court?

10 Marks Question

12 With reference to the powers and jurisdiction of the High Court, answer the following questions.

(i) State any three appellate jurisdiction of the High Court.

(ii) Mention any three distinction between court of the District Judge and Session Court.

(iii) Explain the terms.

(a) Judicial Review

(b) Court of Record

01 The First War of Independence and Growth of Nationalism

TREND ANALYSIS 3 YEARS

Average No. of Questions Across all Sets

Topic	Types of Questions	2023	2020	2019
TOPIC 01 First War of Independence	1 Mark	2	–	–
	2/3 Marks	1	–	1
	4 Marks	–	–	–
	10 Marks	2	1	–
TOPIC 02 Growth of Nalionalism	1 Mark	2	–	–
	2/3 Marks	1	–	1
	4 Marks	–	–	–
	10 Marks	–	–	–

India got independence from British rule on 15th August, 1947, but the fundamental struggle that led to freedom had been a long drawn process. The culmination of traditional opposition to British rule came with the First War of Independence in 1857, in which millions of peasants, artisans and soldiers participated.

The first hundred years of British rule in India from 1757 to 1857, were marked by the British victories and the rapid expansion of their dominion in India.

Beginning of the Revolt of 1857

- In 1856, the British authorities decided to replace the old fashioned musket (called the 'Brown Bess') by the new **Enfield rifle**. The cartridges to be used in the rifle were greased with fat. The loading process of the Enfield rifle involved bringing the cartridge to the mouth and biting off the top greased paper with the mouth.
- A rumour spread out, that the cartridges were greased with the fat of pigs and cows. Soldiers believed that, these cartridges were intentionally greased with animal fat to hurt their religious sentiments.
- The revolt first began at Barrackpore, when most of the Indian soldiers refused to use the grease cartridges. As a result, a Brahmin soldier of the 34th Native Infantry at Barrackpore, named **Mangal Pandey** led an attack on the adjutant of 34th Native Infantry on 29th March, 1857.
- After this incident, Mangal Pandey was arrested and hanged on **8th April, 1857**. Within a month of this incidence, uprisings started in **Meerut, Delhi, Kanpur, Lucknow, Jhansi** and at many other places.

Events at Meerut

The mutiny started at Meerut on **10th May, 1857**. The occasion was the punishment of some sepoys for their refusal to use the greased cartridges. They broke open jails, murdered Europeans, burnt their houses and marched to Delhi. They seized the city and proclaimed the aged **Mughal Emperor Bahadur Shah II** as the Emperor of India.

Events at Delhi

After reaching Delhi, they killed many British soldiers and surrounded the entire city. The loss of Delhi, lowered the respect of the British army. So, in order to achieve their respect again, Sir **John Nicholson** besieged Delhi with the help of loyal Sikh soldiers.

In the end, the British surmounted Delhi and the old emperor Bahadur Shah was taken prisoner. As a punishment, he was ordered life imprisonment and deported to Rangoon, where he died in 1862.

Events at Lucknow

Begum Hazrat Mahal, the wife of the Nawab of Awadh led the uprising at **Lucknow** on 30th May, 1857. The city was recaptured by the British in March, 1858. Begum Hazrat Mahal fled towards the Nepal Frontier.

Events at Kanpur

The War of Independence was led by **Nana Sahib** at Kanpur. He wanted to get his pension from the government, which they were paying to the last Peshwa Baji Rao II. But now the British refused to grant it. Nana Sahib was the adopted son of the last Peshwa Baji Rao II and at that time there was a policy called the **Doctrine of Lapse** applied by the Governor-General Lord Dalhousie.

Lord Dalhousie annexed few states like—Jhansi, Udaipur, Kanpur, Satara, etc., by using this policy. Being a brave and determined General, Nana Sahib opposed this policy. But in the end, on 17th June, 1857 General Havelock captured Kanpur after defeating Nana Sahib.

Note Kunwar Singh (Bihar), Rani Laxmi Bai (Jhansi), Tantia Tope (Naha Sahib's General), Khan Bahadur Khan (Bareilly), Maulvi Ahmedullah (Faizabad), Azimullah Khan (Fatehpur), etc., were the other leaders, who took command of the movement.

Causes of the Revolt

The Revolt of 1857 is an important landmark in the history of India, which occurred during the Governor-Generalship of **Lord Canning**. The Revolt of 1857 was a combination of political, economical, socio-religious, military and many other causes.

Political Causes

Some of the political causes of the revolt were as follows

(i) Lord Dalhousie's **Policy of Annexation** and the **Doctrine of Lapse** were the significant causes. As per the Doctrine of Lapse, heirs adopted without the consent of the company, could inherit only the private property of the deceased ruler and not his territory, which would come under the company's rule. They made the British administration very unpopular and the rulers of the different states as bitter enemies of the British.

(ii) The British refused to grant pension to Nana Sahib, as he was the adopted son of Peshwa Baji Rao II. Avadh was annexed in 1856, on charges of maladministration. Satara, Jhansi, Nagpur and Sambalpur were annexed owing to the Doctrine of Lapse.

(iii) All the Indian states had either been annexed or had entered into alliances with the company in 1856. The British had become the supreme power and the Indian princes were reduced to puppets.

(iv) **Lord Dalhousie**, the Governor-General of India, annexed many Indian states to the company using the Doctrine of Lapse.

(v) The rulers of Indian states believed that their states were not annexed by the application of Doctrine of Lapse, but due to **lapse of all morals** on the part of the East India Company.

(vi) In 1849, Lord Dalhousie announced that the successors of Bahadur Shah Zafar would not be permitted to use the Red Fort as their palace. They were required to shift to a place near the Qutab Minar.

(vii) After 7 years, in 1856, Lord Canning announced that after the death of Bahadur Shah Zafar, his successors would not be allowed to use the imperial titles with their names and would be known as mere princes. This decision of the British hurt the feelings of the Muslims, consequently Bahadur Shah began plotting against them.

Socio-Religious Causes

Some of the socio-religious causes of the revolt were as follows

(i) The British Government's attempt to interfere in the social and religious life of the Indians led to widespread fear among the masses.

(ii) The combined effect of British Expansionist Policies, Economic Exploitation and Administrative changes adversely affected the Indian society as a whole.

(iii) British social reforms like Abolition of Sati (1829), Legalisation of Widow Remarriage (1856) etc., hurt the sentiments of the orthodox and conservative people.

(iv) The orthodox Indians felt humiliated to note that in the railway compartments brahmins and people from the backward classes were made to sit side by side.

Economic Causes

The most important reason for the popular discontent was the economic exploitation by the British. The economic exploitation took the following forms

(i) The East India Company made huge profits at the expenses of the people of India. The company purchased textiles, indigo, foodgrains and spices from India and sold them abroad at exorbitant prices.

(ii) By buying and exporting Indian goods, the company encouraged their production in India. But gradually, the Indian textiles began to compete with the textiles manufactured in England. The British put pressure on the East India Company to forbid the sale of Indian textiles in England. The British Government then put restrictions on the import of Indian textiles besides imposing heavy import duties on such goods.

(iii) People moved to cities to find employment, which was very difficult to get. Peasants were forced to pay tax in cash, which pushed them into the hands of the moneylenders, as tax was collected even during the famines.

(iv) Indigo, tea, jute, cotton and opium were crops, which the British wanted the Indians to grow. If the peasants planted anything else, their crops were destroyed and cattle were carried off as a punishment.

(v) The British Economic Policies also affected the upper and the middle classes of the society. The **Inam Commission**, appointed in 1852 in Bombay, confiscated as many as 20000 estates. This drove the landed aristocracy to poverty without benefitting the peasantry, which suffered due to the exorbitant land revenue. It was claimed by the merchants, moneylenders and the new owners of these estates.

Military Causes

Military causes that led to the revolt were as follows

Several factors contributed to a change in the attitude of the Indian soldiers towards the company. The discrimination with Indian soldiers was one of the causes of the revolution.

(i) The Indian and British soldiers were not treated equally. The salary of the Indian soldiers was too meagre to support their families, while the duties of both the British and the Indian soldiers were more or less similar.

(ii) The British Parliament passed the **General Service Enlistment Act** in 1856, which decreed that the Indian soldiers could be sent overseas on duty. This act did not take into account the sentiment of the Indian soldiers. Indian soldiers dreaded sea voyage and considered it against their customs.

(iii) Indians were of the belief that, the British were invincible, but the British were beaten in the First Afghan War (1838-42). This convinced the Indian soldiers that the British could also be defeated. This gave courage to the Indian soldiers to wage a war against the British rule.

Consequences of the Revolt

End of the Company's Rule

This act abolished the Board of Control and Court of Directors of the Company and the responsibility of the Government of India was passed on to a separate minister, who was known as the Secretary of state for India. The Governor General was made the **Viceroy**, who dealt with the Nawabs, the Rajas and other native Princes. **Lord Canning** was declared as the **first Viceroy of India**.

Queen Victoria's Proclamation

The first significant result of the Revolt was the end of the rule of the East India Company in India. The Queen's proclamation incorporating the transfer of governance from East India Company to the British crown was made public at Allahabad, on 1st November, 1858, by Lord Canning, the first Viceroy of India.

The proclamation declared that the British would not interfere in their internal matters except in the case of 'misconduct' and 'anarchy'. After the proclamation of the queen, the policy of 'Doctrine of Lapse' was abolished.

Relations with Princely States

There was a change in the policy of the new government towards the Indian Princes, in order to make them loyal to the British. It assured them that all the treaties entered with the company would be honoured. Their territories would not be annexed to the British crown. They were given the right to adopt sons and successors.

End of Peshwaship and the Mughal Rule

The war also ended the Peshwaship and the Mughal rule. As Nana Sahib, the adopted son of Peshwa Baji Rao II, who had taken part in the war could not be traced, the office of the Peshwa was abolished. Similarly, the title of Mughal Emperor was also abolished with the death of Bahadur Shah II in 1862.

Policy of Divide and Rule

After 1858, the British continued their policy of 'Divide and Rule' by giving special protections and concessions to the Princely States, encouraging hatred and ill-feelings among the Hindus and the Muslims, so that the people of India could never challenge the British authority.

Changes in the Army

The Indian Army had been mainly responsible for the crisis of 1857. After the revolt, it was thoroughly reorganised and built up on the policy of 'division and counterprise'.

The strength of the European troops in India was increased from 45000 to 65000 and the number of Indian troops was reduced from 238000 to 140000. All big troops and artillery departments were reserved for the Europeans. Discrimination on the basis of caste, region and religion was practised in the recruitment to the army. Newspapers, journals and nationalist publications were prevented from reaching the Indian army to keep them separated from the rest of the population.

Economic Exploitation

The Revolt of 1857 ended an era and sowed the seeds of a new era *i.e.*, the era of Territorial Expansion gave place to the era of Economic Exploitation. India became a typical colony of the British, by exporting raw materials and importing British goods. Peasants, rural artisans etc., were impoverished under the British rule.

Growth of Nationalism

The origination of nationalism is one of the most distinguishing features of the second half of the 19th century. It originated from the concepts of nationalism and right of self-determination initiated by the French Revolution, the socio-religious reform movements in India, as an off shoot of modernisation introduced by the British in India, and as a reaction of the Indians to the British colonial policies.

Factors Promoting the Growth of Nationalism

Repressive colonial policies, socio-religious reform movements, rediscovery of India's past, influence of Western education, role of press, modern means of transport and communication etc., are responsible for the growth of nationalism in India.

The Economic Factors Responsible for Growth of Nationalism

(i) Agricultural India was made an economic colony to serve the interests of Industrial England.

(ii) India was made to accept readymade British goods either duty free or at nominal duty rates, while Indian products were subjected to high import duties in England.

(iii) The British capital invested in Indian markets especially in railway, shipping, oil exploration, tea and coffee plantations etc., was used to get huge profits and were sent to England.

(iv) The export of raw materials and foodgrains deprived the country of her agricultural surplus and raised the prices of raw materials.

(v) The salaries and allowances of the English, who served in the administration and the army were paid out from Indian resources.

(vi) The drain included the salaries, incomes and savings of the Englishmen and the British expenditure in India on the purchase of military goods, office establishment, interest on debts, unnecessary expenditure on the army, etc.

Growth of Political Association

- **Raja Ram Mohan Roy** was the pioneer of political movements in India. He was the first Indian to focus the attention of the Englishmen on the grievances of the Indians and to ask for remedial measures.
- The first political association to be started in India was the **Land Holder's Society** in Kolkata in 1838. Many public associations like the Bengal British India Society, British Indian Association, East India Association, London Indian Society and Indian Association wer started in different parts of India.
- In 1877, a Grand Delhi Durbar was organised by **Lord Lytton**, which proclaimed Queen Victoria as the Empress of India. Lord Lytton introduced the Vernacular Press Act (1878) and Indian Arms Act (1879), which were protested against by Surendranath Banerjee.

Rediscovery of India

Sir William Jones founded the **Asiatic Society of Bengal** to encourage oriental studies. The Asiatic Society got many Indian classics translated into English and these translations introduced the ancient Indian culture to the Western world.

The works of various European scholars contributed to the rediscovery of India's glorious history. Archaeological excavations also helped in adding knowledge about ancient Indian culture.

Influence of Western Education

- The British introduced Western education in India through the medium of English to serve their own representatives. They wanted to train Indian people as clerks so as to run their own administration.
- The British wanted to rear their culture and conquer the goodwill of the educated Indians. But it produced results, which were against their expectations.
- Western education, through the study of European history, political thought and economic ideas, gave the educated Indians a rational, secular, democratic and national outlook. The slogan–**Equality, Liberty and Fraternity** of the American and the French Revolutions, impressed all the educated Indians.
- English language played a leading part in this process. It was through this language that the Indians from different parts of the country could meet and exchange ideas. English gave them a linguistic unity.
- Through Western education, social and national consciousness of Indians was awakened by the revolutionary ideas of the liberal thinkers like Rousseau, Mazzini and Thomas Paine.

Role of the Press

A large number of newspapers were started in the later half of the 18th century. Some of the prominent newspapers were The Amrit Bazar Patrika, The Bengali, The Tribune, The Pioneer, The Times of India, The Hindu and The Statesman in English. The press played an enormous role in fostering national unity and creating consciousness among the Indians.

Repressive Colonial Policies

The British colonial power followed a repressive policy against Indians

- **Lord Lytton** Viceroys like **Lord Lytton** (1876-1880) and **Lord Curzon** (1899-1905) took many repressive policies due to which the Indians were resented and nationalism grow among them.
- **Ilbert Bill** The Ilbert Bill of 1883 abolished judicial disqualification on the basis of racial distinction. This bill allowed the trail of Europeans by Indian Judges for criminal offences. The law provoked a strong criticism among the educated Indians.

The Vernacular Press Act

The Vernacular Press Act forbade the vernacular papers to publish any material against the British Government. This act was not applicable to English newspapers. In 1881, this was repealed by Lord Ripon.

Modern Means of Transport and Communication

The first railway line connecting **Mumbai** with **Thane** was laid down in 1853. By 1869, more than 6000 kms of railways had been built, extending to nearly 45000 km by 1905. Besides encouraging trade and commerce, the railways facilitated the growth of nationalism.

Socio-Religious Reform Movement

The second half of the 19th century witnessed the rise of many religious and social reformers in India. Reformers like Raja Ram Mohan Roy, Swami Dayananda Saraswati, Swami Vivekananda and Jyotiba Phule played an important role in the growth of nationalism through their reform movements.

Contributions of Raja Ram Mohan Roy and Jyotiba Phule

- Raja Ram Mohan Roy was the greatest social and religious reformer of the 19th century, who established the **Brahmo Sabha** in 1828, which was later renamed as **Brahmo Samaj**. Raja Ram Mohan Roy is also called as the **Father of Modern India**. The Brahmo Samaj believed in 'Monotheism' or 'Worship of One God'.
- Jyotiba Phule was an urban-educated member of a so-called low caste. In 1854, he established a school for untouchables and started a private orphanage for the widows. He founded the **Satya Shodhak Samaj** in 1873, with the aim of securing social justice for the weaker sections of the society.

The Indian National Association and the East India Association

- In 1883, Surendranath Banerjee convened the All India National Conference at Kolkata. It was a provincial organisation. It offered a model to the Indian National Congress, which was formed two years later.

- The **East India Association** was founded in London in 1866 by **Dadabhai Naoroji**. The association provided information on all the Indian subjects to the British citizens and the Members of Parliament. The association had its branches in Mumbai, Kolkata and Chennai.

Indian National Congress

The Indian National Congress was formed by **Allan Octavian Hume** (AO Hume), an Englishman and a retired civil servant, in association with various national leaders, who called for a conference in Pune in December, 1885.

The First Congress Session

It was held at Gokuldas Tejpal Sanskrit College, Mumbai from 28th December to 31st December, 1885 under the presidentship of **Womesh Chunder Bonnerjee**. It was attended by 72 delegates. The Viceroy Lord Dufferin, favoured the formation of the Congress because he wanted it to act as a **safety-valve** for popular discontent, thereby, safeguarding the British interests in India.

The prime objectives of Indian National Congress (INC) as per Womesh Chunder (WC) Bonnerjee were to promote friendly relations between nationalist political workers from various parts of country and to develop the feeling of national unity.

The Second Congress Session

It was held at Kolkata in 1886 under the presidentship of **Dadabhai Naoroji**, some of the delegates were also received by Lord Dufferin as distinguished visitors to the capital.

The Surat Session (23rd Session)

- It was held in 1907 under the presidentship of **Rashbihari Ghosh**. There was a dispute between the Early Nationalists and the Assertive Nationalists of the Congress regarding the methods of agitation in Bengal after its partition.
- The Assertive Group was excluded from the Congress nearly for a decade. It was only in 1916, that the two wings of the Congress were united at the Lucknow Session.

Objectives of the Indian National Congress

The objectives of Indian National Congress were as follows

(i) Promotion of close relations of nationalistic workers in different parts of the country.

(ii) Evolution and consolidation of a feeling of national unity, irrespective of caste, religions, etc.

(iii) Presentation of popular demands before the government.

(iv) Training and organisation of public opinion in the country.

PYQs Previous Years' Questions

1 Mark Questions

Multiple Choice Questions

1. Which of these was not an aim of the Indian National Congress? *(ICSE Specimen 2023)*

(a) To train and organise public opinion in the country.

(b) To promote friendly relations between nationalists political workers.

(c) To make the world aware of the true nature of the British.

(d) To formulate popular demands and present them before the government.

Ans. (*c*) To make the world aware of the true nature of the British.

2. .... announced that the successors of Bahadur Shah could not use imperial titles. *(ICSE Specimen 2023)*

(a) Lord Canning (b) Lord Wellesley

(c) Lord Dalhousie (d) Lord Ripon

Ans. (*a*) Lord Canning

3. Which of these is not a repressive policy of Lord Lytton? *(ICSE Specimen 2023)*

(a) Arms Act (b) Ilbert Bill

(c) Vernacular Press Act (d) Grand Delhi Durbar

Ans. (*b*) Ilbert Bill

4. Complete the given analogy.

Jyotiba Phule : Satya Shodhak Samaj : : Raja Ram Mohan Roy : : ? *(ICSE Specimen 2023)*

(a) Arya Samaj (b) Brahmo Samaj

(c) Satya Shodhak Samaj (d) Prarthana Samaj

Ans. (*b*) Brahmo Samaj

5. Which statement does not apply to the Subsidiary alliance? *(ICSE Specimen Semester I 2021)*

(a) The kings virtually lost their powers

(b) It was introduced by Lord Dalhousie

(c) The kings had to maintain the British army at their cost

(d) They had a British resident in their court

Ans. (*b*) It was introduced by Lord Dalhousie

6. The year in which the Congress was established *(ICSE Specimen Semester I 2021)*

(a) 1885 (b) 1856

(c) 1898 (d) 1886

Ans. (*a*) 1885

7. .... was denied pension under the Doctrine of Lapse. *(ICSE Specimen Semester I 2021)*

(a) Zeenat Mahal (b) Baji Rao II

(c) Bahadur Shah Zafar (d) Nana Saheb

Ans. (d) Nana Saheb

8. The General Service Enlistment Act implied that soldiers *(ICSE Specimen Semester I 2021)*

(a) would not be given promotions

(b) would have to travel overseas to fight

(c) would be given less salaries

(d) would not be given extra allowance

Ans. (*b*) would have to travel overseas to fight

9. In 1857, the Hindu and Muslim soldiers refused to use the new cartridges because *(ICSE Specimen Semester I 2021)*

(a) they were greased with cow and pig fat

(b) they were paid less salaries

(c) they were forced to go abroad on duty

(d) they were ill fed

Ans. (*a*) they were greased with cow and pig fat

10. Match the following. *(ICSE Specimen Semester I 2021)*

	List I		List II
A.	Jyotiba Phule	1.	Indian National Congress
B.	Raja Ram Mohan Roy	2.	Forward Bloc
C.	Subhash Chandra Bose	3.	Brahmo Samaj
D.	AO Hume	4.	Sathya Shodhak Samaj

Codes

	A	B	C	D		A	B	C	D
(a)	1	2	3	4	(b)	2	1	4	3
(c)	3	4	1	2	(d)	4	3	2	1

Ans. (*d*)

11. Which of these statements is not associated with Jyotiba Phule? *(ICSE Semester I 2021)*

(a) He established schools for girls

(b) He established the Brahmo Samaj

(c) He established the Satya Shodhak Samaj

(d) He was against the caste system

Ans. (*b*) He established the Brahmo Samaj

12. Who was the founder of the Indian National Congress? *(ICSE Semester I 2021)*

(a) AO Hume (b) WC Bonnerjee
(c) Dadabhai Naoroji (d) Gopal Krishna Gokhale

Ans. (*a*) AO Hume

2/3 Marks Questions

1. Mention any two repressive policies of Lord Lytton. *(ICSE 2023, 2017)*

Ans. Two repressive colonial policies of Lord Lytton were

(i) **Vernacular Press Act (1878)** This act forbade vernacular papers to publish any material that instigated Indians against the British.

(ii) **Indian Arms Act (1879)** This act made it a criminal offence for Indians to carry arms without licence.

2. Mention any two ways in which the British ill-treated the Indian soldiers. *(ICSE Specimen 2023)*

Ans. Two ways in which the British ill-treated the Indian soldiers are

- They were racially discriminated against by the Britishers which further led to growth of discontentment among the Indian sepoys in the ranks of company's troops.
- The Indian soldiers had a lesser salary as compared to their British counterparts. British soldiers were also given preference in terms of promotions.

3. What was the General Service Enlistment Act ? *(ICSE 2019, 2014)*

Ans. The British Parliament passed the General Service Enlistment Act in 1856. According to this act, the Indian soldiers in the East India Company could be sent overseas on duty.

4. Name each of the organisations founded by Jyotiba Phule and Raja Ram Mohan Roy. *(ICSE 2019)*

Ans. The organisation founded by Jyotiba Phule is Satya Shodhak Samaj in 1873. Raja Ram Mohan Roy founded the Brahmo Sabha in 1828, which was later renamed as Brahmo Samaj.

5. When and why was Awadh annexed by Lord Dalhousie? *(ICSE Specimen 2018)*

Ans. Lord Dalhousie annexed Awadh to the British territory under the pretext that the state of Awadh was not properly governed on 13th February, 1856.

6. Give two factors that gave rise to nationalism in India in 19th century. *(ICSE Specimen 2018)*

Ans. Two factors that gave rise to nationalism in India in the 19th century were

(i) The British introduced Western education in India which inspired Indians and made them politically conscious and disillusioned with the British policies.

(ii) Indian National Congress was founded in 1885 which helped in uniting the people of India.

7. Name the two Presidents under whom the first two sessions of the Indian National Congress were held. *(ICSE 2018)*

Or Name the Presidents who presided over the first two sessions of the Indian National Congress. *(ICSE 2016)*

Ans. WC Bonnerjee was the President of the first session of the Indian National Congress held at Bombay. The second session of the Indian National Congress was held under the presidentship of Dadabhai Naoroji at Calcutta.

8. Mention any two economic factors responsible for the growth of nationalism in India. *(ICSE 2018, 2011)*

Ans. Two economic factors responsible for the growth of nationalism in India were

(i) The British shipped India's agricultural products to England at a cheap rate while supplying machine made goods produced in England to India. This ruined the Indian cottage industries and caused unemployment.

(ii) Even during famines and epidemics, the British Government did nothing to help the victims of such calamities.

9. What is meant by Doctrine of Lapse? *(ICSE Specimen 2017)*

Other Similar Questions

Or Why did the Doctrine of Lapse become a political cause for the Revolt of 1857?

Or Explain the term 'Doctrine of Lapse'.

Ans. According to the Doctrine of Lapse heirs adopted without the consent of the company, could inherit only the private property of the deceased ruler and not his territory, which would come under the company's rule. The prominent states, which became victims to the doctrine were Jhansi, Satara, Jaipur, Sambalpur, Udaipur and Nagpur. Thus, it became a political cause for the Revolt of 1857.

10. Name the two main associations that were the precursors of the Indian National Congress. ***(ICSE 2017,2010)***

Ans. The two precursors of the Indian National Congress were

(i) East India Association founded by Dadabhai Naoroji in 1866 in London.

(ii) Indian Association established by Surendranath Banerjee in 1876 in Calcutta.

11. What impact did the uprising of 1857 have on the Mughal rule? ***(ICSE 2016)***

Ans. The uprising of 1857 ended the Mughal rule and the title of Mughal Emperor was also abolished with the death of Bahadur Shah II in 1862.

12. Mention two administrative changes that the British Government brought about regarding the East India Company's rule in India. ***(ICSE 2015)***

Ans. The two administrative changes brought by British Government regarding the East India Company's rule in India

(i) After revolt of 1857, the governance of India was transferred from the East India Company to the British crown in 1858. The crown was made directly responsible for the management of Indian affairs.

(ii) The policy relating to the Princely States was changed and they were assured that all treaties that they had with the East India Company would be honoured. The Doctrine of Lapse was abolished and the Princely States were allowed to adopt sons as successors.

13. Mention any two contributions of Jyotiba Phule in preparing the ground for the National Movement. ***(ICSE 2015)***

Ans. The two contributions of Jyotiba Phule in preparing the ground for the National Movement.

(i) In 1873, Jyotiba Phule established the 'Satyashodhak Samaj' to attain equal rights for peasants and the lower class.

(ii) He promoted widow remarriage and worked for the education of women.

14. When was the Indian National Congress established? Who presided over its first session? ***(ICSE 2014, 2009)***

Ans. The Indian National Congress was established in 1885 by AO Hume.

Womesh Chunder Bonnerjee was the President of its first session. The first session of the Congress was attended by 72 delegates from all parts of India, including some eminent persons like Dadabhai Naoroji, Pherozeshah Mehta, Badruddin Tyabji, etc.

15. State any two political causes responsible for the First War of Independence. ***(ICSE 2014)***

Ans. There were many political causes responsible for the First War of Independence. Two of them are as follows

(i) Lord Dalhousie's 'Policy of Annexation' and 'Doctrine of Lapse'.

(ii) British disrespect shown to Bahadur Shah II.

16. What was the role of the press in promoting nationalistic sentiments among the Indians? ***(ICSE 2014)***

Ans. The introduction of Printing Press in India was an event of revolutionary significance in promoting nationalistic sentiments amongst the Indians. It played an important role in carrying ideas to the people. During the later half of the 19th century, a large number of newspapers were started. These papers fostered patriotism and ideas of liberty and justice in our country.

The press was a powerful factor in building and developing a strong nationalistic sentiment among the Indians.

17. What was the influence of Western education on the minds of the educated Indians in the 19th century? ***(ICSE 2013, 2009)***

Ans. The influences of Western education were as follows :

(i) Through the study of European history, political thought and economic ideas, educated Indians had an access to the ideas of Liberty, Nationality, Equality, rules of Law and Self-government.

(ii) Social awareness and national consciousness among Indians were brought by the revolutionary ideas of the liberal thinkers like Rousseau, Mazzini and Thomas Paine.

18. What was Nana Sahib's grievance against the British? ***(ICSE 2012, 2003)***

Ans. Nana Sahib was the adopted son of the last Peshwa Baji Rao II. The British refused to grant him pension, which they were paying to Peshwa Baji Rao II.

19. There were various factors that promoted the growth of nationalism in India in the 19th century. Give the meaning of 'nationalism' in this context. ***(ICSE 2011)***

Ans. Nationalism was the most successful political force of the 19th century. Nationalism is a feeling of oneness which the people feel about their nation. It was a result of a new social and economic force which had put an end to feudalism.

20. Mention two objectives of the Congress as enumerated by WC Bonnerjee. ***(ICSE 2011, 2006)***

Ans. The objectives of Indian National Congress, which were declared by the WC Bonnerjee in December, 1885, were as following

(i) To promote friendly relations between Nationalist political workers from various parts of the country.

(ii) To develop and consolidate the feelings of national unity, irrespective of caste, religion or province.

21. Mention any two social reforms advocated by the British, which affected the religious traditions of the Indian people. ***(ICSE 2009)***

Ans. Widow Remarriage Act and Abolition of Sati were the two major social reforms advocated by the British, which affected the religious traditions of the Indian people.

22. Name two leaders of the Indian National Congress in its early years. ***(ICSE 2008)***

Ans. Dadabhai Naoroji and Surendranath Banerjee were the two famous leaders of the Indian National Congress in its early years.

23. State two factors responsible for the growth of nationalism in India. ***(ICSE 2007, 2006)***

Ans. Two important factors responsible for the growth of nationalism in India were as follows :

(i) Repressive colonial policies of the British Empire.

(ii) Socio-religious Movements of India in the 19th century.

24. Mention any two social reforms suggested to the British by Raja Ram Mohan Roy. ***(ICSE 2006)***

Ans. Raja Ram Mohan Roy was the father of Indian Renaissance and the prophet of Indian Nationalism. His efforts to abolition of Sati and support of Western education made him immortal as a social reformer.

25. Mention two economic factors, which became the causes of the First War of Independence, 1857. ***(ICSE 2005)***

Ans. Two economic factors were

(i) Heavy taxation, forced evictions, discriminatory tariff policy against Indian products and destruction of traditional handicrafts that hit peasants and artisans.

(ii) India was forced to export at cheaper rates, raw materials like raw cotton and raw silk that the British industries needed urgently and also plantation products like indigo, tea and foodgrains which were in short supply in Britain.

26. Mention one reason for the unhappiness of the Indian soldiers in the British army before 1857. ***(ICSE 2004)***

Ans. The British Parliament passed the General Service Enlistment Act in 1856, according to which, Indian soldiers could be sent overseas on duty. This act did not take into account the sentiment of the Indian soldiers, who dreaded such voyages.

27. Name the last Mughal Emperor of India before the British crown declared India to be its colony. ***(ICSE 2004)***

Ans. Bahadur Shah Zafar was the last Mughal Emperor of India. After his death, the British crown declared India to be its colony.

28. How did the English language play a leading role in the growth of nationalism in India? ***(ICSE 2004)***

Ans. The English language spread all over India, which gave the educated Indians a common language in which they could communicate with one another. In the absence of such a common language, it would have been very difficult to come on a common platform and to organise a movement of a pan India character.

29. Under which pretext and when was Awadh annexed to the Company's Dominions? ***(ICSE 2003)***

Ans. Lord Dalhousie annexed Awadh to the Company's Dominions on the pretext of alleged misrule on 13th February, 1856.

30. The Act of 1858 ended the East India Company's rule and the Government of India was transferred to the British Queen. Who became the first Viceroy under this act? ***(ICSE 2003)***

Ans. The Act of 1858 ended the rule of the East India Company and the Government of India was transferred to the British Queen by the proclamation of Queen Victoria. Lord Canning became the first Viceroy under this act on 1st November, 1858.

31. Name the policy used by Lord Dalhousie for the extension of British territories in India. ***(ICSE 2002)***

Ans. The policy of 'Doctrine of Lapse' was used by Lord Dalhousie for the extension of British territories in India.

32. Why was the War of 1857 hailed as the 'First War of National Independence'? *(ICSE 2002)*

Ans. The War of 1857 was hailed as the 'First War of Independence' because it provided an inspiration to the leaders and to the people to fight for the independence from the British rule and millions of soldiers, peasants and artisans participated in it.

33. Name the first President of the Indian National Congress. *(ICSE 2002)*

Ans. Womesh Chunder (WC) Bonnerjee was the first President of the Indian National Congress (INC).

34. Where and when was the first session of the Indian National Congress held? *(ICSE 2001)*

Ans. The first session of the Indian National Congress was held at Gokuldas Tejpal Sanskrit College, Mumbai from 28th to 31st December, 1885.

4 Marks Questions

1. Read the passage given below and answer the questions that follow. *(ICSE Semester I 2021)*

India's First War of Independence, better known as the Indian Rebellion of 1857, began on, 10th May in the year 1857. The first martyr of the revolt was Mangal Pandey and the war was the result of accumulation of many factors over time. The rebellion of 1857 is considered the first blow that came to shatter the British rule in India. Some epicenters of the revolt were- Kanpur, Lucknow, Aligarh, Agra, Delhi and Jhansi. Due to all the epicenters being far from each other, there was a communication gap between the leaders of different parts of India. Due to the rebellion having no central leadership, it got limited to some parts of India only. Rebels did not have enough weapons and finance whereas British people had advanced weapons and enough finance.

(i) Identify the immediate cause of the above revolt.
(a) The General Service Enlistment Act
(b) The inhuman treatment of indigo cultivators
(c) The Subsidiary Alliance
(d) The incident of greased cartridges

Ans. (*d*) The incident of greased cartridges

(ii) Which policy of expansion led to the annexation of Awadh?
(a) Subsidiary Alliance (b) Doctrine of Lapse
(c) Pretext of alleged misrule (d) Outright wars

Ans. (a) Subsidiary Alliance

(iii) Which of these is a socio-religious cause of the revolt?
(a) Taxing religious places
(b) Decay of cottage industries
(c) Drain of wealth
(d) Exploitation of economic resources

Ans. (*a*) Taxing religious places

(iv) The British showed total disregard towards the soldiers. In this context, which of the following statements is not true?
(a) They were deprived of allowances.
(b) They were forced to go overseas on duty.
(c) They were given the same salaries as that of the British soldiers.
(d) The chances of promotion were very bleak.

Ans. (*c*) They were given the same salaries as that of the British soldiers.

2. What were the four aims of the Congress? *(ICSE 2014)*

Ans. Four aims of the Congress were as follows

(i) To develop the friendly relations between Nationalist political workers from different parts of the country.
(ii) To promote and consolidate the feelings of national unity irrespective of caste, religion or province.
(iii) To formulate popular demands and present them before the government.
(iv) To train and organise the public opinion in the country.

10 Marks Questions

1. The India Nationalists described the Great Uprising of 1857 as the First War of Independence. With reference to this, answer the following questions. *(ICSE 2023)*

(a) Mention any three policies used by the British to expand their political power in India.
(b) The Revolt of 1857 is also known as the sepoy Mutiny. Mention any three military causes which led to the uprising.
(c) Mention any four economic causes of the revolt.

Ans. (a) The British used both battle and strategic policies to gain control over India.

(i) They used their financial strength to indebt local rulers and gradually surrendered their territories. Where this did not work, they used force and battles.

(ii) The British official also adopted policies to annex territories

(iii) The expansion policies included the subsidiary alliance surprise of lapre.

(b) Military causes that led to the revolt were as follows

(i) The Indian and British soldiers were not treated equally. The salary of the Indian soldiers was too meagre to support their families, while the duties of both the British and the Indian soldiers were more or less similar.

(ii) The British Parliament passed the General Service Enlistment Act in 1856, which decreed that the Indian soldiers could be sent overseas on duty. Indian soldiers dreaded sea voyage and considered it against their customs.

(iii) Indians were of the belief that, the British were invincible, but the British were beaten in the First Afghan War (1838-42). This gave courage to the Indian soldiers to wage a war against the British rule.

(c) The most important reason for the popular discontent was the economic exploitation by the British. The economic exploitation took the following forms

(i) The East India Company made huge profits at the expenses of the people of India. The company purchased textiles, indigo, foodgrains and spices from India and sold them abroad at exorbitant prices.

(ii) By buying and exporting Indian goods, the company encouraged their production in India. But gradually, the Indian textiles began to compete with the textiles manufactured in England. The British put pressure on the East India Company to forbid the sale of Indian textiles in England. The British Government then put restrictions on the import of Indian textiles besides imposing heavy import duties on such goods.

(iii) People moved to cities to find employment, which was very difficult to get. Peasants were forced to pay tax in cash, which pushed them into the hands of the moneylenders, as tax was collected even during the famines.

(iv) Indigo, tea, jute, cotton and opium were crops, which the British wanted the Indians to grow. If the peasants planted anything else, their crops were destroyed and cattle were carried off as a punishment.

2. The culmination of discontent against the British rule came with the Great Revolt of I857.With reference to this, answer the following questions.

(ICSE Specimen 2023)

(a) What was the Doctrine of Lapse? Name the queen who became a victim of this policy.

(b) Mention any three economic causes of the revolt.

(c) Mention any four administrative changes made by the British after the revolt.

Ans. (a) According to Lord Dalhousie's Policy of Doctrine of Lapse, the adopted heirs of kings could neither inherit King's title nor his property. This created dissatisfaction among the Kingdoms of Satara, Jhansi, Nagpur and Sambalpur which were annexed this way.

Rani Lakshmi Bai, the queen of Jhansi became a victim of this policy. Her adopted son Anand Rao was not considered as a lawful successor to the throne under the Doctrine of Lapse. This further led to the annexation of Jhansi Kingdom by the Britishers.

(b) For three economic causes of the 1857 revolt, refer to Q. 1 (c) of 10 marks questions.

(c) Four administrative changes made by the British after the revolt are as follows

(i) The revolt ended the rule of East India Company by the Government of India Act of 1858.

(ii) The Queen's Proclamation incorporating the transfer of governance from the East India Company to the British crown was made public at Allahabad on 1st November, 1858, by Lord Canning.

(iii) Doctrine of Lapse was abolished and right to adopt sons and successors were given to the states.

(iv) The strength of the European troops in India was increased from 45000 to 65000 and the number of Indian troops was reduced from 238000 to 140000.

3. By 1857, conditions were ripe for a mass uprising in the form of the Great Revolt of 1857. In this context, explain the following. ***(ICSE 2020)***

(a) Any three economic causes for the Revolt of 1857.

(b) Any three military causes.

(c) Any three political causes of the revolt.

Ans. (a) For three economic causes for the Revolt of 1857, refer to Q. 1 (c) of 10 marks question.

(b) For three military causes for the Revolt of 1857, refer to Q. 1 (b) of 10 marks questions.

(c) The political causes for the Revolt of 1857 were
   (i) The British Policy of effective control and gradual extinction of the native Indian states was one of the major grievances of the Indian rulers.
   (ii) The policy of 'Doctrine of Lapse' and 'Policy of Annexation'.
   (iii) The Annexation of Awadh on the pretext of alleged misgovernance.

Examiner's Comment

- The subparts (a), (b) and (c) of this question were attempted well by most of the candidates.

Suggestion for Students

- Explain the causes of the Revolt of 1857 under sub-headings such as, Economic causes, Military causes and Political causes.

4. With reference to the First War of Independence, 1857, answer the following questions. ***(ICSE Specimen 2018)***

(a) Give three causes for the resentment of the sepoys against the British.

(b) Mention three economic causes that caused unrest among Indians.

(c) State four changes introduced in the organisation of the army after the First War of Independence.

Ans. (a) Three causes for the resentment of the sepoys against the British are
   (i) Indian and British soldiers were not treated equally. Indian soldiers were poorly paid, ill-fed and provided poor accommodation.
   (ii) The General Service Enlistment Act of 1856 made it compulsory for Indian soldiers to go overseas on duty. This was strictly objected by Indians on religious ground.
   (iii) The wages of the Indian soldiers were inadequate to support their families. On the other hand, the British soldiers received more than eight times the salary of the Indian soldiers.

(b) Three economic causes that caused unrest among Indians are
   (i) Heavy taxation, forcibly evictions, discriminatory tariff against the Indian products.
   (ii) The transfer of wealth from India to England for which India got no proportionate economic returns.
   (iii) Inhuman treatment of Indigo cultivators.

(c) Four changes introduced in the organisation of the army after the First War of Independence were
   (i) The strength of the European troops in India was increased and the number of Indian troops were reduced.
   (ii) All Indian artillery units with the exception of a few mountain batteries were disbanded.
   (iii) The general principle adopted was the number of Indian sepoys should not exceed twice that of the European.
   (iv) The earlier policy of excluding Indians from the officer corps was strictly maintained.

5. Numerous causes gave rise to the First War of Independence and its consequences led to several changes in the British Government in India. In this context, answer the following. ***(ICSE 2018)***

(a) Explain any three political causes of the Revolt of 1857.

(b) Briefly explain the immediate cause of the Great Revolt.

(c) State any four changes in the administration of the British Government as a consequence of the revolt.

Ans. (a) For three political causes, refer to Q. 3 (c) of 10 marks questions.

(b) The immediate cause of the Revolt of 1857 was the introduction of new Enfield Rifle in the Indian army which needed a cartridge having a greased paper cover. This paper cover had to be bitten off before loading the cartridge into the rifle. Rumours were spread that the grease was made from beef and pork fat.
The soldiers felt that it was a move by the British to defame their religion. Mangal Pandey urged his fellow soldiers not to use the rifle. On 29th March 1857, he attacked his officers in Barrackpore. He was later hanged and this marked the beginning of the sepoy revolt in Meerut which later spread to other parts of North India.

(c) The changes introduced in the administration of the British territories in India were
   (i) The rule of the East India Company was transferred to the British Crown.
   (ii) The Governor-General of India now came to be known as the Viceroy of India.
   (iii) Government of India Act was passed by British Parliament. Due to this Act, the responsibility to govern India was transferred to the Queen of England and the British Parliament.

(iv) This act abolished the Board of Directors of the Company and the responsibility of the Government of India was passed on to a separate minister in the British Parliament known as Secretary of State.

Examiner's Comment

- Most of the candidates wrote three causes of the Revolt of 1857 correctly. However, a few mentioned other causes instead of political causes.
- Majority of the candidates explained the immediate cause of the Great Revolt correctly barring a few exceptions who explained the immediate causes of the First World War instead of the Great Revolt.
- Majority of the candidates stated all the changes brought about by the British after the Revolt of 1857 rather than stating the administrative changes only as asked in the question.

Suggestions for Students

- Read and understand the question before attempting it.
- Learn that the results of the Revolt of 1857 are different from the administrative changes.

6. Many factors contributed to the growth of nationalism in India, in this context, explain the relevance of the following ***(ICSE Specimen 2017)***

(a) Contributions of socio-religious reformers.

(b) Repressive policies of the British.

(c) Economic exploitation.

Ans. (a) The contributions of the socio-religious reformers and their movements were enormous to the onset of Indian Nationalism in the following ways

(i) Swami Dayananda and Vivekananda proclaimed the superiority of Indian culture and civilisation. The reformers also condemned untouchability and the caste systems, which led to the ideas of equality and brotherhood, thereby attracting the so called lower castes.

(ii) Emanicipating and leading the causes of women made the women to participate in the National Movement as well.

(iii) Swami Dayananda Saraswati was the first to use the word *'Swaraj'* thereby protesting against the British Domination of India.

(iv) The Reform Movement not only promoted a feeling of an Indianism and a spirit of nationalism, but also created a new consciousness and built a new society devoid of privileges based on caste, creed or religion.

(b) The repressive policies of the British were countless, which further provoked nationalism in India. Some of them were as follows

(i) Organisation of Grand Delhi Durbar and spending lakhs of rupees on the same (by Lord Lytton) but not spending a penny on the Indians facing a famine.

(ii) The introduction of the Vernacular Press Act (1878), which forbade the vernacular papers to publish any material which might excite feelings of dissatisfaction against the British Government and also of the Indian Arms Act (1879), which made it a criminal offence (only for the Indians) to carry arms without license.

(iii) Maximum age limit for the Civil Services examination reduced from 21 years to 19 years.

(iv) Removal of the import duties on British textiles.

(v) The Ilbert Bill Controversy, where the Britishers wanted to defend their special privileges and resented what the Bill had i.e. to abolish judicial disqualification based on race distinctions.

(c) Economic exploitation by the British was something that was resented most by the Indians. Each section of the society was discontented with their economic policies. These policies were as follow

(i) They took away a major part of the produce of the peasants and their land revenue taxes were too high and unbearable.

(ii) The raw materials were exported to the industries of Britain, thereby reducing the markets in India and crippling the native artisans and craftsmen.

(iii) The Indian working class was exploited by the English factory owners.

(iv) There were very few employment opportunities and even fewer chances of promotion and of a better pay to the Indians.

7. With reference to the rise of 'national consciousness' in India, explain the following. ***(ICSE 2017)***

(a) The influence of Western education.

(b) Any three contributions of Raja Ram Mohan Roy.

(c) The development of modern means of transport and communication.

Ans. (a) The influences of Western education were as follows

(i) Through the study of European history, political thought and economic ideas, educated Indians had an access to the ideas of liberty, nationality, equality, rules of law and self-government.

(ii) Social awareness and national consciousness among Indians were brought by the revolutionary ideas of the liberal thinkers like Rousseau, Mazzini and Thomas Paine.

(iii) Learning the English language helped the Indians from different parts of the country to meet and exchange ideas as it gave them a linguistic unity. They could converse in a common language and thus understand each other better.

(b) Raja Ram Mohan Roy was the greatest social and religious reformer of the 19th century. His contributions are as follows

(i) Raja Ram Mohan Roy helped the British to understand the custom of Sati and got it abolished in 1829.

(ii) He advocated the cause of women education. He wanted women to be given the right to inherit property.

(iii) He established Brahmo Sabha, which later became Brahmo Samaj to struggle against the caste discrimination prevailing in society which included the evil of untouchability.

(c) The developments of modern means of transport and communication are as follows

(i) The first railway line connecting Mumbai with Thane was laid in 1853. By 1869, more than 6000 kms of railways had been built, extending to nearly 45000 km by 1905. Besides encouraging trade and commerce, the railways facilitated the growth of nationalism.

(ii) The development of the modern postal system helped to unify the country. A cheap uniform postage rate brought about a transformation in the social education and the intellectual and political life of Indians. Circulation of national literature and transmission of messages became possible through the operation of post offices.

8. Explain the causes of the Great Revolt of 1857 with reference to the following. ***(ICSE 2016, 2011, 2002)***

(a) Any three political causes
(b) Any three military causes
(c) Any four economic causes

Ans. (a) For answer, refer to Q. 3 (c) of 10 marks questions.

(b) For answer, refer to Q. 3 (b) of 10 marks questions.

(c) For four economic causes, refer to Q 1 (c) of 10 marks questions.

9. Describe the results of the First War of Independence, with reference to the following. ***(ICSE 2009)***

(a) Policy towards the Indian Princes
(b) Rise of Nationalism in India
(c) Changes in the Administrative Set-up of the British Territories in India

Ans. (a) **Policy towards the Indian Princes**

(i) The Proclamation of Queen Victoria declared that the British Government would not annex the Indian states. It assured them that all treaties entered into with the company would be honoured.

(ii) The Proclamation declared that the British would not interfere in their internal matters except in the case of 'misconduct' and 'anarchy'. However, they were asked to restrict their armies.

(iii) After the Proclamation of the Queen, the policy of 'Doctrine of Lapse' was abolished.

(b) **Rise of Nationalism in India**

(i) The war of 1857 was a great struggle of the Indians for freedom. It aroused national feelings and paved the way for the rise of the National Movement which ultimately won freedom for India in 1947.

(ii) It served as the source of inspiration for the struggle for freedom and the war also became a symbol of challenge to the mighty British, as man's inborn desire for freedom cannot be subdued.

(iii) The heroic struggle also established valuable traditions of resistance to the British rule. Due to the First War of Independence the Indian people realised that unless, they wake up from the slumber, they can't achieve Independence.

(c) For answer, refer to Q. 5 (c) of 10 marks questions.

10. Several factors led to the Revolt of 1857. With reference to this, explain each of the following.

(a) Discontentment of the Sepoys. *(ICSE 2007)*

(b) Resentment of the Rulers of the Native States against the British.

(c) Unhappiness of the Indian Artisans and Craftsmen

Ans. (a) **Discontentment of Sepoys** Several factors were responsible for the discontentment of Indian soldiers. These are as follows

(i) Indian and British soldiers were not treated equally. Indian soldiers were poorly paid, ill-fed and provided poor accommodation. British military authorities forbade the sepoys from wearing caste or sectarian marks beards or turbans and they showed disregard for the sentiments of the sepoys.

(ii) The General Service Enlistment Act of 1856, made it compulsory for Indian soldiers to go overseas on duty. This was strictly objected to by Indians on religious grounds.

(iii) The wages of the Indian soldiers were inadequate to support their families. On the other hand, the British soldiers received more than eight times the salary of the Indian soldiers.

(b) **Resentment of the Rulers of the Native States against the British**

A tricky method was adopted by the British to gain control over the rulers of the Native States. They struck at the very root of their existence by the Doctrine of Lapse. According to this policy, if a ruler died without his heir, his adopted son could neither inherit the throne nor the title and the state would be annexed to the British empire using the doctrine.

Lord Dalhousie annexed would be Satara, Jhansi and Nagpur and also Jaipur, Udaipur and Sambalpur. And where this policy could not be applied, the pretext of mismanagement in the governance of the state was done like in the case of Awadh. These discriminating actions of the British caused widespread resentment among the Native Rulers.

(c) **Unhappiness of the Indian Artisans and Craftsmen**

Heavy duties on the Indian silk and cotton textiles in Britain destroyed the Indian industries. On the other hand, British goods were imported into India at a nominal duty. As a result of the British Policy of making India a raw material producing country, Indian handicrafts and cottage industries were ruined. Thousands of craftsmen and artisans were thrown out of employment. The manufacturers of silk and cotton goods got no profits from their work and began to look for other means of livelihood. The miserable condition of the workmen became a potent cause of resentment against the British rule.

11. "Numerous causes were at work in causing the great upsurge of 1857." *(ICSE 2005)*

Explain the following with reference to the above statement.

(a) The Introduction of the Railways and Telegraphs

(b) The Introduction of the Enfield Rifles

(c) The Laws that interfered with the religious customs of the people

HINT *Dear students, the above question just requires to mention and explain the causes of Revolt of 1857 with the help of reference points given below.*

Ans. (a) **The Introduction of the Railways and Telegraphs**

(i) The rapid spread of modern civilisation made people afraid and suspicious.

(ii) Peoples spread the rumour that the telegraph poles were erected for the purpose of hanging people who opposed the British rule in India.

(iii) The orthodox Indians felt humiliated to note that in the railway compartments, brahmins and people from the backward classes were made to sit side by side.

(iv) This practice, they believed, was intentionally introduced in order to defile their caste and religion.

(v) Modern innovations threatened the old social rules and produced unrest among many common people in India.

(b) The introduction of Enfield Rifles was the immediate cause of the revolt. In 1856, the British authorities decided to replace the old fashioned musket by the new 'Enfield Rifles'. There was a rumour that the cartridges of these rifles were greased with the fat of cows and pigs. The loading process of the Enfield rifles involved bringing the cartridge to the mouth and biting off the top greased paper with the mouth. Both the Hindu and Muslim sepoys refused to use the cartridges, as they felt that the English were defiling their religion.

(c) **The Laws that Interfered with the Religious Customs of the People**

(i) The laws allowing conversion from Hinduism to Christianity to inherit their ancestral property.

(ii) Religious sentiments of the Indians were hurt by the official policy of taxing lands belonging to temples and mosques.

(iii) Laws to abolish the Sati System in 1829.

(iv) The introduction of the Widow Remarriage Act (1856) and the opening of Western education to girls were not welcomed by the masses.

12. The First War of Independence led to several changes. With reference to this, explain ***(ICSE 2003)***

(a) The Rights Granted to the Indian Princes and Chiefs

(b) The Reorganisation of the Army

(c) The changes introduced in the Administrative Set-up of the British Territories in India

Ans. (a) **The Rights Granted to the Indian Princes and Chiefs**

The Policy of Annexation and the Doctrine of Lapse were abandoned. Some of the Indian princes had remained loyal to the British and had helped them in suppressing the uprisings. All the treaties between the princes and the company were decided to be respected. The British promised not to annex any territory and gave the Indian rulers the right to adopt heirs. The Indian princes became junior partners of the British crown because they were promised that they would continue as rulers of their states.

(b) **The Reorganisation of the Army**

The strength of the European troops in India was increased, and the number of Indian troops was reduced. The strength of European troops in India was increased from 45000 to 65000 and the number of Indian troops reduced from 238000 to 140000. All Indian artillery units (with the exception of a few mountain batteries) were disbanded. Practically the same ratio was maintained till the First World War. The general principle adopted was the number of Indian sepoys should not exceed twice that of the European troops.

The earlier policy of excluding Indians from the officer corps was strictly maintained.

(c) For answer, refer to Q. 5 (c) of 10 marks questions.

13. The First War of Independence of 1857, was the culmination of peoples' dissatisfaction with the British rule. In this context, enumerate the following causes. ***(ICSE 2002)***

(a) The Economic Causes (b) The Military Causes

Ans. (a) For answer, refer to Q. 1 (c) of 10 marks questions.

(b) For answer, refer to Q. 3 (b) of 10 marks questions.

CHAPTER TEST

01 Mark Questions

1 When did Queen Victoria announced the transfer of power from the company to the British Crown?
(a) 15th November, 1858 (b) 1st November, 1858
(c) 1st November, 1857 (d) 15th November, 1857

2

Indian National Congress	Presided by
First Session	Womesh Chandra Bannerjee
Second Session	?

(a) Dadabhai Naoroji (b) AO Hume
(c) Rash Behari Ghosh (d) Surendranath Banerjee

3 Who was the first Viceroy of India?
(a) Lord Dalhousie (b) Lord Dufferin
(c) Lord Canning (d) Lord Wellesley

4 Raja Ram Mohan Roy was the greatest social and religious reformer of the 19th century who established the .... in 1828.
(a) Prarthana Samaj (b) Dharma Sabha
(c) Satya Shodhak Samaj (d) Brahmo Sabha

5 The East India Association was founded in London in 1866 by ....
(a) Dadabhai Naoroji (b) Raja Ram Mohan Roy
(c) Surendranath Banerjee (d) Jyotiba Phule

Answers

1. (b) | 2. (a) | 3. (c) | 4. (d) | 5. (a)

02 Marks Questions

6 Mention any two political cause of the Revolt of 1875.

7 State any two socio-religious cause of the responsible for the First War of Independence.

8 What was the main provision of the General Service Enlistment Act of 1856?

9 Mention any two objective of the Indian National Congress.

10 Marks Question

10 The factor promoting the growth of nationalism in India. With reference to the growth of nationalism, answer the following questions.

(i) Mention any four economic factors responsible for the growth of nationalism.

(ii) What do you mean by Ilbert Bill? State any two repressive policies of Lord Lytton.

(iii) What was the role of Press in the growth of nationalism in India?

02

The Early Nationalists and Assertive Nationalism

TREND ANALYSIS 3 YEARS

Topic	Average No. of Questions Across all Sets: Types of Questions	2023	2020	2019
TOPIC 01 Early Nationalists	1 Mark	1	–	–
	2/3 Marks	–	1	1
	4 Marks	1	–	–
	10 Marks	1	–	–
TOPIC 02 Assertive Nationalists	1 Mark	–	1	1
	2/3 Marks	1	1	–
	4 Marks	–	–	–
	10 Marks	1	–	–

The Early Nationalists (or the Moderates)

- In the years from 1885 to 1905, the Congress was led by a group of leaders, who were called **Early Nationalists** or **Moderates**. The Moderates were drawn from the educated middle class consisting of professionals like lawyers, barristers, teachers and officials.
- The Moderates or the Early Nationalists were included from all parts of the country—WC Bonnerjee, Rash behari Ghosh, Surendranath Banerjee from Bengal, Pandit Madan Mohan Malviya from Uttar Pradesh and some other Moderates were from Maharashtra and Gujarat like— Dadabhai Naoroji, Gopal Krishna Gokhale, Justice Ranade, Pherozeshah Mehta, etc.

Belief of the Early Nationalists

The Early Nationalist leaders believed in moderate politics and in loyalty to the British crown. They asked for any constitutional and other reforms within the framework of the British rule as they had faith in the British sense of justice and fair play.

Their demands were moderate in nature. They thought that Englishmen are willing to put India on the path of democracy and self-governance. They praised British for English language and the modern means of communication and transport.

Objectives/Demands of the Early Nationalists

The objectives of the Early Nationalists were as follows :

Constitutional Demands

The Moderates wanted a larger share in the government of their country. They believed that eventually India should go more towards democratic self-government. Moderates demanded the expansion of the Legislative Council and Legislative Assemblies both at the centre and in the provinces.

Economic Demands

The Moderates also wanted a reduction in land revenue and protection of peasants against the unjust demands of the zamindars. They demanded for the development of banking industrial growth by the protection of trade.

Administrative Demands

The Moderates demanded for the **Indianisation of services** through simultaneous Indian Civil Service Examinations in England and India. They wanted to repeal the Arms Act and the Licence Act and also wanted to spread primary education among the maximum population of India.

They demanded for the complete separation of the Executive and the Judiciary, wider employment of Indians in higher ranks and also wanted to gradually move towards Democratic self-government of India.

Other Demands

Moderates demanded the industrial growth through trade protection. It means that a heavy tax should be imposed on imported goods and the government should give out loans for the development of iron, coal, paper and sugar industries in India.

Criticism of the Early Nationalists

The Moderates failed to draw the maximum people into the mainstream of the National Movement. Their field of influence was very limited to the urban educated Indians. Their leadership was confined by the particular professional groups like–lawyers, doctors, journalists and teachers, etc.

Methods of Struggle and Achievements of the Early Nationalists

- Relying on constitutional and peaceful methods and avoiding violence and confrontation, the Early Nationalists made good use of the three P's —Petitions, Prayers and Protest, to accomplish their objectives.
- Early Nationalists aroused the feeling of one nation, and they trained people in politics by popularising the ideas of Democracy, Civil liberties, Secularism and Nationalism, etc.

  Following reforms were led by the efforts of moderates

  (i) In 1886, the Public Service Commission was appointed by the British.

  (ii) A Resolution was passed by the House of Commons in 1893 for simultaneous examination of the ICS in London and India.

  (iii) In 1895, the British Government appointed the **Welly Commission** on Indian expenditure, under Sir Reginald Earle Welhy.

  (iv) In 1892, the Indian Council Act was passed by the British.

Official Attitude towards the Congress

- In the initial stage of the Congress, the British Government favoured the Congress. In fact, a few government officials like **Sir William Wedderbwin, Sir Henry Cotton** also attended the First Session of the Congress.
- In 1887, **Lord Dufferin** attacked the National Congress in his speech and ridiculed it as representing only a microscopic minority of the people. British officials criticised the National Congress and branded its leaders as **'disloyal babus'** and **'violent villains'**.

Prominent Early Nationalist Leaders

Dadabhai Naoroji (1825-1917)

Dadabhai Naoroji generally known as the '**Grand Old Man of India**' was looked upon as India's unofficial ambassador during his stay in England. He was elected to the Bombay Municipal Corporation and later, to the Town Council. He was the founder of Bombay Association. The newspaper ***Rast Goftar*** was edited by him.

In 1865, he founded the London India Society in collaboration with WC Bonnerjee. The theory of Drain was presented by him in his book **Poverty and Un-British Rule in India**. After spending years collecting statistics, Dadabhai propounded that "The inevitable consequences of foreign domination is the drain of wealth of the subject nation to the country of the rulers." Dadabhai proved that the average annual income of an Indian was barely ₹ 20.

Naoroji was thrice elected as the President of Congress. The credit for demanding Swaraj from the Congress platform for the first time (1906) goes to him. In England during the year 1892, he presented the cause of the Indians in the house.

In 1866, he established the **East India Association** in London. The East India Association soon became popular and its branches were set-up in Calcutta, Bombay and Madras.

Gopal Krishna Gokhale (1866-1915)

Gopal Krishna Gokhale was influenced by the ideals of Justice Ranade. He joined the Deccan Education Society, which was founded by Justice Ranade.

Gokhale presided over the Varanasi Session of the INC in 1905. In the year 1905, he founded the **Servants of India Society** and went to England and Africa. Srinivas Shastri and Hridaynath Kunzru were some of the important members of the society.

Surendranath Banerjee (1848-1925)

Surendranath Banerjee was a nationalist leader, popular journalist and also a dedicated educationist, who advocated the use of constitutional methods for the attainment of India's goals.

He was the first Indian to qualify for the **Indian Civil Services** Examination, and was elected from the Bengal Council four times. The Arms Act, the Vernacular Press Act and the lowering of age for appearing in the ICS Examination from 21 to 19 years were all opposed by him. He also opposed the **Morley-Minto Reforms** and the **Partition of Bengal.**

Surendranath Banerjee protested against the Arms Act and the Vernacular Press Act.

Assertive Nationalism
(or the Extremists or the Radicals)

In the years from 1905 to 1918, there emerged a new and younger group of leaders within the Congress, who did not agree with the methods and ideology of the Moderates, this group of leaders came to be known as Assertive Nationalists. The three prominent leaders of the Assertive groups were **Bal Gangadhar Tilak, Lala Lajpat Rai** and **Bipin Chandra Pal.**

They belonged to the famous trio **Lal-Bal-Pal.** The difference in the ideologies and in the methods to voice their anger also led to a huge arguement between the Early Nationalists and the Assertive Nationalists. While the Moderates wanted to gain Swaraj through constitutional means, the extremists wanted to do so through putting pressure on the government. This episode at the Indian National Congress, was a reason for the **Surat Split** (1907).

Main Causes of the Rise of Assertive Nationalism

The main causes of the rise of Assertive Nationalism were as follows

(i) Restrictions on Indians for their own natural rights.
(ii) Britishers were responsible for the bad economic conditions of India.
(iii) To make Indians aware about their self-respect and rights to freedom of speech, and right of property, etc.
(iv) Unfavourable policies of the British Government.

Objectives of the Assertive Nationalists

National freedom was the sole programme and objective of the Assertive Nationalists. The immediate attainment of **Swaraj** was the main objective of the Assertive Nationalists.

Methods of the Assertive Nationalists

Passive resistance, non-cooperation with the British Government by boycotting government services, courts, schools and colleges, promotion of Swadeshi and Boycott of foreign goods, etc., were the methods of the Assertive Nationalists.

Achievements of the Assertive Nationalists

The true character of the British Rule was exposed by the Assertive Nationalist. They promoted self-reliance by Swadeshi and Boycott Movements. Many educational institutions were established also by them. They brought the middle classes into the National Movement.

Prominent Assertive Leaders

Bal Gangadhar Tilak

He was known as the father of Assertive Nationalism. Lokmanya Tilak was the uncompromising leader of the Assertive group. He was influenced by Agarkar, Ranade and Dadabhai Naoroji. The two newspapers, **The Kesari** (in Marathi) and **The Maratha** (in English) were launched by him. He organised the **Ganpati festival** to propagate nationalist ideas (1893) and the **Shivaji festival** (1895) to encourage young Maharashtrians. He was deported to Mandaly Jail (Burma) for writing seditious articles. He started the **Home Rule League in 1916**. He wrote *Gita Rahasaya.* Tilak asserted, 'Swaraj is my birth-right and I shall have it'.

No-rent campaigns were also organised by him. Due to his efforts Congress passed the resolution of Swadeshi, Boycott, Swaraj and National Education.

Bipin Chandra Pal

He discarded orthodox Hinduism and entered Brahmo Samaj and visited England and America. He founded **English weekly** and **New India**. He led the Swadeshi Movement. He carried the gospels of Boycott, Swadeshi, National Education, Swaraj and of Passive Resistance. He started journal named Vande Mataram.

Pal was known as the **father of revolutionary thought in India.** He gave a strong speech so to repeal the Arms Act. He also opposed the caste system and other rigiditions connected to the same.

He advocated widow remarriage. According to him educating women was the most effective way of elevating their position.

Lala Lajpat Rai

Under the influence of Arya Samaj, Lajpat Rai founded the National School of Lahore. Lala Lajpat Rai joined Congress in 1888 and remained its member till the end of his life. He presided over the **AITUC** (All India Trade Union Congress) in 1920 in its opening session. He also started a newspaper named **The Young India**. He boycotted the **Simon Commission** and demonstrated against it at Lahore.

During which, he was brutally assaulted by the police to which he subsequently succumbed. Lala Lajpat Rai was also referred to as **Punjab Kesari** or **Sher-e-Punjab**.

His contributions as an educationist and a writer are immense. Lalaji started 'Punjabi' from Lahore. He also published Urdu daily 'Vande Mataram' and English weekly named 'People'. Along with 'Young India' he also published 'The Call to Young India', 'England's Debt to India' and 'The Political Future of India'.

He is also credited with writing a book on national education that called for a reform of the prevalent educational system.

Differences between Moderates (Early Nationalists) and Extremists (Assertive)

Moderates	**Extremists**
Their social base was consisted of Zamindars and upper middle class in towns.	Their social base consisted of educated and lower middle classes in towns.
Moderates were loyal to British crown.	Extremists believed that British crown was unworthy for claiming Indian loyalty.
They demanded constitutional reforms and share for Indians in services.	They demanded swaraj or self rule for Indians.
Moderates insisted the use of Constitutional methods only.	They used extra constitutional methods like a boycott and passive resistance.

PYQs Previous Years' Questions

1 Marks Questions (MCQ)

Multiple Choice Questions

1. The main objective of the Assertive Nationalists was …………… *(ICSE 2023)*
   (a) constitutional agitation
   (b) peaceful protests
   (c) Purna Swaraj
   (d) self-government under British rule

Ans. (c) Purna Swaraj

2. Identify the Early Nationalist leader. *(ICSE 2023)*
   (a) Gopal Krishna Gokhale
   (b) Bipin Chandra Pal
   (c) Jyotiba Phule
   (d) Bal Gangadhar Tilak

Ans. *(a)* Gopal Krishna Gokhale

3. Which of the following statements about Early Nationalists is false? *(ICSE Semester I 2021)*
   (a) Their leaders were Dadabhai Naoroji and Gopal Krishna Gokhale.
   (b) They believed in constitutional means of protest.
   (c) They wanted self-government under British rule.
   (d) They wanted to launch violent agitations against the British.

Ans. *(d)* They wanted to launch violent agitations against the British.

4. Which of the following is a method of the Assertive Nationalists? *(ICSE Semester I 2021)*
   I. Swadeshi II. Boycott
   III. Passive Resistance IV. Revivalism

   Codes
   (a) I (b) II
   (c) III and IV (d) All of these

Ans. *(d)* All of these

5. Replace the underlined word and correct the statement. *(ICSE Semester I 2021)*
   Surendranath Banerjee presided over the Second Session of the Indian National Congress.
   (a) Dadabhai Naoroji
   (b) WC Bonnerjee
   (c) Rash behari Ghosh
   (d) Badruddin Tyabji

Ans. *(a)* Dadabhai Naoroji

2/3 Marks Questions

1. Mention any two contributions of Bipin Chandra Pal in promoting Nationalism. *(ICSE 2020)*

Ans. The contributions of Bipin Chandra Pal were as follows
(i) He started the newspaper 'New India' in 1914.
(ii) He was the main architect of the Swadeshi Movement.

2. State any two methods adopted by the Early Nationalists in the National Movement. *(ICSE 2020)*

Ans. The two methods adopted by the Early Nationalists in the National Movement were
(i) They arranged lectures in different parts of England to create public opinion in favour of Indians.
(ii) A British committee of the Indian National Congress was set-up in 1889.

3. Name the two books that Dadabhai Naoroji authored explaining the drain of India's wealth. *(2019)*

Ans. Two books of Dadabhai Naoroji explaining the drain of India's wealth are
(i) Poverty of India
(ii) Poverty and Un-British rule in India

4. Write any two contributions of Lala Lajpat Rai to the National Movement. *(ICSE 2019)*

Or Mention two important contributions of Lala Lajpat Rai. *(ICSE 2014)*

Ans. Two important contributions of Lala Lajpat Rai were as follows
(i) Lala Lajpat Rai was popularly known as 'Punjab Kesari' or 'Sher-e-Punjab'. He founded 'Punjabi', 'Vande Mataram' (Urdu Daily) and 'People' (English Weekly).
(ii) He joined the Congress in 1888 and remained its member till the end of his life. He was elected as the President of Congress in 1920. He became the first President of the All Indian Trade Union Congress (AITUC) in 1920.

5. Name the nationalist who said, 'Swaraj is my birth-right and I shall have it'. State any one of his contributions to the National Movement. *(ICSE 2018, 2007)*

Or Who said 'Swaraj is my birth-right and I will have it'? *(ICSE 2000)*

Ans. Bal Gangadhar Tilak said 'Swaraj is my birth-right and I shall have it'. Tilak was the first nationalist leader who openly declared the demand for 'Swaraj'. He started the Home Rule League at Pune, in 1916 for attaining self-government.

6. Mention any two objectives of the Early Nationalists. ***(ICSE Specimen 2017)***

Ans. Two objectives of the Early Nationalists were as follow

(a) Constitutional reforms like the abolition of Indian Council, or increase in the membership of Indians in the local bodies etc.

(b) Complete separation of the Executive and the Judiciary.

7. Mention any two causes for the rise of Assertive Nationalism. ***(ICSE 2015)***

Ans. Two causes for the rise of Assertive Nationalism were

(a) Restrictions on Indians for their own natural rights.

(b) Britishers were responsible for the bad economic conditions of India.

8. Who exposed the Economic Exploitation of India through his book 'Poverty and Un-British Rule in India'? ***(ICSE 2013)***

Ans. Dadabhai Naoroji exposed the Economic Exploitation of India through his book 'Poverty and Un-British Rule in India'.

9. Mention two reasons for the faith of the Moderates in the British sense of justice. ***(ICSE 2012)***

Ans. Two reasons for the faith of the Moderates in the British sense of justice were as follows

(i) The Moderates thought that the Englishmen thought about progressing India and putting it on the path of democracy and self-governance.

(ii) The Moderates thought that English rule had conferred benefits upon them, especially the English language and the modern means of communication and transport.

10. Mention any two achievements of the Moderates. ***(ICSE 2011, 2002)***

Ans. The two achievements of the Moderates were as follows

(i) They trained people in politics by popularising the ideas of democracy, civil liberties, secularism and nationalism.

(ii) They created national awakening among the people that they belonged to one common country. This made Indians conscious of the bonds of common political, economic and cultural interests that united them.

11. What were the two methods adopted by the radical nationalists in the freedom struggle? ***(ICSE 2010)***

Ans. Swadeshi and Boycott were the two methods, which were adopted by the radical nationalists in the freedom struggle.

12. Mention two acts against which Surendranath Banerjee protested. ***(ICSE 2008)***

Ans. The Arms Act and The Vernacular Press Act were protested against by the Surendranath Banerjee.

13. Name the Congress leader, who died after being assaulted by the British in his demonstration against the Simon Commission's recommendation. ***(ICSE 2008)***

Or Name the national leader, who succumb to a Lathi charge during the protest movement against the Simon Commission. ***(ICSE 2004)***

Ans. Lala Lajpat Rai was the Congress leader, who died after being assaulted by the British in his demonstration against the Simon Commission's recommendation.

14. Mention two contributions of Dadabhai Naoroji to the Indian Movement. ***(ICSE 2006)***

Ans. Two contributions of Dadabhai Naoroji were as follows

(i) In 1865, he founded the London India Society in collaboration with WC Bonnerjee.

(ii) He presented the 'Drain Theory' in his book 'Poverty and Un-British Rule in India'.

15. Name the Moderate leader who explained the economic 'Drain Theory' during the colonial times. ***(ICSE 2004)***

Ans. Dadabhai Naoroji explained the economic 'Drain Theory' during the colonial times.

16. Who started the paper 'The Young India'? ***(ICSE 2003, 2000)***

Ans. Lala Lajpat Rai started the paper 'The Young India'.

17. Who was called 'The Grand Old Man of India'? ***(ICSE 2001)***

Ans. Dadabhai Naoroji was called 'The Grand Old Man of India.'

18. Name any two leaders among the Moderates. *(ICSE 2000)*

Ans. Two leaders of the Moderates were as follows
(i) Dadabhai Naoroji
(ii) Surendranath Banerjee

4 Marks Questions

1. Look at the picture given below and answer the questions that follow. *(ICSE 2020)*

(i) Identify the leaders in the picture.
(a) Surendranath Banerjee, Dadabhai Naoroji, Gopal Krishna Gokhale
(b) Dadabhai Naoroji, Lala Lajpat Rai, Bipin Chandra Pal
(c) Gopal Krishna Gokhale, Bal Gangadhar Tilak, Dadabhai Naoroji
(d) Lala Lajpat Rai, Bal Gangadhar Tilak, Bipin Chandra Pal

Ans. (d) Lala Lajpat Rai, Bal Gangadhar Tilak, Bipin Chandra Pal

(ii) Which group of Congress did they belong to?
(a) Early Nationalists
(b) Assertive Nationalists
(c) Revolutionaries
(d) Swarajists

Ans. (b) Assertive Nationalists

(iii) What was their main objective?
(a) Attainment of Poorna Swaraj
(b) Self-Government under British Rule
(c) Abolition of India Council
(d) Demand for Provincial Government for Indians

Ans. (a) Attainment of Poorna Swaraj

(iv) What are the methods associated with them?
(a) Prayers and Protests
(b) Swadeshi and Boycott
(c) Sending deputations of Indian leaders to Britain
(d) Sending petitions to the British Government

Ans. (*b*) Swadeshi and Boycott

2. What were the four aims of the Congress? *(ICSE 2014)*

Ans. There were several aims of the Congress party. Some of them were as follows
(i) To develop the friendly relations between Nationalist political workers from different parts of the country.
(ii) To promote and consolidate the feelings of national unity irrespective of caste, religion or province.
(iii) To formulate popular demands and present them before the British Government.
(iv) To train and organise the public opinion in the country.

3. Why were the Early Congressmen called Moderates? *(ICSE 2013)*

Ans. The Early Congressmen were called Moderates, because
(i) early Moderates believed in loyalty to the British crown.
(ii) they had faith in the British sense of justice and fair play. Their attitude was not anti-British.
(iii) they believed that the British rule had many benefits. e.g., it aided in cleansing social ills like Sati, Untouchability and Child Marriage.
(iv) the method of Petitions, Prayers and Protests were used by the Early Moderates.

4. How did Moderates differ from the Assertive Nationalists in realising their objectives? *(ICSE 2013)*

Or Discuss the differences between the philosophy of Moderate and Extremist.

Ans. Differences between the Moderates and Assertive Nationalists were as follows
(i) Moderates wanted to achieve self-governance and they strove for autonomy within the empire and not for absolute independence. The Assertive Nationalists aimed at nothing short of Swaraj.
(ii) In terms of the basic beliefs, the Moderates looked to England for inspiration and guidance. They had an unlimited faith in the British benevolence whereas aggressive nationalists had no faith in the goodness of the British or in their assurance to the Indians.
(iii) The moderates had faith in the British sense of justice and fair play. The Assertives rejected British rule and held it responsible for the poverty of the Indian people.

(iv) Moderates were inspired by the ideas of Western philosophers. Assertives drew their inspiration from the Indian past.

(v) Moderates believed in constitutional methods and worked within the framework of the law. Whereas, aggressive Nationalists were radical in their approach. Their demands were aggressive.

5. How did Tilak bring a new wave in Indian politics that was distinct from the Early Congressmen? *(ICSE 2013)*

HINT *Dear students, this question simply ask you to explain the contribution of Bal Gangadhar Tilak in Indian freedom struggle.*

Ans. (i) Bal Gangadhar Tilak is known as the 'Father of the Assertive Nationalism'. He was a fearless fighter and had no faith in the methods of prayers and petitions.

(ii) He started two newspapers, 'The Kesari' (Marathi) and 'The Maratha' (English), both of which made bitter attacks on the Government. He used his newspapers as powerful weapons to spread discontent against the British rule.

(iii) He preached the idea of Swadeshi, Boycott and Prohibition, later on these ideas were followed by Mahatma Gandhi.

(iv) It was his conviction that independence would come to India only when the Indians were strong enough to snatch it from the British hands.

(v) He was the first Nationalist leader, who sought close contact with the masses.

(vi) It was under his influence that, the Congress in its annual session in 1906, had to pass resolutions regarding Swaraj. He said 'Swaraj is my birth-right and I shall have it'.

7 Marks Questions

1. With reference to nationalism, explain each of the following *(ICSE 2008)*

(a) Contributions of Bipin Chandra Pal.

(b) How did the British react when the Indian National Congress was founded? Why did their attitude change later?

Ans. (a) **Contributions of Bipin Chandra Pal**

Bipin Chandra Pal is known as the 'Father of the Revolutionary Thought' in India. He joined the Congress in 1886 and made a forceful speech in Madras to repeal the Arms Act. In the role of a journalist, he worked for 'Bengal Public Opinion', 'The Tribune' and 'New India' to propagate his brand of nationalism. He opposed the caste system and other rigidities concerning inter-dining and inter-mixing.

He advocated Widow remarriage. Educating women, he believed, was the most effective way of elevating their position. To establish equality in society, he wanted to tax the rich more heavily than the poor.

He demanded forty-eight hours of work in a week and an increase in the wages. During the Anti-Partition Movement, he toured several parts of the country with the messages of Boycott and Swadeshi.

(b) Initially, the British Government looked upon the Congress Movement with favour and welcome the formation of the Indian National Congress. A few government officials attended the First Session of the Congress and took part in its deliberations.

In fact, A.O. Hume, the founder of the Congress was himself a retired British civil servant. It was felt by the British rulers that the supressed anger or popular demands of the Indians can be given a safe outlet through a political platform.

They thought that this will prevent the recurrence of revolt from the Indians. But the official attitudes soon changed. Lord Dufferin, tried to divert the National Movement, by suggesting Hume that the Congress should devote itself to social rather than political affairs. But the rising popularity of the Congress and the increasing demands of the Nationalists from the British rulers led to a change in the British policy towards the Congress. Gradually, the British Government became indifferent to the meetings and demands of the Congress.

In 1887, Lord Dufferin attacked the National Congress in his speech and ridiculed it as representing only 'a microscopic minority of the people' and called the demands of the Congress as 'eminently unconstitutional'. British officials criticised the National Congress and branded its leaders as 'disloyal babus' and 'violent villains'.

10 Marks Questions

1. With reference to first and second phase of the Indian National Movement, answer the following. *(ICSE Specimen 2023)*

(a) What was the objective of the Assertive Nationalists? Mention any two contributions of Bal Gangadhar Tilak.

(b) Who partitioned Bengal? State any two actual reasons behind the partition.

(c) Mention any four methods used by the Early Nationalists.

Ans. (a) Following were the objectives of the Assertive Nationalists

- To make Indians aware about their self-respect and rights to freedom of speech and right of property, etc.
- Fight against unfavourable policies of the British Government.
- To make a nationwide presence of the movements.

Two contributions made by Bal Gangadhar Tilak are

- He organised the Ganapati Festival and Shivaji Festival to encourage nationalist ideas.
- He started the Home Rule League in 1916 and also stated 'Swaraj is my birth right and I shall have it'.

(b) The British Viceroy in India, Lord Curzon carried out the Partition of Bengal which was implemented on 16th October, 1905. This partition led to separation of large Muslim areas from the large Hindu areas.

The two actual reasons behind the Partition of Bengal are as follows

- To bring administrative efficiency in Bengal province as it was very large.
- To destroy the political influence of educated middle class.

(c) Four methods used by the Early Nationalists are as follows

- They made use of three P's i.e. Petitions, Prayers and Protests. They sent petitions, requests and letters of protest to the British Government to look into the problems of the Indians.
- The Early Nationalists relied on constitutional and peaceful methods in order to achieve their aim. They believed that if the demands of Indians were just, the British would grant them their demands.
- The Early Nationalists adopted the method of sending deputation for the fulfillment of its programme and to divert the attention of the British Government towards Indians.
- They organised annual sessions, meetings and discussions for generating political consciousness among the masses so that the government could take proper actions.

2. The Second half of the 19th centrury witnessed the growth of a strong feeling of Nationalism. With reference to the statement, answer the following. *(ICSE 2019)*

(a) Write any three repressive colonial policies of the British.

(b) State any three ways in which the Press played an important role in developing nationalism amongst Indians.

(c) Explain briefly any three differences in the methods adopted between the Early Nationalists and Radicals, in the National Movement.

Ans. (*a*) Three repressive colonial policies of the British were

(i) Agricultural India was made an economic colony to serve the interests of Industrial England.

(ii) India was made to accept readymade British goods either duty free or at nominal duty rates, while Indian products were subjected to high import duties in England.

(iii) The British capital invested in Indian markets especially in railway, shipping, oil exploration, tea and coffee plantations, etc was used to get huge profits and were sent to England.

(b) The role played by the Press in developing nationalism amongst Indians was as follow

(i) It played an important role in carrying ideas to the people.

(ii) During the later half of the 19th century, a large number of newspapers were started. These papers fostered patriotism and ideas of liberty and justice in our country.

(iii) The Press was a powerful factor in building and developing a strong nationalistic sentiment among the Indians.

(c) For answer, refer to Q 4 of 4 marks questions.

Examiner's Comment

- Most of the candidates were able to attempt this question quite well. However, some candidates were not sure whether to write the repressive policies of Lord Curzon or Lord Lytton.
- Most of the candidates were able to answer this question correctly. A few candidates, however, only mentioned the names of the books and the newspapers.
- Majority of the candidates mentioned the beliefs and aims of the Early Nationalists and Radicals rather than mentioning the methods adopted by them in the National Movement. Most of the candidates were not clear regarding the objectives, beliefs and methods of both the groups.

Suggestions for Students

- Learn the time frame of repressive policies during the early part and later part of the 19th century.
- Explain the role of books and newspapers in developing nationalism amongst Indians.
- Learn to read and understand the question carefully. The demand of the question must be understood before writing its answer.

3. With reference to the growth of Nationalism, answer the following questions. *(ICSE Specimen 2018)*

(a) Mention two associations which served as the forerunners (precursors) of the Indian National Congress. Who were the founders of the two associations?

(b) Differentiate between the methods adopted by the Early Nationalists and the Radical Nationalists.

(c) State two contributions of Gopal Krishna Gokhale and Lala Lajpat Rai.

Ans. (a) Two associations which served as the forerunners of the Indian National Congress were

(i) **The East India Association** It was founded by Dadabhai Naoroji in London in 1866.

(ii) **Indian Association of Calcutta** It was founded in 1876 by Surendranath Banerjee.

(b) For answer, refer to Q. 4 of 4 marks questions.

(c) Two contributions of Gopal Krishna Gokhale were

(i) Established the Servants of Indian Society. This society trained men to devote their lives to the cause of the country.

(ii) He presided the Varanasi session of the Congress in 1905.

For two contributions of Lala Lajpat Rai, refer to Q. 4 of 2/3 marks questions.

4. The Assertive Nationalists lost faith in the methods and ultimate success of the Early Nationalists. In the light of this statement, briefly describe *(ICSE Specimen 2017)*

(a) Basic beliefs of Assertive Nationalists.

(b) Difference between their methods and those of the Early Nationalists.

(c) Any two contributions made by Bal Gangadhar Tilak and Lala Lajpat Rai.

Ans. (a) The beliefs of the Assertive Nationalists differed from those of the Early Nationalists.While the Early Nationalists strove for autonomy within the empire, the Assertive, aimed at complete independence or Swaraj. And while the Early Nationalists had faith in the British sense of justice and fair play and were inspired by the ideas of the Western philosopheres (thus having a positive outlook towards the British) the Assertives bluntly rejected the British rule, holding it responsible for India's poverty, thereby drawing their inspiration from India's past.

(b) While the Early Nationalists believed in and sticked to the constitutional methods to propose any requirement, the Assertives believed in adopting non-violent resistance and vigorous political actions to achieve their aims. They did not want to beg for, but claim their rights. They advocated courage, self-confidence and a spirit of sacrifice to achieve their goal of Swaraj and asked the people to refuse to cooperate with the government and to boycott government service, courts, schools and colleges.

(c) **Contributions of Bal Gangadhar Tilak**

- He used the traditional religious Ganapati festival to propagate Nationalist ideas, through songs and speeches in 1893.
- He also started two newspapers -Maratha and Kesari, which voiced his ideas well. He also established a Home Rule League at Pune in 1916 to attain self-government.

For Contributions of Lala Lajpat Rai, refer to Q. 4 of 2/3 marks question.

5.

(A)

(B)

(a) Identify the persons 'A' and 'B' given above. To which section of the Congress did each belong and what were their ultimate objectives?

(b) Highlight three different methods of struggle adopted by each section of the Congress.

(c) State the contributions of the person 'B' in the freedom struggle. *(ICSE 2009)*

Ans. (a) **Person in picture 'A' is Gopal Krishna Gokhale**
He belonged to the Moderate section of the Congress. He was influenced by the ideals of Justice MG Ranade.
The moderates wanted to achieve self-governance and they strove for autonomy within the British empire and not for absolute independence. They believed in constitutional methods and worked within the framework of the law.
Person in picture 'B' is Lala Lajpat Rai, one of the Assertive leaders of the Congress.
The main objective of the Assertive Nationalists was the immediate attainment of 'Swaraj'. This meant complete independence and not just self-government, as was in the colonies of Australia and New Zealand, etc.

(b) Methods of struggle adopted by each section of the Congress were as follows

(i) **Methods of Moderates**
The Moderates relied on constitutional and peaceful methods and avoided violence and confrontation. They believed in the three P's—Prayers, Petitions and Protests to achieve their objectives. They had full faith in the British sense of justice and fair play and believed that India needed a balanced representation of its demands before the British rulers. Therefore, they did not follow a policy of confrontation but highlighted their problems in the following manner

- They held meetings where speeches were made and resolutions for popular demands were passed.
- They made use of the press to carry out a criticism of the government policies.
- They sent memorandums and petitions to the government officials and to the British Parliament.

(ii) **Methods of the Assertives**
The main focus of the Assertive Nationalists was to get a larger share for Indians in the administration of their country and to end Britain Economic Exploitation of India. They favoured the use of force and revolutionary methods for achieving their aims.
They adopted the following methods for the struggle are as follows

- The Assertive leaders believed in adopting the policy of non-violent resistance and vigorous political action to achieve their aims.
- They mainly relied on the strength of their masses. They converted the National Movement into a Mass Movement. They aroused the masses by influencing them with their sacrifices and sufferings.
- Assertive Nationalists received self-respect by referring to India's past glory. These leaders planned the National Movement on people's religious beliefs. The Assertive Nationalists tried to enlist the students in their service, when the British Government threatened to take disciplinary action against the students, the national leaders advocated national universities that were free from government control.

(c) **Contributions of Lala Lajpat Rai in the Freedom Struggle**

(i) He started a monthly magazine 'The Young India', to spread the message of the right of India to attain Swaraj. Through this magazine, he propagated his ideas of Radical Nationalism among the people of India.

(ii) He opened orphanages, hospitals and schools. He set-up 'Servants of the People Society' for the welfare of the downtrodden and outcastes.

(iii) He was assaulted by a British sergeant while demonstrating against the Simon Commission in Lahore in 1928. This incident fuelled Anti-British passion and enraged revolutionaries.

(iv) He inspired Indians to take action against the British rulers rather than following the three P's — Prayers, Petitions and Protests for this purpose. He delivered many seditious speeches and for the same was arrested and deported to prison for six months for the same.

6. Read the extract given below and answer the questions that follow.

'.... the Indians, who actively worked for the creation of an all-India political organisation represented new social forces that were increasingly opposed to the exploitation of India for British interests. They needed an organisation that would fight for India's political and economic advancement.' — From 'Freedom Struggle'. *(ICSE 2007)*

(A)

(B)

(a) In the context of the above, identify the two individuals in Pictures (A) and (B), who were the early leaders of the organisation to be for.

(b) How did the person in picture (B) explain the Economic Exploitation of India for British interests?

(c) Name the organisation, which was to be formed. What were the objectives behind the formation of this political body?

(d) Explain the major ideological differences, which emerged amongst the leaders within the first twenty years of the foundation of this organisation.

Ans. (a) Picture (A) — Gopal Krishna Gokhale and Picture (B) — Dadabhai Naoroji

(b) Dadabhai Naoroji exposed the economic ills of the Indian economy and criticised the British rule for its bad effects on the Indian economy. His views on Indian economy are given in his work titled 'Poverty and Un-British Rule in India'. His famous 'Drain Theory' explained how India's wealth was being 'drained' to England through various ways.

(c) The Indian National Congress was the organisation that was to be formed.

For the objectives of the Indian National Congress, refer to Q. 2 of 4 marks questions.

(d) The method popularly known as Constitutional Agitation method was followed by the Early Liberal Nationalists.

The Moderates carried their agitations by the following methods which were as follows

(i) They made use of the Press to carry out a criticism of the government policies.

(ii) They made use of three P's—Petitions, Prayers and Protests.

(iii) They held meetings in towns, cities and the countryside.

(iv) Resolutions and distributions of leaflets and pamphlets.

(v) Preparing memorandum for the Government Committees and sending them.

(vi) They merely wanted to mitigate the evils of British rules and not to terminate it.

7. With reference to the role of the Moderates in arousing National awakening in India, answer the following questions. *(ICSE 2002)*

(a) Name the Moderates leaders why were they called so?

(b) Who was known as 'India's unofficial ambassador in England'? What were his views on the cause of poverty in India? Mention his achievements in strengthening Indian nationalism.

Ans. (a) Dadabhai Naoroji, WC Bonnerjee, Madan Mohan Malviya, Gopal Krishna Gokhale, Justice Ranade and Pherozeshah Mehta were some major Moderate leaders. They were called Moderate leaders because by nature, their demands were Moderate along with their methods, which were constitutional as well.

(b) Dadabhai Naoroji, the 'Grand Old Man of India', was known as India's unofficial Ambassador in England, and can be viewed as the architect who laid the foundation of the Indian Freedom Struggle. He sacrificed his career and his family for the country.

His views on why poverty occurred in India and how the wealth of the Indians was gradually drained to Britain have been published. As the years passed, Dadabhai grew more and more disillusioned with the 'fair-minded' British.

After spending years collecting statistics, Dadabhai propounded the 'Drain Theory'. Dadabhai proved that the average annual income of an Indian was barely ₹ 20. Examining the import and export figures for 37 years, he proved that India's exports exceeded its imports by ₹ 50 crore (approximately $ 135 million) annually.

CHAPTER TEST

01 Mark Questions

1 Identify the famous personality who is known as the "Grand Old Man of India".

(a) Sardar Patel (b) Dadabhai Naoroji
(c) Gopal Krishna Gokhale (d) Bal Gangadhar Tilak

2

The Maratha Newspaper	Bal Gangadhar Tilak
New India Newspaper	?

(a) Bipin Chandra Pal (b) Lala Lajpat Rai
(c) Gopal Krishna Gokhale (d) Surendranath Banerjee

3 Name the personality who founded the servants of India society in 1905.

(a) Dadabhai Naoroji (b) WC Bonnerjee
(c) Gopal Krishna Gokhale (d) Bal Gangadhar Tilak

4 .... was the first Indian to quality for the Indian Civil Service Examination and was elected from the Bengal Council four times.

(a) Gopal Krishna Gokhale (b) Lala Lajpat Rai
(c) Bal Gangadhar Tilak (d) Surendranath Banerjee

5 Which of the following statements about Extre mists (Assertive) Nationalists is false?

(a) They demanded Swaraj or self rule for India.
(b) The used extra constitutional methods like a boycott and passive resistance.
(c) They wanted self-government under British rule.
(d) Their leaders were Bipin Chandra Pal and Lala Lajpat Rai.

Answers

1. (b) | 2. (a) | 3. (c) | 4. (d) | 5. (c)

02 Marks Questions

6 Mention any two methods of the Extremists (Assertives) proposed for attaining independence.

7 State any two achievements of Early Nationalists.

8 Mention any two contributions of Bal gangadhar Tilak in promoting Nationalism.

9 What are the objective of the Rise of Assertive Nationalism?

10 Marks Question

10 With reference to the role of the Extremists in arousing national awakening in India, answer the following questions.

(i) Name the prominent Extremist leaders. Why were they called so?

(ii) Who was known as the father of revolutionary thought in India? Mention any three contribution in strengthening Indian nationalism.

(iii) How International events become the major factor in the growth of the Assertive Nationalism? Discuss.

03

The Partition of Bengal & Formation of the Muslim League

TREND ANALYSIS 3 YEARS

Average No. of Questions Across all Sets

	Types of Questions	2023	2020	2019
TOPIC 01 Partition of Bengal	1 Mark	1	–	–
	2/3 Marks	–	1	–
	4 Marks	–	–	–
	10 Marks	–	–	–
TOPIC 02 Formation of Muslim league	1 Mark	1	–	–
	2/3 Marks	1	–	–
	4 Marks	–	–	–
	10 Marks	–	–	–

The era of Lord Curzon's office as the Viceroy (1899-1905) started with controversies. The Partition of Bengal (1905) was one of his administrative measures which resulted in strong resentment. Provoking people against the British was made an offence as per the Curzon's Act of 1898.

The **Calcutta Corporation Act** (1899) increased the number of Englishmen on the list of official members of the corporation.

Scheme of Partition

The area of Bengal was very large and it was most densely populated and because of this, it was difficult to administer the same efficiently. On 20th July 1905, Lord Curzon announced the division of the Province of Bengal.

The scheme of the Partition of Bengal was implemented on 16th October, 1905.

Lord Curzon's Motive Behind the Partition

- Administrative necessity was the main motive cited by the British behind the Partition of Bengal.
- The partition of the state was intended to curb Bengali influence by not only placing Bengalis under two administrations, but by reducing them to a minority in Bengal itself.
- Curzon's real motive behind the partition was to break **the growing solidarity of Bengali Nationalism**. Another motive was to drive a wedge between the Hindus and the Muslims.

- The partition was meant to foster divisions on the basis of religion. East Bengal would be predominantly a Muslim majority state and Paschim Bangal would have a Hindu majority.

Causes Behind the Partition of Bengal

- According to the British administrators, the main objective behind the Partition of Bengal was that, it was an administrative necessity. They explained that the Province was very large, hence it was to be divided.
- At that time, Bengal was the main centre of Indian Nationalism. So, the British expected to regulate the rising tide of Nationalism by the division of Bengal.
- The main reason for the Partition of Bengal was to destroy the political influence of the educated middle class among whom, the Bengali 'intelligensia' were the most prominent.

The Anti-Partition Movement

- The Partition of Bengal was opposed by the Indian National Congress and the Nationalists of Bengal. Various sections of the population like the landholders, merchants, lawyers, students and women rose up in opposition to the division of their province.
- Many protest meetings were organised by the prominent leaders like Surendranath Banerjee, Krishna Kumar Mitra, PC Ray, BC Pal and Ananda Mohan Bose. Both the Moderates and the Assertive Nationalists cooperated with one another during the course of the movement. Some newspapers like **Bengali, Hitabadi** and **Sanjibani** played an important role.
- On 7th August, 1905, the Anti-Partition Movement was initiated in the town hall of Calcutta. A massive demonstration against the partition was organised on that day.

Lord Curzon's Reaction

Curzon hoped to achieve double advantages with this partition, which are as follows

- To split up and thus weaken the Nationalist Movement.
- To create a Mohammedan province where Islam and its followers could be pre-dominant.

Nationalist Reaction

Reactions of the Nationalists to the Partition of Bengal were as follows

- The Partition of Bengal led to a mighty upsurge, which brought people and political leaders together. The nationalists were opposed to the Partition of Bengal.
- The streets of Kolkata were full of the cries of Vande Mataram, which became the theme song of the National Movement.
- They celebrated 16th October as the 'Day of Mourning.' The newspapers 'The Bengalee' and the 'Amrit Bazar Patrika' criticised the government severely.
- People of Bengal tied rakhis on one another's wrists as the symbol of unbreakable unity of the Bengalis.

People's Reaction

People's reactions to the Partition of Bengal were as follows

- On 16th October, 1905, the Partition of Bengal came into effect. This day was declared to be a day of **National Mourning** by the Nationalists. It was also observed as a **day of fasting**.
- The singing of Vande Mataram (Written by Bankim Chandra Chatterjee) was forbidden in the streets of Bengal. The leaders of the movement were ill-treated. Hindu and Muslims tied *rakhis* on one another's wrists as the symbol of unbreakable unity and the ceremony of Raksha Bandhan was celebrated in a new way.

Impact of the Anti-Partition Movement

The Partition of Bengal led people towards the idea of Swadeshi and Boycott and the people now lost their faith in the justice of British. The agitation of Anti-Partition backfired the plans of Lord Curzon.

Repressions by the Britishers against the Anti-Partition Movement

Following were the main steps taken for repressions by the Britishers

(i) Thousands of people were arrested and put behind bars.

(ii) Lathi charge became common.

(iii) Lala Lajpat Rai, Sardar Ajit Singh, Surendranath Banerjee and many other leaders got arrested.

(iv) Institutions were warned to stop participating in the movement.

(v) Grants of many suspected institutions were cancelled.

(vi) Crying of 'Vande Mataram' was strictly forbidden.

(vii) Government made use of several repressive measures such as the Prevention of Seditious Meeting Act, the Explosive Substance Act, the Criminal Law Amendment Act and the Newspaper Act.

Swadeshi and Boycott Movements and their Impact

- The Boycott and Swadeshi Movements had their genesis in the Anti-Partition Movement, which was started to oppose the British's decision to divide Bengal. With the start of the Swadeshi Movement the Indian National Movement took a major leap forward.
- Swadeshi, as a purely economic measures for the development of the industries, had been preached by some nationalists like Gopal Rao Deshmukh, GV Joshi and MG Ranade of Maharashtra and Rajnarain Bose, etc. In the year 1896, **Bal Gangadhar Tilak** had led a full fledged Boycott campaign.
- On 7th August, 1905, a resolution to Boycott British goods was adopted at a meeting of the INC held in Kolkata. It was started as a purely economic measure for the development of the Indian industry.
- The Swadeshi and Boycott movements brought into politics new classes of people. They encouraged the indigenous industries. This movement provided employment to many craftsmen in the indigenous industries.
- The Assertive Nationalists played an important role during the National Movement. They clarified its objectives, taught people self-reliance and prepared the social base of the movement by including the middle class, the students, the youth and also women. Thus, these movements with a wide social base paved the way for future Mass Movement led by Gandhiji.

Surat Split (1907)

- In December, 1906, at Kolkata, the Indian National Congress under the leadership of Dadabhai Naoroji adopted 'Swaraj' as the goal of the Indian people.
- The Assertive Nationalists wanted to extend the Swadeshi and Boycott to the rest of India and make it a vehicle for a full fledged political mass struggle leading to Swaraj, but the Moderates did not approve it for the whole of India and wanted it to be continued only in Bengal.
- In the year 1907, the Annual Session of the Congress was held in Surat. Assertive Nationalists wanted to adopt revolutionary methods as announced by them, but the Moderates were not in favour of such methods.
- The INC split into two groups at the Surat session, the Extremists were led by Bal Gangadhar Tilak, Lala Lajpat Rai and Bipin Chandra Pal and the Moderates were led by Gopal Krishna Gokhale.
- The Extremist Nationalists proposed the name of Lala Lajpat Rai as the President of the Surat Session whereas the Early Nationalists proposed the name of Rashbihari Ghosh. Finally, the Extremist Nationalists were expelled from the Congress.

Formation of the Muslim League (1906)

In December, 1906, the All India Muslim League was set-up by Nawab Salimullah at Dhaka. The **1st session** of Muslim League took place in **Dhaka** in 1906 and the first President of this session was **Sir Sultan Muhammad Shah (Agha Khan III)**. The League supported the Partition of Bengal, opposed the Swadeshi Movement and demanded special safeguards for its community and separate electorates for Muslims. This led to communal differences between the Hindus and the Muslims.

Factors Leading to the Formation of the Muslim League and its Objectives

In India, the Hindus and the Muslims had lived together for centuries, and there prevailed some sort of unity between the two. Such a unity between the two communities posed a danger to British imperialism.

The following factors were responsible for the formation of the Muslim League

Loss of Sovereignty by Mughal Rulers

In India, after the dethroning of Mughal rulers, the British established their supremacy. The Mughals were the followers of Islam. Due to this, the Muslims became bitter enemies of the British. Muslim took part in the Wahabi Movement. The aim of this movement was restoring the Islamic rulers in India.

British Policy of Divide and Rule

After the First War of Independence in 1857, the British became apprehensive of the safety and stability of their empire in India. In the war of 1857, both the Hindus and the Muslims took part in a large number. Britishers saw the unity between the Hindus and the Muslims as a threat to them. To check the growth of a United National feeling in India and to encourage communal and separatist tendencies in Indian politics, they decided to follow the policy of **Divide and Rule**.

The Muslims were made to fight with the Hindus, with one class or caste used against the other and the high caste Hindus were excited against the low caste Hindus and the Sikhs alike.

British tried to create hatred among the Hindus and the Muslims by portraying Muslim rulers as plunders and Hindu rulers as cruel kings to their Muslim subjects. They tried to spread communal hatred through the use of press, posters, literature and public platform.

Relative Backwardness of the Muslim Community in Education, Trade and Industry

After 1858, the Muslims were consciously discriminated by the British Government, holding them responsible for the uprising of 1857. Muslims were also discriminated in the recruitment of Civil and Military Services.

Objectives of the Muslim League

The objectives of the Muslim League were as follows

(i) To promote feeling of loyalty among the Indian Muslims towards the British Government.

(ii) To protect the political and other rights of the Muslims and present them before the government in a mild language.

(iii) One of the main objectives of the Muslim League was to keep the Muslim intelligensia away from the mainstream of the National Movement.

Impact of the Muslim League on the National Movement

- Initially the Muslim League stood apart from the National Movement, opposed the Anti-Partition Movement and the Swadeshi and Boycott Movements.
- The radical and nationalist ideas among the Muslims were promoted by a group of educated and young men. Among them the most prominent were Maulana Abul Kalam Azad, Habib-ur-Rahman, Hakim Ajmal Khan and Mazhar-ul-Haq.
- In the World War I, when the safety of Turkey was threatened, Indians reacted and anti-British sentiments started to grow among the Muslims. As a result many more radical young Muslims like Maulana Mohammed Ali, Hakim Ajmal Khan and Mazhar-ul-Haq joined the Nationalists towards the common cause. The emergent section of Nationalists Muslims changed the attitude of the Muslim League towards the Congress. The Lucknow Pact was signed in 1916.
- In 1930, the demand for Pakistan was raised by the Muslim League and in the 1940 Session of the Muslim League at Lahore, Jinnah put forward his **Two Nation Theory**. Ultimately, the activities of the League brought about the creation of Pakistan in 1947.

PYQs Previous Years' Questions

1 Mark Questions

Multiple Choice Questions

1. Complete the given analogy.
Formation of Congress : 1885 : : Formation of Muslim League : ? *(ICSE 2023)*
(a) 1905 (b) 1906
(c) 1907 (d) 1908

Ans. (b) 1906

2. The plan of Partition of Bengal was proposed by .... *(ICSE 2023)*
(a) Lord Canning (b) Lord Dalhousie
(c) Lord Curzon (d) Lord Ripon

Ans. (c) Lord Curzon

3. The nationalists felt Bengal was partitioned .... *(ICSE Specimen Semester I 2021)*
(a) to divide Hindus and Muslims
(b) for effective administration
(c) to stop the spread of Swadeshi
(d) to help the Muslims

Ans. (a) to divide Hindus and Muslims

4. Which of the following is not the aim of the Muslim League? *(ICSE Specimen Semester I 2021)*
(a) To develop and consolidate the feelings of national unity among Muslims.
(b) To protect and advance the political rights of Muslims.
(c) To promote among Muslims of India, support for the British Government.
(d) To prevent hostilities between Muslims and other communities

Ans. (*a*) To develop and consolidate the feelings of national unity among Muslims.

5. Which of the following was a nationalist perspective of the Partition of Bengal? *(ICSE Semester I 2021)*
(a) There were only Hindus in West Bengal.
(b) To divide the Hindus and Muslims.
(c) There were many riots in Bengal.
(d) It was an administrative necessity as Bengal was a large territory.

Ans. (*b*) To divide the Hindus and Muslims.

6. When was Bengal partitioned? *(ICSE Semester I 2021)*
(a) 1905 (b) 1907
(c) 1906 (d) 1911

Ans. (*a*) 1905

7. From the given list, identify the objective of the Muslim League. *(ICSE Semester I 2021)*
(a) To train and organise public opinion in the country.
(b) To promote friendly relations between nationalists political workers.
(c) To promote among Muslims of India support for the British Government.
(d) To agitate through constitutional means.

Ans. (*c*) To promote among Muslims of India support for the British Government.

Very Short Answer Questions

1. Who wrote 'Vande Mataram'? *(ICSE 2003)*

Ans. Vande Mataram was written by Bankim Chandra Chatterjee.

2. Mention one reason for the rise of Militant Nationalism in India. *(ICSE 2002)*

Ans. The Division of Bengal led to the rise of Militant Nationalism in India.

3. When was the decision regarding the Partition of Bengal officially announced? *(ICSE 2000)*

Ans. The decision regarding the Partition of Bengal was officially announced on 16th October, 1905.

2/3 Marks Questions

1. State any two objectives of the Muslim League. *(ICSE 2023, Specimen 2023, ICSE 2018)*

Or State any two objectives of the All-India Muslim League. *(ICSE Specimen 2017)*

Ans. The two objectives of the Muslim League were as follows
(i) To promote feeling of loyalty among the Indian Muslims towards the British Government.
(ii) To protect the political and other rights of the Muslims and present them before the government in a mild language.

2. Why is 16th October, 1905 regarded as an important day in the history of the Indian National Movement? *(ICSE 2020)*

Ans. 16th October, 1905 is regarded as an important day in the history of Indian National Movement because on this day, Bengal was partitioned which separated Eastern parts of Bengal from the rest of the Bengal. It was announced on 19th July, 1905 by Viceroy of India, Lord Curzon. This day was observed as day of mourning throughout Bengal.

3. When and by whom was Bengal partitioned? *(Specimen 2017)*

Or When was Bengal partitioned? Name the Viceroy responsible for it. *(ICSE 2011)*

Ans. On 20th July, 1905, Lord Curzon announced the division of the province of Bengal into the following two provinces

(i) Eastern Bengal and Assam

(ii) The rest of Bengal

4. Briefly explain the terms 'Swadeshi' and 'Boycott'. *(ICSE Specimen 2017)*

Ans. Swadeshi means 'of one's own country' aimed at the promotion of indigenous industries for strengthening the nation.

Boycott means 'abstaining from the purchase of British goods'.

For example, not buying any foreign goods or even using any titles or even working for them.

5. State two reasons given by Lord Curzon to justify the Partition of Bengal. *(ICSE 2016)*

Other Similar Questions

Or What were Curzon's two real motives behind the Partition of Bengal?

Or How did Lord Curzon justify the Partition of Bengal?

Ans. On 20th July, 1905, Lord Curzon announced the division of the province of Bengal by giving two important reasons as follows

- Administrative necessity because the province of Bengal was too big for efficient administration.
- Another reason was to foster division on the basis of religion to crush the nationalist spirit of Bengal. East Bengal would be predominantly a Muslim majority state and West Bengal would have a Hindu Majority.

6. State any two repressive policies of Lord Curzon. *(2012)*

Ans. The two repressive policies of Lord Curzon were

(i) He passed the act of 1898 which made it an offence to provoke people against the British.

(ii) He passed the Calcutta Corporation Act in 1899 which reduced the strength of elected members from India, giving majority to the British.

Additional Info

Other repressive policies of Lord Curzon were

- He passed the Indian Universities Act of 1904 which imposed strict official control over the Indian Universities as he considered them as the centres of Indian nationalism.
- He partitioned Bengal on communal lines into East and West Bengal.

7. Three factors leading to the formation of the Muslim League. *(ICSE 2008)*

Ans. Three factors leading to the formation of Muslim League were as follows

(i) The unity between Hindus and Muslims was seen by the Britishers after the Revolt of 1857 and during the Partition of Bengal. To check the growth of nationalism, the Britishers encouraged the formation of the Muslim League.

(ii) The Communal and Separatist trend of thinking grew among the Muslims to some extent because of their relative backwardness in education, trade and industry.

(iii) Sir Syed Ahmad Khan was a great educationist. He opposed the formation of Indian National Congress. He worked as a guiding force for the Muslims to form a separate organisation.

10 Marks Questions

1. One of Lord Curzon's administrative measures that resulted in a strong resentment from the masses was the Partition of Bengal in 1905. In this context, answer the following questions. *(ICSE 2012)*

(a) What was Lord Curzon's argument in favour of the Partition of Bengal? How did the nationalists interpret Lord Curzon's motives?

(b) How did the people react to the Partition of Bengal?

(c) What was the impact of the Swadeshi Movement on the Indian industries?

Ans. (a) **Curzon's argument in favour of the Partition of Bengal** Curzon justified the Partition of Bengal Presidency, saying that the area of Bengal was very large and it was also the most thickly populated province in British India. And it was difficult for the British to administer the same efficiently. Hence, according to Lord Curzon, Partition of Bengal was an 'administrative necessity.'

The Interpretation of Nationalists The Indian nationalists clearly saw the design behind the partition and condemned it. They thought that this was done in order to divide or break the Hindu—Muslim unity, they felt that administrative efficiency could have been better secured to stop the tide of Nationalism, to curb Bengali influence by not only placing Bengalis under the administration, but by reducing them to a minority in Bengal.

(b) People's reactions to the Partition of Bengal were as follows

(i) On 16th October 1905, the Partition of Bengal came into effect. The leaders of the Protest Movement declared it a day of 'National Morning' throughout Bengal. It was observed as a 'day of fasting.'

(ii) The streets of Kolkata were full of the cries of 'Vande Mataram', which became the theme song of the National Movement.

(iii) They tied rakhis on each other's wrists to show their bonds of love and unity.

(iv) People showed their anger by boycotting foreign goods. They observed fasts and pledged support to the Nationalists for forcing the government to cancel the partition.

(c) Swadeshi and Boycott Movements marked the beginning of a new era in India's freedom. The Swadeshi Movement gave a great stimulus to the Indian industries, particularly the weaving industries. These movements brought into politics many new classes of people without any distinction of caste and creed.

Textiles mills, match and soap factories came up quickly all over the country. All this gave impetus to the Nationalists poetry, prose and journalism and education gave India a national orientation in the vernacular media. Swadeshi Movement led to the establishment of first Steel Company of India, 'Tata Steel' in Bihar in 1911.

2. To some extent Lord Curzon was responsible for the anti-partition agitation into a Mass movement. In this context, answer the following questions. ***(ICSE 2006)***

(a) What was Lord Curzon's argument in favour of the Partition of Bengal? How did the nationalists interpret Lord Curzon's motives?

(b) How did the people express their unhappiness against this decision of the British?

(c) Explain the terms Swadeshi and Boycott in the context of the National Movement in India.

Ans. (a) For answer, refer to Q. 1 (a) of 10 marks questions.

(b) For answer, refer to Q. 1 (b) of 10 marks questions.

(c) In the year 1905, the Swadeshi and Boycott Movements started as a part of the agitation against the Partition of Bengal. Swadeshi literally means of 'one's own country'. The aim of the Swadeshi Movement was the promotion of indigenous industries for strengthening the nation. Boycott Movement meant 'abstaining from the purchase of British goods'.

These movements were started with a view to accelerate the pace of the freedom struggle. Swadeshi was a weapon forged by the people to achieve industrial and economic regeneration. The Boycott Movement was more comprehensive and a four-fold programme of Boycott was advocated.

3. Bengal was partitioned in the year 1905 by Lord Curzon. In the light of this, describe briefly. ***(ICSE 2004)***

(a) The motives of Lord Curzon behind the partition.

(b) The measures taken by the British to crush the Anti-Partition Movement.

(c) The reasons given by the British to justify the Partition of Bengal.

Ans. (a) The motives of Lord Curzon behind the partition were as follows

(i) The main motive for the Partition of Bengal according to British rulers was administrative necessity. They said that the province of Bengal was too big to be efficiently administered by a 'Single Provincial Government.'

(ii) The partition of the state was intended to curb Bengali influence by not only placing Bengalis under two administrations, but by reducing them to a minority in Bengal itself.

(iii) Curzon's real motive behind the partition was to break 'the growing solidarity of Bengali Nationalism'. Another motive was to drive a wedge between the Hindus and the Muslims.

(iv) The partition was meant to foster divisions on the basis of religion. East Bengal would be pre-dominantly a Muslim majority state and Paschim Bengal would have a Hindu majority.

(b) The government banned processions and meetings, curbed the newspapers by rigorous Press laws and imprisoned the leaders of the movement without trial. The government took all measures to suppress the students.

The government made use of several repressive measures such as the Prevention of Seditious Meeting Act, the Explosive Substances Act, the Criminal Law Amendment Act and the Newspapers Act. The singing of Vande Mataram was forbidden in the streets of Bengal. The leaders of the movement were ill–treated. Some leaders were tried for seditious writing in various papers. The educational institutions were warned that if they did not prevent their students from participating in the Boycott Movement, their grants-in-aid would be stopped.

(c) For answer, refer to Q. 5 of 2/3 marks questions.

4. The Partition of Bengal in 1905 was intended to check the rising tide of Indian Nationalism and to break the Hindu-Muslim unity in Bengal. In this context, state the following. ***(ICSE 2002)***

(a) Reaction of the Nationalists to the Partition of Bengal.

(b) Reaction of the British against the agitators.

Ans. (a) Reactions of the Nationalists to the Partition of Bengal were as follows

(i) The Partition of Bengal led to a mighty upsurge which brought people and political leaders together. The Nationalists were opposed to the Partition of Bengal.

(ii) The streets of Kolkata were full of the cries of Vande Mataram, which became the theme song of the National Movement.

(iii) They celebrated 16th October as the 'day of Mourning.' The newspapers 'The Bengalee' and the 'Amrit Bazar Patrika' criticised the government severely.

(iv) People of Bengal tied rakhis on one another's wrists as the symbol of unbreakable unity of the Bengalis.

(b) The government used all kinds of repression. Thousands of people were arrested and put behind the bars. Lathi charge were common on peaceful and non-violent protesters. Many leaders i.e., Lala Lajpat Rai, Sardar Ajit Singh, Surendranath Banerjee, etc were arrested. Institutions were stopped to take part in the movement. Those institutions, who were in suspicion, their grants were cancelled, even crying of Vande Mataram was forbidden.

5. With reference to the Partition of Bengal in 1905, answer the following questions. ***(ICSE 2001)***

(a) Why was Bengal partitioned?

(b) What was the reaction of the people to the partition?

Ans. (a) For answer, refer to Q. 5 of 2/3 marks questions.

(b) For answer, refer to Q. 1 (b) of 10 marks questions.

CHAPTER TEST

01 Mark Questions

1 The Partition of Bengal was done mainly ....

(a) for the development of Bengal
(b) to weaken the growth of Nationalism in Bengal
(c) for administrative convenience
(d) to divide the Hindus and Muslims

2

'The Bengalee' Newspaper	Surendranath Banerjee
'Sanjibani' Newspaper	?

(a) Ananda Mohan Bose (b) Krishna Kumar Mitra
(c) Raja Ram Mohan Roy (d) Bipin Chandra Pal

3 Identify the famous personality who composed the song Vande Mataram.
(a) Bipin Chandra Pal (b) Rabindranth Tagore
(c) Bankim Chandra Chatterjee (d) Krishna Kumar Mitra

4 Who was the Viceroy of India when Bengal was partitioned for the first time in 1905?
(a) Lord Curzon (b) Lord Hardinge
(c) Lord Dufferin (d) Lord Wellesley

5 In December, 1906 the All Indian Muslim League was founded at .... by Nawab Salimullah.
(a) Calcutta (b) Lahore
(c) Delhi (d) Dhaka

Answers

1. (b) | 2. (b) | 3. (c) | 4. (a) | 5. (d)

02 Marks Questions

6 Mention any two objective of the Muslim League.

7 State any two factors that led to the formation of the Muslim League.

8 What were the two reasons behind the Partition of Bengal?

9 Mention any two reactions of the Nationalists to the Partition of Bengal.

10 Marks Questions

10 Lord Curzon announced the division of the province of Bengal on 20th July, 1905, with reference to the Partition of Bengal, answer the following questions.

(i) Mention any three cause behind the partition of Bengal.

(ii) What are the main steps taken for repressions by the Britishers against the Anti-partition movements?

(iii) Mention any four Lord Curzon's motive behind the Partition of Bengal.

04

The Lucknow Pact

TREND ANALYSIS 3 YEARS

TOPIC 01 Lucknow Pact

Average No. of Questions Across all Sets

Types of Questions	2023	2020	2019
1 Mark	1	–	–
2/3 Marks	–	–	–
4 Marks	–	–	–
10 Marks	–	–	–

The era of the First World War (1914-1919) was full of enormous nationalist political activities in India. The events occurred during the First World War and the prevalent sentiments were responsible for the signing of Lucknow Pact between the Indian National Congress and the Muslim League. This era was also known for the establishment of the **Home Rule League** and the **August Declaration**.

Lucknow Pact was an agreement, that took place between the Indian National Congress (INC) and the Muslim League in 1916. The Congress and the League held their annual sessions simultaneously, in Lucknow.

Lucknow Pact (1916)

Efforts were being made to bring the Congress and the Muslim League to reach an agreement on the scheme of political reforms in India. In 1915, both of them met at Bombay, where the leaders of both the parties forged a joint plan of post-war constitutional reforms.

In 1916, there were simultaneous sessions of both the Congress and the League at Lucknow, where the joint scheme of political reforms was put forward and adopted by both parties in 1916. This agreement so signed by them came to be known as the Lucknow Pact.

Causes of Lucknow Pact

- There shall be a self-government in India. Muslims should be given 1/3 rd representation in the Central Government.
- There should be separate electorates for all the communities, until a community demanded joint electorates. System of weightage to minority political representation should be adopted.
- The number of the members of Imperial Legislative Council was to be 150, of which 4/5th were to be elected and 1/5th nominated. 1/3 rd of the elected members were to be Muslims.

- At the Provincial level, 4/5th of the members of the Legislative Council should be elected and 1/5th should be nominated. All members except those nominated, should be elected directly on the basis of Adult Franchise.
- The salaries of the Secretary of State for Indian affairs should be paid by the British Government, not from Indian funds. Out of the two secretaries, one should be Indian and other should be their own member. The Executive should be separated from the Judiciary.
- In Viceroy Executive Council, half the members were to be Indian, elected by the members of the Imperial Legislative Council.
- The Judiciary, in every province, shall be placed under the control of the highest court of that province and shall be separated from the Executive.

Circumstances Leading to the Lucknow Pact

The following circumstances were responsible for the Lucknow Pact, 1916

International Events

During the Balkan wars, the policy of Britishers was not sympathetic to Turkey. In the First World War, Britain was fighting against Turkey, which was the holy place of all Muslims. Because of this, the Muslim League was unhappy with the British in the First World War. The Caliph or the ruler of Turkey was the **religious head** of the Muslims, so Muslims automatically were upset with British.

National Events

There were various national events, which changed the behaviour of the Muslim League, like the Partition of Bengal was cancelled by the British. Nationalist Muslims like, Abul Kalam Azad, Ali Brothers spread nationalist ideas among the Muslims. Some prominent Muslim leaders were arrested under the **Seditious Meeting Act**.

A Compromise Between the Two Fractions of the Congress

The Lucknow Pact also manifested the establishment of cordial relations between the two prominent groups of the Indian National Congress (*i.e.,* between the Extremists and the Moderates).

The Extremists were led by **Bal Gangadhar Tilak** and the Moderates were led by **Gopal Krishna Gokhale**. Tilak rejoined the Congress in 1916 and he played a major role in resolving differences between the Congress and the Muslim League.

Significance of the Lucknow Pact

The Lucknow Pact is considered important as for the first time the Congress and the Muslim League had come up with a joint programme, which the British found difficult to ignore. The fear of Hindu-Muslim unity made the British to rethink their policies and they introduced different measures to placate the Indians.

Therefore, the government felt it necessary to pacify the Indians by the declaration of 20th August, 1917, which promised a policy of gradual development of self-government institutions in India.

Drawbacks of the Lucknow Pact

- The wishes of the masses were not considered, the Pact was confined only to the educated and to the rich Hindus and Muslims. It emphasised the separate political existence for the Hindus and the Muslims. It did not resolve the deadlock between the Executive and the Legislatures.
- **Communal Veto** in legislation was provided by this pact. Because no Legislature could proceed with any bill, if 3/4th of the members of particular community opposed it. The government's repressive policy followed the Declaration of August, 1917.
- The Congress lost its secular character by accepting separate electorates for Muslims and hence, paved the way for communal tension in the future.

PYQs Previous Years' Questions

1 Mark Questions

Multiple Choice Question

1. The Lucknow Pact was signed between ....
(a) the British and the Congress *(ICSE 2023)*
(b) the Congress and the Muslim League
(c) the Early and the Assertive Nationalists
(d) the Muslim League and the British

Ans. (b) the Congress and the Muslim League

2/3 Marks Questions

1. Mention the significance of the Lucknow Pact of 1916. *(ICSE Specimen 2018)*

Other Similar Questions

Or Mention two reasons why the Lucknow Pact is considered important in the history of the Indian National Congress.

Or The Lucknow Pact is remembered for two main reasons, state the reasons.

Or Mention one reason why the year 1916 is considered very important in the history of the Indian National Congress.

Ans. Significance of the Lucknow Pact of 1916 were
(i) In the Lucknow Pact, for the first time, the Congress and the Muslim League agreed to compromise on same areas for their common good.
(ii) The Lucknow session and the signing of the Lucknow Pact brought about a unity between the Assertive Nationalists and the Early Nationalists.

2. Name the famous pact that demonstrated the unity between the Congress and the Muslim League. When was it signed? *(ICSE 2016)*

Ans. The Lucknow Pact was the famous pact that demonstrated the unity between the Congress and the Muslim League, with a joint programme. This pact was signed in 1916.

3. What was the importance of the Lucknow Pact of 1916? *(ICSE 2013)*

Or Why was the signing of the Lucknow Pact an important event towards the growth of unity in India? *(ICSE 2004)*

Ans. Lucknow Pact played an important role, as it brought about a unity between the Hindus and the Muslims. Both the communities agreed to compromise on some areas for their common good. Congress compromised on its secular character by accepting the scheme of Separate Electorates for Muslims.
The Muslim League accepted the principles of election and the majority rule. As a result of this pact, the Hindus and the Muslims worked together from 1916 to 1922.

4. With reference to the Lucknow Pact of 1916, answer the following questions *(ICSE 2002)*
(i) What were the terms of the Lucknow Pact?
(ii) Why was this Pact important?

Ans. (i) Two terms of Lucknow Pact were as follows
(a) The Indian Council of the Secretary of State, operating from England should be abolished.
(b) 4/5th of the members of the Provincial Legislature should be directly elected and 1/5 th should be nominated. The number of members in the province were laid down in the scheme.

(ii) The Lucknow Pact is considered important as for the first time the Congress and the Muslim League had come up with a joint programme, which the British found difficult to ignore. The fear of Hindu-Muslim unity made the British to rethink their policies and they introduced different measures to placate the Indians. Therefore, the government felt it necessary to pacify the Indian by the declaration of 20th Aug, 1917, which promised a policy or gradual development of self-government institutions in India.

CHAPTER TEST

01 Mark Questions (MCQ)

1 Lucknow Pact is associated with which of the following annual session of INC?
(a) 1914 (b) 1915
(c) 1916 (d) 1917

2 Who among the following was the chief architect or reconciliation between the Extremists and Moderates?
(a) Annie Besant (b) Gopal Krishna Gokhale
(c) Bal Gangadhar Tilak (d) Mohammad Ali Jinnah

3 The Congress for the first time accepted the system of separate electorate for Muslims in the year ....
(a) 1932 (b) 1914 (c) 1915 (d) 1916

4 Who played a major role in resolving differences between the Congress and the Muslim League?
(a) Bal Gangadhar Tilak (b) Gopal Krishna Gokhale
(c) Mahatma Gandhi (d) Lala Lajpat Rai

5 Complete the given analogy.
Gopal Krishna Gokhale : INC Session 1905 ::
Ambica Charan Mazumdar :: ?
(a) INC Session, 1910 (b) INC Session, 1916
(c) INC Session, 1915 (d) INC Session, 1917

Answers

1. (c) | 2. (a) | 3. (d) | 4. (a) | 5. (b)

02 Marks Questions

6 Mention any two factors which brought the Muslim League and the Congress closer by the year 1916.

7 State any two features of the Lucknow Pact.

8 Mention any two major drawback of Lucknow Pact.

9 What are the causes of the Lucknow Pact?

10 Marks Question

10 The Lucknow Pact was an agreement between the INC and the Muslim League. With reference to the Lucknow Pact, answer the following questions.

(i) What was the significance of the Lucknow Pact?

(ii) Mention any three constitutional provisions of Lucknow Pact.

(iii) Mention any three reasons why the Lucknow Pact is considered important in the history of the Indian National Congress.

05

Mahatma Gandhi and the National Movement

TREND ANALYSIS 3 YEARS

Average No. of Questions Across all Sets

Topic	Types of Questions	2023	2020	2019
TOPIC 01 Mahatma Gandhi	1 Mark	–	–	–
	2/3 Marks	–	–	–
	4 Marks	–	–	–
	10 Marks	–	–	–
TOPIC 02 Movements of Mahatma Gandhi	1 Mark	4	–	–
	2/3 Marks	1	1	–
	4 Marks	–	–	–
	10 Marks	2	1	1

Mahatma Gandhi

Mohandas Karamchand Gandhi was one of the prominent leaders of Indian Nationalism during British-ruled India. He was popularly known as **Bapu or Mahatma**. The Indian National Movement was dominated by him from 1919 to 1948. That is why, the nation regards him as the **Father of the Nation**.

Early Life of Mahatma Gandhi

- Mohandas Karamchand Gandhi was born in **Porbandar**, in the Kathiawad district of Gujarat on **2nd October, 1869**. His father Karamchand Gandhi was the Diwan of the Rajkot State. His mother's name was Putli Bai and Gopal Krishan Gokhale was his political guru.
- From 1893 to 1914, Mahatma Gandhi spent his time in South Africa and during this period, he was engaged in a heroic struggle against the racist authorities in South-Africa. He formed the Natal Indian Congress and suffered imprisonment.
- Mahatma Gandhi returned to India in January, 1915. His heroic fight for Indians in South-Africa was well-known. His novel method of Satyagraha had yielded good results. The idea of Satyagraha emphasised on the power of truth and the need to search for the truth.

Some Significant Movements

Champaran Satyagraha (1917)

After arriving in India, Mahatma Gandhi successfully organised the Satyagraha movement at various places. In 1916, he travelled to Champaran in Bihar to inspire the peasants to struggle against the repressive plantation system. Here, indigo planters were forced to grow indigo at least on 3/20th of their land part and to sell it at a fixed price made by the Britishers.

Ahmedabad Satyagraha (1918)

In 1918, Mahatma Gandhi intervened in a dispute between the workers and the mill owners of Ahmedabad. He advised the workers to go on a strike and to demand a 35% increase in their wages. He undertook a fast until death, which pressurised the mill owners and they agreed to increase the wages.

Kheda Satyagraha (1918)

Crops failed in the Kheda district of Gujarat, but the government refused to remit land revenues and insisted on its full collection.

Gandhiji supported the peasants and advised to withhold the payment of revenues till their demand of its remission gets fulfilled. Ultimately, the government was forced to arrive at a settlement with the peasants. **Sardar Vallabhbhai Patel** accompanied Gandhiji in this movement.

Non-Cooperation Movement (1920)

This movement was the first mass based movement under Gandhiji. In his famous book **Hind Swaraj** (1919), Mahatma Gandhi declared that British rule was established in India with the cooperation of Indians and had survived only because of their cooperation.

If Indians refused to cooperate, British rule in India would collapse within one year and Swaraj would be achieved. Congress passed the resolution in its Calcutta Session in September, 1920.

Objectives of the Non-Cooperation Movement

The Non-Cooperation Movement was launched to press the following demands

(i) The Khilafat issue.
(ii) The redressal of the Punjab wrongs.
(iii) The attainment of Swaraj.
(iv) Boycotting of the elections to the Legislatures by not putting up the candidates.
(v) Foreign clothes burnt in market places.
(vi) Lawyers leaving their legal practice.
(vii) Measures to promote Hindu-Muslim unity, removal of untouchability and Harijan welfare.

Programmes of Non-Cooperation Movement

The following programmes of resistance were adopted in the Non-Cooperation Movement

- **Boycott Programmes** Boycott of Legislatures, law courts, schools, colleges and all institutions having connection with the British.
- **Swadeshi Programmes** Adoption of Swadeshi and Khadi by reviving hand-spinning and hand-weaving clothes in the country. Revive the Hindu-Muslim unity. Removal of untouchability for the welfare of Harijan .

Suspension of the Non-Cooperation Movement

The incident at **Chauri Chaura,** a village of Gorakhpur district in Uttar Pradesh occurred on 5th February, 1922. Gandhiji, a believer in **Ahimsa** was greatly shocked at these incidents and he withdrew the Non-Cooperation Movement on 12th February, 1922.

Impact of the Non-Cooperation Movement

Although, the Non-Cooperation Movement failed to achieve any of its immediate objectives, its ultimate impacts were as follows

(i) The Indian National Movement, for the first time in history, acquired a real mass base with the participation of different sections of the Indian society.
(ii) It instilled a new confidence among the people and transformed the Congress from a deliberative assembly into a moral fighting force.
(iii) It fostered Hindu-Muslim unity by merging the Khilafat Movement with this movement.

It also led to the formation of the Swaraj party after CR Das and Motilal Nehru suggested to remove the boycott on entering the Legislative Councils and argued that they should enter it and obstruct their work for the Non-Cooperation Movement to be more effective. It was this party, that questioned the coming of Dyarchy also leading to the Simon Commission.

Causes that led to the Non-Cooperation Movement

Khilafat Movement (1919)

The Caliph (or Khalifa) Sultan of Turkey was looked upon by the Muslims as their religious head.

During the First World War, the safety and welfare of Turkey was threatened by the British, thereby weakening the Caliph's position. Therefore, Indian Muslims adopted aggressive anti-British attitude.

Rowlatt Act (1919)

This act was passed in 1919, which gave the government enormous powers to repress any political activities and allowed the detention of any political revolutionary without trial for 2 years.

The act gave unbridled powers to the government. The act caused a wave of anger among the people.

Jallianwala Bagh Tragedy (13th April, 1919)

A public meeting was held on **13th April, 1919** in a park called Jallianwala Bagh in Amritsar to protest against the arrest of leaders like **Dr Saifuddin Kitchlu** and **Dr Satyapal,** where **General Dyer** ordered open fire on the peaceful crowd and killed plenty of people.

The massacre was a turning point in the Indo-British relations and inspired the people of India to provide a more intense fight for freedom.

Civil Disobedience Movement (1930)

It was started by Gandhiji in March, 1930 in accordance with the decision taken at the Lahore Session of the Congress for 'Poorna Swaraj'.

Impact of the Civil Disobedience Movement

- It shattered people's faith in the British Government. It received the will to fight the elections. It laid the social roots for the freedom struggle and popularised the new methods of propaganda like the prabhat pheris, pamphlets, etc.
- The Dandi March was significant indeed. Violation of the salt laws was soon followed by the defiance of forest laws in Maharashtra, Karnataka and the Central Provinces and the refusal to pay the rural 'chaukidari tax' in Eastern India. It ended the monopoly of the British over salt manufacturing.

Causes of the Civil Disobedience Movement

Simon Commission (1927)

This commission was constituted under **Sir John Simon** in November, 1927 to review the functioning of the constitutional system in India and to suggest any changes and the need for any further constitutional reforms. Indian leaders opposed the commission as there were no Indians in it.

When the commission arrived in India in 1928, it was greeted with the slogan **Simon Go Back**. The Muslim League and the Hindu Maha Sabha decided to support the Congress. The British used brutal suppression and police attacks to break the popular opposition.

Nehru Report (1928)

A committee was set-up under the chairmanship of **Motilal Nehru** to determine the principles of the Constitution before actually drafting it. The chief architects of the report were **Motilal Nehru and Tej Bahadur Sapru.**

This was after Lord Birkenhead had justified the exclusion of Indians in the Simon Commission owing to the fact that they were not united and could not arrive at an agreed scheme of reforms. The recommendations of Nehru Report evoked lively debate concerning the goal of Indian Dominion Status or Complete Independence.

Declaration of Poorna Swaraj

- All parties including the Congress and the Muslim League participated in the demonstrations. In an effort to win over them, the Viceroy Lord Irwin announced in October 1929, a vague offer of **Dominion Status for India.**

Lahore Session (1929)

- In December 1929, under the presidency of Jawaharlal Nehru, the **Lahore Congress** formalised the demand of Poorna Swaraj or full Independence for India. It was also declared that 26th January, 1930 would be celebrated as the **Independence Day**.

Events of the Civil Disobedience Movement

- The movement started with the **Dandi March** on 12th March, 1930.
- On 31st January, 1930, Gandhiji sent a letter to Viceroy Irwin stating eleven demands. Irwin was unwilling to negotiate, then Gandhiji took the decision along with 78 followers and started a march from the Sabarmati Ashram on 12th March, 1930 for Dandi, the coastal town of Gujarat.

Gandhi Irwin Pact (1931)

Mahatma Gandhi and Lord Irwin concluded an agreement at Delhi on 5th March, 1931 known as the Gandhi Irwin Pact.

The pact made the British Government concede some demands, which were

(i) To withdraw all ordinances and end prosecutions.
(ii) To release all the political prisoners.
(iii) To restore the confiscated properties of the Satyagrahis.
(iv) To permit the free collection or manufacture of salt.

Second Round Table Conference

- It was held in **London** during the Viceroyalty of Lord Willington during September to December, 1931 and Gandhiji attended it on behalf of the Indian National Congress.
- The Conference, however, failed as Gandhiji could not agree with British Prime Minister Ramsay MacDonald on his policy of Communal Representation and the refusal of the British Government for the basic Indian demand for freedom. The Conference closed on 1st December, 1931 without any concrete resultsProgrammes of the Civil Disobedience Movement
- The movement included violation of salt laws, non-payment of taxes and revenues, Boycott of foreign cloth, british goods and liquor.
- The movement was followed by violation of forest laws in Maharashtra, Karnataka and the Central Provinces.
- People refused to pay the rural Chaukidari tax in Eastern India.
- People joined hartals, demonstrations and the campaign to boycott foreign goods and refused to pay taxes.
- Satyagraha was adopted by many Indians.

Quit India Movement (1942)

On 8th August, 1942, the Congress in its meeting at Gowaliya tank near Bombay, passed a resolution known as Quit India Resolution, whereby Gandhiji asked the British to quit India and gave a call for **Do or Die** (We shall either free India or die in the attempt) to his countrymen.

Causes of the Quit India Movement

The events which led to the passing of the Quit India Movement include

Failure of the Cripps Mission

The mission did not bring with it any promise of independence and did not grant the right of self-determination to the Muslims. Also, the Indians were upset with the mission as its proposals had provisions, which could divide India into hundreds of independent provinces. Gandhiji referred to it as a 'Post-dated cheque on a failing bank.'

The Threat of the Japanese

- In 1942, the Japanese Army attacked Myanmar and marched towards India. This threat (of a Japanese invasion) convinced the Indian leaders of the need to throw away the Britishers from India immediately.
- On 9th August, 1942, all prominent leaders like Gandhiji, Nehru, Patel, etc., were arrested, but the others like (JP Lohiya, Aruna Asaf Ali, Usha Mehta, etc) continued the revolution for struggle.
- Violence spread throughout the country. Several government offices were destroyed and damaged, the telegraph wires were cut and communication was paralysed.
- Parallel government was established in some places like Balia, Uttar Pradesh (by Chittu Pandey), etc. The first parallel government was established in Bengal by **Satish Samant Satara** and in Maharashtra (by YB Chavan and Nana Patil), which was the longest term parallel government.

Note The Quit India Resolution was adopted by the Congress Working Committee at Wardha in July 1942. The British put down the movement with ruthless brutality. Gandhiji and other important leaders were arrested and the Congress was declared illegal.

Events Leading to the Quit India Movement

- **Resignation** The Congress ministries resigned in October 1939, when the Viceroy without consulting the Indians, declared that India was at war with Germany during the Second World War. This led to a political deadlock in the country.

  The Muslim League was jubilant over the resignation of the Congress Ministries. It celebrated the day as a **day of deliverance** and **thanks giving** . In 1940, the Muslim League demanded the division of India into two autonomous States.
- **August Offer** During the era of the Second World War, the International compulsions forced the British Government to seek some settlement with the Congress. So, the August Offer was made by Lord Linlithgow. The offer proposed Dominion Status for India after the war.
- **Quit India Resolution** It was adopted by the Congress Working Committee at Wardha on 14th July, 1942. According to the resolution, it was proposed that the Congress would start a non-voilent movement under the leadership of Gandhiji.

Significance of the Quit India Movement

It demonstrated the depth of the nationalist feeling in India and the capacity of Indians for struggle and sacrifice. It made clear to the British that they would no longer be able to rule India against the wishes of its people. It also strengthened the Congress Socialist Party to a huge extent.

PYQs Previous Years' Questions

1 Mark Questions

Multiple Choice Questions

1. People protested against the .... because it had seven British members and no Indian representation in act. *(ICSE 2023)*
(a) Simon Commission (b) Lucknow Pact
(c) Illbert Bill (d) Cabinet Mission

Ans. (a) Simon Commission

2. .... was one of the causes of the Quit India Movement. *(ICSE 2023)*
(a) Failure of the Second Round Table Conference
(b) Rowlatt Act
(c) Mountbatten Plan
(d) Failure of the Cripps Mission

Ans. (d) Failure of the Cripps Mission

3. The Khilafat Movement was started in India by .... *(ICSE Specimen 2023)*
(a) Ali Brothers (b) Mahatma Gandhi
(c) Jinnah (d) Sir Sayyid Ahmed Khan

Ans. (*a*) Ali Brothers

4. The Non-Cooperation Movement was suspended due to the .... *(ICSE Specimen 2023)*
(a) Gandhi -Irwin Pact
(b) Chauri-Chaura Incident
(c) Cripps Mission
(d) Rowlatt Act

Ans. (*b*) Chauri-Chaura Incident

5. Complete the given analogy.
Simon Commission : Civil Disobedience Movement : : Cripps Mission : ? *(ICSE Specimen Semester I 2021)*
(a) Non-Cooperation Movement
(b) Anti-Partition Movement
(c) Quit India Movement
(d) Khilafat Movement

Ans. (*c*) Quit India Movement

6. Mahatma Gandhi signed a pact with .... to end the Civil Disobedience Movement. *(ICSE Specimen Semester I 2021)*
(a) Lord Mountbatten (b) Lord Irwin
(c) Lord Wavell (d) Stafford Cripps

Ans. (*b*) Lord Irwin

7. Identify the clauses of the Rowlatt Act. *(ICSE Specimen Semester I 2021)*
(a) In camera trial
(b) Arrest people with a warrant
(c) Vernacular Press must not publish anything against the British
(d) Compulsory License for arms

Ans. (*c*) Vernacular Press must not publish anything against the British

8. The Civil Disobedience Movement was launched in .... *(ICSE Specimen Semester I 2021)*
(a) 1929 (b) 1920
(c) 1930 (d) 1942

Ans. (*c*) 1930

9. Which of these statements is not associated with the Jallianwala Bagh Massacre? *(ICSE Semester I 2021)*
(a) It happened in the year 1919.
(b) General Dyer was responsible for this massacre.
(c) It became a cause for the Non-Cooperation Movement.
(d) It became a cause for the Civil Disobedience Movement.

Ans. (*d*) It became a cause for the Civil Disobedience Movement.

10. What was the cause for the sudden suspension of the Non-Cooperation Movement? *(ICSE Semester I 2021)*
(a) Repressive measures of the British
(b) The Chauri-Chaura Incident
(c) The Gandhi-Irwin Pact
(d) Jallianwala Bagh Massacre

Ans. (*b*) The Chauri-Chaura incident

11. How did the Lahore Session of 1929 lead to the Civil Disobedience Movement? *(ICSE Semester I 2021)*
(a) The Declaration of Poorna Swaraj was passed
(b) Subhash Chandra Bose was made the President of the Congress
(c) Simon Commission recommendations were accepted
(d) Congress passed a resolution to begin the Civil Disobedience Movement

Ans. (*a*) The Declaration of Poorna Swaraj was passed

12. Complete the given analogy. *(ICSE Semester I 2021)*

Non-Cooperation Movement : 1920 : : Civil Disobedience Movement : ?

(a) 1919 (b) 1932

(c) 1931 (d) 1930

Ans. (*d*) 1930

13. What were the causes of the Quit India Movement? *(ICSE Semester I 2021)*

(a) Failure of Simon Commission and Rowlatt Act.

(b) Failure of the Cripps Mission and Declaration of Poorna Swaraj.

(c) Growing Unemployment and Jallianwala Bagh Massacre.

(d) Failure of Cripps Mission and Japanese threat.

Ans. (*b*) Failure of the Cripps Mission and Declaration of Poorna Swaraj.

2/3 Marks Questions

1. What are the causes of the Quit India Movement? *(ICSE Specimen 2023)*

Ans. Causes of the Quit India Movement are

- The failure of Cripps Mission to guarantee or provide any kind of constitutional remedy to the problems of India led to the Indian National Congress calling it for a mass Civil-Disobedience Movement.
- Difficulties due to the Second World War such as high prices of essential commodities fostered resentment against the British Government.

2. Name any two leaders of the Khilafat Movement. *(ICSE 2020)*

Other Similar Questions

Or Name the leaders of the Khilafat Movement that was launched in India to champion the cause of the Caliph of Turkey.

Or Who were the leaders of the Khilafat Movement?

Ans. Two leaders of Khilafat Movement were Maulana Azad and Hakim Ajmal Khan.

3. State any two causes for the Non-Cooperation Movement. *(ICSE 2020)*

Ans. Causes that led to the Non-Cooperation Movement were

(i) Crimes Act was introduced in the Central Legislature in February, 1919. This act authorised the government to imprison any person without trial and convict him in a court.

(ii) A peaceful crowd gathered at the Jallianwala Bagh in Amritsar on 13th April, 1919 to protest against the arrest of leaders like Dr Saifuddin Kitchlu and Dr Satyapal. Without much warning, General Dyer ordered the army to open fire at this peaceful crowd. This event shocked Gandhiji and he decided to stop every cooperation with the British Government at every level.

4. State any two causes that led to the Civil Disobedience Movement in 1930. *(ICSE 2018, 2002)*

Ans. Two causes that led to the Civil Disobedience Movement in 1930 were

(i) A resolution was passed at the Lahore Session of Congress in 1929, which declared Poorna Swaraj to become the objective of the Congress.

(ii) An 'Eleven Points Ultimatum' was served by Gandhiji on the British Government. After the government's failure to negotiate, Gandhiji started the Civil Disobedience Movement.

5. What was the Khilafat Movement? *(ICSE 2017)*

Ans. The Caliph (Khalifa) or Sultan of Turkey was looked upon by the Muslims as their religious head. During the First World War, the safety and welfare of Turkey was threatened by the British, thereby weakening the Caliph's position. To restore his position, the Muslims of India adopted an aggressive anti-British attitude and launched the Khilafat Movement in 1919.

6. State any two provisions of the Rowlatt Act passed by the government in 1919. *(ICSE 2017)*

Or Why was the Rowlatt Act (1919) passed? *(ICSE 2007)*

Ans. The Rowlatt Act was passed by the British Government in 1919. Two main provisions of this act were

(i) It gave the government enormous powers to repress any political activities.

(ii) It allowed the detention of any political revolutionary without trial for 2 years.

7. Why did Mahatma Gandhi start his historic march to Dandi? *(ICSE 2017)*

Ans. Mahatma Gandhi believed that salt tax and the monopoly of the government on salt production should be abolished. To achieve this goal on 12th March, 1930, Gandhiji along with his 78 followers began the historic 'Dandi March'. The march started from Gandhiji's ashram in Sabarmati to the Gujarati coastal town of Dandi.

8. Why was the Congress Session held at Lahore in 1929 significant to the National Movement? ***(ICSE 2016)***

Ans. The Congress Session held at Lahore in 1929 was significant to the National Movement because the Congress at this session under the presidency of Jawaharlal Nehru, passed a resolution declaring Poorna Swaraj (complete Independence) to be the goal of the National Movement. It was also declared that 26th January, 1930 would be celebrated as the Independence Day.

9. Who is regarded as the political guru of Mahatma Gandhi? Give a reason for him being considered as the Mahatma's Guru. ***(ICSE 2015)***

Ans. Gopal Krishna Gokhale is regarded as the political guru of Mahatma Gandhi. Gandhiji considered him as Guru because Gokhale believed that politics could be a means. of service to the people of India and that political work should be done in the spirit of religion.

10. Why was the Simon Commission rejected by the Congress? ***(ICSE 2015)***

Ans. The Simon Commission was rejected by the Congress on the following basis

(i) All members of this commission were Europeans. (whites) and no Indian was associated with it.

(ii) This was seen by the Congress as a violation of the principle of self-determination and a deliberate insult to the self respect of the Indians..

11. Mention any one provision of the Gandhi-Irwin Pact signed in 1931. ***(ICSE 2014)***

Ans. One of the provisions of the Gandhi-Irwin Pact was the withdrawal of all the ordinances and prosecutions.

12. State the two methods of political struggle evolved by Mahatma Gandhi as a part of the National Movement. ***(ICSE 2009)***

Or Name the two important methods adopted by Gandhiji in the freedom struggle. ***(ICSE 2002)***

Ans. The two methods of political struggle evolved by Mahatma Gandhi were the following

(i) Gandhiji promoted the use of Satyagraha which was the moral force of truth and non-violence. The Satyagraha Movement of Gandhiji was directed against the British system of exploitation and not the British people individually or collectively.

(ii) Gandhiji advocated the Non-Violence Movement. According to him, non-violence is not a negative but a positive and active force. It is the virtue of the strong and not of the weak, which requires benevolence and sympathy.

13. On what assurances did Gandhiji withdraw the Civil Disobedience Movement? ***(ICSE 2008)***

Ans. Gandhiji's withdrawal of the Civil Disobedience Movement was on the basis of the following assurances from the British Government

(i) Withdrawal of all the ordinances and the prosecutions.

(ii) Releasing the political prisoners, except those guilty of violence.

14. When and by whom was the Civil Disobedience Movement launched? ***(ICSE 2004)***

Ans. The Civil Disobedience Movement was launched by Mahatma Gandhi in 1930.

15. Why was the Civil Disobedience Movement of March (1930) withdrawn? ***(ICSE 2003)***

Ans. The Civil Disobedience Movement (1930) was withdrawn because of the Gandhi-Irwin Pact.

16. Why was the Dandi March undertaken? ***(ICSE 2001)***

Ans. Dandi March was undertaken so that Lord Irwin would concede to the demands, that Gandhiji had put forward (in his ultimatum).

10 Marks Questions

1. Look at the picture given below and answer the following questions. ***(ICSE 2023)***

(a) Name the march being led by Gandhiji in the above picture. Which movement did this march launch ?

(b) What were the three causes of the Non-Cooperation Movement ?

(c) Mahatma Gandhi and Lord Irwin signed a pact in 1931. Mention any two conditions that the Congress agreed to and two conditions that the British Government agreed to according to this pact.

Or (i) Identify the event in the above picture and briefly explain any two causes that led to this event.

(ii) Programmes of the movement.

(iii) Impact of the movement. ***(ICSE Specimen 2017)***

Ans. (a) The march was Dandi March. It led to the beginning of Civil Disobedience Movement.

(b) Causes that led to the Non-Cooperation Movement were

(i) Crimes Act was introduced in the Central Legislature in February, 1919. This act authorised the government to imprison any person without trial and convict him in a court.

(ii) A peaceful crowd gathered at the Jallianwala Bagh in Amritsar on 13th April, 1919 to protest against the arrest of leaders like Dr Saifuddin Kitchlu and Dr Satyapal.

(iii) Economic hardship due to World War I caused a lot of economic hardships to the people. Prices of goods increases leads to resentment against the government.

(iv) A resolution was passed at the Lahore Session of Congress in 1929, which declared Poorna Swaraj to become the objective of the Congress.

Suspension of the Non-Cooperation Movement

The incident at **Chauri Chaura,** a village of Gorakhpur district in Uttar Pradesh occurred on 5th February, 1922. Gandhiji, a believer in **Ahimsa** was greatly shocked at these incidents and he withdrew the Non-Cooperation Movement on 12th February, 1922.

(c) Mahatma Gandhi and Lord Irwin concluded an agreement at Delhi on 5th March, 1931 known as the Gandhi-Irwin Pact.

The pact made the British Government agreed to some demands, which were

(i) To release all the political prisoners.

(ii) To permit the free collection or manufacture of salt.

Under this pact, the Congress agreed to

(i) Suspend the Civil Disobedience Movement.

(ii) Take part in the Second Round Table Conference.

Or The event shown in the given picture belongs to Dandi March.

(i) Two causes of this event were as follow

(a) The Simon Commission, which was though composed to investigate the need for further constitutional reforms, did not have even a single Indian member, but all British members. This came to be seen as a violation of the principle of self-determination and a deliberate insult to the self-respect of the Indians.

(b) The unwillingness of the British Government to negotiate on the 'Eleven Point Ultimatum' that Gandhiji handed over to Lord Irwin, containing demands such as, abolition of the salt tax, deduction in the land revenues, etc.

(ii) The Dandi March was an initiation of the Civil Disobedience Movement, that involved

(a) Defiance of Salt Laws.

(b) Boycott of liquor.

(c) Boycott of foreign cloths and British goods of all kinds.

(d) Non-payment of taxes and revenues.

(iii) The impacts of the movement were as follow

(a) It caused a tide of patriotic rising in the country. The government withdrew the ban on the Congress in 1934.

(b) It widened the base of the freedom struggle.

(c) It made people understand the significance of the principles of non-violence.

(d) New methods of propaganda were popularised. For example, Prabhat Pheris, Pamphlets etc.

Additional Info

Other impacts of the movement were

- It led to the introduction of the Government of India Act, 1935, which introduced the principle of a Federation and the principle of Provincial Autonomy.
- The leadership of Birla and the 'Harijan Sevaksangh' changed the social conditions. Depressed classes were given entry into the temples and started having access to wells.
- It brought women participators to the fore.
- The movement also revived the will to fight the elections.

2. The mass phase of the National Movement led to the freedom of India. With reference to this phase, Answer the following questions. ***(ICSE Specimen 2023)***

(a) What were the causes of the Civil Disobedience Movement? Name the march which marked the beginning of this movement.

(b) Mention any three causes of the Non-Cooperation Movement.

(c) Mention any four clauses of the Mountbatten Plan.

Ans. (a) Following were the causes of the Civil Disobedience Movement

- Formation of the Simon Commission at that time when exports were declined and peasants found it difficult to sell their harvest and pay their revenue. Indian leaders opposed this Commission as there were no Indians. in it.
- A vague offer of Dominion Status for India in an unspecified future Constitution was offered by Lord Irwin in October 1929.
- Salt March or Dandi March marked the beginning of the Civil Disobedience Movement to abolish the salt tax.

(b) For answer, refer to Q. 1 (b) of 10 marks questions.

(c) Four clauses of the Mountbatten Plan are as follows

- Partition of India into two different and sovereign states i.e. India and Pakistan.
- The plan provided Partition of Punjab and Bengal. ' Princely States were given the choice of joining either of the two countries or to remain independent.
- Creation of a Boundary Commission to decide the boundary of two dominions.
- The provinces of Assam, Bengal and Punjab were also to be divided.

3. With reference to the mass phase of the National Movement under the leadership of Gandhi, ans.wer the following. ***(ICSE 2020)***

(a) Briefly explain the Dandi March of 1930.

(b) State any three reasons for the launching of the Quit India Movement.

(c) Explain any four significant effects of the Quit India Movement.

Ans. (a) 'Dandi March' was undertaken by Gandhiji in response to British disapproval of his 'Eleven Point Ultimatum'. He began this march from Sabarmati Ashram to Dandi, the coastal town of Gujarat.

The two features of 'Dandi March' were as follows

(i) It marked the beginning of the Civil Disobedience Movement.

(ii) By Dandi March, Gandhiji broke the salt laws because the salt-tax affected all sections of society especially poor.

(b) The reasons for launching the Quit India Movement were

(i) **Congress Ministers Resignation** Ministries were formed by Congress in the United provinces, Central provinces, Odisha, Bihar, Madras and Bombay. In protest against the decision of the government to join the Second World War and its refusal to liberate India, the Congress resigned.

(ii) **The August Offer** The British Government made a new offer to the Congress known as the August Offer on 8th August, 1940. Congress rejected the offer as too much constitutional independence was given to the minorities. The League also rejected the offer because it did not talk about the formation of the separate state of Pakistan.

Reasons for launching Quit India Movement

- Congress Ministers Resignation
- The August Offer
- Cripps Mission and its Failure

(iii) **Cripps Mission (1942) and its Failure** Prime Minister Winston Churchill sent Sir Stafford Cripps, a seasoned diplomat with some proposals of constitutional reforms. This proposal did not satisfy the leaders. Failures of Cripps Mission led to disappointment and bitterness among Indians.. Gandhiji felt that it was the correct time to launch the final struggle for freedom.

(c) The significant effects of the Quit India Movement were

(i) It demonstrated the depth of the nationalist feelings in India and the great capacity for struggle and sacrifice that the people had developed.

(ii) It was obvious that the British would no longer found it possible to rule India against the wishes of the people.

(iii) It was a mass uprising before attaining independence. People from all the parts of India took part in the processions and demonstrations. The Hindus, Muslims, Sikhs, Christians. and Parsis and even people from the Princely States participated.

(iv) The emergence of Parallel Government in various places of India like Ballia in Uttar Pradesh, Midnapur in Bengal and Satara in Maharashtra took place.

Examiner 's Comment

- Most candidates were able to narrate the Dandi March of 1930 well.
- Several candidates wrote the reasons for the launching of the Quit India Movement such as 'economic distress', while some wrote the causes of other mass movements led by Gandhi such as the Non-Cooperation Movement and the Civil Disobedience Movement.
- Most of the candidates answered this question correctly. However, a few jumbled up the parts with the impact of the Non – Cooperation Movement and the Civil Disobedience Movement.

Suggestions for Students

- Narrate the event-the historic Dandi march from Sabarmati to Dandi and the subsequent violation of the salt Law point wise.
- Explain the political reasons in India as well as in the International arena during 1942 .
- Understand the three major Gandhian movements-Causes, Course and Consequences.

4. With reference to the picture given below, answer the following questions. ***(ICSE 2019)***

(a) (i) Identify the memorial built for those who were killed in this incident.

(ii) Where did this incident take place ?

(iii) Name the movement launched by Gandhi in 1920 as a consequence.

(b) Explain briefly the reason for the suspension of this particular movement by Gandhi in 1922.

(c) State any four impacts of the movement.

Ans. (a) (i) This monument was established in 1951 by the Government of India in Amritsar, to commemorate the Jallianwala Bagh Massacre.

(ii) The massacre took place in the Jallianwala Bagh on 13th April, 1919 where a large number of people assembled on the day of Baisakhi.

(iii) Mahatma Gandhi started Non-Cooperation Movement in 1920 as a consequence of this incident.

(b) A violence incident at Chauri Chaura, a village of Gorakhpur district in Uttar Pradesh occurred on 5th February, 1922. Gandhiji, a believer in Ahimsa was greatly shocked at these incidents due to which he withdrew the Non-Cooperation Movement on 12th February, 1922.

(c) The impacts of the Non-Cooperation Movement were as follows

(i) The Indian National Movement, for the first time in history, acquired a real mass base with the participation of different sections of the Indian society.

(ii) It instilled a new confidence among the people and transformed the Congress from a deliberative assembly into a moral fighting force.

(iii) It fostered Hindu-Muslim unity by merging the Khilafat Movement with this movement.

(iv) It led to the formation of the Swaraj party under the leadership of CR Das and Motilal Nehru.

5. The advent of Mahatma Gandhi on the Indian political scene gave a new direction to the freedom struggle. In this context, answer the following. ***(ICSE Specimen 2018)***

(a) What were the causes which led to the launching of the Non-Cooperation Movement?

(b) Why did Gandhiji withdraw the Non-Cooperation Movement?

(c) What was the impact of the Non-Cooperation Movement?

Ans. (a) Causes which led to the launching of the Non-Cooperation Movement were

(i) The Muslim of India decided to force Britain to change its Turkish policy and Khilafat Committee was formed. Gandhiji decided to start Non-Cooperation in support of Khilafat Movement.

(ii) Rowlatt Act was passed hurriedly through imperial Legislative Council in spite of unanimous opposition of the Indian members, Gandhiji wanted non-violent civil disobedience against such laws.

(iii) Jallianwala Bagh massacre on 13th April led to sudden start of Non-Cooperation Movement.

(b) The Non-Cooperation Movement was non-violent, but an unfortunate incident brought the movement to an end. On 5th February, 1922 a procession of 3,000 peasant were fired upon by the police at Chauri Chaura. Gandhiji, a firm believer of non-violence, was shocked and decided to call off the movement immediately.

(c) For answer, refer to Q. 4 (c) of 10 marks questions.

6. The Quit India Resolution in 1942 was one of the final calls given by Gandhiji for the British to leave India. Moving towards Independence, Lord Mountbatten's Plan was significant. In this context, ans.wer the following questions.

(ICSE 2018, 2014, 2013, 2003)

(a) State two reasons for the launching of the Quit India Movement.

(b) Give any three effects of the Quit India Movement launched by Gandhiji in 1942 that was significant to the last phase of the National Movement of India.

(c) Give any four clauses of the Mountbatten Plan of 1947.

Ans. (a) For answer, refer to Q. 3 (b) of 10 marks questions.

(b) For answer, refer to Q. 3 (c) of 10 marks questions.

(c) For answer, refer to Q. 2 (c) of 10 marks questions.

Examiner's Comment

- Several candidates, instead of stating the reasons for the launching of the Quit India Movement, wrote the reasons for launching the other movements like Civil Disobedience Movement and Non-Cooperation Movement.
- Most of the candidates were able to write the correct answer. Some candidates wrote only two effects and repeated the same points in different forms.
- Most of the candidates wrote the correct clauses of the of the Mountbatten Plan of 1947. A few candidates got confused between the Mountbatten Plan and the Indian Independence Act / the Cabinet Mission Plan.

Suggestions for Students

- Explain the causes and consequences of all the movements launched by Mahatma Gandhi.
- Elucidate about the Cabinet Mission Plan, Mountbatten Plan and the Indian Independence Act.
- Learn that the country was divided according to the Mountbatten Plan and finally the British Parliament passed the Indian Independence Act which provided the basis for the creation of India and Pakistan.

7. Through various National Movements, Gandhiji mobilised public support to win freedom for India. In this context, state the following. ***(ICSE 2016)***

(a) Any three causes for Gandhi to launch the Non-Cooperation Movement.

(b) The name given to the uprising of 1942. Two reasons for launching this mass uprising.

(c) The impact of the Non-Cooperation Movement in India's freedom struggle.

Ans. (a) Three causes for Gandhi to launch the Non-Cooperation Movement are as follows

(i) **Rowlatt Act, 1919** This act gave the British Government enormous powers to repress any political activities and allowed the detention of any political revolutionary without trial for 2 years.

(ii) **Jallianwala Bagh Tragedy** A public meeting was held on 13th April, 1919 in Amritsar where General Dyer ordered open fire on the peaceful crowd and killed over 300 people.

(iii) **Khilafat Movement, 1919** The Caliph or Sultan of Turkey was looked upon by the Muslims as their religious head. During the First World War, the safety and welfare of Turkey was threatened by the British. To restore the power of the Caliph, the Muslims adopted an aggressive anti-British attitude.

Three causes of Non-Cooperation Movement
- Rowlatt Act, 1919
- Jallianwala Bagh Tragedy
- Khilafat Movement, 1919

(b) The name given to the uprising of 1942 was Quit India Movement wherein Gandhiji asked the British to quit India and gave a call for 'Do or Die'.
For reasons for launcing the Quit India Movement, refer to Q. 3 (b) of 10 marks questions.

(c) For answer, refer to Q. 4 (c) of 10 marks questions.

8. In 1930, Mahatma Gandhi's demands were rejected by the British, as a result of which he launched the Civil Disobedience Movement. In this context, explain the following. *(ICSE 2015, 2011, 2002)*

(a) Name the famous march undertaken by Gandhiji. Where did he begin this march? State two of its features.

(b) The Gandhi-Irwin Pact as a consequence of this movement.

(c) Significance of the Second Round Table Conference.

Ans. (a) The 'Dandi March' was undertaken by Gandhiji in response to British disapproval of his 'Eleven Point Ultimatum'. He began this march from Sabarmati Ashram to Dandi. The two features of 'Dandi March' were

(i) It marked the beginning of the Civil Disobedience Movement.

(ii) Gandhiji broke the salt laws because the salt tax affected all sections of society, especially the poor.

(b) The Civil Disobedience Movement resulted in the signing of a pact between Gandhiji and Lord Irwin, the Viceroy, in March 1931 to call off the Civil Disobedience Movement, stop the boycott of British goods as well as release of all persons imprisoned due to the movement.

(c) The Second Round Table Conference was a significant event. It was held in London during the Viceroyalty of Lord Willington from September to December 1931. Gandhiji attended it on the behalf of Indian National Congress. The conference reached a deadlock on the minority issue and the question of Independence or setting up a responsible government receded into the background.

9. In the Nagpur Session (1920), the Congress ratified the resolution to launch the Non-Cooperation Movement under the leadership of Gandhiji. In this context, answer the following questions. *(ICSE 2014)*

(a) What were the objectives which the Non-Cooperation Movement sought to achieve?

(b) What do you understand by the term Non-Cooperation?

(c) Explain the impact of the Non-Cooperation Movement in India's struggle for freedom.

Ans. (a) Objectives of the Non-Cooperation Movement were as follows

(i) The issue of Khilafat.

(ii) The redressal of the Punjab wrongs.

(iii) The attainment of Swaraj.

Additional Info

Some other important objectives of Non-Cooperation Movement were

- Burning of foreign clothes
- Lawyers boycotting legal practice
- Removal of untouchability and Harijan.

(b) Non-Cooperation is a way of protesting, in which one does not cooperate with the evil-doer, Gandhiji asked the people not to assist the Foreign Government to rule over them.

(c) For answer, refer to Q. 4 (c) of 10 marks questions.

10. The Congress Working Committee passed the famous Quit India Resolution at Wardha in July, 1942. With reference to this, answer the following questions. *(ICSE 2013)*

(a) What were the reasons for the passing of this resolution?

(b) What was the British Government's reaction to the Quit India Movement?

(c) What was the impact and significance of this movement?

Ans. (a) For answer, refer to Q. 3 (b) of 10 marks questions.

(b) **Reaction of the British Government to the Quit India Movement** The government resorted to severe measures to crush the Quit India Movement. The press was completely muzzled. The demonstrating crowds were machine gunned and even bombed from the air. Prisoners were tortured. The police and secret police reigned. Nearly 10000 people were killed and 60000 people were arrested by the end of 1942. The military took over many towns and cities.

Rebellious villages had to pay huge sums as punitive fines and the villagers had to undergo mass floggings. India had witnessed such intense repression since the First War of Independence, 1857. Gandhiji was detained at the Agha Khan Palace in Pune and other prominent leaders were sent to jail in Ahmednagar Fort. In the end, the government succeeded in crushing the movement.

(c) For answer, refer to Q. 3 (c) of 10 marks questions.

11. Gandhiji introduced new ideas in politics and adopted new methods to give a new direction to the Political Movement. In this context, ans.wer the following questions. *(ICSE 2012)*

(a) Gandhiji's Doctrine of Satyagraha.

(b) Gandhiji's social ideas.

(c) Which mass struggle was launched by him on non-violent lines in 1920? Explain in brief the programmes of such a campaign.

Ans. (a) **Gandhiji's Doctrine of Satyagraha** Gandhi introduced the Satyagraha, which was a method of agitation and protest based on truth and non-violence. It was a Passive resistance consisting of defiance of laws, non-payment of taxes, boycott of government institutions, etc. Gandhiji's Satyagraha Movement was directed against the British system of exploitation and not against the British people individually or collectively.

These experiments in Satyagraha brought Gandhiji into a close touch with the masses, with both the peasants in the rural areas and the workers in the urban areas. In course of time, he became the symbol of the poor and the downtrodden, whose authenticity could not be questioned or doubted.

(b) **Gandhiji's Social Ideas** The whole philosophy of Gandhiji was based on non-violence. According to Gandhiji, 'Truth and non-violence is the weapon of strong, mighty and powerful individuals'. Gandhiji always used mass movements as weapon of protest. He realised that movement which involved rural, urban, men, women, educated, uneducated are more liable to have an effect. He launched many movements for gaining freedom, but none of them was violent. During the Non-Cooperation Movement, he suspended the movement, when it was on its zenith just because of the Chauri-Chaura Incident, in which 22 policemen were burnt alive.

(c) In the year 1920, Non-Cooperation Movement was started by Gandhiji.

Although, the Non-Cooperation Movement failed to achieve any of its immediate objectives, its ultimate gains were as follows

(i) The National Movement became a Mass Movement.

(ii) It instilled new confidence among the people.

(iii) It transformed Congress from a deliberative assembly into a moral fighting force.

(iv) It fostered the unity between the Hindus and Muslims, by merging the Khilafat Movement with this movement.

(v) It shattered the myth that the British rule was for the betterment of the Indians.

(vi) It promoted social reforms. Several steps were taken in the direction of prohibition of Sati.

12. The Civil Disobedience Movement was significant in the history of the National Movement. In this context, write briefly on the following points *(ICSE 2011)*

(a) The circumstances leading to the Civil Disobedience Movement

(b) The Second Round Table Conference

(c) The Gandhi-Irwin Pact

Ans. (a) The Lahore Session of Indian National Congress, 1929 had declared a resolution of Poorna Swaraj or complete independence, as ultimate objectives of the Congress. The earlier demand of dominion was rejected by Lord Irwin. At this time, steps were initiated to start a programme of disobedience and 26th January, 1930 was celebrated as a Day of Poorna Swaraj. Gandhiji then openly made eleven demands, for fulfilling people's welfare. On receiving a negative response from the Viceroy, the Civil Disobedience Movement was launched by Gandhiji.

It aimed at forcing the government to meet the Indian demands. Gandhiji started the movement with his famous Dandi March on 12th March, 1930 which continued till 6th April, 1930 and extended from the Sabarmati Ashram to Dandi on the Gujarat coast.

(b) For answer, refer to Q. 8 (c) of 10 marks questions.

(c) The Satyagraha Movement could not be suppressed by the government, through Tej Bahadur Sapru and Jayakar started negotiations with Gandhiji in jail. This resulted in the signing of a pact by Gandhiji and Lord Irwin, the Viceroy, in March 1931, popularly called as the Gandhi-Irwin Pact. According to it, the government agreed to

(i) withdraw all ordinances and end prosecutions.

(ii) release all political prisoners, except those guilty of violence.

(iii) permit peaceful picketing of liquor and foreign cloth shops.

(iv) restore the confiscated properties of the Satyagrahis.

(v) permit the free collection or manufacture of salt by persons near the sea coast.

13. The Simon Commission was appointed in November, 1927 by the British Government. Subsequently, the Civil Disobedience Movement began. In this context, ans.wer the following questions. ***(ICSE 2010)***

(a) Why was the Simon Commission appointed by the British Government? Why did the Congress boycott the commission?

(b) The Civil Disobedience Movement was launched by Gandhiji with his famous Dandi March on 12th March, 1930. Mention the significance of this historic event.

(c) Why did Gandhiji call off the Civil Disobedience Movement and later renew it?

Ans. (a) In November, 1927, the British Government appointed the Indian Statutory Commission, which was popularly known as the Simon Commission (after the name of its Chairman Sir John Simon) to investigate the need for further constitutional reforms. This commission was composed by the seven British members of Parliament. Simon Commission was boycotted by the Congress on the following bases.

(i) All members of this commission were Europeans. (whites) and no Indian was associated with it.

(ii) This was seen as a violation of the principle of self-determination and a deliberate insult to the self–respect of the Indians.

(b) Significance of the Dandi March were as follows

(i) The movement spread rapidly. Violation of Salt Laws over the country was soon followed by defiance of forest laws in Maharashtra, Karnataka and the Central Provinces and the refusal to pay the rural Chaukidari tax in Eastern India.

(ii) The British Government was put out of gear in many places. e.g., Midnapore in Bengal.

(iii) The monopoly of the British over the salt was abolished by this movement.

(c) The Civil Disobedience Movement was called off by Gandhiji because of the Gandhi-Irwin Pact, signed between Gandhiji and Viceroy Lord Irwin. In this pact, Irwin agreed to some of the demands of Gandhiji, like the abolition of salt tax, release of political prisoners, permit peaceful picketing of liquor, etc. After this, Gandhiji agreed to call off the Civil Disobedience Movement and attend the Second Round Table Conference in London. When Gandhiji came back from London, he renewed the movement again because of the failure of the Second Round Table Conference. Gandhiji sought an interview with Viceroy Willington. The interview was refused post, which he continued with his movement.

14. In 1919, Gandhiji plunged into India's struggle for freedom. He guided the affairs of the Indian National Congress with new techniques. Through various National Movements, he got the public support to win freedom for India. In this context, explain the following. ***(ICSE 2009)***

(a) The reasons leading to the Non-Cooperation Movement.

(b) Which resolution was passed on 8th August, 1942 leading to a mass struggle on non-violent lines? State any two reasons behind the launching of this movement.

(c) The impact of the Non-Cooperation Movement in India's struggle for freedom.

Ans. (a) For answer, refer to Q. 1 (b) of 10 marks questions.

(b) On 8th August, 1942, the All India Congress Committee passed the Quit India Resolution. The proposal of Quit India Movement was adopted at Wardha in July, 1942.

For reasons behind the launching of Quit India Movement, refer to Q. 3 (b) of 10 marks questions.

(c) For answer, refer to Q. 4 (c) of 10 marks questions.

15. ***(ICSE 2006)***

(a) Identify the two male personalities in the picture given above. Mention any four ideological tenets of the Indian leader.

(b) Explain the reason behind the launching of the Khilafat Movement in India. Why were the Khilafat and Non-Cooperation Movements merged in 1920?

(c) Why was the Non-Cooperation Movement withdrawn? How did this decision lead to the formation of the Swaraj Party?

Ans. (a) Lord Mountbatten and Mahatma Gandhi are the two male personalities in the above picture. Satyagraha, Boycott, Swadeshi, Non-violence, Mass movements, etc were the ideological tenets of the Indian leader.

(b) **Khilafat Movement in India** In the World War I, Turkey was defeated and the Ottoman empire was divided. The Sultan of Turkey, who was the Caliph, was deprived of all authority. The Caliph was looked upon by a large section of Muslims as their religious head. This angered the Indian Muslims and they started an agitation known as Khilafat Movement, under the leadership of the Ali Brothers-Muhammad Ali and Shaukat Ali, Maulana Azad, Hakim Azmal Khan and Hasrat Mohani. The Khilafat and Non-Cooperation Movements were merged in 1920 in order to bring about Hindu-Muslim unity.

(c) The Non-Cooperation Movement was withdrawn because of the tragedy in Chauri Chaura, a village in Gorakhpur district in Uttar Pradesh, occurred on 5th February, 1922. A procession of about 3000 peasants marched to the police station to protest against the police officer, who had beaten some volunteers picketing a liquor shop. This infuriated the demonstrators and they set the nearby police station on fire, killing 22 policemen who were inside the police station. Gandhiji realising his Non-Cooperation Movement turning out to be violent withdrew the movement which demoralised the Congress Party. This action of Gandhiji was severely criticised by the leaders like Motilal Nehru and Lala Lajpat Rai.

Formation of the Swaraj Party Some of the leaders like Motilal Nehru and CR Das suggested that the nationalists should end the boycott of the Legislative Council. They should enter them and obstruct every work of the council. They felt that by doing like this, they would be continuing the Non-Cooperation Movement in a more effective form. All those leaders, who supported the council entry programme formed a party called Swaraj Party or the Congress Khilafat Swaraj Party.

16. Read the passage given below and answer the questions that follow. ***(ICSE 2005)***

On 7th and 8th August in Bombay the All-India Congress Committee considered and debated in public the resolution, the Committee resolves therefore to sanction, the starting of a mass struggle on non-violent lines under the inevitable leadership of Gandhiji. The resolution was finally passed late in the evening of 8th August, 1942. A few hours later, in the early morning of 9th August, a large number of arrests were made in Bombay and all over the country.
(From : The Discovery of India — Jawaharlal Nehru)

(a) What is meant by 'mass struggle on non-violent lines'? Which resolution was passed on the 8th August, 1942 leading to a mass struggle on non-violent lines?

(b) State any three reasons behind the launching of the August Movement (1942).

(c) Discuss any four consequences of the 1942 Movement.

Ans. (a) The term mass struggle means. peaceful protest, demonstration and strikes by the public. The Indian National Movement , for the first time in history, acquired a real mass base movement during the Non-Cooperation Movement with the participation of different sections of Indian society, such as peasants, workers, students, teachers and women.
The Quit India Resolution was passed on 8th August, 1942.

(b) Reasons behind the launching of the August Movement (1942) were as follows

(i) The Cripps Mission did not bring with it the promise of Independence in the near future. The League opposed the creation of a single union. The proposals did not accept Pakistan specifically. They did not grant the right of self-determination to Muslims. The Indians. were also not happy at the proposals of Cripps Mission because proposals contained such provisions which could divide India into hundreds of independent provinces. Gandhi opposed the Declaration and urged the Working Committee to reject it. He described the Cripps proposals as a 'post-dated cheque on a failing bank.'

(ii) In the year 1942, the Japanese Army attacked Myanmar and marched towards India. The threat of Japanese invasion of India convinced the Indian leaders that for

India's safety, the British should withdraw from India immediately. Gandhiji believed that the presence of the British in India is an invitation for Japan to invade India. Gandhiji asked the British to quit India, because Gandhiji also felt that an orderly and peaceful withdrawal of the British could save India from the internal anarchy and also an external aggression.

(iii) The Congress believed that the British were supporting the League and if they leave India, the people could sort out their differences. The Indian National Congress wanted the immediate withdrawal of the British to save India from the Japanese Invasion.

(c) For answer, refer to Q. 3 (c) of 10 marks questions.

17. The Indian National Congress, at its Nagpur Session, in 1920 decided to launch the Non-Cooperation Movement. In this context, explain the following *(ICSE 2004)*

(a) Meaning of the Non-Cooperation Movement.

(b) Methods and programmes of the movement.

(c) Reasons for the withdrawal of the movement.

Ans. (a) For answer, refer to Q. 9 (b) of 10 marks questions.

(b) For answer, refer to Q. 11 (c) of 10 marks questions.

(c) For answer, refer to Q. 15 (c) of 10 marks questions.

18. In the context of the Civil Disobedience Movement, explain the importance of the following *(ICSE 2004)*

(a) The Simon Commission (1927)

(b) Nehru Report (1928)

(c) The Lahore Session of the Indian Congress (1929)

Ans. (a) **The Simon Commission** (1927) The activities of the Swaraj Party had induced the British Government to review the working of the Dyarchy System introduced by the Montague-Chelmsford reforms of 1919 and to report as to what extent can representative government be introduced in India. The Simon Commission was appointed by the British Government in November, 1927. All members of this commission were Europeans. (whites) so the Indian political leaders decided to boycott the commission. The Muslim League and the Hindu Mahasabha decided to support the Congress decision. The government used brutal suppression and police attacks to break the popular opposition.

(b) **Nehru Report** (1928) Lord Birkenhead, the Secretary of State for India, justified the exclusion of Indians. in the Simon Commission. According to him, the Indians. were not united and could not arrive at an 'agreed scheme of reforms'. To refute this charge, an All Parties Conference was convened in 1928 to take up the challenge posed by Lord Birkenhead.
The committee was set-up under the chairmans.hip of Motilal Nehru to determine the principles of the Constitution before actually drafting it. The chief architects of the report were Motilal Nehru and Tej Bahadur Sapru. The recommendation evoked a lively debate concerning the goal of India-Dominion Status or Complete Independence.

(c) For answer, refer to Q. 14 (a) of 10 marks questions.

19. Various circumstances were responsible for the Non-Cooperation Movement started by Gandhiji. In this context, write short notes on the following *(ICSE 2003)*

(a) Rowlatt Act, 1919

(b) Jallianwala Bagh Tragedy

(c) Khilafat Movement

Ans. (a) **Rowlatt Act, 1919** During the Viceroyalty of Lord Chelmsford, a Sedition Committee was appointed by the government in 1918 with Justice Rowlatt, which made certain recommendations to curb seditious activities in India. The Rowlatt Act, 1919, gave unbridled powers to the government to arrest the impression suspects, without trial. The act caused a wave of anger among the people. Even before the act was passed, popular agitation began against it. Gandhiji decided to fight against this act and he gave a call for Satyagraha on 6th April, 1919. He was arrested on 8th April, 1919. This led to further intensification of the agitation in Delhi, Ahmedabad and Punjab.

(b) **Jallianwala Bagh Tragedy** The arrest of Dr Saifuddin Kitchlu and Dr Satyapal on 10th April, under the Rowlatt Act in connection with Satyagraha caused serious unrest in Punjab. A public meeting was held on 13th April, 1919 in a park called Jallianwala Bagh in Amritsar where thousands of people including women and children assembled. Before the meeting could start, General O' Dyre ordered indiscriminate heavy firing on the crowd and the people had no way out to escape. As a result, hundreds of men, women and children were killed and more than 1200 people wounded. The massacre was a turning point in Indo-British relations and inspired the people to provide a more unrelating fight for freedom.

(c) For answer, refer to Q. 15 (b) of 10 marks questions.

20. Trace the programme and progress of the Civil Disobedience Movement under the leadership of Mahatma Gandhi with reference to the following

(a) The Dandi March of 1930 *(ICSE 2002)*

(b) Gandhi-Irwin Pact of 1931

(c) The Second Round Table Conference of 1931

Ans. (a) **The Dandi March of 1930** To achieve the goal of complete independence, Gandhi launched the Civil Disobedience Movement. Along with 78 followers, Gandhi started his famous march from the Sabarmati Ashram on 12th March, 1930 for Dandi (Navsari district) to break the Salt Law. Gandhi covered a distance of 240 miles in 24 days (12th March 5th April). On reaching the seashore on 6th April, he broke the Salt Law by picking up salt from the seashore. By picking a handful of salt, Gandhi inaugurated the Civil Disobedience Movement, a movement that was to remain unsurpassed in the history of Indian National Movement.

The movement became so powerful that it sparked off patriotism even among the Indian soldiers in the Army. The Garhwal soldiers refused to fire on the people at Peshawar. Gandhiji was arrested on 5th May, 1930.

This was followed by another round of boycott of foreign goods and it took the nationwide Civil Disobedience shape in which women also participated. Soon, thereafter, repressive measures such as mass arrests, lathi charge, police firing etc., happened. About 100000 people went to jail.

(b) For answer, refer to Q. 12 (c) of 10 marks questions.

(c) For answer, refer to Q. 8 (c) of 10 marks questions.

21. The Civil Disobedience Movement was significant in the history of the National Movement. With reference to this movement, write short notes on *(ICSE 2001)*

(a) Circumstances leading to the Civil Disobedience Movement

(b) Gandhi-Irwin Pact, 1931

Ans. (a) For answer, refer to Q. 12 (a) of 10 marks questions.

(b) For answer, refer to Q. 12 (c) of 10 marks questions.

22. The resolution to launch the Non-Cooperation Movement was adopted at the Nagpur Session of the Indian National Congress 1920. In this context, explain the following. *(ICSE 2000)*

(a) What is meant by 'Non-Cooperation'? Give one example.

(b) What was the impact of the Non-Cooperation Movement on the National Movement?

Ans. (a) For answer, refer to Q. 9 (b) of 10 marks questions.

(b) For answer, refer to Q. 4 (c) of 10 marks questions

CHAPTER TEST

01 Mark Questions

1 Which of the following programmes resistance were adopted in the Non-Cooperation Movement?
(a) Boycott
(b) Swadeshi
(c) Both (a) and (b)
(d) None of the above

2 Who among the following is the author of the Book 'Hind Swaraj' ?
(a) Mahatma Gandhi
(b) Jawaharlal Nehru
(c) Bal Gangadhar Tilak
(d) Gopal Krishna Gokhale

3 Mahatma Gandhi and Lord Irwin concluded an agreement at Delhi on ………… known as the Gandhi-Irwin Pact.
(a) 5th March, 1930 (b) 5th March, 1931
(c) 5th February, 1930 (d) 5th February, 1931

4 The Simon Commission arrived in India in ……………, it was greeted with the slogan 'Simon Go Back'.
(a) 1928 (b) 1927 (c) 1929 (d) 1930

5 Complete the given analogy.
Chauri-Chaura Incident : 5th February, 1922 :: Dandi March : ?
(a) 12th March, 1929 (b) 12th February, 1930
(c) 12th March, 1930 (d) 12th February, 1929

Answers

1. (c) | 2. (a) | 3. (b) | 4. (a) | 5. (c)

02 Marks Questions

6 Mention any two terms/provisions of the Gandhi-Irwin Pact?

7 Why did Gandhiji suspended the Non-Cooperation Movement?

8 What are the impact of Civil Disobedience Movement?

9 Mention any two provisions of the Rowlatt Act, 1919.

10 Marks Question

10 With reference to the mass phase of the National Movement under the leadership of Mahatma Gandhi, Answer the following questions.
(i) Mention any three cause of the Quit India Movement.
(ii) State any three significance of the Quit India Movement.
(iii) Write a short notes on
(a) Khilafat Movement
(b) The Dandi March of 1930

06

The Forward Bloc, The INA, Independence and Partition of India

TREND ANALYSIS 3 YEARS

Average No. of Questions Across all Sets

		Types of Questions	2023	2020	2019
TOPIC 01	Forward Bloc and INA	1 Mark	–	–	–
		2/3 Marks	–	1	–
		4 Marks	–	–	–
		10 Marks	1	–	–
TOPIC 02	Independence & Partition	1 Mark	1	–	–
		2/3 Marks	1	–	1
		4 Marks	–	–	–
		10 Marks	1	–	–

Forward Bloc

All India Forward Bloc was a left wing nationalist political party in India. On account of his differences with Mahatma Gandhi and the Congress Working Committee, Subhash Chandra Bose founded the Forward Bloc. It emerged as a faction within the Indian National Congress in 1939, led by **Subhash Chandra Bose**. The first INA collapsed in December before it was revived under the leadership of Subhash Chandra Bose in 1943 and proclaimed the army of Bose's Argi Hukumat-e-Azad Hind.

Subhash Chandra Bose

- Subhash Chandra Bose was one of the greatest freedom fighters of India. He was born on 23rd January, 1897 at Cuttack in Orissa. Having been completed his studies in India, he went to England and passed the **Indian Civil Services Examination.**
- The Non-Cooperation Movement of Mahatma Gandhi attracted Subhash Chandra Bose and he became an active worker of the Freedom Movement. Gandhiji criticised when he withdrew the Non-Cooperation Movement in 1922.

- He was unanimously elected as the President of the Congress at the **Haripura** (Gujarat) Session in 1938. Subhash Chandra Bose inaugurated the **Indian National Planning Committee** in December, 1938.

Contribution of Subhash Chandra Bose in INA

- **Setting up Provisional Government of Free India** Netaji Subhash Chandra Bose founded the Provisional or Interim Government of Free India (Arzi Hukumat-e-Azad Hind) at Singapore on 21st October, 1943. The objective of the Provisional Government of Free India was to establish a permanent national government of Azad Hind. Netaji transferred the headquarters of the Provisional Government to **Rangoon** which had a strategic importance as Myanmar was close to India's Eastern Border where INA would reach easily.
- **Declaration of War** On 23rd October, 1943, the cabinet of the Provisional Government called a meeting where it was decided to start war against Britain and USA. Netaji himself broadcast this decision on radio.

Objectives of the Forward Bloc

The main objective of the Forward Bloc was liberation of India with the support of workers, peasants, youth and other organisations.

Indian National Army (INA)

- The outbreak of the war in South-East Asia in 1941 caused a great stir among the Indians in those regions. Indians, living in the territories captured by Japan, organised themselves into association, with the objective of contributing to the Liberation of India and serving the interest of the overseas Indians during critical period.
- The Japanese, after defeating the British in South-East Asia, took a number of Indian soldiers as Prisoners of War. In March 1942, a conference of Indians was held in Tokyo and they formed the Indian Independence League.
- At the Bangkok Conference (June, 1942), Rash behari Bose was elected the President of the League. INA was formed by **Mohan Singh**. Subhash Chandra Bose had escaped to Berlin in 1941 and set-up an Indian League there.
- In July, 1943, he joined the INA at Singapore. There Rash behari Bose handed over the leadership to him. Provisional Government of Free India and the INA were formed by Subhash Chandra Bose in Singapore on 21st October, 1943. Subhash Chandra Bose gave the call to his soldiers 'Give me blood and I shall get you freedom.' He gave the slogans **Delhi Chalo** and **Jai Hind**.
- The INA gave a tough fight to the British forces in the Assam hills and succeeded in capturing Ukhral and Kohima. However, the surrender of Japan in the Second World War sealed the fate of the INA. The INA failed in its political mission, but it set an inspiring example of patriotism.

Contributions of the INA

The contributions of the INA to the National Movement were

(i) It inspired uprisings against the British in the armed forces of the country.

(ii) As Hindus, Muslims and Sikhs in the INA fought as Indians, it indicated that Indians who waged an armed battle against the British were not at all affected by communal division.

Objectives of the INA

The main objectives of the Indian National Army are as follows

(i) To organise an armed revolution and to fight the British army of occupation with modern arms.

(ii) To organise a provisional government of free India in order to mobilise all forces effectively.

(iii) Total mobilisation of India's manpower and money for a total war was one of the main objectives of INA.

(iv) The motto of the INA was **Unity, Faith and Sacrifice**.

Achievements of INA

The two achievements of INA are

- In early 1944, three units of the **Azad Hind Fauj** (INA) took part in the attack on the North-Eastern parts of India to oust the British from India. It captured Mowdok, an outpost situated South-East of Chittagong and advanced up to the frontier of India. They captured the strong military post of Klang Klang.
- They raised the Tricolor Flag for the first time on the liberated Indian soil on 19th March, 1944 in Kohima (Nagaland).

Independence and Partition of India

In the Lahore Session of the Muslim League in 1940, the demand for Pakistan came up. The name of Pakistan came from beginning letters of Punjab, the Afghan Province, Kashmir and Sindh and from Baluchistan was taken the last syllable.

Wavell Plan and Shimla Conference

(4th June-14th July, 1945)

- The war situation in Europe improved in the beginning of the year 1945. India's goodwill was however, needed as the war against Japan was expected to last for about 2 years.
- The British Government was compelled to come forward with some sort of plan to satisfy the Indians After consulting the British Government on the Indian problem, Lord Wavell, the Viceroy of India, issued a statement known as **Wavell Plan**.

Proposal of the Plan

Viceroy's Executive Council would consist of an equal number of Hindus and Muslims. Only the Commander in Chief and the Viceroy would be British. Once the important political parties agree to the basics, a new Constitution would be framed by the Indians themselves. And India like other dominions would have a British High Commissioner.

Mountbatten Plan (3rd June, 1947)

- In March 1947, Lord Mountbatten replaced Lord Wavell. He announced his plan on 3rd June, 1947. His earlier plan regarding Balkanisation of the country was abandoned for this 3rd June plan. It offered a key to the political and constitutional deadlock created by the refusal of Muslim League to join the **Constituent Assembly** formed to frame the Constitution of India.
- The Plan provided for the creation of a Boundary Commission to settle the boundaries of the two dominions in case partition was decided upon.
- Mountbatten's formula was to divide India, but to retain maximum unity. The country would be partitioned, but so would be Punjab and Bengal, so that the limited Pakistan that emerged, would meet both the Congress and the League position to some extent. Its acceptance by the Congress and the **Muslim League** resulted in the birth of the Pakistan.

Clause of the Mountbatten Plan

India was to be partitioned into two independent and sovereign states namely India and Pakistan. The plan provided for the Partition of Punjab and Bengal. The Princely States were given the choice of joining either of the two new States—India or Pakistan.

Acceptance of Mountbatten Plan by the Congress

The Mountbatten Plan was accepted by the Congress because

- the large-scale of communal riots 'that engulfed the whole country convinced all that the only solution to communal problem lay in the Partition of India.
- the League had joined the Interim Government to obstruct and not to cooperate. Experience of working with the League had convinced the Congress that it could not have a joint administration with the League.
- the leaders felt that partition would rid the Constitution of separate electorates and other undemocratic procedures. India could evolve a truly secular and democratic polity.
- the only alternative to partition was a federation with a weak centre. A smaller India with a strong central authority was better than a bigger state with a weak centre.

Indian Independence Act (1947)

- The Bill containing the provisions of the Mountbatten Plan of 3rd June, 1947 was introduced in the British Parliament and was passed as the Indian Independence Act, 1947. The act laid down detailed measures for the Partition of India and the speedy transfer of political powers to the new government of India and Pakistan.
- This act marked the end of the British rule in India and the Dominions of India and Pakistan came into existence on 15th August, 1947.

Clauses of the Indian Independence Act

The main clauses of the act were as follows

- **Two New Dominions** India would be partitioned and two Independent Dominions India and Pakistan would be created from 15th August, 1947. The act provided legislative supremacy of both the dominions.
- The territories of the two dominions were divided in such terms that Pakistan would comprise Sindh, British Baluchistan, North-West Frontier Province, the West Punjab and East Bengal. India was to comprise all the remaining territories included in the British India. The exact boundaries of the dominions would be determined by a Boundary Commission.

- **Provisions of Partitions** Both Bengal and Punjab would be divided, if so desired by the people. The Provincial Assemblies of the two parts would meet separately representing Hindu majority districts and Muslim majority districts and would decide through a majority vote whether they wanted the division of province or not.

  A plebiscite would be held in North-West Frontier Province (NWFP) as well as in Sylhet district (Muslim majority area) in East Bengal to determine whether they would like to join Pakistan or India. (Both these provinces joined West and East Pakistan respectively).
- **Governor-General for Each Dominion** There would be a Governor-General, who would be appointed by the British king on the advice of the Cabinet of the concerned dominion.
- **Constituent Assemblies to Serve as Central Legislatures** The Constituent Assemblies of both the dominions were to act as the Central Legislatures and would have full power to make laws for their respective dominion. They would act as sovereign bodies for legislative purposes.

PYQs Previous Years' Questions

1 Mark Questions (MCQ)

1. Which of the following clauses was not a part of the Indian Independence Act of 1947? ***(ICSE Specimen 2023)***
   (a) There would be a Governor-General for each dominion.
   (b) The country would be divided into two Dominions.
   (c) The British Parliament had legislative control over India.
   (d) There would be a division of army and assets.

Ans. (*c*) The British Parliament had legislative control over India.

2. The Supreme Commander of the Indian National Army ***(ICSE Specimen Semester I 2021)***
   (a) Subhash Chandra Bose (b) Rash Behari Ghosh
   (c) Jawaharlal Nehru (d) Lord Wavell

Ans. (*a*) Subhash Chandra Bose

3. Which of these was not a provision of the Indian Independence Act, 1947? ***(ICSE Specimen Semester I 2021)***
   (a) There would be a Governor-General for each Dominion.
   (b) There would be no division of the army.
   (c) The office of the Secretary of State was abolished.
   (d) The jurisdiction of the British Parliament would end.

Ans. (*b*) There would be no division of the army.

4. Replace the underlined word to correct the statement. Unity, Faith, Sacrifice was the motto of the <u>Forward Bloc</u>. ***(ICSE Specimen Semester I 2021)***
   (a) Indian National Congress (b) Indian National Army
   (c) East India Association (d) The Muslim League

Ans. (*b*) Indian National Army

5. To reorganise agriculture and industry on socialist lines was an aim of: ***(ICSE Specimen Semester I 2021)***
   (a) Indian National Congress
   (b) The Indian National Army
   (c) The Forward Bloc
   (d) The Muslim League

Ans. (*c*) The Forward Bloc

6. Which of the following was an objective of the Indian National Army? ***(ICSE Semester I 2021)***
   (a) To formulate and present the demands to the government.
   (b) To make the world aware of the true nature of British rule in India.
   (c) Total mobilisation of Indian manpower and money for a total war.
   (d) To establish Home Rule in India.

Ans. (*c*) Total mobilisation of Indian manpower and money for a total war.

7. Which of the following was a reason for the acceptance of the Mountbatten Plan? ***(ICSE Semester I 2021)***
   (a) The British forced the Congress to accept the plan.
   (b) The Muslim League would cooperate in the governance.
   (c) The only alternative to partition was a Federation with a weak centre.
   (d) The Princely States wanted to accept the plan.

Ans. (*c*) The only alternative to partition was a Federation with a weak centre.

8. Identify the famous slogan of Subhash Chandra Bose. *(ICSE Semester I 2021)*

(a) Give me blood and I shall give you freedom
(b) Swaraj is my birth-right and I shall have it
(c) Do or Die
(d) Vande Mataram

Ans. (*a*) Give me blood and I shall give you freedom

9. Which of the following is not a clause of the Indian Independence Act of 1947? *(ICSE Semester I 2021)*

(a) All treaties made with the British would lapse.
(b) The army and assets would belong only to India.
(c) The Constituent Assemblies would serve as Central Legislatures.
(d) The Princely States were free to associate themselves with either dominion.

Ans. (*b*) The army and assets would belong only to India.

2/3 Marks Questions

1. Give two reason for the acceptance of the Mountbatten Plan by the Congress. *(ICSE Specimen 2023)*

Or Write any two reasons for the acceptance of the Mountbatten Plan by the Congress. *(ICSE 2019)*

Or Why was Mountbatten's Plan finally accepted by the Congress? *(ICSE 2016)*

Ans. The Mountbatten Plan was accepted by the Congress because

- the large-scale of communal riots 'that engulfed the whole country convinced all that the only solution to communal problem lay in the Partition of India.
- the League had joined the Interim Government to obstruct and not to cooperate. Experience of working with the League had convinced the Congress that it could not have a joint administration with the League.

2. Mention any two objectives of the Forward Bloc. *(2020, Specimen 2018)*

Ans. The objectives of the Forward Bloc were

(i) To unite all the left-wing sections within the Congress under one head and to develop an alternative leadership.
(ii) To liberate India with the support of workers, peasant, youths and all radical organisations.

3. State any two provisions of the Indian Independence Act of 1947 that was to decide the fate of the Princely States. *(ICSE 2019)*

Or Mention any two provisions of the Indian Independence Act, 1947. *(ICSE Specimen 2018, ICSE 2005)*

Ans. Two provisions of the Indian Independence Act, 1947 were as follows

(i) India would be partitioned and two independent dominions India and Pakistan would be created on 15th August, 1947.
(ii) The territories of the two dominions were divided in such terms that Pakistan would comprise Sindh, British, Baluchistan, North-West Frontier Province, the West Punjab and East Bengal.

4. Give any two contributions of Subhash Chandra Bose. *(ICSE Specimen 2018)*

Or Mention two contributions of Subhash Chandra Bose to India's freedom struggle. *(ICSE 2011)*

Ans. Two contributions of Subhash Chandra Bose were

(i) Subhash Chandra Bose was a freedom fighter. A new party called Forward Bloc was established by him to bring all the left-wing parties under one roof.
(ii) Subhash Chandra Bose was the founder of Indian National Army, INA's main aim was to organise an armed revolution against British.

5. Name the last Viceroy of India. State any one of the provisions of the Indian Independence Act of 1947. *(ICSE 2018, ICSE 2008, ICSE 2004)*

Ans. Lord Mountbatten was the last Viceroy of India. One provision of the Indian Independence Act, 1947, was the Partition of British India divided into two independent nations, India and Pakistan.

6. Mention any two clauses of the Mountbatten Plan. *ICSE Specimen 2018)*

Ans. Two clauses of the Mountbatten Plan were as follow

(i) The country was to be divided into two dominions i.e. India and Pakistan.
(ii) The Partition of Bengal and Punjab was to take place, if the Legislative Assemblies of the provinces would decide in the favour of the same.

7. Mention any two objectives of the Indian National Army. *(ICSE 2017, ICSE 2014)*

Ans. Two objectives of Indian National Army were

(i) To organise an armed revolution and to fight the British army with modern arms.

(ii) To organise a provisional government of free India in order to mobilise all forces effectively.

8. Mention any two contributions of the INA to the National Movement. *(ICSE 2016)*

Ans. Two contributions of INA to the Indian Freedom Movement are as follows

(i) The INA inspired uprisings in the armed forces of the country.

(ii) As Hindus, Muslims and Sikhs in the INA fought as Indians, the INA demonstrated that those who waged an armed battle against the British were not at all affected by communal division.

9. Who founded the Forward Bloc? Mention any one of its objectives. *(ICSE 2015)*

Or Name the party formed by Subhash Chandra Bose. What was its immediate objective? *(ICSE 2012, ICSE 2002)*

Ans. The Forward Bloc was formed by Subhash Chandra Bose. The main objective of the Forward Bloc was liberation of India with the support of workers, peasants, youth and other organisations.

10. What were the two proposals related to the Princely States in the Mountbatten Plan? *(ICSE 2013)*

Other Similar Questions

Or Mention the proposals for the Princely States in the Mountbatten Plan of 1947.

Or What has been stated about the Princely States in the Indian Independence Act of 1947?

Ans. The two proposals related to the Princely States in the Mountbatten Plan were as follows

(i) All treaties and agreements made by the British with reference to states would lapse from 15th August, 1947.

(ii) They would be free to associate themselves with either of the two dominions or to remain independent.

11. How were the prisoners reorganised as Indian National Army after the capture of british Indian Soldiers by Japanese? *(ICSE 2008)*

Ans. Japanese captured Indian soldiers in South-East Asia. During this time Britain's defeats aroused great hopes among Indian soldiers, which led to the formation of the Indian Independence League by Rash Behari Bose. A conference which was held in the Tokyo, took a decision to form an Indian National Army.

12. Mention two proposals of the Wavell Plan. *(ICSE 2008)*

Ans. Two proposals of the Wavell Plan were as follows

(i) The plan, which chiefly concerned Viceroy's Executive Council proposed certain changes in the structure of the Council. The Executive Council would be constituted giving a balanced representation to the main communities in it, including equal representation to Hindus and Muslims.

(ii) The Constitution of India would be framed by the Indians themselves.

13. Name the military organisation formed by Subhash Chandra Bose. *(ICSE 2004)*

Ans. Indian National Army was the military organisation formed by Subhash Chandra Bose.

10 Marks Questions

1. The heroism of Indians was revealed by the courage of Subhash Chandra Bose and the Indian National Army. With reference to this, answer the following questions. *(ICSE 2023)*

(a) Mention any three objectives of the Forward Bloc.

(b) Mention any three contributions of Subhash Chandra Bose.

(c) Who was the founder of the Indian National Army? Mention any three of its objectives.

Ans. (a) The objectives of the Forward Bloc were

(i) To unite all the left-wing sections within the Congress under one head and to develop an alternative leadership.

(ii) To liberate India with the support of workers, peasant, youths and all radical organisations.

(iii) In the domain of foreign policy, the Forward Bloc stood for world peace, disarmament, friendly relations with socialist countries, non-alignment and a new economic order.

(b) The three contributions of Subhash Chandra Bose are

(i) Netaji Subhash Chandra Bose founded the Provisional or Interim Government of Free India (Arzi Hukumat-e-Azad Hind) at Singapore on 21st October, 1943.
The objective of the Provisional Government of Free India was to establish a permanent national government of Azad Hind.

(ii) Netaji transferred the headquarters of the Provisional Government to Rangoon which had a strategic importance as Myanmar was close to India's Eastern Border where INA would reach easily.

(iii) On 23rd October, 1943, the cabinet of the Provisional Government called a meeting where it was decided to start war against Britain and USA. Netaji himself broadcast this decision on radio.

(c) Mohan Sing was the founder of Indian National Army. The main objectives of the Indian National Army are as follows

(i) To organise an armed revolution and to fight the British army of occupation with modern arms.

(ii) To organise a provisional government of free India in order to mobilise all forces effectively.

(iii) Total mobilisation of India's manpower and money for a total war was one of the main objectives of INA.

2. With reference to the Partition Plan, answer the following. ***(ICSE 2020)***

(a) (i) Name the last Viceroy of India.

(ii) State any two reasons for him to come to India.

(b) Mention any three proposals under his plan.

(c) State any four reasons for the Congress to finally accept the plan.

Ans. (a) (i) Refer to Q. 5 of 2/3 marks questions.

(ii) Lord Mountbatten come to India due to the following reasons

- To solve the dispute between the Muslim League and the Indian National Congress. It offered a key to the political and constitutional deadlock created by the refusal of the Muslim League to join the Constituent Assembly formed to frame the Constitution of India.
- To divide India, but retain maximum unity.

(b) The proposals under Mountbatten Plan were

(i) India would be divided into two dominions, i.e. India and Pakistan.

(ii) A referendum or plebiscite would be held in the North-West Frontier Province to ascertain whether the people in the area wanted to join India or not.

(iii) The Princely States would have the choice of joining either of the two dominions or to remain independent.

(c) All-Indian Congress Committee accepted the Mountbatten Plan for the four following reasons

(i) The most important reason for this acceptance was the safety of the Indians. The large scale of communal riots that engulfed the whole country convinced all the Congress leaders that the only solution to communal problem lay in the Partition of India.

(ii) The Muslim League had joined the Interim Government to obstruct and not to co-operate. Experience of working with the League had convinced the Congress that it could not have a joint administration with the League.

(iii) After partition, India could avoid Constitution of separate electorates and other undemocratic procedures and could evolve as a truly secular and democratic polity.

(iv) The Congress leaders realised that the extension of the British rule would be harmful to Indians. By applying 'Divide and Rule' policy the Britishers not only divided Hindu and Muslim community in our country, but they also instigated the native rulers of Indian states to remain independent. Thus, for the betterment of the people Congress leaders accepted partition.

Examiner's Comment

- This question was well attempted by the candidates.
- Majority of the candidates answered this part of the question correctly. However, some candidates wrote about the Cabinet Mission Plan or the Provisions of the Indian Independence Act.
- Some candidates found it difficult to write four reasons why the Congress finally accepted the plan.

Suggestions for Students

- Study each and every event related to the Partition Plan of India thoroughly to the students.
- Understand the Cabinet Mission Plan, the Mountbatten Plan and the Provisions of the Indian Independence Act of 1947.
- Study the clauses of above-mentioned Plans /Act thoroughly and present them in a factual manner.

4. Study the picture given below and answer the following questions. ***(ICSE 2018)***

(a) Identify the leader given in the picture. Name the political party and the Military Organisation that he formed.

(b) State any three objectives of the political party that he founded.

(c) Mention any four objectives of the Military Organisation that he formed.

Ans. (a) The above picture belongs to Subhash Chandra Bose, one of the most respected and prominent leaders of the Indian Freedom Movement. Forward Bloc was the political party he formed and the Indian National Army (INA) was a Military Organisation formed by him.

(b) For answer, refer to Q. 1 (a) of 10 marks questions.

(c) Four objectives of the Indian National Army were

(i) To mobilise all the forces effectively to lead the Indian people to regain their freedom.

(ii) To prepare the Indian people inside and outside India for a modern armed struggle against the British.

(iii) To organise a provisional government of free India.

(iv) Total mobilisation of India's manpower and money against the British.

Examiner's Comment

- All the candidates were able to identify the leader given in the picture. They were also able to name the political party and the Military Organization founded by Subhas Chandra Bose.
- Majority of the candidates, instead of stating the objectives of the Forward Bloc, mentioned the objectives of the Indian National Army.
- Many candidates, instead of mentioning the objectives of the Indian National Army either mentioned the objectives of the Forward Bloc or a mix of the objectives of both Forward Bloc and the Indian National Army.

Suggestions for Students

- Learn to identify the pictures of important leaders and teach them the contributions of these leaders in the freedom struggle.
- Study the differences between the objectives of the Forward Bloc and the Indian National Army.
- Emphasise on keywords and create mind maps and train the students also to make their own mind maps for better retention.

5.

With reference to the picture given above, answer the following. ***(ICSE 2014)***

(a) Identify the Viceroy in the picture.

(b) Why was he sent to India?

(c) How did he plan to solve the communal problem existing in India?

(d) Why did the Congress accept the plan? State three reasons to justify its acceptance.

Ans. (a) Lord Mountbatten is depicted in the given picture.

(b) For answer, refer to Q. 2 (a) (ii) part of 10 marks questions.

(c) In the struggle for India's partition, riots broke out in Kolkata, Punjab, Assam and the North-West frontier province. Mountbatten put his plan for the Partition of India before the 'big seven' leaders-Nehru, Patel, Kripalani, Jinnah, Liaquat, Nishtar and Baldev Singh. After many consultations with them, Mountbatten came to the conclusion that the sooner the power was transferred, the better for all. He was convinced that India was to be partitioned and transfer of power to Indians could only be on the basis of partition of the country.

(d) For answer, refer to Q. 2 (c) of 10 marks questions.

6.

(a) Identify the event in the above picture. Name the lady seen in the given picture. Mention the year when the event took place.

(b) What were the main provisions of the Indian Independence Act?

(c) Mention the reasons that made the Congress accept the partition proposals. ***(ICSE 2011)***

Ans. (a) The event is that of the Transfer of Power ceremony. The lady shown in the picture is Edwina Mountbatten. This event took place in the year 1947.

(b) The Indian Independence Act was passed by the British Parliament on 1st July, 1947.

The main provisions of this act were

(i) The act laid down the procedure for the Partition of India.

(ii) It laid down the measures for the speedy transfer of power to the Government of India and Pakistan.

(iii) The act proposed the post of Governor-General for each dominion.

(iv) As per the act, the Constituent Assemblies of each dominion were to act as the Central Legislatures.

(c) For answer, refer to Q. 2 (c) of 10 marks questions.

7. With reference to the Indian National Army, answer the following questions. ***(ICSE 2008)***

(a) Explain three measures taken by Subhash Chandra Bose to establish a Socialist Society.

(b) What were the three decisions taken at the Tokyo Conference?

(c) Explain any three contributions of Subhash Chandra Bose to the National Movement.

Ans. (a) The three measures taken by Subhash Chandra Bose to establish a Socialist Society were as follows

(i) Reorganisation of agriculture and industry on socialist lines.

(ii) Abolition of the zamindari system.

(iii) Introduction of a new monetary and credit system.

(b) At the Tokyo Conference, the decisions were as follows

(i) To expand and strengthen the Indian Independence League.

(ii) To form under the overall command of the league an Indian National Army (INA), an army for Indian liberation.

(iii) To hold a conference at Bangkok to consolidate these decisions.

(c) For, answer, refer to Q. 1 (b) of 10 marks questions.

8. In the political scenario of 1939, important developments took place in India and abroad. In this context, answer the following questions. ***(ICSE 2007)***

(a) Who was the founder of the 'Forward Bloc'? Why was this organisation formed?

(b) Why did Sir Stafford Cripps come to India? Why was the Quit India Movement launched?

(c) Explain any four proposals made by Lord Mountbatten to settle the Independence issue for India.

Ans. (a) For answer, refer to Q. 9 of 2/3 marks questions.

(b) The Cripps Mission wanted to break the political deadlock in India, which had resulted due to the British needing Indian support in the Second World War which was denied by the Indians.

Under the following circumstances, the Quit India Movement was launched by the Gandhiji to force the British out of the country.

(i) The Cripps Mission failed to solve the constitutional problems of India. Cripps Mission did not bring with it the promise of independence in near future.

(ii) The Cripps Mission proposed that India would be given a dominion status. It did not propose any immediate transfer of power.

(iii) In 1942, the Japanese Army attacked Myanmar and marched towards India. The threat of Japanese invasion of India convinced the Indian leaders that for India's safety, the British should withdraw from India immediately. Gandhiji believed that the presence of the British in India is an invitation of Japan to invade India. He asked the British to quit India.

(c) For answer, refer to Q. 2 (b) of 10 marks questions.

9. With reference to the Indian National Army, answer the following questions. ***(ICSE 2000)***

(a) Mention the circumstances which led to the formation of the Indian National Army.

(b) Summarise the contributions of Subhash Chandra Bose to the National Movement.

Ans. (a) The outbreak of the war in South-East Asia in 1941 caused a great stir among the Indians in those regions.

Indians, living in territories captured by Japan, organised themselves into association, with the objective of contributing to the Liberation of India and serving the interest of the overseas Indians during the critical period.

The Indian National Army (INA) formed in the Indian Independence League to free India with Japanese support, held a conference at Tokyo and later at Bangkok and gave a concrete shape to the Indian National Army which consisted of Indian Prisoners of War.

Captain Mohan Singh was the Commander in Chief and Rash behari Bose was elected the President. The INA was later led by Subhash Chandra Bose who got support from the Japanese who were advancing towards India to remove the Britishers from India.

(b) Refer to Q 1 (b) of 10 marks questions.

CHAPTER TEST

01 Mark Questions

1 Name the famous personality who founded the Forward Bloc.
(a) Subhash Chandra Bose
(b) Jawaharlal Nehru
(c) Mahatma Gandhi
(d) Rash behari Ghosh

2 Which of the following statements is correct about the Subhash Chandra Bose?
(a) He was born on 23rd January, 1897 at Cuttack, Orissa.
(b) He went to England and passed the Indian Civil Services Examination.
(c) He was elected as the President of the Congress at the Lahore Session in 1929.
(d) He inaugurated the Indian National Planning Committee in December, 1938.

3 Complete the given analogy.
Congress session in 1939 : Tripuri :: Congress Session in 1938 : ?
(a) Haripura (b) Lahore
(c) Amritsar (d) Nagpur

4 Complete the given analogy.
Forward Bloc : 1939 :: Indian Independence League : ?
(a) Rash Behari Bose (b) Mohan Singh
(c) Subhash Chandra Bose (d) Kartar Singh

5 Subhash Chandra Bose announced the establishment of provincial government of Free India on ....
(a) 21st October, 1940 (b) 21st October, 1942
(c) 21st October, 1941 (d) 21st October, 1943

6 The formula for transfer of sovereignty to India in 1947 was known as ....
(a) Wavell Plan (b) Cripps Plan
(c) Mountbatten Plan (d) Radcliffe Plan

Answers

1. (a) 2. (c) 3. (a) 4. (a) 5. (d) 6. (c)

02 Marks Questions

7 What are the main objective of the Forward Bloc?

8 Mention any two objectives of the Indian National Army.

9 State any two clause of the Indian Independence Act.

10 Mention any two contribution of Subhash Chandra Bose to Indian's Freedom struggle.

10 Marks Question

11 Look at the picture given below and answer the following questions.

(i) Identify the event in the above picture. Name any two features of the plan devised by the man in the centre. Why was he sent to India?
(ii) How did he plan to solve the communal problem existing in India?
(iii) Mention any four reason that made the Congress accept the plan.

07

The First World War and the Rise of Dictatorships

TREND ANALYSIS 3 YEARS

		Average No. of Questions Across all Sets			
		Types of Questions	2023	2020	2019
TOPIC 01	First Word War	1 Mark	1	–	–
		2/3 Marks	–	1	1
		4 Marks	–	–	–
		10 Marks	1	–	–
TOPIC 02	Rise of Dictatorships	1 Mark	1	–	–
		2/3 Marks	–	–	–
		4 Marks	–	–	–
		10 Marks	–	–	–

First World War

The First World War began in Europe, in the year 1914. Its extent was over the entire world including Asia, Africa and the Pacific. This period witnessed innovations in the methods of destruction and defence, which in turn termeds the period as 'the First World War'.

Causes of the First World War

Militant Nationalism

This was the result of Aggressive Nationalism, Economic Competition and International Tension, which emerged in Europe in the second half of the 19th century. Aggressive nationalism basically meant the immense love and interest for one's own country and hatred towards the other countries.

Fierce economic competition meant cut-throat commercial ambitions of the European nations, which ended up with an armed conflict amongst all the other nations, further leading to international tension and problems across the world.

Imperialism

The expansionist policies in the name of nationalism led to the rise of imperialism. Imperialism occurs when a strong nation takes over a weaker nation or region and dominates its economic, political and cultural life. These types of colonies were governed and administered by the imperial nation through its puppet government.

The main focus of the British imperialism was to expand its trade by exploiting the resources of its colonies such as India, Sri Lanka, Myanmar, South Africa, Egypt, Caribbean Islands and many parts of Africa.

Division of Europe into Two Hostile Groups

In Europe, there were two kinds of states, first was **Single nation states** like–France, Holland and Germany, which were based on common languages and common traditions that they shared.

And the other kind were the **Imperial states** consisting Austria-Hungarian empire and the Russian empire, who spoke different languages and had different cultural traditions.

Sarajevo Crisis (Immediate Cause)

One of the major causes of the First World War was the assassination of Archduke Francis Ferdinand, the heir to the throne of Austria-Hungary at Sarajevo, capital of Bosnia on 28th June, 1914. The assassination was planned and carried out by a secret society of the extremist Serbian nationalists called the **Black Hand** or the **Union of Death**.

Results of the War

This war altered the whole political scenario as well. Three ruling dynasties Romanov, Hohenzollern and Hapsburg were destroyed in this war. The rule of the Ottomans came to an end. Austria, Hungary, Czechoslovakia and Yugoslavia became separate independent states.

Treaty of Versailles

- It was signed between the Allies and Germany on 28th June, 1919 at the Paris Conference. This treaty had great territorial rearrangements, which changed the political map of the world by giving a serious blow to monarchy and developed democracy in Europe.
- This treaty not only affected substantial territorial changes, but also reduced the military strength of Germany.

  Some of the terms of the Treaty of Versailles are as follows

  (i) Germany was declared guilty of aggression.

  (ii) It was required to pay for the loss and the damages incurred by the Allies, which came to be around 33 billion dollars. Germany also lost her merchant ships.

  (iii) Rhine Valley was decided on to be demilitarised.

  (iv) Germany lost Alsace Lorraine to France, Eupen-et-Malmedy to Belgium, and Schleswig to Denmark. Danzing became a free port.

  (v) The coal mines in the German area called Saar were ceded to France.

  (vi) The German army and navy were severely restricted.

Note The most important development was the formation of the League of Nations which aimed to create a mechanism to prevent future wars and to promote International cooperation.

Objectives of the League of Nations

Objectives of the League of Nations were as follows

(i) States were prohibited from entering into secret treaties and alliances.

(ii) Member states were restricted to maintain huge armies, warships and destructive armaments.

(iii) The major aim of the League of Nations was to settle disputes among the member states and to maintain peace and order.

(iv) The League of Nations was supposed to promote political, social, cultural and economic cooperation among the member states.

(v) All the states were to respect each other's independence.

(vi) The member states had to heed to the directions of the League against any state trying to disturb world peace and order. But unfortunately, the League came to an end when Hitler committed an aggression on Poland, which marked the start of Second World War in 1939-1945.

Rise of Dictatorships

19th century witnessed different styles of governance, amongst which dictatorship was also one of those. Many intellectuals expressed their satisfaction and agreed for the prevalence of dictatorship.

Fascism

- Fascism means *Union* or *League* and has been derived from the Italian word *fascio*. Fascism has been described as 'power in one hand'. It is a form of dictatorship, where all the power is in one hand and it is compulsory for all the others to respect its orders.
- Italy and Germany ruled on the basis of Fascism, which was regarded as a Nationalistic, Anti-communistic and an Anti-democratic movement.

Rise of Mussolini

- Mussolini started as a socialist, but later converted to an anti-socialist due to the realisation that he could get finance from the industrialists. Different groups called **Fascios** who wore black uniform and known as the **black-shirts** were formed by Mussolini.
- They believed in violence and captured factories, police stations, municipalities, etc. The conference of the Fascist party was held at Naples in 1922.

  Mussolini demanded for the following conditions

  (i) Inclusion of 5 members of the Fascist party in the Cabinet.

  (ii) New elections to be announced.

(iii) Firm reaction of the government on its Foreign Policy.
(iv) Implementation of the economic reforms as soon as possible.

- These demands were not focussed upon by the Italian Government so Mussolini marched towards Rome. He formed a new government with Emmanuel III and designated fascists as **Prefects** and **Chief Officers**.
- The Government of Italy was handed over to the Fascists as the ruling classes considered Democracy and Socialism as threats to their power.

Mussolini regained the islands of Rhodes, Dodecanese as well as Fiume. He turned Albania into a protectorate of Italy and entered into commercial and diplomatic treaties with France and Russia. He captured Abyssinia in 1936.

Causes for the Rise of Fascism in Italy

Fascism came into existence with the objective of handling the challenges faced by Italy. The following factors contributed to the rise of Fascism in Italy

Discontentment after the Treaty of Versailles Italy was not satisfied with the Treaty of Versailles, because it could not get any part of the German or the Turkish empire.

Economic Crisis Italy was very much affected by the First World War. It suffered losses in each and every respect-life and property, trade and commerce, supply shortage of foodgrains, etc.Fascists favoured equal control over all sections of society. They wanted to control capitalists, industrialists, labourers, landlords, peasants and artisans

Political Instability No party enjoyed majority in elections. Six coalition governments were formed in Italy. No party was able to deal properly with the problems of unemployment, strikes and riots.

Class Conflicts The First World War led to an increase in class conflicts. The major issue was whether the government or the economic system would favour elites or would they work in favour of the less privileged majorities.

Threat of Socialism or Communism Threat of anarchists and communists ignited the atmosphere with revolutionary ideas. The common masses desired a powerful leadership for establishment of peace and prosperity.

Failure of the League of Nations The League of Nations was created after the First World War. But since it could not control the rise of dictatorship, it failed.

Leadership Provided by Mussolini Mussolini with his charismatic personality won the confidence of his countrymen. He was regarded as the 'Duce' which means the leader.

Objectives of Fascism

The main objectives of Fascism were as follows

(i) It was an anti thesis of democracy.
(ii) It supported the notion of **one party** and **one leader**.
(iii) It favoured equal control in all the sections of the society.
(iv) They focussed on nationalism and on individual institutions.
(v) They believed that the interests of the States must get precedence over individual interests as the individual gets all the rights from the state.

End of Fascism in Italy

Italy was defeated in the Second World War, ending the career and the life of Mussolini. In 1945, he was executed which ended Fascism in Italy.

Impact of Fascism

Fascism impacted Italy both positively and negatively.

Its positive impacts were as follows

(i) Mussolini's work improved the conditions of Italy. Many administrative and economic reforms were setting up of hydroelectric power plants, bringing of more lands under cultivation, etc., were undertaken.
(ii) Measures to reduce unemployment were undertaken.
(iii) Eradication of illiteracy by making provisions for education was done.
(iv) Various steps were taken to increase the military might of the country. Military training was made necessary.
(v) Treaty of Lateran was signed between the Pope and Mussolini. Roman Catholic religion was made the State Religion.
(vi) Aggressive Foreign policy was formulated.
(vii) Mussolini became the dictator to military and civil powers. All political parties lost their existence except Mussolini's party.

The negative impacts of Fascism were as follows

(i) It curbed political freedom.
(ii) System of Jury was abolished.
(iii) Special courts with fascist civilian and military officers were empowered to decide on political cases.
(iv) Press was censored.
(v) The freedom of Speech and that of organising meetings was also prohibited.

Nazi Dictatorship in Germany

After the defeat in the First World War, fresh elections were held in January, 1919 at Weimar. A new Constitution was adopted by Germany. The people were dissatisfied with the problems faced by them and conducted riots and made attempts to seize the power.

Role of Hitler

- Adolf Hitler, ranked Corporal, joined 'the German Workers Party' and soon became its leader and changed its name to **National Socialist Party** or the **Nazi Party**. Nazi party had two groups. One working for saving its party members and to break the meeting of the opposition parties. The other group wore **black shirts** and their duty was to save their party leaders.
- Hitler planned to capture power through a march on Berlin and was arrested. He lost in the elections in July, 1932 and was later offered chancellorship by President Hindenburg, where he formed his first Nazi Government on 30th January, 1933.
- Nazi party was not able to win majority, so he assumed dictatorial powers. Hitler abolished the Constitution and became the dictator of Germany. Germany got defeated by Allied powers. Hitler committed suicide and this ended Nazism in Germany.

Causes for the Rise of Nazism in Germany

- The Versailles Treaty forced Germany to cede their territories to France, Belgium, Poland and Denmark and also pay heavy reparation which humiliated the Germans Bolshevik Revolution created inclination of Germans towards Communism and Hitler warned people not to become the servants of Russian masters.
- Versailles Treaty created an economic deadlock because of the raised tariffs against the German goods, which created an economic crisis. It was felt that only a strong leadership could restore the past prestige of Germany which led to Militant Nationalism.
- Nazi party rose due to the absence of a strong opposition party. The agenda and the principle of Nazi party was propagated by the members of the volunteer corps.
- Hitler was known for moulding public opinion and was a gifted orator, who captivated the Germans by his emotional speeches.

Objectives of Nazism

The main objectives of Nazi Movement were as follows

(i) To use force and brutality.
(ii) To extol war.
(iii) To exalt nationalism.
(iv) To despise Internationalism, Peace and Democracy.
(v) To uphold racial supremacy of the Germans.
(vi) To advocate the rule by a great leader from a single party.

Impact of Nazism

Establishment of a Totalitarian State Hitler finished all the opposition parties and controlled the authority of the Nazi party. He concentrated all the power in his hands and suppressed all the oppositions. He altered the federal system into a unitary government. Hitler also became the Governor of Prussia all by himself. He abolished all the political parties, imposed a ban on the press, public speeches, etc. He also formed the Gestapo, a secret police to keep check on the activities of the citizens.

Economic Reforms Hitler launched the First Five Year Plan to increase production and improve the economy.

Following steps were taken in this regard

(i) Factories were set-up to provide work to the labourers.
(ii) Industrial and agricultural production and trade were encouraged.
(iii) Strikes were banned.
(iv) A food corporation was created.
(v) Imports and exports were controlled to maintain favourable trade balance.

Militarism and Compulsory Military Training Creation of more employment was done through increasing military training.

Repudiation of Peace Treaties Hitler openly condemned the Treaty of Versailles. Policy of territorial expansion and fortification of Germany was resorted to.

Acquisition of Territories Hitler acquired more and more territories for the Germans. He tried to expand in the South and East of Europe as that region was economically useful for Germany. He also reclaimed the territory of Saar and Rhineland from France and annexed Austria by force in 1938.

Racial Supremacy Hitler presented Germans as the 'Master Race' or the superior race, which would rule all the inferior races.

Similarities between the Ideologies of Fascism and Nazism

Following were the main similarities between the ideologies of Fascism and Nazism

(i) Favoured Totalitarian rule.
(ii) Against Democratic political system.
(iii) Both believed in State Supremacy, which could suppress Fundamental Rights and individual freedom.
(iv) To uphold one party and one leader.
(v) Belief in aggressive nationalism and imperialism.
(vi) War regarded as an instrument of national interests.
(vii) To uphold anti-communist, anti-democratic rule.

PYQs Previous Years' Questions

1 Marks Questions

1. The immediate cause of the First World War was .... *(ICSE 2023)*
   (a) Imperialism (b) Alliance system
   (c) Sarajevo Crisis (d) Arms Race

Ans. (c) Sarajevo Crisis

2. Which of the following is a common ideology of Fascism and Nazism? *(ICSE Specimen 2023)*
   (a) To believe in democracy
   (b) To encourage political systems
   (c) To uphold one party and one leader
   (d) To support communism.

Ans. (c) To uphold one party and one leader

3. Which of the following was not a common ideology of the dictators? *(ICSE Specimen Semester II 2022)*
   (a) Faith in totalitarian rule
   (b) One party and One Leader
   (c) Faith in Communism
   (d) Aggressive Nationalism and Imperialism

Ans. (c) Faith in Communism

2/3 Marks Questions

1. Name the two alliances formed in Europe during the First World War. *(ICSE Specimen Semester II 2022)*

Ans. The two alliances formed in Europe during the First World War are

(a) **Triple Alliance** In 1882, Germany and Austria-Hungary strengthened their bond by forming the Triple Alliance with Italy.

All three nations pledged support should any of them be attacked by France. If any member found itself at war with two or more nations at once, the alliance would come to their aid.

(b) **Triple Entente** It was formed in 1907 to counter the effects of the formation of the Triple Alliance among Russia, France and Britain.

2. Name the two countries which came under dictatorship after the First World War. Name the dictators. *(ICSE Specimen Semester II 2022)*

Ans. The two countries which came under dictatorship after the First World War were Italy and Germany. The two dictators were Benito Mussolini (ruler of Italy) and Adolf Hitler (ruler of Germany).

3. Explain the Sarajevo Crisis. *(ICSE Specimen Semester II 2022)*

Ans. The Sarajevo crisis was a series of interrelated military and diplomatic escalations in 1914 among the major powers of Europe (i.e. Austria and Serbia) leading to the outbreak of First World War. The crisis began on 28th June, 1914, was the reiterating reaction of the assassination of Archduke Francis Ferdinand and his wife.

This dual murder was planned by a terrorist outfit 'Union of Death' or popularly known as Black Hand. This group aimed at uniting all the South Slavs in Serbia. Thus, they killed the Prince who was the heir of Austria- Hungarian Empire. Due to this incident, on 23rd July, 1914, Austria sent an ultimatum to Serbia as it wanted the conspirators to be caught and handed over to the Austrian Government.

4. What was meant by the term 'imperialism', as a cause for World War I? *(ICSE 2020)*

Ans. Imperialism occurs when a strong nation takes over a weaker nation or region and dominates its economic, political and cultural life. In 19th century, aggressive and fierce economic competition gave rise to fear, confusion, insecurity and mutual hatred in Europe. This was followed by expansionist policies which led to rise of imperialism and further led to First World War.

5. Why was the League of Nations established ? *(ICSE 2019)*

Or Mention any two aims of the League of Nations. *(ICSE 2008)*

Ans. The League of Nations was established with the following objectives

- All the States of the world were prohibited from entering into any secret treaties and alliances.
- The member states were not supposed to maintain huge armies, warships and/or destructive armaments.

6. Give any two similarities between the ideologies of Nazism and Fascism. *(ICSE 2018)*

Or Mention two similarities between the ideologies of Fascism and Nazism. *(ICSE Specimen 2017)*

Or State any two similarities between Nazism and Fascism. *(ICSE 2007)*

Ans. Two similarities between the ideologies of Nazism and Fascism were as follows

(i) Both were anti-people and anti-democratic.

(ii) Both advocated aggressive nationalism and imperialism.

7. Explain briefly the causes of First World War with reference to nationalism and imperialism. ***(ICSE 2018)***

Ans. Causes of First World War with reference to nationalism and imperialism were

(i) Militant Nationalism was one of the major reasons of the First World War. It included building a huge army and appointing a powerful class of military and naval officers.

(ii) France and Britain built large colonial empires in Asia and Africa. Germany, Italy and Japan competed with other powers to establish their colonies.

(iii) Colonies added to the power and prestige of the European nations. This led to clash of interests among these countries.

8. Explain the immediate cause of the First World War. ***(ICSE Specimen 2017, 2017, 2013)***

Ans. The immediate cause of the First World War was the Sarajevo Crisis. In June 1914, Archduke Francis Ferdinand, the heir-apparent to the throne of Austria, went on an official visit to Sarajevo, the capital of Bosnia. There on 28th June, 1914, he and his wife were shot dead. The assassination was planned and carried out by a secret society of the extremist Serbian nationalists called the 'Black Hand'. After that many European countries declared war against each other and the First World War started.

9. What is the meaning of 'Fascism'? ***(ICSE 2015)***

Ans. The word 'Fascism' has been derived from the Italian word 'Fascio' which means 'a bundle of rods', symbolising strength. Fascism means 'autocracy' or 'dictatorship' in which the power of the state is vested in one man only and it is obligatory for all the others to obey his orders.

10. Name the two rival blocs formed in Europe before World War I. ***(ICSE 2015)***

Ans. The two rival blocs formed in Europe before World War I were

(i) Allied Powers Britain, France, Russia.

(ii) Imperialist Powers Germany, Austria and their allies.

11. Mention any two terms of the Treaty of Versailles signed on 28th June, 1919. ***(ICSE 2014)***

Ans. The main terms of the Treaty of Versailles were as follows

(i) The treaty declared Germany guilty of aggression.

(ii) The area of the Rhine valley was to be demilitarised and the German Territory West of Rhine was to be occupied by the Allied Troops for 15 years.

12. How much did Germany have to pay as war reparation charges according to the Treaty of Versailles? ***(ICSE 2010)***

Ans. 33 billion dollars had to be paid as war reparation charges by Germany according to the Treaty of Versailles.

13. Mention any two important consequences of the First World War. ***(ICSE 2009)***

Ans. The consequences of the First World War were as follows

(i) A number of people, those killed in the war, are estimated at about 9 million, that is about one-seventh of those who participated in it.

(ii) The expenditure on the Allied side was nearly 41000 million pounds and that on the German side over 15000 million pounds.

14. How did the Sarajevo Crisis in 1914 lead to the First World War? ***(ICSE 2006)***

Ans. Archduke Francis Ferdinand, the heir to the throne of Austria-Hungary was assassinated at Sarajevo, capital of Bosnia on 28th June, 1914. The assassination was organised by a secret society called 'Black Hand' or 'Union of Death' formed by extremist Serbian nationalists, whose aim was to unite all Serbians into a single Serbian State.

15. Name the countries that formed the Allied Powers. ***(ICSE 2006)***

Ans. Britain, France, United States of America (USA) and Russia formed the Allied Powers.

16. State two underlying Principles of Fascism. ***(ICSE 2005)***

Ans. Two Principles of Fascism were as follows

(i) Fascism was the antithesis of democracy. Fascists believed that democracy was not suitable for the country because it widens the gulf between the poor and the rich.

(ii) Fascists favoured equal control over all sections of society. They wanted to control capitalists, industrialists, labourers, landlords, peasants and artisans.

4 Marks Question

1. Mention any four terms of the Treaty of Versailles which affected Germany after World War I. ***(ICSE 2017)***

Ans. The main terms of the Treaty of Versailles were as follows

(i) The treaty declared Germany guilty of aggression.

(ii) Germany was required to pay for the losses and damages suffered by the Allies during the war. The amount of reparations was fixed at 33 billion dollars. Germany had to cede her merchant ships to the Allies as compensation. It had to supply huge quantities of coal to France, Italy and Belgium for 10 years.

(iii) The area of Rhine Valley was to be demilitarised and the German territory West of the Rhine was to be occupied by the Allied Troops for 15 years.

(iv) The newly created state of Poland got back all its territories lost in the war. To provide Poland with a port, Danzig was internationalised and kept as a free city under the protection of the League of Nations.

Additional Info

Some of the other restrictions on Germany due to Treaty of Versailles included

- The coal mines in the German Area called Saar were ceded to France.
- German army and navy were severely restricted.

10 Marks Questions

1. Look at the picture given below and answer the following questions. ***(ICSE Specimen 2023)***

(a) Identify and briefly explain the above incident.

(b) Mention any four conditions imposed on Germany in the Treaty of Versailles.

(c) Name the organisation established to maintain peace after the First World War. Mention any three of its objectives.

Ans. (a) The picture shows the murder of the Austrian Archduke Francis Ferdinand. The Austrian prince Archduke Francis Ferdinand was assassinated in the Sarajevo city capital of Bosnia on 28th June, 1914. The murderer was a Serbian from a terrorist outfit. Austria blamed Serbia and declared war on Serbia on 28th July, 1914. Serbia was supported by Russia.

(b) Four conditions that were imposed on Germany in the Treaty of Versailles are

(i) German power was severely restricted and monarchy ended.

(ii) The German Army was restricted to a force of 1,00,000 soldiers in a maximum seven infantry and three cavalry divisions.

(iii) Germany was required to pay for the loss and damages incurred by the Allies, which came to be around 33 billion dollars.

(iv) The manpower of German Navy was not to exceed 15000, including men for the fleet, coastal defences, signal stations, administration, other land services, etc.

(c) The League of Nations was established to maintain peace after the First World War in 1920.

Objectives of the League of Nations are as follows

(i) The major aim of the League of Nations was to settle disputes among the member states and to maintain peace and order.

(ii) The League of Nations was supposed to promote political, social, cultural and economic cooperation among the member states.

(iii) All the states were to respect each other's independence.

2. The First World War had a devastating effect on the world and caused unprecedented destruction. With reference to the First World War, answer the following questions. ***(ICSE Semester II 2022)***

(a) Name the signatory countries of the Triple Entente.

(b) What is meant by the term Imperialism?

(c) Explain the immediate cause of the First World War.

(d) What was the amount of war reparation that Germany had to pay the allies? Mention any two terms of the Treaty of Versailles which affected the German military.

Ans. (a) The signatory countries of the Triple Entente were Russia, Britain and France. During the First World War, Canada, Australia, Italy, Japan and the United States joined the Entente.

(b) Imperialism refer to state policy by which powerful nation establish its control over their nation by political social interest.

(c) For answer, refer to Q. 8 of 2/3 marks questions.

(d) The amount of war reparation that Germany had to pay the allies was 33 billion dollars.

The terms of Treaty of Versailles (1919) which affected the German Military were

(i) Germany lose all colonial empire.

(ii) Germany had to accept the war guilt and compelled to pay heavy sum.

(iii) The coal mines in the German area called Saar ceded to France.

3. *(ICSE 2016)*

(a) Identify the leader in the picture. Give two examples to state that the leader followed an expansionist policy.

(b) State three factors that led to the rise of Fascism.

(c) State four similarities between the ideologies of Nazism and Fascism.

Ans. (a) Benito Mussolini is depicted in the given picture. Two important examples to state that the leader followed an expansionist policy are as follows

(i) Mussolini used to say 'Italy must expand or perish'. He regained the Island of Rhodes, Dodecanese as well as the city of Fiume.

(ii) He turned Albania into a protectorate of Italy and captured Abyssinia in 1936.

(b) Three factors that led to the rise of Fascism are as follows

(i) **Discontent After the Treaty of Versailles** Italy was not satisfied with the Treaty of Versailles because it could not get any part of Germany or the Turkish empire.

(ii) **Failure of the League of Nations** The League of Nations was established to maintain peace in the world and to prevent wars. But it proved weak and failed to check the rise of dictatorship.

(iii) **Leadership Provided by Mussolini** Mussolini with his charismatic personality, won the confidence of his countrymen. His speeches praised the past glories of Italy.

Additional Info

Some other factors that led to therise of Fascism in Italy were

- Political Instability
- Class Conflict
- Threat to Socialism and Communalism
- Failure of League of Nations

(c) Four similarities between the ideologies of Nazism and Fascism are as follows

(i) Both believed in aggressive nationalism and imperialism.

(ii) Both favoured totalitarian rule.

(iii) Both believed in state supremacy, which could suppress Fundamental Rights and individual freedom.

(iv) Both upheld intensely nationalistic, anti-communist and anti-democratic rule.

4. With reference to the First World War, answer the following questions. *(ICSE 2011)*

(a) Explain any three causes of the First World War.

(b) Mention three points under the Treaties of Versailles, which affected Germany.

(c) What were the objectives of the League of Nations?

Ans. (a) The following were the causes of the First World War

(i) **Militant Nationalism** In the later half of the 19th century, Militant Nationalism emerged in Europe. It meant outright wars by the European countries to achieve their goals. Militant nationalism was caused by Aggressive Nationalism, Economic Competition and International Tension. The spirit of nationalism was a strong driving force in European politics of the 19th century. Thus, the whole atmosphere was charged with narrow militant nationalism and inter-state rivalries.

Causes of the First World War

- Militant Nationalism
- Race for Armament
- The Immediate Cause

(ii) **Race for Armaments** The mad race for armaments, which began soon after the Franco-Prussian war was one of the reasons, which led to the First World War. Every major power began stockpiling armaments in the name of self-defence and preservation of peace. As a result if one country increased its armaments, other countries were compelled to do the same. It filled the atmosphere with fear, apprehension and mutual hatred.

(iii) **The Immediate Cause** The Sarajevo incident was the immediate cause of the First World War. It is related to the assassination of the heir apparent to the throne of Austria, Archduke Francis Ferdinand and his wife on 28th June, 1914 in Sarajevo where they were shot dead.

(b) For answer, refer to Q. 1 of 4 marks question.

(c) For answer, refer to Q. 1 (c) of 10 marks questions.

5. There were several far reaching consequences as a result of the First World War. In this context, answer the following. ***(ICSE 2010)***

(a) Explain how the First World War brought about a change in the political scenario of the world?

(b) What did France gain from the Treaty of Versailles?

(c) How was the war responsible for the rise of Fascism and Nazism in Italy and Germany respectively?

Ans. (a) Three ruling dynasties namely the Romanov, Hohenzollern and Hapsburg were destroyed in this war. The rule of Ottomans came to an end. Austria, Hungary, Czechoslovakia and Yugoslavia became separate independent states. These political changes were the main scenario of the First World War.

(b) France gained the following from the Treaty of Versailles

(i) The coal mines in the German area called 'Saar' were given to France for 15 years and the area was to be governed by the League of Nations.

(ii) Some regions of South-East Africa like Togo and Cameroons were also given to France.

(iii) Alsace Lorraine captured from France in the Franco-Russian War (1871) was returned to France.

(c) **Rise of Fascism**

The word 'Fascism' has been derived from the Italian word 'Fascio' which means 'union' or 'league'. Fascism means Autocracy or Dictatorship where the power of the state is vested in one man only and it is obligatory for all the others to obey his orders. Fascism emerged as a movement in the post First World War period not only to meet the challenges of the International Communist Movement, but also to tackle the various problems that Italy confronted.

Economic crisis in Germany and Italy, like heavy losses, unemployment, shortage of foodgrains at the end of war etc., came to the fore. Industrialisation had not progressed and unemployment was on the rise. Even the employed working class felt the pinnacle of inflation with low wages and poor working conditions and there were frequent strikes and agrarian riots.

Rise of Nazism

The factors which contributed to the growth of Nazism were as follows

(i) Defeat in the First World War and the conditions imposed by the Treaty of Versailles made the German feel humiliated and helpless. Many territories of Germany were now shared by the European powers.

(ii) The German economy was ruined by the First World War. The heavy burden of war penalties had made the recovery of Germany more difficult. Germany had to borrow heavily from other countries. Inflation and unemployment went hand in hand. Thus, between 1924 and 1933, the Nazi party ranks were swelling with German youth.

(iii) The Nazi party rose due to the absence of a strong opposition party. The agenda and the principle of Nazi party was propagated by the members of the volunteer corps.

(iv) Hitler was known for moulding public opinion and was a gifted orator, who captivated the Germans by his emotional speeches.

6. The World witnessed a 'Great War' in the years between 1914-1918. In this context ***(ICSE 2007)***

(a) Discuss any three reasons which led to the war in 1914.

(b) Mention three clauses of the Treaty of Versailles.

(c) Explain how the Treaty of Versailles was responsible for the outbreak of the Second World War.

Ans. (a) Reasons for the war in 1914 were as follows

(i) Militant nationalism which aggravated the mechanism of keeping armies and navies and also the estab3lishment of a class of military and naval officers.

(ii) Division of Europe into two hostile powers was equally responsible for the war.

(iii) There was a mad race for armaments in the name of self-defence and preservation of place.

(b) Three clauses of the Treaty of Versailles were as follows

(i) Germany was to pay 33 billion dollars as a fine, to the Allies.

(ii) Its coal mines were ceded to France for 15 years.

(iii) The Germany army and navy were dramatically reduced.

(c) Peace settlement at Paris was made in a spirit of revenge. As a result of the discussions at the Paris conference on 28th June, 1919 the Treaty of Versailles was signed. The German felt that too much injustice had been done them.

The victorious powers had deprived Germany of huge tracts of its territories. Germany was burdened with an immense war indemnity. It was impossible for a German race to forget the consequences of the war, which they had lost so humiliatingly. This fuelled the rise of Nazism in Germany and to enter upon a career of aggression, and ultimately to the Second World War.

7. With reference to the First World War, answer the following questions. ***(ICSE 2005)***

(a) Enumerate any three causes of the First World War.

(b) What were the objectives of the League of Nations?

(c) Mention three points under the Treaty of Versailles which affected Germany.

Ans. (a) For answer, refer to Q. 4 (a) of 10 marks questions.

(b) For answer, refer to Q. 1 (c) of 10 marks questions.

(c) For answer, refer to Q. 1 of 4 marks question.

CHAPTER TEST

01 Mark Questions (MCQ)

1 Which of the following countries did not take part in the First World War?
(a) Portugal (b) Germany
(c) France (d) England

2 The Treaty of Versailles was signed between the Allies and Germany on .... at the Paris Conference.
(a) 28th July, 1919
(b) 28th June, 1918
(c) 28th March, 1917
(d) 28th June, 1919

3 Complete the given analogy.
Allied Power : France :: Imperialist Power : ?
(a) Britain (b) Russia
(c) Germany (d) United States

4 Which one of the following is the immediate causes of the First World War?
(a) Militant Nationalism
(b) Assassination of Archduke Francis Ferdinand
(c) Imperialism
(d) Secret Alliance

5 Which of the following is/are the main objectives of Nazi movement?
(a) To use force and brutality
(b) To exalt nationalism
(c) Both (a) and (b)
(d) Press was censored

Answers

1. (a) | 2. (d) | 3. (c) | 4. (b) | 5. (c)

02 Marks Questions

6 Mention any two consequence of Nazism in Germany.

7 Name any two objectives of the League of Nations.

8 State any two similarities between Fascism and Nazism.

9 What was meant by the term 'Militant Nationalism' as a cause for First World War ?

10 Marks Question

10 In the post First World War scenario, Italy and Germany experienced the rise of dictatorships. With reference to the First World War, answer the following questions.
(a) Mention any three circumstances that led to the rise of Fascism in Italy.
(b) How did class conflicts lead to the rise of dictatorship that emerged in Italy and Germany after the First World War?
Or How did the decline of democracy help in the rise of dictatorship in Italy and Germany.
(c) Mention any three domestic policies of Hitler.

08

The Second World War

TREND ANALYSIS 3 YEARS

Average No. of Questions Across all Sets

Topic	Types of Questions	2023	2020	2019
TOPIC 01 Second World War	1 Mark	1	–	–
	2/3 Marks	–	3	2
	4 Marks	–	–	–
	10 Marks	1	–	1
TOPIC 02 Cold War	1 Mark	–	–	–
	2/3 Marks	–	–	–
	4 Marks	–	–	–
	10 Marks	–	–	–

The First World War and its harsh peace treaties sowed the seeds for the Second World War. The similarity in its causes and characteristics with those of the First World War were superficial.

Causes of the Second World War

Though the German invasion of Poland was the immediate cause for the outbreak of the war, the real causes were much deeper and varied in character. These were as follows:

Dissatisfaction with the Treaty of Versailles

- The treaty by which the First World War came to an end, created more problems than it had solved. Germany had to cede many of its territories and many new nations were created. The treaty was based on the spirit of revenge and was forced on Germany.
- German colonies were forcibly taken away and divided among the victors. Germany, so that Poland could reap benefits, was divided into two parts. Germany was burdened with huge war indemnities, her military power also got reduced.
- This humiliation gave rise to the spirit of revenge and Germany started looking for an opportunity to do away with the harsh treaty. Hence, the war became inevitable.

Rise of Fascism and Nazism

- The rise of extreme nationalism in Italy and Germany in the form of Fascism and Nazism, respectively contributed to the causes which led to the Second World War.
- Italy wanted to revive the glory of the old Roman Empire and joined **Anti-Comintern Pact in 1937** and formed a 10 years alliance with Germany in 1939.

- Mussolini established Dictatorship in Italy and demonstrated nation's imperialistic designs by attacking Abyssinia. Hitler wanted to re-establish the prestige of Germany. He flouted the military causes of the Treaty of Versailles and declared re-armament in 1936 and started regaining its lost territories on all frontiers.
- In 1938, Hitler annexed **Austria** and dismembered **Czechoslovakia**. Thus, both the leaders through their acts, furthered the war.

Japanese Invasion of China

- Japan's ambitions rose after the First World War and she was determined to dominate the far East. In 1931, Japan invaded Manchuria and occupied it, despite the League's opposition. Japan also started an undeclared war against China in the same year.
- Japan joined the Berlin-Rome axis to form the **Berlin-Rome-Tokyo axis** to further its policy of expansion and conquest. In 1933, Japan left the League of Nations and started occupying the British and American properties in China.
- Britain and France felt that this appeasement policy could be used to weaken China and thus, started following the same. Thus, a war was inevitable under these circumstances.

Failure of the League of Nations

- The League of Nations was created to prevent future wars. However, the USA did not join the League, which proved to be a blow to the League. Even those, who joined the League were not interested in the principle of collective security.
- The League succeeded in allaying the threat of war in cases, where the parties involved were small nations, but did nothing when Poland, with the backing of France seized a part of Lithuania in 1920.
- In 1923, Italy refused to submit to the League's intervention and settled the dispute with Greece by direct mediation of Great Britain and France. Thereafter in every crisis, the League was either defied or ignored.
- League's authority was flouted by Japan, when it seized Manchuria in 1931 and by Italy, when it conquered Ethopia in 1936.
- Countries of Europe lost faith in League's usefulness as it failed to maintain International peace. Therefore, they themselves entered into mutual political and military alliances.

Hitler's Invasion of Poland

- Germany lost its port city of Danzing, which was given to Poland as a part of the Treaty of Versailles. The city was mainly inhabited by Germans. Poland was accused of committing atrocities against Germans living there.
- On 1st September, 1939, the German armies marched into Poland. France and Britain gave an ultimatum to Germany. In reply, Germany attacked France. On 3rd September, Britain and France declared war against Germany. Thus, the invasion of Poland marked the beginning of the Second World War.

Chronology of Major Events

Year	Event
1939	• 1st September- German armies marched into Poland. • 3rd September- Britain and France declared war on Germany. • Soon after, USSR attacked Eastern Poland.
1940	• Latvia, Estonia and Lithuania became republics of the USSR. • April-Germany completed its conquest of Norway and Denmark. • May-Germany completed the conquest of Belgium and Holland. • June-France fell into German hands. • August-German Air Force began bombing on Britain.
1941	• June-Hitler invaded Soviet Union. • 8th December-America joined the war.
1942	• August-Hitler targeted Stalingrad. • November-Soviet counter-attacked, Germans surrendered.
1945	• April-Allied Powers attacked Germany from both the sides. • 7th May-Hitler committed suicide. • 8th May-Day of celebration of Victory in Europe. • 2nd September-Japan surrendered unconditionally.

Spread of the War

Germany, Italy and Japan formed an alliance and were called the **Axis Powers**. Their opponents, led by Britain, France and the USA became the **Allied Powers**.

The World War engulfed each country of Europe one after another. Only Sweden, Switzerland, Spain, Portugal and Turkey remained neutral until the last.

Consequences of the Second World War

Defeat of Axis Powers

- Upto the middle of 1942, Axis Powers met with remarkable success and captured large territories in Europe, Africa and Asia. However, in November 1942, Allied Forces recaptured African territories lost by France. This was followed by their victory over Italy. Italy made an unconditional surrender and signed an armistice.
- In March 1945, the Allied forces moved across the Rhine and dealt a death-blow to the German forces. Hitler was so disappointed that he committed suicide on 30th April, 1945.
- The Allied Forces, after Germany's defeat, turned their attention towards Japan. Japan had occupied Hong Kong, Philippines, Singapore, Myanmar, parts of new Guinea and Indonesia.
- After bombings on Hiroshima and Nagasaki, Japan offered to surrender on the terms of **Potsdam declaration** on 10th August and the war came to an end. After the war, the Axis Powers had to face the following consequences
  - (i) Germany was divided into zones under the army of each of the Allied Powers.
  - (ii) The Federal Republic of Germany (West Germany) was administered by UK, France and the USA.
  - (iii) German Democratic Republic (East Germany) was administered by the Soviet Union.
  - (iv) Japan and Italy also became very weak. American army was to occupy Japan until 1952. All lands acquired by Japan, since 1895, were taken away.

Formation of the UN

The failure of the League and the horrors of the World Wars led to a meeting of the Big Three- Roosevelt, Churchill and Stalin at Yalta in February 1945. They resolved to convene a conference of the representatives of all the nations at San Francisco to draw up the Charter of the UN. This led to establishment of the **United Nations Organisation** on **24th October, 1945**.

Cold War

- Though, the USA and the Soviet Union fought together in co-operation during the World War, the apparent harmony between the two declined and old suspicion and ideological differences came to the forefront.
- Both the countries did not engage in actual fights, but there was a state of extreme political tension between the two. This state of tension is known as the **Cold War**, an atmosphere with no armed struggle, but the prevalence of a cold hostility. All these results divided the world into two blocs.

The Democratic and Capitalist Bloc

It is led by the USA. This bloc believed in Liberal Democracy based on Capitalism. America tried to maintain her influence by giving economic aid to different countries.

The Communist Bloc

It is led by the USSR, and was also called the Eastern Bloc or the Soviet Bloc. It believed in Communism based on Marxist theory. This bloc considered the Western style Democracy as a force, meant only for the rich and upper middle class. Thus, the whole Europe got divided into two power blocs. These two blocs openly propagated against each other, each from its own view points.

PYQs Previous Years' Questions

1 Mark Questions

1. Hitler attacked Poland because he wanted to .... *(ICSE Specimen 2023)*

(a) seize the coal mines (b) militarise the Rhine valley
(c) regain the Danzing port (d) control the trade

Ans. (*c*) regain the Danzing port

2. The signatory countries of the Triple Alliance were .... *(ICSE Semester-II 2022)*

(a) Germany, France, Italy
(b) France, Britain, Russia
(c) Germany, Italy, Austria Hungary
(d) Britain, Russia, Italy

Ans. (*c*) Germany, Italy, Austria Hungary

3. The Treaty of Versailles mandated Germany to pay a war reparation of .... *(ICSE Specimen Semester II 2022)*

(a) 35 billion dollars (b) 40 billion dollars
(c) 33 billion dollars (d) 50 million pounds

Ans. (*c*) 33 billion dollars

4. Which of these countries was not part of the Berlin-Rome-Tokyo Axis? *(ICSE Specimen Semester II 2022)*

(a) Germany (b) Italy
(c) Japan (d) France

Ans. (*d*) France

2/3 Marks Questions

1. Mention any three ways in which the Treaty of Versailles benefitted France. *(ICSE Specimen Semester II 2022)*

Ans. Three ways through which the Treaty of Versailles benefitted France are

(i) Through the Treaty of Versailles got France more colonies as all the German colonies were taken and given to Britain and France.

(ii) As per the demand made by France, the Rhineland, the area between France and Germany was demilitarised. The Germany army could no longer get into this territory.

(iii) On the security ground also, France was at the gaining end to some extent. As per the treaty, German could only have 1,00,000 men in the army and six battleships. No submarines and air force was allowed too.

2. Give any two reasons for the rise of Fascism. *(ICSE2020)*

Ans. The reasons for the rise of Fascism were

(i) Italy joined the Allies in the First World War to gain territories of Turkey and Germany. But, the Treaty of Versailles failed to give its Southern Tyrol, Trentino, coastal areas of Dalmatia and Albania.

(ii) First World War made Italy weak in economic field. The war ruined the life of common people, trade, business, etc.

3. Explain briefly three reasons for the dissatisfaction with the Treaty of Versailles. *(ICSE 2020)*

Ans. The reasons for the dissatisfaction with the Treaty of Versailles were

(i) Germany had been forced to sign this treaty and had to pay heavy war compensation.

(ii) Italy was not favoured by Allies for the compensation of war. So, the Italians felt that they had won the war but lost the peace.

(iii) The Treaty of Versailles was a dictated and imposed treaty by the victorious countries on the defeated countries.

4. State any three consequences of the Second World War. *(ICSE 2020)*

Ans. The consequences of the Second World War were as follows

(i) Germany was divided into zones under the army of each of the Allied Powers.

(ii) The Federal Republic of Germany (West Germany) was administered by UK, France and the USA.

(iii) German Democratic Republic (East Germany) was administered by the Soviet Union.

5. State any two objections imposed by the Treaty of Versailles on the German military power. *(ICSE 2019)*

Ans. The two objections imposed by the Treaty of Versailles on the German military power were

(i) German colonies were forcibly taken away and divided among the victors.

(ii) Germany was burdened with huge war indemnities, her military power also got reduced.

6. Name the signatory countries of the Triple Alliance. ***(ICSE 2019)***

Ans. The signatory countries of Triple Alliance are Germany, Austria-Hungary and Italy. The three countries promised to assist each other if any of them should be attacked.

7. What is understood by the 'Policy of Appeasement' followed by Britain and France towards Germany? ***(ICSE Specimen 2018)***

Ans. It is a diplomatic policy of making political or material concessions to an enemy power in order to avoid conflict. Britain and France tried to make Germany and Hitler happy with this policy. They hoped that by meeting his demand, he would be satisfied and there would not be any war.

8. Name the countries that formed the Axis Bloc, during World War II. ***(ICSE 2018)***

Ans. Germany, Italy and Japan formed the Axis Bloc during World War II.

9. Give the reason as to why Japan invaded China? ***(ICSE 2017)***

Ans. Japan's ambitions rose after the First World War and it was determined to dominate the far East. In 1931, Japan invaded Manchuria and occupied it. In the same year, it started an undeclared war against China.

10. Explain the consequences of the Second World War with reference to the Cold War. ***(ICSE 2017)***

Ans. The consequences of the Second World War with reference to the Cold War were

(i) Though the USA and the Soviet Union fought together in co-operation during the World War, the apparent harmony between the two declined and old suspicion and ideological differences came to the forefront afterwards.

(ii) Both the countries did not engage in actual fights, but there was a state of extreme political tension between the two. This state of tension is known as the Cold War, an atmosphere with no armed struggle, but the prevalence of a cold hostility. This divided the world into two power blocs.

11. What made Japan surrender to the Allies in August, 1945? ***(ICSE 2016)***

Ans. Japan made surrender to the Allies in August, 1945 due to following reasons

(i) On 6th and 9th August, the United States dropped atomic bombs on Hiroshima and Nagasaki, Japan.

(ii) On 9th August, the Soviet Union declared war on Japan. Thus, Japan on 15th August, 1945 offered to surrender to the Allies on the terms of Potsdam declaration and the war came to an end.

12. Explain how the ideologies of Fascism and Nazism led to the Second World War. ***(ICSE 2014)***

Ans. **Fascism** Italy did not gain much from the Treaty of Versailles and wanted to revive the glory of the old Roman Empire. Italy demonstrated her imperialistic ambitions by attacking Abyssinia and also joined the Anti-Comintern Pact in 1937. The League of Nations also couldn't take any action against Italy.

Nazism Hitler wanted to re-establish the prestige of Germany to avenge the humiliation it faced after the Treaty of Versailles. He flouted many clauses of the treaty and declared re-armament. Germany showed its imperialistic ambitions by annexing Austria.

Thus, Fascism and Nazism drove the countries of the world towards another World War.

13. How did the Japanese invasion on China create conditions for the outbreak of the war? ***(ICSE 2014)***

Ans. Japan's ambition to control far East was another cause of the war. It intervened in Manchuria in 1931 and in spite of the League's opposition, occupied it. That marked the beginning of undeclared war on China by Japan.

Japan joined Berlin-Rome axis to form the Berlin-Rome-Tokyo axis to further its policy of expansion. In 1933, it left the League and started occupying the British and American properties in China. Britain and France felt that this appeasement policy could be used to weaken China and thus, started following the same. Thus, a war was inevitable under such circumstances.

14. State how each of the following factors were the causes of the Second World War. ***(ICSE 2011)***

(i) The failure of the League of Nations.

(ii) The Aggressive Nationalism of Germany.

Ans. (i) The League was created after the First World War to prevent future wars. However, the League only succeeded in cases, where the parties were small nations. In 1923, there was a threat of war between Italy and Greece. Italy refused to submit to the League's intervention. Thereafter, the League was either defied or ignored.

Moreover, the member nations were more concerned about their own interests.

Besides, the League also failed to maintain international peace and the countries lost faith in its usefulness. Thereafter, they themselves entered into mutual alliances.

(ii) Germany, under the Nazi Government of Hitler wanted to revive its past glory and also to avenge the humiliating Treaty of Versailles. Hitler declared re-armament in 1936 and started regaining its lost territories on all frontiers.

He annexed Austria, occupied Rhineland and dismembered Czechoslovakia. He also set his eyes on Danzing and Poland. This aggressive policy of Germany was the main cause of the Second World War. When it attacked Poland to stop Germany, Britain and France declared a war on Germany.

15. With the surrender of Japan, the Second World War was finally over. The war had far reaching consequences, against this background, write short notes on ***(ICSE 2005)***

(i) Effect of Second World War on Japan.

(ii) The division of Germany.

Ans. (i) After Second World War, Japan became very weak and was decided to be governed by conquering forces. It was to be occupied by America till 1952. After that Japan was to resume managing their own affairs. The Emperor Hirhito was left on the throne, though some of its power was retained by the Japanese Parliament. Japan was reduced to the pre-1895 territorial extent and the lands acquired after that were taken away from her.

(ii) The last German armies surrendered on 7th May, 1945 and the next day was celebrated as the day of celebration of victory. The victors divided Germany into two zones each under the army of allied nations. These zones were

Federal Republic of Germany (FRG), commonly known as the West Germany, was administered by United Kingdom, France and the USA with Bonn as the capital.

German Democratic Republic (GDR), known as East Germany, was administered by the Soviet Union with East Berlin as the capital.

4 Marks Questions

1. State any four causes that led to the Second World War. ***(ICSE 2018)***

Ans. Four causes that led to the Second World War were

(i) There was dissatisfaction in Italy and Germany with the terms of the Treaty of Versailles.

(ii) The rise of Fascism in Italy and Nazism in Germany caused them to wage war on their neighbours as both opposed democracy and believed in a totalitarian state.

(iii) The Policy of Appeasement by Britain and France towards Germany and Italy made them more belligerent.

(iv) The League of Nations failed to fulfill its purpose.

2. Explain the consequences of the Second World War with reference to the formation of the United Nations. ***(ICSE 2014)***

Ans. The destruction caused by the war, both to the human life and property, surpassed all the other wars. The failure of League of Nations to stop the Second World War forced the Big Three *i.e.*, Roosevelt (USA President), Churchill (British Prime Minister) and Stalin (Premier of USSR) to meet.

In their meeting at Yalta in February 1945, they resolved to convene a meeting to draw up a Charter of the United Nations. Efforts thereafter, finally resulted into establishment of the United Nations on 24th October, 1945.

3. Write short note on division of the world in two Power Blocs. ***(ICSE 2005)***

Ans. Towards the end of the Second World War, the apparent harmony between the USA and the Soviet Union declined and old suspicion and ideological differences came to the forefront. Both the countries did not resort to overt clashes, but treated each other with hostility. This led to the division of world into two power blocs which were

(i) Capitalist Bloc led by the USA, which believed in Liberal Democracy based on Capitalism.

(ii) Communist Bloc led by the USSR, which believed in Communism based on Marxist theory. Both the Blocs openly propogated against each other and left no opportunity to weaken their opponent. But at the same time, both made efforts to prevent another war

10 Marks Questions

1. The world war marked a turning point in the history of the world. With reference to this period, answer the following questions. ***(ICSE 2023)***

(a) Mention any three similarities between the ideologies of Fascism and Nazism.

(b) State the three consequences of the Second World War.

(c) Mention any four causes of the Second World War.

Ans. (a) Three similarities between the ideologies of Nazism and Fascism were as follows

(i) Both were anti-people and anti-democratic.

(ii) Both advocated aggressive nationalism and imperialism.

(iii) Both had a view that state is supreme and it could suppress all the fundamental rights and freedoms of individuals.

(b) For answer, refer to Q. 4 of 2/3 marks questions.

(c) For answer, refer to Q. 1 of 4 marks questions.

2. Look at the picture given and answer the questions that follow. ***(ICSE Semester II 2022)***

(a) Identify the leader in the picture. What was the name given to the form of dictatorship practiced by him?

(b) State any two similar ideologies of the dictators.

(c) What was the immediate cause of the Second World War? Mention any two reasons for it.

(d) Explain how the Japanese invasion of China became a cause for the Second World War.

Ans. (a) The given picture belongs to Adolf Hitler, the Chancellor of Germany. The form of dictatorship practiced by Adolf Hitler was 'Nazism'.

(b) The two similar ideologies of the dictators are

(i) Anti-people and anti-democratic.

(ii) Advocated aggressive nationalism and imperialism.

(c) The invasion of Poland by Germany (1st September, 1939) became the immediate cause of the Second World War.

Two reasons for the immediate cause of the Second World War are

(i) German dissatisfaction with Treaty of Versailles and Poland.

(ii) Conquered the port of danzing.

(d) For answer, refer to Q. 13 of 2/3 marks questions.

3. With reference to the Rise of Dictatorships and the Second World War, answer the following. ***(ICSE 2019)***

(a) State any three reasons for the rise of Fascism in Italy.

(b) Explain any three consequences of World War II.

(c) Name the two rival blocs that fought against each other during World War II and state its signatory countries.

Ans. (a) Three reasons for the rise of Fascism in Italy were

(i) Italy wanted to revive the glory of the old Roman Empire.

(ii) It joined Anti-Comintern Pact in 1937 and formed a 10 years alliance with Germany in 1939.

(iii) Mussolini established dictatorship in Italy and demonstrated the nation's imperialistic designs by attacking Abyssinia.

(b) For answer, refer to Q. 4 of 2/3 marks questions.

(c) Germany, Italy and Japan formed an alliance and were called the Axis Powers. Their opponents, led by Britain, France and the USA became the Allied Powers.

The World War engulfed almost all the countries of Europe one after the another. Only Sweden, Switzerland, Spain, Portugal and Turkey remained neutral until the end.

4.

(ICSE Specimen 2018)

(a) Identify the above picture and with which war was it associated? Mention the year of the incident.

(b) Mention three causes that led to the war.

(c) State any two consequences of the war.

Ans. (a) The given picture is associated with the atomic bomb drop on 9th August, 1945 on Nagasaki, Japan.

(b) Three causes that led to the war were

(i) The Treaty of Versailles was a peace treaty, which was signed at the end of the First World War, but it lead to gross dissatisfaction among the countries especially, Germany and Italy.

(ii) Many nations follow aggressive nationalism and it became a race to win over foreign land in Europe. Germany waged war to grab areas which were lost from them during the First World War. Japan attacked Manchuria and many cities fell into the hands of the Japanese.

(iii) League of Nations was set-up to make peace over the world. It was decided by world leaders to make such organisation that can resolve all the international disputes. The League lacked universal representation. The permanent members opposed decision which were against their own interests. It has no military force to act against any wrong action. Germany and Italy started foreign aggression to regain the lost regions and the world followed it later.

(c) For answer, refer to Q. 4 of 2/3 marks questions.

5. With reference to the Second World War, explain the following ***(ICSE Specimen 2017)***

(a) Any two causes of the war.

(b) Impact of the Treaty of Versailles.

(c) The Cold War.

Ans. (a) For answer, refer to Q. 1 of 4 marks questions.

(b) The treaty had marked a humiliating defeat for Germany. It had stripped Germany of its territories, declaring her guilty of aggression. Germany was to pay the war indemnities, lost the area of the Rhine valley, Alsace Lorraine went to France, Danzing became a free port. Even her coal mines (Saar) were ceded to France. Her army got reduced significantly.

However, the most significant impact that the treaty had, was that it sowed the seeds of the Second World War. It angried, rather urged Germany and Italy to raise a war against its humiliating terms.

(c) The Cold War, between the USA and the Soviet Union, emerged as a result of the Second World War. Their harmony declined and old suspicion and ideological differences came to the forefront. Though, there was no fighting, there was a prevalence of a political tension.

Cold War refers to an atmosphere with no armed struggle, but where the rivals continue maintaining diplomatic relations, along with a hostility. It also involves an arms race i.e. piling up arms and weapons, etc.

CHAPTER TEST

01 Mark Questions

1 Which of the following options is/are the immediate cause of the Second World War?
(a) German dissatisfaction with Treaty of Versailles and Poland
(b) Japanese invasion of China
(c) Both (a) and (b)
(d) None of the above

2 Choose the correct option.

Capitalist Bloc led by	USA
Communist Bloc led by	?

(a) USSR (b) Britain (c) France (d) Canada

3 Identify the name of countries which became republics of the USSR in 1940.
(a) Latvia (b) Estonia
(c) Lithuania (d) All of these

4 Which among the following countries was the first Axis Power to surrender in Second World War?
(a) Japan (b) Italy
(c) Germany (d) Romania

5 Which of the following conferences adopted the United Nations charter on 26th January, 1945?
(a) London Conference (b) Yalta Conference
(c) Tokyo Conference (d) San Francisco Conference

Answers

1. (c) | 2. (a) | 3. (d) | 4. (b) | 5. (d)

02 Marks Questions

6 Mention any two important consequences of the Second World War.

7 What is meant by the Cold War? Mention any one characteristics of the Cold War.

8 State any two reasons why did America drop the atom bombs on the cities of Hiroshima and Nagasaki.

9 What happened to Germany after her defeat in the Second World War?

10 Marks Question

10 With reference to the cause of the Second World War, answer the following questions.
(i) State any four factors that led to the rise of Fascism and Nazism.
(ii) Mention any three factors that led to the failure of the League of Nations.
(iii) What are the cause of the Hitler's invasion of Poland. Discuss.

09

United Nations Organisation and Its Major Agencies

TREND ANALYSIS 3 YEARS

	Average No. of Questions Across all Sets			
	Types of Questions	2023	2020	2019
TOPIC 01 United Nations & its Organs	1 Mark	–	–	–
	2/3 Marks	–	1	1
	4 Marks	–	–	–
	10 Marks	2	–	1
TOPIC 02 Main Agencies of UN	1 Mark	–	–	–
	2/3 Marks	–	–	–
	4 Marks	–	–	–
	10 Marks	1	–	–

Destructive and horrifying experiences of the two World Wars made the world realise the necessity of a peace maintaining organisation more powerful than the previous ones *e.g.,* the League of Nations. The efforts finally took shape at **San Francisco** on 24th October, 1945 with the emergence of the **United Nations Organisation** (UNO).

Establishment of the UNO

- The two World Wars left a legacy of misery and depression in nearly every country. Millions of people lost their lives and many others became disabled, homeless and unemployed, apart from the millions of dollars that were spent during the war.
- The League of Nations was established with a promise of peace, but it had failed to prevent another war. All the countries feared, that another World War might lead to the end of the world as destructive weapons, like atom bombs, were now invented and already used.
- The world was divided in two Power Blocs, both having opposite ideologies. All the above mentioned events gave the world leaders a purpose to form a more powerful, transparent and impartial organisation, which would be able to resolve the differences between the countries/blocs amicably and save the mankind from any further destructions.

Origin of the UNO

- The leaders of the Allied powers comprising Great Britain, France, Soviet Union, United States and China realised the potential danger of wars on humanity, during the war period. Thus, there were talks about setting up a World Organisation.

- The formation of the UN had a huge history behind it, with many such efforts being already taken in the past. American President Roosevelt pointed out four freedoms-those of **Worship, Speech, Freedom from Wars** and **Freedom from Fears** as the basis of Peace.
- **The London Declaration, 1941**, proposed by the representatives of New Zealand, Canada, Australia, South Africa and Britain, aimed at forming a World Organisation more powerful than the League of Nations.
- **The Atlantic Charter of August, 1941** required all signatories to accept peaceful settling of disputes, recognising equality and sovereignty of nations and also, the right of each nation to choose its own form of government and trying to preserve peace and security. This was signed by the British Prime Minister, Winston Churchill and the American President, Roosevelt.
- **Washington Declaration of 1942** also aimed for peace, declaring to accept the principles of the Atlantic charter. It were finally, after all these preceding conferences and declarations, the **Moscow declaration** (which laid the foundation of the UN), the Dumbarton Oaks Conference (1944) (where the Draft of the Charter was prepared) and the Yalta Conference in 1945 (where it was conceded that the membership would be open to all peace loving states) and also the San Francisco Conference, that finally lend the shape to the UN as it is today.
- The Organisation formally came into existence on **24th October, 1945**, when the Charter was ratified by 29 nations, including 5 permanent members of the Security Council.

Note 24th October, since 1945, has being celebrated every year as the United Nations Day. Disarmament, Decolonisation and Development are the three new objectives set by the UN.

Purposes/Objectives of the United Nations

Objectives of the United Nations are as follows

(i) To maintain International Peace and Security.

(ii) To develop friendly relations among nations, based on the respect for the principle of equal rights and self-determination of people.

(iii) To achieve International Co-operation in solving various International, Economic, Social, Cultural or Humanitarian problems.

(iv) To be a centre for harmonising the actions of nations in the attainment of goals.

Principles of the United Nations

Principles of the United Nations are as follows

(i) To respect the sovereign equality of all its members.

(ii) All members should fulfil, in good faith, the obligations assumed by them.

(iii) They should settle their international disputes by peaceful means.

(iv) They would refrain from threat or use of force against any state.

(v) They should give the United Nations every assistance in any action it takes.

(vi) The organisation should ensure, that states, which are not members of the United Nations, act in accordance with these principles.

(vii) The United Nations shall not intervene in the domestic, i.e., the internal affairs of any state.

Headquarters and the Flag of the United Nations

- All the organs of the United Nations are based in New York, USA, except the **International Court of Justice**, which is located at **the Hague** in **Netherlands**.
- The UN flag is light blue in colour and is portrayed in white. At its centre is the **UN Emblem**, a polar map of the world, embraced by twin olive branches. The flag was adopted on **20th October, 1947**.

Official Languages and Membership

Arabic, Chinese, English, French, Russian and Spanish are the official languages of the UNO. However, any documents are written only in the working languages-English and French.

50 members who took part in the San Francisco Conference, signed and approved the Charter and became the original members of the United Nations.

All peace-loving nations can be admitted to the UN. These countries are admitted by the General Assembly upon the recommendation of the Security Council by a 2/3rd majority of votes. It should be noted that India was one of those 50 members who took part in the conference and has been an active participator in all the peace-keeping endeavours of the UN.

Organs of the United Nations

The General Assembly

The work of the UN is determined by the will of the majority of the members as expressed in Resolutions adopted by the Assembly.

The General Assembly is the main deliberative organ of the UN. All the members of the UN are members of the General Assembly. Each state has 5 representatives in the General Assembly, but each state has only one vote.

Composition and Session

The regular session of the General Assembly begins each year on the 3rd Tuesday in September and continues usually until the 3rd week of December.

At the beginning of each regular session, the Assembly elects a new President, 21 Vice-Presidents and the Chairmen of the Assembly's six main committees.

The Presidency of the Assembly rotates each year among the **five groups of states** : Africa, Asia, Eastern Europe, Latin America and Caribbean and Western Europe and other states. This rotation of Presidency is done so as to ensure equitable geographical representation.

Powers and Functions of the General Assembly

The powers and functions of the General Assembly are as follows

(i) To consider and make recommendations on the principles of co-operation, in the maintenance of international peace and security.

(ii) To discuss any question relating to international peace and security and to make recommendations on it.

(iii) To make recommendations for the peaceful settlements of disputes.

(iv) To receive and consider reports from the Security Council and other organs of the UN.

(v) To consider and approve the budget of the UN and to apportion the contributions among members.

(vi) To elect the non-permanent members of the Security Council, the Economic and Social Council and the Trusteeship Council and to elect the judges of the International Court of Justice.

(vii) To appoint the Secretary-General on the recommendation of the Security Council.

(viii) To discuss and make recommendations on any issue affecting the powers and functions of any organ of the UN.

(ix) To make recommendations to promote International, Political, Social and Economic co-operation.

The Security Council

It is the executive body of the United Nations. It has the primary responsibility for the maintenance of International peace and security.

Composition

The Council consists of 15 members out of which 5 members China, France, Russia, Britain and the USA are permanent. The non-permanent members are elected from Afro-Asian countries (5 Members), Latin America (2 Members), West European and other countries (2 Members) and East European countries (1 Member).

Each member of the Security Council has one vote. The permanent members have the Veto power *i.e.,* a **negative vote**. However, abstinence for voting does not amount to a negative vote or a veto.

Note These non-permanent members are elected by the General Assembly by a 2/3*rd* majority for a term of 2 years.

Powers and Functions of the Security Council

The powers and functions of the Security Council are as follows

(i) To maintain International peace and security in accordance with the principles and purposes of the UN.

(ii) To investigate any dispute or situation and to take military action against an aggressor, and to recommend terms of settling disputes and any methods of adjusting against them.

(iii) Formulating plans to regulate armaments.

(iv) To call on members to apply economic sanctions and other measures other than force, to prevent or stop aggression.

(v) To recommend to the General Assembly for the appointment of the Secretary-General and to elect the Judges of the International Court of Justice together with the General Assembly.

(vi) To determine existence of any threats and to recommend actions for the same.

(vii) To recommend the admission of new members.

(viii) To exercise the trusteeship functions of the United Nations in strategic areas. One of the peace keeping forces of the UN is working in Afghanistan as **UN Assistance Mission in Afghanistan** (UNAMA), which is deeply concerned about the rising number of civilian deaths and injuries.

The International Court of Justice

It is the principal judicial organ of the UN. Its headquarter is at the **Hague** (Netherlands). The Court has a dual role to settle in accordance with International law, to settle the legal disputes submitted to it by the states, to give advisory opinions on legal questions referred to it, to modify International laws etc.

Composition and Qualification

- The Court composes of 15 judges elected for a term of 9 years by the UN General Assembly and Security Council sitting independently. Elections are held every 3 years for 1/3rd of the seats.
- A retiring judge may be re-elected.
- The judges must possess the qualifications required in their respective countries for appointment to the highest judicial offices.

Powers and Functions of the International Court of Justice

- Only the Member States may apply to and appear before the Court. The Court decides cases in accordance with International treaties and conventions in force, and is competent to entertain a dispute if the parties so involved agree for it.
- The advisory procedure of the Court is open only to its 5 organs and 16 other authorised agencies of the UN family. The Court plays a significant role in the codification of International laws. The Court may recommend appropriate procedures/methods of settlement during or at the end of the case.

The Economic and Social Council (ECOSOC)

It is responsible for promoting higher standards of living, full employment and economic and social progress. It has 54 members elected for 3 years by the General Assembly. The Council deals with initiating research and reports on economic, health, social, educational and even cultural matters.

The Trusteeship Council

It is in charge of all the territories administered by the League of Nations under the mandate system before the Second World War.

The Secretariat

It is the **Chief Administrative Office** of the UN. It consists of the Secretary General and other staff appointed by him. Its main function is to co-ordinate and supervise the activities of the UN organs. It organises seminars and co-ordinates the work of the organs and agencies.

Major Agencies of the UN

There are **18 specialised agencies** and **14 major programmes** to achieve economic and social progress.

1. United Nations Children's Fund (UNICEF)

- UNICEF stands for United Nations International Children's Emergency Fund. Later on, its name was changed to United Nations Children's Fund, but its acronym continued.
- It was created by the General Assembly, during its first session, to provide long range benefits to the children of all developing countries. It is governed by a 36-member executive board. Its headquarter is in **New York**.
- The agency depends on voluntary contributions made by different governments, by private agencies, through sale of greeting cards and *via* other fund raising campaigns, to finance its projects.
- UNICEF was also awarded the **Nobel Prize for Peace** (1965) and the **Indira Gandhi Prize for Peace** (1989).

Functions of UNICEF

The functions of UNICEF are as follows

(i) It works for the protection of children in respect of their survival, health and well being. It also supports child-immunisation programmes.

(ii) It provides funds for training the personnel, including health and sanitation workers, teachers and nutritionists, etc.

(iii) It provides technical supplies, equipments and other aids to villages.

(iv) It assists governments to plan, develop and extend community services.

(v) It provides help to children and mothers in case of emergencies.

(vi) It makes efforts to prevent diseases like TB, Malaria, eye diseases, skin diseases, etc.

2. World Health Organisation (WHO)

It is the specialised agency for health established on 7th April, 1948 with the objective of achieving the highest possible level of health for all. Its headquarter is at **Geneva** in **Switzerland**. Its main aim is to help the government raise the standards of public health and medical research.

Functions of WHO

The functions of WHO are as follows

(i) It helps countries to improve their health system by building up infrastructure.

(ii) It gives important drugs needed for medical care. It launches programmes to immunise children against 6 major diseases-Measles, Diphtheria, Tetanus, Tuberculosis, Polio and Whooping cough.

(iii) It promotes research to cure and prevent diseases.

(iv) It works towards providing safe drinking water and adequate waste disposal.

(v) It organises conferences, seminars and training activities for health care personnel.

(vi) It aims at fighting diseases and preventing them from spreading.

(vii) It publishes health journals to create health consciousness among people.

Achievements of WHO

Some of the achievements of WHO in the field of health are as follows

(i) 80% of immunisation coverage has been achieved.

(ii) Significant reduction in Diarrhoeal deaths.

(iii) Rare occurrences of Cholera and Plague.

(iv) Eradication of Smallpox.

(v) Management of Leprosy etc.

3. United Nations Educational, Scientific and Cultural Organisation (UNESCO)

It was established on 4th November 1946, with the main objective to contribute to peace and security in the world, by promoting collaboration among nations through education, science, culture and communication. Its headquarters is at Paris.

Functions of UNESCO

The main functions of UNESCO are as follows

(i) Removal of illiteracy by encouraging adult education, distance education and open school education.

(ii) Financial assistance for the education of disabled children. It also lays special emphasis on the education of women and girls.

(iii) Encouragement of scientific education by providing regional training centres.

(iv) Advices about the production of textbooks, syllabus and teacher-training.

(v) Helps to set-up library systems and also gives fellowships.

Scientific Activities

Scientific activities undertaken by UNESCO are as follows

(i) It promotes research in fields like Geology, Mathematics, Physics and Oceanography.

(ii) It helps in correcting the imbalances in scientific and technological manpower, so existing.

(iii) It encourages the study of Social Sciences in order to focus attention on combating all forms of discrimination, improving the status of women and helping the youth in solving their problems.

(iv) It also organises conferences to bring scientists together.

(v) It circulates information through journals. **Courier** is the official monthly magazine of UNESCO.

Communication

It assists developing countries to develop communication and has set-up regional networks for the same. It upholds the freedom of the press and independence of the Media. It disseminates information about Human Rights and also sets up projects on mass communication.

Preservation of Cultural Heritage

Following are the measures taken by UNESCO to preserve the Cultural Heritage

(i) It provides technical advice and assistance, equipments and funds for the preservation of monuments and other works of art.

(ii) It aims to protect the world inheritance of books, works of arts and rare manuscripts.

(iii) It gives encouragement to artistic creations in Literature and Fine Arts.

PYQs Previous Years' Questions

1 Mark Questions

Multiple Choice Questions

1. The International Court of Justice consists of .... judges. **(ICSE 2023, ICSE Specimen Semester II 2022)**

(a) 9 (b) 15

(c) 10 (d) 20

Ans. (b) 15

2. The non-permanent members of the Security Council are elected by the members of .... **(ICSE Specimen Semester II 2022)**

(a) General Assembly

(b) International Court of Justice

(c) the Trusteeship Council

(d) the Secretariat

Ans. (a) General Assembly

3. Which of the following countries is not a permanent member of the Security Council? **(ICSE Semester II 2022)**

(a) France (b) China

(c) Germany (d) Britain

Ans. (c) Germany

4. The full form of UNESCO is **(ICSE Semester II 2022)**

(a) United National Education, Scientific and Cultural Organisation

(b) United Nations Economic, Scientific and Cultural Organisaton

(c) United Nations Educational, Social and Cultural Organisation

(d) United Nations Educational, Scientific and Commercial Organisation

Ans. (a) United National Education, Scientific and Cultural Organisation

5. The Security Council consists of ...... non-permanent members. **(ICSE Semester II 2022)**

(a) fifteen (b) ten (c) five (d) six

Ans. (b) ten

Very Short Answer Questions

1. State the most important reason for the formation of the UNO. **(ICSE 2004)**

Ans. The main reason for the formation of the UNO is to maintain world peace and to secure the world from another war.

2. Where is the permanent headquarter of the International Court of Justice located? **(ICSE 2004, 2001)**

Ans. The headquarter of the International Court of Justice is located at the Hague in Netherlands.

3. State one way in which the UNICEF raises funds. **(ICSE 2004)**

Ans. UNICEF raises funds from selling greeting cards and through various fund raising campaigns.

4. What is meant by the term 'Veto Power' which is enjoyed by the permanent members of the UN? **(ICSE 2003)**

Ans. It is a negative vote with reference to any matter. No matter can be referred or passed, if any member uses the veto power.

5. When did the United Nations officially come into existence? **(ICSE 2002)**

Ans. On 24th October, 1945, the United Nations formally came into existence.

6. Give one of the functions of the General Assembly of the United Nations. **(ICSE 2001)**

Ans. The General Assembly elects the judges of the International Court of Justice along with the Security Council.

7. WHO is a specialised UN agency devoted to a specific cause. What is this cause? **(ICSE 2000)**

Ans. World Health Organisation is an agency working towards achieving the highest level of health for all the people.

8. Name the principal judicial organ of the UN. **(ICSE 2000)**

Ans. International Court of Justice is the principal judicial organ of the UN.

2/3 Marks Questions

1. Give the full form of UNICEF and UNESCO. **(ICSE Specimen Semester II 2022)**

Or State the full forms of the following agencies of the United Nations. UNICEF and UNESCO.

Ans. UNICEF stands for United Nations Children's Fund while UNESCO stands for United Nations Educational, Scientific and Cultural Organisation.

2. Mention any two functions of WHO. *(ICSE Specimen Semester II 2022)*

Ans. Two functions of the World Health Organisation (WHO) are

(i) It helps countries to improve their health system by building up infrastructure.

(ii) It organises conferences, seminars and training activities for health care personnel.

3. Name the two International Organisations that were formed, one as a consequence of World War I and the other after World War II. *(ICSE 2020)*

Ans. The International Organisations formed as a consequence of First World War was League of Nations and as a consequence of Second World War was United Nations.

4. What is meant by the term Veto power? *(ICSE 2019)*

Or What is meant by the term 'Veto Power' which is enjoyed by the permanent members of the Security Council? *(ICSE 2011)*

Ans. Veto power means to block or reject the vote. The permanent members (VSA, China America, Russia and UK) of the UN Security Council have the power to reject and block decisions taken by other members.

5. What do you understand by the term 'Human Rights'? *(ICSE Specimen 2017)*

Ans. Human Rights are those freedoms, which ought to be available to all persons, irrespective of their religion, race, caste, sex, nationality or any of them.

6. Mention any two functions of UNESCO in the field of education. *(ICSE 2017)*

Ans. Two functions of UNESCO in the field of education are

(i) Removal of illiteracy by encouraging adult education, distance education and open school education.

(ii) Financial assistance for the education of disabled children. It also lays special emphasis on the education of women and girls.

7. The UNO was established to maintain peace and promote social progress and better standards of life with more freedom. With reference to this, explain the following. *(ICSE 2013, 2009, 2004)*

(i) Explain the composition of the Security Council.

(ii) The functions of the Security Council related to maintaining World Peace.

Ans. (i) The Security Council comprises of 5 permanent members and 10 non-permanent members elected for a term of 2 years. It is the executive body of the United Nations.

(ii) The functions of the Security Council related to maintaining World Peace are as follows

(a) The Security Council investigates any dispute or situation which might lead to International friction.

(b) It recommends methods of adjusting any such dispute and the terms of settlement.

(c) The Council can call on members to apply economic sanctions and other measures not involving the use of force to prevent or stop aggression.

(d) The Council can take military action against an aggressor.

8. Who appoints the Secretary General of the United Nations? *(ICSE 2012)*

Ans. The Secretary General of the United Nations is appointed by the General Assembly on the recommendation of the Security Council.

9. Study the picture given below and answer the questions that follow. *(ICSE 2012)*

(i) Where are the headquarters of this organisation located? Who all can be its members?

(ii) Name the principal Judicial organ of this organisation and explain its composition.

Ans. (i) The headquarters of the United Nations are situated at New York in the USA.

Its membership is open to all peace loving countries who believe in the principles of the United Nations (UN). Countries are admitted by the General Assembly by a majority of 2/3rd votes.

(ii) The International Court of Justice is the principal judicial organ of the United Nations situated at the Hague in Netherlands.

The Court consists of 15 judges elected for a term of 9 years. It may not include more than one judge from any nationality. Elections are held every 3 years for 1/3 rd of the seats. The Court elects its President and Vice-President for 3 years.

10. Mention the big five countries that constitute the permanent members of the Security Council (USA). *(ICSE 2010)*

Other Similar Questions

Or Name the permanent member countries of the Security Council.

Or Name the countries that are permanent members of the Security Council.

Ans. The five permanent members of the Security Council are Britain, France, Russia, China and the United States of America (USA).

11. Explain three vital roles that the WHO plays in combating diseases. *(ICSE 2010)*

Ans. Vital roles that the WHO plays in combating diseases are as follows

(i) It helps the countries to build up infrastructure in the health sectors.

(ii) It promotes research to cure and prevent diseases.

(iii) It gives important drugs needed for medical care. e.g., it launched a programme to immunise children against 6 major diseases.

12. Where is the headquarter of the WHO located? Mention any one function of the Security Council. *(ICSE 2009)*

Ans. The headquarter of the WHO is located at Geneva in Switzerland. The Security Council formulates plans for the establishment of a system to regulate armaments.

13. Mention any three objectives of the United Nations. *(ICSE 2009)*

Ans. Three objectives of the United Nations are as follows

(i) To develop friendly relations among nations.

(ii) To achieve International co-operation in solving problems.

(iii) To be a centre for harmonising the actions of nations in the attainment of these common aims.

14. Mention any three functions of the International Court of Justice. *(ICSE 2008)*

Ans. Three functions of the International Court of Justice are as follows

(i) The Court plays a significant role in the codification of International Law.

(ii) The Court's jurisdiction extends to disputes pertaining to the interpretation of International Law.

(iii) It also advises the authorised bodies to request for any opinion.

15. Explain the composition of the International Court of Justice. *(ICSE 2008, 2003)*

Ans. For answer, refer to Q. 9(ii) of 2/3 marks questions.

16. Which agency of the UN looks after the interests of the children in the world? What was the original purpose of setting up this agency? *(ICSE 2007)*

Ans. United Nations International Children Emergency Fund (UNICEF) looks after the interests of the children in the world. The original purpose of setting up this agency is to help the urgent needs of children in post war Europe.

17. The World has seen the damages caused by the two World Wars. The aim of the United Nations Organisation is to save the succeeding generations from the scourge of another war. With reference to this, answer the following. *(ICSE 2006)*

(i) Explain any three functions of the General Assembly.

(ii) Mention any three important functions of UNESCO.

Ans. (i) The functions of the General Assembly are as follows

(a) To consider and make recommendations on the principles of co-operation.

(b) To discuss questions relating to International peace and security.

(c) To discuss and make recommendations on any question within the scope of the Charter of the UN.

Additional Info

Other functions of General Assembly are

- To initiate studies and make recommendations to promote International co-operation.
- To make recommendations for peaceful settlement of disputes.
- To receive and consider reports from the Security Council.
- To consider and approve the budget of the UN.
- To elect the non-permanent members of the Security Council, the Economic and Social Council and the Trusteeship Council and to elect the judges of the International Court of Justice.

(ii) The three important functions of the UNESCO are as follows

(a) Removal of illiteracy by encouraging adult education, distance education and open school education.

(b) Financial assistance for the education of disabled children, women and girls.

(c) It provides technical advice and assistance, equipments, and funds for the preservation of monuments and other work of arts.

18. Explain briefly any one peace keeping operation of the UN Security Council. ***(ICSE 2004)***

Ans. One of the UN peace keeping forces is working in Afghanistan as UN Assistance Mission in Afghanistan (UNAMA), which is deeply concerned about the rising number of civilian deaths and injuries.

19. What does the WHO do to achieve its objective for ensuring 'Health for all'? ***(ICSE 2003)***

Ans. To ensure 'Health for all', WHO undertakes many functions, which include

(i) It helps countries to improve their health systems by building up infrastructure.

(ii) It gives important drugs for medical care.

(iii) It works towards providing safe drinking water and adequate waste disposal.

Additional Info

Other functions that WHO undertakes are

- It aims at fighting diseases and preventing them from spreading.
- It publishes health journals to create health consciousness among people.
- It organises conferences, seminars and training for health care personnel from different countries.

20. Mention any two ways by which the Security Council maintains international peace. ***(ICSE 2002)***

Ans. Two ways by which the Security Council maintains international peace are as follows

(i) By calling on members to apply economic sanctions and by taking other measures to prevent or stop aggression.

(ii) By taking military action against an aggressor.

21. What were the objectives behind setting up the UNESCO? ***(ICSE 2002)***

Ans. The main objective behind the setting up of UNESCO is to contribute to peace and security in the world by promoting collaboration among nations through education, science, culture and communication.

4 Marks Questions

1. Explain the role of the UNESCO in the development of Science and Technology. ***(ICSE 2013)***

Ans. The scientific activities undertaken by the UNESCO are as follows

(i) It organises seminars and conferences of scientists of various countries and circulates information through journals, press and exhibition.

(ii) It promotes research in fields of Geology, Mathematics, Physics and Oceanography.

(iii) It helps in correcting the imbalance in scientific and technological manpower that exists.

(iv) It encourages the study of Social Sciences in order to focus attention on combatting all forms of discrimination.

2. Study the picture below and answer the question that follow. Identify the organisation associated with the emblem above and mention any three principles of this organisation. ***(ICSE 2012)***

Ans. The above emblem belongs to the United Nations Organisation. In order to fulfill the purpose for which UNO was established, the members shall act in accordance to some principles

(i) To respect the sovereign equality of all its members.

(ii) They should settle their international disputes by peaceful means.

(iii) They should refrain from threat or use of force against any state.

(iv) They should give the UN every assistance in any action it takes.

(v) The United Nations shall not intervene in the domestic i.e., the internal affairs of any state.

3. The UN, apart from its main organs also work through its allied agencies. In this context, mention four functions of the Security Council in maintaining peace. ***(ICSE 2010)***

Ans. For answer, refer to Q.7 (ii) of 2/3 marks questions.

4. Name the organisation associated with the above emblem. Mention any three functions of this organisation. ***(ICSE 2008)***

Ans. The emblem is associated with the World Health Organisation (WHO). For functions of the WHO, refer to Q.19 of 2/3 marks questions.

5. Mention any four functions of the General Assembly. ***(ICSE 2004, 2003)***

Ans. For answer, refer to Q. 17 (i) of 2/3 marks questions.

6. The aim of the UN is to safeguard the world from the scourge of war. In this context, describe briefly the composition of the Security Council. ***(ICSE 2000)***

Ans. For composition of the Security Council, refer to Q.7(i) of 2/3 marks questions.

5/6 Marks Questions

1. With reference to the agencies of the UN, give the main functions of the World Health Organisation. ***(ICSE 2001)***

Ans. For answer, refer to Q. 19 of 2/3 marks questions.

2. The horrors of the two World Wars led to the formation of the United Nations Organisation, while the formation of the Non-Aligned Movement followed later. In this context, answer the following. ***(ICSE 2017)***

(a) Mention any three aims and objectives of the United Nations Organisation.

(b) Explain any three functions of the Security Council.

Ans. (a) For answer, refer to Q.13 of 2/3 marks questions.

(b) For answer, refer to Q. 7 (i) of 2/3 marks questions.

3. Describe briefly the functions of the General Assembly. ***(ICSE 2000)***

Ans. Refer to Q. 17 (i) of 2/3 marks questions.

10 Marks Questions

1. The United National Organisation aims to maintain international peace. With reference to its organs and agencies, answer the following. ***(ICSE 2023)***

(a) What is the composition of the Security Council ?

(b) Mention any three functions of the General Assembly.

(c) Mention any three functions of UNESCO.

Ans. (a) For composition of the Security Council, refer to Q. 7(i) of 2/3 marks questions.

(b) For answer refer to Q. 17 (i) of 2/3 marks questions.

(c) For answer refer to Q.17 (ii) of 2/3 marks questions.

2. The United Nations Organisation was established to maintain peace in the world. With reference to this organisation, answer the following questions. ***(ICSE Specimen 2023)***

(a) What is the composition of the Security Council?

(b) Mention any three functions of the International Court of Justice.

(c) What is the full form of UNESCO? Mention any three of its functions.

Ans. (a) For answer, refer to Q. 7 (i) of 2/3 marks questions.

(b) For answer, refer to Q. 14 of 2/3 marks questions.

(c) UNESCO stands for United Nations Educational, Scientific and Cultural Organisation.

For functions of the UNESCO, refer to Q. 17(ii) of 2/3 marks questions.

3. Look at the picture given and answer the questions that follow. ***(ICSE Specimen Semester II 2022)***

(a) Which organisation does this emblem represent? Where is its headquarters?

(b) Mention any two objectives of this organisation.

(c) Mention any three functions of the General Assembly.

(d) What is the composition of the Security Council?

Ans. (a) The emblem represents the United Nations Organisation.

The headquarters of United Nations is situated at New York City in the USA.

(b) For answer, refer to Q. 13 of 2/3 marks questions.

(c) For answer, refer to Q. 17 (i) of 2/3 marks questions.

(d) For answer, refer to Q. 7 (i) of 2/3 marks questions.

4. With reference to the United Nations Organisation, answer the following questions. ***(Semester II 2022)***

(a) State any two objectives of the United Nations Organisation.

(b) How many judges is the International Court of Justice composed of? What is their term?

(c) Mention any three functions of the General Assembly.

(d) What is the full from of WHO? Mention any two of its functions.

Ans. (a) For answer, refer to Q. 13 of 2/3 marks questions.

(b) The International Court of Justice composed of 15 judges. Their term is 9 years. Elections held every 3 years for 1/3rd of the seats.

(c) For answer, refer to Q. 17 (i) of 2/3 marks questions.

(d) The full form of WHO is World Health Organisation. For functions of WHO, refer to Q.19 of 2/3 marks questions.

5.

2020

(a) Name the organisation associated with the above emblem. Mention any two of its objectives.

(b) Mention any three functions of WHO, as its agency.

(c) Name the principal judicial organ of this organisation and explain its composition.

Ans. (a) The organisation which is associated with the given emblem is United Nations.

For objectives of UN, refer to Q. 6 of 2/3 marks questions.

(b) For answer, refer to Q. 19 of 2/3 marks questions.

(c) For answer, refer to Q.9 (ii) of 2/3 marks questions.

Examiner's Comment

- Most of the candidates named the organization associated with the Emblem correctly. However, a few candidates confused the emblem with that of the 'WHO'. A few candidates did not mention the two objectives correctly.
- This part of the question was answered well by most candidates barring a few who mixed up the functions of WHO with the functions of UNICEF, as some health and hygiene related functions are similar.
- Some candidates confused the Principal Judicial Organ of the United Nations with the General Assembly and the Security Council.

Suggestions for Students

- Develop the skills in students to identify pictures. Give them practice by giving several pictures to identify, including emblems and logos, wherever necessary, within the scope of the syllabus.
- Emphasise on the differences between the UNICEF and the WHO.
- Discuss that the United Nations has six principal organs of which the International Court of Justice is the principal judicial organ. Explain its composition.

6. The necessity to maintain international peace led to the establishment of the United Nations Organisation. With reference to the statement, answer the following. ***(ICSE 2019)***

(a) Write any three functions of UNESCO that preserves our cultural heritage.

(b) State the composition of the Security Council.

(c) Write any four functions of the General Assembly.

Ans. (a) UNESCO was established on 4th November 1946, with the main objective to contribute to peace and security in the world, by promoting collaboration among nations through education, science, culture and communication. The main functions of UNESCO are as follows

(i) To encourage policy-makers to promote the participation of women in political, legislative, social, economic and cultural processes.

(ii) To promote youth participation in political, legislative, social, economic and cultural processes.

(iii) To support and strengthen, through partnerships and networks, the contribution of civil society organisations in promoting democracy and respect for human rights.

(b) For answer, refer to Q. 7 (i) of 2/3 marks questions.

(c) For answer, refer to Q. 17 (i) of 2/3 marks questions.

Examiner's Comment

- Many candidates instead of writing the functions of the UNESCO which preserve our Cultural Heritage, wrote its general functions relating to education and science.
- Majority of the candidates stated the composition of the Security Council correctly, barring a few candidates who wrote the composition of the General Assembly.
- Attempted well by most of the candidates. However, a few candidates mixed up the functions of the General Assembly with that of the Security Council.

Suggestions for Students

- Explain with examples, the functions of UNESCO regarding education, science and culture.
- Train students to present facts while answering questions relating to composition of the Security Council.
- Ensure that students learn at least five notable functions of the General Assembly and other organs of the UN.

7. With reference to the United Nations, answer the following questions. ***(ICSE Specimen 2018)***

(a) Write the full form of UNESCO. Mention two of its functions in the field of education.

(b) What is the composition of the International Court of Justice?

(c) What is meant by 'veto power'? Give three functions of the Security Council.

Ans. (a) UNESCO stands for United Nation Educational, Scientific and Cultural Organisation.
For functions of UNESCO in the field of education, refer to Q. 6 of 2/3 marks questions.

(b) For composition of International Court of Justice, refer to Q. 9 (ii) of 2/3 marks questions.

(c) Each of the 5 permanent members has the power to vote a decision. By application of this right, a permanent member may reject any decision at the Security Council is held once a month, but in case of Emergency, it can be held whenever required.
Three functions of the Security Council are
(i) To recommend the admission of new members.
(ii) To take military action against an aggression.
(iii) To exercise the trusteeship function of the United Nations in strategic areas.

8. With reference to the United Nations and its specialised agencies, answer the following questions. ***(2018)***

(a) Mention any three functions of the International Court of Justice.

(b) State the composition of the General Assembly.

(c) State any two functions of the UNICEF and any two functions of WHO.

Ans. (a) For answer, refer to Q. 14 of 2/3 marks questions.

(b) The General Assembly is the main organ of the UNO, and all members of the UNO are members of General Assembly. Each state has five representatives in the General Assembly, but each state has one vote. All member countries of the UNO are members of the General Assembly.

(c) Two functions of UNICEF are
(i) It works for the protection of children in respect of their survival, health and well beings. It also supports child immunisation programmes.
(ii) It provides technical supplies, equipment and other aids to villages.
For two functions of WHO, refer to Q. 19 of 2/3 marks question.

Examiner's Comment

- Several candidates did not write three functions of the International Court of Justice correctly. They mixed-up the functions of the United Nations and the Security Council.
- Majority of the candidates stated the composition of the General Assembly correctly. A few candidates, however, wrote the composition of the Security Council.
- Most of the candidates stated the functions of the UNICEF and WHO correctly. However, some candidates, instead of writing the functions of UNICEF wrote the functions of UNESCO.

Suggestions for Students

- Explain to the students thoroughly the functions of the International Court of Justice.
- Teach the composition and functions of the organs of United Nations by drawing a flow chart.

9. With reference to the United Nations, examine the following ***(ICSE Specimen 2017)***

(a) Main objectives.

(b) Any three functions of the General Assembly.

(c) Composition of the Security Council and any two of its functions.

Ans. (a) For answer, refer to Q. 13 of 2/3 marks questions.

(b) For answer, refer to Q. 17 (i) of 2/3 marks questions.

(c) For composition of Security Council, refer to Q. 7 (i) of 2/3 marks questions.
For two functions of the Security Council, refer to Q. 7 (c) of 10 marks questions.

10. With reference to the United Nations and its related agencies, answer the following questions. ***(2016)***

(a) Explain any three functions of the WHO.

(b) State the composition of the International Court of Justice.

(c) State any four functions of the General Assembly.

Ans. (a) For answer, refer to Q. 19 of 2/3 marks questions.

(b) For answer, refer to Q. 9 (ii) of 2/3 marks questions.

(c) For answer, refer to Q.17 (i) of 2/3 marks questions.

11. The United Nations was established to be an effective peace keeping international organisation. In this context, explain the following. ***(2015)***

(a) Its objectives and purposes.

(b) The meaning of Human Rights as incorporated in the Human Charter.

(c) Name the agency that the UN set up to deliver relief to children and mothers after World War II. State any three of its functions.

Ans. (a) The objectives and purposes of United Nations.

(i) To maintain International Peace and Security.

(ii) To develop friendly relations among nations, based on the respect for the principle of equal rights and self-determination of people.

(iii) To achieve International Cooperation in solving various international, economic, social, cultural or humanitarian problems.

(iv) To be a centre for harmonising the actions in the attainment of goals.

(b) Meaning of Human Rights as Incorporated in the Human Charter Human Rights are the inalienable Fundamental Rights, which every human being is entitled to have, simply for being a human.

(c) The United Nations International Children's Emergency Fund (UNICEF) was created by the UN General Assembly to deliver relief to children and mothers after World War II.

Following are the functions of UNICEF

(i) UNICEF works for the protection of children in respect to their survival, health and well-being.

(ii) It provides funds for training the personal including health and sanitation workers, teachers and nutritionists.

(iii) It provides help to children and mothers in emergencies arising from natural calamities, civil strifes and epidemics.

CHAPTER TEST

01 Mark Questions (MCQ)

1 Which of the following is/are the official language of the United Nations Organisation?
(a) English
(b) Chinese
(c) Spanish
(d) All of the above

2 Which of the following statements is incorrect about International Court of Justice?
(a) It is the principal judicial organ of the United Nations.
(b) The headquarter of the International Court of Justice is located at the Hague, Netherlands.
(c) The Court composes of 15 judges elected for a term of 5 years by the UN General Assembly and Security Council.
(d) The elections are held every 5 years for $\frac{1}{3}$rd of the seats.

3 The ……………… consist of 15 members out of which 5 members China, France, Russia, Britain and USA are permanent.
(a) General Assembly
(b) Security Council
(c) Secretariat
(d) Trusteeship Council

4 What is the full form of UNICEF?
(a) United Nations International Children's Emergency Fund.
(b) United Nations International Collaboration Emergency Fund.
(c) United Nations International Care Emergency Fund.
(d) United Nations International Control Emergency Fund.

5

UNESCO Headquarters	New York
WHO Headquarters	?

(a) Moscow (b) Paris
(c) Hague (d) Geneva

Answers

1. (d) | 2. (c) | 3. (b) | 4. (a) | 5. (b)

02 Marks Questions

6 Mention any two objectives of the United Nations.

7 Name the six principal organs of the United Nations.

8 State any two functions of the General Assembly.

9 What are the two functions of UNESCO in the field of culture?

10 Marks Question

10 The United Nations apart from its main organs also work throug its allied agencies. With reference to this, answer the following questions.
(i) When was WHO established? Mention any two objectives of the WHO.
(ii) State any three functions of UNICEF.
(iii) Mention any four principles of the United Nations.

10

Non-Aligned Movement

TREND ANALYSIS 3 YEARS

TOPIC 01 Non-Aligned Movement

Average No. of Questions Across all Sets

Types of Questions	2023	2020	2019
1 Mark	2	–	–
2/3 Marks	–	–	–
4 Marks	–	1	1
10 Marks	–	–	–

Concept of Non-Aligned Movement

The concept of Non-Aligned Movement came into existence during the Cold War period, when Asia and Africa decided to remain non-aligned and did not join any power blocs. Non-alignment refers to the International policy of a sovereign state according to which it does not align itself with any of the power blocs.

Features of the Non-Alignment

The main features of Non-Alignment are as follows :

(i) It is not aligned to any power blocs and it is against military alliances like NATO, SEATO, Warsaw Pact etc.

(ii) The belief, that each country has the complete freedom to take independent foreign policy decisions.

(iii) Non-alignment stands for action rather than passivism and it judges an issue on merit and is for the freedom and justice of people.

(iv) It actively participates in the politics among nations.

Factors Responsible for the Non-Alignment

The main factors responsible for Non-Alignment are as follows

(i) Global tension caused by Cold War.

(ii) Struggle against Imperialism and Neo-Colonisation.

(iii) Right of independent judgement.

(iv) Use of moderation in relations to all big powers.

(v) Restructuring international economic order.

(vi) Formation of a collective force.

Principles of NAM

The principles, became the guidelines for NAM. These five principles were as follows

(i) Mutual non-interference in each-other's internal affairs.

(ii) Mutual non-aggression.

(iii) Equality for mutual benefit.

(iv) Mutual respect for each other's territorial integrity and sovereignty.
(v) Peaceful co-existence.

First NAM Summit

It was held in September, 1961 at **Belgrade** in **Yugoslavia**. This was attended by 25 Afro-Asian and one European country.

Objectives of NAM

The main objectives of NAM are as follows

(i) To eliminate causes that could lead to war.
(ii) To protect the newly independent countries of Asia and Africa from colonial domination.
(iii) To oppose Colonialism, Imperialism and Racial discrimination.
(iv) To support sovereign equality of all States.
(v) To advocate peaceful settlement of International disputes and protect human rights and the environment.
(vi) To strengthen the United Nations as an organ of world peace.

Achievements of NAM

The main achievements of NAM are as follows

(i) NAM helped in solving tensions between the two power blocs and brought an end to the Cold War.
(ii) NAM acted against the arms race of the superpowers during the Cold War years.
(iii) NAM supports the cause of International peace, justice and freedom.

NAM advocated the **new International economic order** and the **first UN conference** on trade and development. NAM has made the developed countries realise that the continued deprivation of the third world would affect the economy of the world and its prosperity.

Future of NAM

NAM stands for a broader objective of international peace as well as independence of the foreign policy of each sovereign state. It is an effective forum for seeking economic justice.

With the emergence of Neo-Colonialism, NAM has become even more relevant. NAM still continues to be a positive, dynamic and constructive movement aimed at achieving Universal peace, Disarmament and Development.

Architects of NAM

The founding fathers of NAM were **Josip Broz Tito** of Yugoslavia, **Jawaharlal Nehru** of India and **Gamal Abdel Nasser** of Egypt. The term NAM was coined by Jawaharlal Nehru in 1954 in Colombo, Sri Lanka.

PYQs Previous Years' Questions

1 Mark Question

Multiple Choice Questions

1. The term Non-Alignment means .... *(ICSE Semester II 2022)*
   (a) not to form any new alliance
   (b) not to align with any of the power blocs
   (c) not to participate in the world affairs
   (d) to be part of military alliances

Ans. (*b*) not to align with any of the power blocs

2. Which of these leaders was an architect of the Non-Aligned Movement ? *(ICSE 2023)*
   (a) Joseph Stalin (b) Abdel Nasser
   (c) Winston Churchill (d) Franklin Roosevelt

Ans. (*b*) Abdel Nasser

3. Identify the founders of Non-Aligned Movement.
   (a) Nasser, Tito, Nehru *(ICSE Specimen 2023)*
   (b) Naseer, Nehru, Stalin
   (c) Churchill, Stalin, Tito
   (d) Tito, Sukarno, Roosevelt

Ans. (*a*) Nasser, Tito, Nehru

2/3 Marks Questions

1. What is meant by the term Non-Alignment? Name any two founders of the Non-Aligned Movement. *(ICSE Specimen Semester II 2022)*

Ans. Non-Alignment refers to the international policy of a sovereign state on the basis of which it does not align itself with any of the power blocs.

The two founders of the Non-Aligned Movement are Prime Minister Pandit Jawaharlal Nehru of India and President Josip Broz Tito of Yugoslavia.

Some other founders of Non-Aligned Movement include President Sukarno of Indonesia, President Kwame Nkrumah of Ghana and President Colonel Gamal Abdel Nasser of Egypt.

2. Mention any three objectives of the Non-Aligned Movement. *(ICSE Specimen Semester II 2022)*

Ans. The three objectives of the Non-Aligned Movement are

(a) To serve as a forum of political coordination of the developing countries to promote and defend their common interests in the system of international relations.

(b) To promote unity, solidarity and cooperation between developing countries based on shared values and priorities agreed upon by consensus.

(c) To build a New Economic International Economic Order (NIEO) based on equity, equality and justice.

3. What is meant by the term 'Non-Aligned Movement'? *(ICSE 2015)*

Ans. Non-Aligned Movement refers to the international policy of a sovereign state according to which it does not align itself with any of the power blocs.

4. Name the two architects of NAM. *(ICSE 2013)*

Ans. The two architects of NAM are as follows
   (i) Josip Broz Tito of Yugoslavia.
   (ii) Jawaharlal Nehru of India.

4 Marks Questions

1. Mention any four chief architects of the Non-Aligned Movement. *(ICSE 2020)*

Ans. The main architects of Non-Aligned Movement were as follows
   (i) Prime Minister Pandit Jawaharlal Nehru of India.
   (ii) President Sukarno of Indonesia.
   (iii) President Josip Broz Tito of Yugoslavia.
   (iv) President Colonel Gamal Abdel Nasser of Egypt.
   (v) President Kwame Nkrumah of Ghana.

2. Explain any four factors that led to the formation of the Non-Aligned Movement. *(ICSE 2019)*

Ans. Four factors that led to the formation of the Non-Aligned Movement were

(i) **Global Tension caused by Cold War** Most of the newly independent countries of Asia and Africa realised that the division of the world into two power blocs might not fulfill their larger interest. Moreover this might endanger world peace. Thus, they adopted a policy of keeping out of alliances in general and military pacts in particular.

Factors that led to the formation of the Non-Aligned Movement
- Global Tension caused by Cold War
- Economic Development
- Struggle against Imperialism and Neo-Colonialism
- Right of Independent Judgement

(ii) **Economic Development** Most of the newly independent countries were facing financial problems and problems related to development. To overcome these problems they needed financial and technical assistance from both the power blocs.

(iii) **Struggle against Imperialism and Neo-Colonialism** These newly independent nations wanted to enjoy their newly acquired freedom and power. They had remained under the big powers for a long period of time. So, they opted for non-alignment.

(iv) **Right of Independent Judgement** The newly independent nations wanted to solve their own problems themselves without any interference from any super power. Thus, they did not want to align with any power bloc.

Additional Questions

1. When and where was the first summit of the Non-Aligned Movement held?

Ans. First Non-Aligned Movement summit was held in September 1961 at Belgrade in Yugoslavia.

2. What are the features of Non-Alignment? Explain any two.

Ans. Two features of Non-Alignment are as follows

(i) It is not aligned to any power blocs.

(ii) It is against military alliances like NATO, Warsaw Pact, etc.

3. State any two objectives of NAM.

Ans. For answer, refer to Q. 2 of 2/3 marks question.

4. State any three achievements of NAM.

Ans. Three achievements of NAM are as follows

(i) It helped in solving tensions between the two power blocs and brought an end to the Cold War.

(ii) It acted against the Arms Race of the superpowers.

(iii) It supported the cause of International peace, justice and freedom.

CHAPTER TEST

01 Mark Questions

1 The concept of Non-Aligned Movement came into existence during the .... period.
(a) World War-I (b) Cold War
(c) World War-II (d) GUIF War

2 The term NAM was coined by .... in 1954 in Colombo, Sri Lanka.
(a) Jawaharlal Nehru (b) Mahatma Gandhi
(c) Subhash Chandra Bose (d) Lala Lajpat Rai

3 Which of the following countries held first Non-Aligned Movement summit?
(a) Egypt (b) Myanmar
(c) Yugoslavia (d) India

4 What is/are the main objective of Non-Alignment Movement?
(a) To eliminate causes that could lead to war
(b) To oppose Colonialism, Imperialism and Racial discrimination
(c) To support sovereign equality of all states
(d) All of the above

5 Who among the following is the founding fathers of Non-Alignment Movement?
(a) Josip Broz Tito (b) Jawaharlal Nehru
(c) Gamal Abdel Nasser (d) All of these

Answers

1. (b)	2. (a)	3. (c)	4. (d)	5. (a)

02 Marks Questions

6 Mention any two achievements of Non-Alignment Movement.

7 What was the Nehru's view about Non-Alignment Movement?

8 State any two reasons that led to the fomation of Non-Alignment movement.

9 What do you understand by Non-Alignment Movement?

10 Marks Question

10 With reference to Non-Aligned Movement, answer the following questions.
(a) Mention any four main factors responsible for the Non-Alignment.
(b) State any four main features of the NAM.
(c) How Non-Alignment is neither neutrality, nor isolation nor non-commitment? Explain.

New Pattern Questions
(Multiple Choice and Case Based Questions)

CIVICS

1. The Lok Sabha and the Rajya Sabha

Multiple Choice Questions

1. Constitution of India provides for a federal system of government. Which among the following statements describe the same?
(a) Written constitution
(b) Single citizenship
(c) Division of powers between centre and state
(d) Single integrated judiciary

Ans. (*c*) Division of powers between centre and state

2. Given below are the details of few Indian citizens.

Candidate	Age	Other Details
A.	25	Has a name in electoral roll
B.	21	Just graduated
C.	40	Bankrupt
D.	75	Retired judge

Which among the following candidate fulfills the criteria to become the member of Lok Sabha?
(a) A (b) B
(c) C (d) D

Ans. (*a*) A

3. Government is facing some issues with finances of the country and wants to be discussed among senior ministers. Where will these issues be discussed?
(a) Cabinet Ministers (b) Ministers of State
(c) Rajya Sabha (d) Deputy Minsters

Ans. (*a*) Cabinet Ministers

4. Identify the differences between Cabinet Ministers and Council of Ministers in India.
P. Cabinet determines the functions of Council of Ministers.
Q. Council of Ministers is collectively responsible to Lok Sabha.
R. Council of Ministers are a part of Cabinet.
S. State Ministers are not a part of Cabinet.
(a) P and Q (b) R and S
(c) Q and R (d) P and S

Ans. (*a*) P and Q

5. Read the two statements below about Supreme Court and select the options that shows correct relationship between A and B.
A. Supreme Court is free to decide its procedure of work.
B. Constitution of India declares Delhi as the seat of Supreme Court.
(a) B contradicts A
(b) B is the reason for A
(c) A is true, but B is false
(d) A and B are independent of each other

Ans. (*d*) A and B are independent of each other

6. Read the two statements given below and select the option that shows the correct relationship between (A) and (R).
Assertion (A) The Speaker of the Lok Sabha presides over the joint sitting of the Houses.
Reason (R) Ordinary bill can only be introduced in Lok Sabha.
Codes
(a) A is true, but R is false (b) R is the reason for A
(c) Both A and R are false (d) Only R is true, A is false

Ans. (*a*) A is true, but R is false

7. The writ in the below mentioned news correctly describes which among the following?

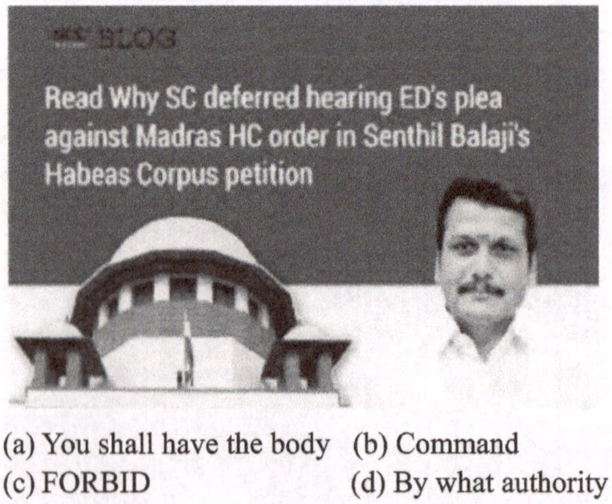

(a) You shall have the body (b) Command
(c) FORBID (d) By what authority

Ans. (*a*) You shall have the body

8. Reshma, a journalist is doing a research on a news related to appointment of Acting Chief Justice. Which Article of Indian Constitution is she likely to research about?

(a) 125 (b) 126
(c) 140 (d) 110

Ans. (*b*) 126

Case Based Question

1. Read the given news carefully

Headline 9 States Assemblies Dissolved, President signs proclamation after late cabinet talks, Government dissolved the assemblies of as many as nine states ruled by non-Congress (I) parties .

Source *Indian Express*

Name and briefly discuss the article using which above action is taken.

Ans. The given action can be taken through Constitutional Emergency under Article 356 if the President receives reports from the Governor stating the inability of the state government to function according to the provisions of the Constitution.

Under such circumstances, President's rule is imposed in the state. The duration of such an emergency is two months. In case the duration has to be increased, it has to be ratified by the Parliament. President's rule in the state can continue for a year.

2. The President and the Vice-President

Multiple Choice Questions

1. All executive orders are issued by the Prime Minister and his Cabinet on the name of the President.

Which statement best describes the above fact?

(a) President is the Head of Government.
(b) President is the Head of Union.
(c) President is the Supreme Commander of Armed Forces.
(d) President is the first citizen of the country.

Ans. (b) President is the Head of Union.

2. Given below are the details of few Indian citizens

Candidate	Age	Other Details
A.	32	Member of Lok Sabha
B.	27	Doctor
C.	36	Eligible for election to Rajya Sabha
D.	45	Bankrupt

Which of the above candidate fulfills the eligibility criteria to become Vice-President of India?

(a) A (b) B (c) C (d) D

Ans. (c) C

3. The Constitutional Emergency can be promulgated if the President receives reports from the Governor stating the inability of the state government to function according to the provisions of the Constitution. Which state was the first to be imposed state emergency?

(a) Karnataka (b) Maharashtra
(c) Punjab (d) Kerala

Ans. (c) Punjab

4. The Vice-President can take over the position of the President under which of the following circumstances?

P. In case of the death of the President .
Q. In case of the resignation of the President.
R. In case of leave of President.
S. In the case of foreign affairs.

(a) P and Q (b) Q and R (c) R and S (d) P and R

Ans. (a) P and Q

5. Read the two statements regarding powers of President

A. When the Lok Sabha is not in session, the President may authorise expenditures out of the Consolidated Fund of the State.

B. The President can declare financial emergency if he feels that the financial credibility or stability of the nation is in danger.

(a) B contradicts A
(b) B is the reason for A
(c) A is true, but B is false
(d) A and B are independent of each other

Ans. (d) A and B are independent of each other

6. Read the two statements given below and select the option that shows the correct relationship between (A) and (R).

Assertion (A) The framers of the Constitution choose the method of indirect election to the office of the President.

Reason (R) The President could become a rival centre of power to the Council of Ministers, if elected directly.

Codes

(a) A is true, but R is false (b) R is the reason for A
(c) Both A and R are false (d) Only R is true, A is false

Ans. (b) R is the reason for A

7. The person below has held which of the following offices?

(a) Vice-President (b) Chairman of Rajya Sabha
(c) Prime Minister (d) Both (a) and (b)

Ans. (d) Both (a) and (b)

8. Parag is studying about all key appointments that are made on the name of the President on the advice of the Prime Minister and his Cabinet. Which among them is not appointed by President?
(a) Chief Justice (b) Attorney General
(b) Governors (d) Vice Chancellors of Universities

Ans. (d) Vice Chancellors of Universities

Case Based Question

1. M Venkaiah Naidu writes: Lessons from Emergency we must not forget

The Emergency serves as a reminder of the importance of upholding democratic principles and protecting the rights and freedoms of individuals.

As the maxim goes, 'Eternal vigilance is the price of liberty' ***Source** Indian Express 24th June, 2023*

Briefly discuss about declaration of Emergency.

Ans. Emergency can be declared if the President feels that the security of India is under threat either because of foreign aggression, civil war or armed rebellion. National emergency should be approved by both Houses of the Parliament within one month by special majority. The emergency cannot continue for more than one month. If the Lok Sabha does not approve the Proclamation of Emergency, the President has to annul his Proclamation.

3. The Prime Minister and the Council of Ministers

Multiple Choice Questions

1. The leader of the majority party in the Lok Sabha is appointed as the Prime Minister. Who appoints the Prime Minister?
(a) President (b) Speaker
(c) Chief Justice (d) Vice-President

Ans. (a) President

2. Consider the following details.

	Candidate	Other Details
A.	Cabinet Ministers	Defence
B.	Ministers of State	Do not participate in Cabinet meetings
C.	Deputy Ministers	?

Fill the above blank with the help of appropriate options given below.
(a) Junior Ministers who assist Cabinet
(b) Ministers of Union Territories
(c) Council of Ministers
(d) None of the above

Ans. (a) Junior Ministers who assist Cabinet

3. They are directly responsible to the Lok Sabha and remain in office as long as they enjoy the support of majority members of the Parliament. If the Lok Sabha passes a vote of No-Confidence Motion against them, they have to resign collectively. Who among the following are 'they' in the above statement?
(a) Cabinet (b) Prime Minister
(c) Opposition (d) Both (a) and (b)

Ans. (d) Both (a) and (b)

4. Identify the correct statements from the statements given below.
P. According to the conventions, only the members of the Parliament are appointed as Ministers.
Q. All important portfolios such as defence, finance and external affairs form the Deputy Ministers.
R. According to the Constitution, the President has to invite the leader of the majority party in the Lok Sabha to form the government.
S. The Deputy Ministers formulate the policies and programmes of the government.
(a) P and Q (b) R and S (c) P and S (d) P and R

Ans. (d) P and R

5. Read the following statements regarding powers and functions of Cabinet.
A. After a decision is taken by the Cabinet Ministers, it is conveyed to the Ministers of State and the Deputy Ministers who implement the policies with the help of the bureaucracy.
B. All important appointments made by the President are decided by the Cabinet under the leadership of the Prime Minister.
(a) B contradicts A
(b) B is the reason for A
(c) A is true, but B is false
(d) A and B are independent of each other

Ans. (d) A and B are independent of each other

6. Read the two statements given below and select the option that shows the correct relationship between (A) and (R).

Assertion (A) The Union Council of Ministers exercises executive authority in the Republic of India.

Reason (R) It consists of junior ministers, called Cabinet Ministers, senior ministers called Ministers of State and Deputy Ministers.

Codes

(a) A is true, but R is false (b) R is the reason for A
(c) Both A and R are false (d) Only R is true, A is false

Ans. (a) A is true, but R is false

7. Identify the appointments made by the below body through the President.

(a) Judge of Supreme Court
(b) Governors of State
(c) Chief Election Commissioner
(d) All of the above

Ans. (d) All of the above

8. Reema is making the list of persons who have been the heads of Government and convey the decisions of Cabinet to the President.
Whom is she referring to?
(a) Deputy Ministers (b) Prime Minister
(c) Governor (d) Home Secretary

Ans. (b) Prime Minister

Case Based Question

1. Read the following news carefully.

Headline PM Modi to chair meeting of Council of Ministers on 3rd, July amid talk of Union Cabinet reshuffle

Prime Minister Narendra Modi will chair a meeting of the Union Council of Ministers on 3rd July, amid talk of a possible Union Cabinet reshuffle ahead of the 2024 Lok Sabha elections.

Source *Times of India 29th June, 2023*

After referring to above news, discuss briefly the legislative functions of Union Cabinet.

Ans. The legislative functions of the Union Cabinet are

- Both Houses also make laws on the Concurrent List. In case of conflicts with the state governments, the laws made by the Union Government are accepted.
- The Houses can make laws on the matters which are not included in any of the three lists. This power is known as residuary powers.
- The Parliament can make laws on the subjects included in the State List during an emergency, when the Rajya Sabha passes a resolution stating that the subject in the State List is of national importance and when two or more states in the Rajya Sabha want laws on the subject in the State List should be made by the Parliament.

4. The Supreme Court

Multiple Choice Questions

1. It is a command issued by court to a public official asking any public body to perform its official duty. Which among the following best describes the above statement?
(a) Habeas Corpus (b) Mandamus
(c) Quo Warranto (d) Certiorari

Ans. (b) Mandamus

2. Consider the following details.

Candidate	Age	Other Details
A.	25	Post Graduate in Law
B.	56	Judge in High Court for 7 years
C.	41	Retired Civil Servant
D.	32	Retired Police Officer

Select the person who fulfills the criteria to become Judge of Supreme Court.
(a) A (b) B (c) C (d) D

Ans. (b) B

3. Read the two statements given below and select the option that shows the correct relationship between (A) and (R).

Assertion (A) A judge of the Supreme Court may resign from his office by writing to the Prime Minister.

Reason (R) Article 126 is associated with the impeachment of the judge of Supreme Court.

Codes

(a) A is true, but R is false (b) R is the reason for A
(c) Both A and R are false (d) Only R is true, A is false

Ans. (c) Both A and R are false

4. Identify the case in which Supreme Court can exercise Judicial Review.
   P. If law infringes fundamental Rights
   Q. If law is against constitutional provisions
   R. If law is made during Emergency
   S. If it is an ordinance by President
   (a) P and Q (b) R and S (c) P and S (d) Q and R

Ans. (a) P and Q

5. Refer to the two statements regarding Supreme Court.
   A. A judge can be removed by the President only on the grounds of proven misbehaviour and incapacity.
   B. Charges against the judges first have to be addressed by the President in front of both Houses of the Parliament and have to be passed by two-thirds majorities of both Houses.
   (a) B contradicts A
   (b) B is the reason for A
   (c) A is true, but B is false
   (d) A and B are independent of each other

Ans. (d) A and B are independent of each other

6. Supreme Court wants to enquire the legality or claim of a Person A to his office. Name the writ that will be issued in this case.
   (a) Mandamus (b) Habeas Corpus
   (c) Quo Warranto (d) Certiorari

Ans. (c) Quo Warranto

7. The below institution was established due to which of the following acts?

   (a) Morley Minto Reforms
   (b) Montagu Chelmsford Reforms
   (c) Government of India Act, 1935
   (d) Pitts India Act

Ans. (c) Government of India Act, 1935

8. Rashi has filed a case in Supreme Court against illegal arrest of her brother. Which writ is she likely to use?
   (a) Habeas Corpus (b) Quo Warranto
   (c) Mandamus (d) Certiorari

Ans. (a) Habeas Corpus

Case Based Question

1. Read the given news carefully.
   Aren't you accountable, My Lord?......
   In the past few days, there has been a striking development which is not of much public interest yetintellectual interest. The Union Government and the Supreme Court have locked horns on the matter on the matter of the appointment of judges in various courts...... ***Source*** *Oraganiser; 27th June, 2023*
   Give any two criteria for the qualification for post of judge in Supreme Court.

Ans. Two criteria for the qualification for post of judges are
- He should been a judge of a High Court for five years or of two and more such courts in succession.
- He should be a distinguished jurist in the opinion of the President.

5. The High Courts and the Subordinate Courts

Multiple Choice Questions

1. The Constitution of India has provided for a High Court for each state. In this sense, which is the only Union Territory that has a High Court?
   (a) Delhi (b) Puducherry
   (c) Daman and Diu (d) Lakshadweep

Ans. (a) Delhi

2. Consider the following details.

Candidate	Age	Other Details
A.	57	Judge for 14 years
B.	66	Lawyer
C.	35	Member of Lok Sabha
D.	52	Magistrate for four years

   Choose the person who fulfills the criteria to become the judge of High Court.
   (a) A (b) B (c) C (d) D

Ans. (a) A

3. Read the two statements given below and select the option that shows the correct relationship between (A) and (R).
   Assertion (A) The revisory jurisdiction is applicable in the case of violation of the principles of natural justice.
   Reason (R) It is not applicable to the injustice or an error of law apparent on the face of the record.
   Codes
   (a) A is true, but R is false (b) R is the reason for A
   (c) Both A and R are false (d) Only R is true, A is false

Ans. (a) A is true, but R is false

4. Which type of jurisdiction is not applicable to High Court?

P Appellate Jurisdiction Q Advisory Jurisdiction
R Writ Jurisdiction S Court of Record

(a) P and Q (b) R and S (c) R only (d) Q and R

Ans. (c) R only

5. Read the following statement regarding Revisory Jurisdiction.

A. The High Court can ask for the record of a case which has been decided by any Subordinate Court.

B. This jurisdiction is applicable to those cases where injustice has been done to the accused, principles of natural justice have been violated and a gross error has been made while delivering justice.

(a) B contradicts A
(b) B is the reason for A
(c) A is true but B is false
(d) B and A are independent of each other

Ans. (d) B and A are independent of each other

8. Sometimes Person X may also act as Deputy Commissioner and District Collector. In that capacity, he maintains law and order and supervises the collection of revenues.

Identify the person X.

(a) Sessions Judge (b) District Judge
(c) SDM (d) Police Commissioner

Ans. (b) District Judge

9. The below High Court of Bombay advises who among the following while appointing any person to the judicial service of the state?

(a) Governor (b) Chief Minister
(c) President (d) Prime Minister

Ans. (a) Governor

10. Rekha has approached a court that deals with civil cases which involve less than ₹ 2000. Appeals against his decision can be made in the Court of the Civil Judge. Which court has she approached to?

(a) Civil Court (b) Sessions Court
(c) Munsif Court (d) Lok Adalat

Ans. (c) Munsif Court

Case Based Question

1. Read the given news carefully.

Telangana: National Lok Adalat to be held on June 10 All kinds of Civil, Compoundable Criminal Cases, Matrimonial disputes, maintenance cases, harassment cases, domestic violence, cases under Sec 138 of Negotiable Instruments Act, Motor Vehicle Accident Claims, etc pending before High Court and Lower Courts can be settled through the Adalat.

***Source** The Siyasat Daily 6 June 2023*

From the above news, deduce the role of Lok Adalat in Indian Judicial System.

Ans. The role of Lok Adalat in Indian Judicial System is

- Lok Adalat means 'court of the people'. It gives legal help and quick justice to people who cannot engage lawyers or bear the cost of legal proceedings.
- The judges of the Lok Adalat are actually counsellors. Lok Adalats are helped by the Legal Aid Committees and help people to solve cases through mutual understanding.
- Lok Adalat help opposing parties to reach a compromise, creating an environment of good will.

HISTORY

1. First War of Independence and Rise of Nationalism

Multiple Choice Questions

1. Subsidiary Alliance was an agreement between British East India Company and Indian Rulers through which these states lost their sovereignty to British. Who among the following introduced Subsidiary Alliance?

(a) Lord Curzon (b) Lord Canning
(c) Lord Wellesley (d) Lord Dalhousie

Ans. (c) Lord Wellesley

2. Given below are the details of few revolutionaries.

Name	Place	Details
Bahadur Shah Zafar	Delhi	Symbol of Revolt
Begum Hazrat Mahal	Lucknow	She was the wife of Nawab of Awadh
Khan Bahadur Khan	Bareilly	Descendent of former ruler of Rohilakhand
Tantia Tope	Awadh	Minister of Rani Lakshmibai

Choose the correct description of the personalities above.
(a) Bahadur Shah Zafar (b) Begum Hazrat Mahal
(c) Khan Bahadur Khan (d) Tantia Tope

Ans. (b) Begum Hazrat Mahal

3. This region was captured by Sir Hugh Rose by assault. Two great leaders including Tantia Tope belonged to this region. Identify the region.
(a) Jhansi (b) Meerut (c) Kanpur (d) Lucknow

Ans. (a) Jhansi

4. Identify the main features of Queen Victoria's proclamation after the Revolt of 1857.
P. Equality among Indians and Europeans
Q. Policy of Non-Intervention
R. Restrictions on Press
S. Increase Indians in Legislative Assembly
(a) P and Q (b) R and S (c) P and S (d) Q and R

Ans. (a) P and Q

5. Read the statements below regarding INA.
A. The practice of sati was banned in 1829 and the Widow Remarriage Act was passed in 1856.
B. The Indians disapproved the British interference in their social system.
(a) B contradicts A (b) B is the reason for A
(c) A is true, but B is false
(d) A and B are independent of each other

Ans. (d) A and B are independent of each other

6. Read the two statements given below and select the option that shows the correct relationship between (A) and (R).

Assertion (A) The political cause of the Revolt of 1857 was disrespect shown to Bahadur Shah Zafar.

Reason (R) The socio-religious cause of the Revolt of 1857 was fears generated by Western Education.

Codes
(a) A is true, but R is false (b) R is the reason for A
(c) Both A and R are false (d) Only R is true, A is false

Ans. (d) Only R is true, A is false

7. The below revolution depicts a revolutionary fighting to defend her state. Identify the British who annexed her state.

(a) Lord Dalhousie (b) Lord Curzon
(c) Lord Wellesley (d) Lord Bentinck

Ans. (a) Lord Dalhousie

8. A student named Rohan is doing a research on a personality who led the Revolt of 1857 from Kanpur. Whom is she doing a research on?
(a) Nana Sahib (b) Tantia Tope
(c) General Bakht Khan (d) Kunwar Singh

Ans. (a) Nana Sahib

Case Based Question

1. Read the excerpt given below and answer the questions that follows.

The great Revolt of 1857 was a momentous struggle against colonial rule in the Indian subcontinent—the most widespread anti-colonial struggle during the nineteenth century. It began in the second week of May and soon encompassed large parts of Northern, Central and Eastern India. Several hundred thousand subjects of the British Indian empire were killed during the revolt. Whereas the British managed to restore their authority in most of the areas where the uprising took place, the final operations continued till the beginning of 1859. The upheaval of 1857-59 was not an isolated event. It was part of a long tradition of resistance to the East India Company (EIC).

Source *Daily Star*

(i) Explain immediate cause of this revolt.
(ii) Mention any three revolutionary fighters and their contribution.
(iii) Discuss any four impacts of this Revolt.

Ans. (i) The immediate cause of this revolt was the British had introduced a new 'Enfield Rifle' in the army. This rifle needed a cartridge which had a greased paper cover. This paper cover had to be bitten off before loading the cartridge into the rifle. Rumours spread that the greased paper was made of beef and pork. The soldiers felt that it was a move by the British to defame their religion.

(ii) The contribution of revolutionaries in the Revolt of 1857 were

- In Delhi General Bakht Khan commanded the Bareilly troops into Delhi and provided leadership to the rebels.
- The leader of the revolt in Awadh was Begum Hazrat Mahal. After the city was recaptured by the British, Begum Hazrat Mahal fled to Nepal.
- In Jhansi, the revolt was laid by Rani Laxmibai, whose state was annexed by Lord Dalhousie on

the basis of the Doctrine of Lapse. She rose against the British and joined the revolt.

(iv) The four impacts of this revolt were

- End of the Company's Rule.
- End of Mughals and Peshwaship.
- The strength of European troops in India was increased.
- European soldiers were posted in key strategic locations.

2. The Early Nationalists and Assertive Nationalism

Multiple Choice Questions

1. The Indian National Congress from its inception in 1885 to 1905 was dominated by the early nationalists. These early nationalists were eminent personalities. Who among the following was not a part of early nationalist?

(a) Dadabhai Naoroji (b) Gopal Krishna Gokhale
(c) Justice Ranade (d) Lokmanya Tilak

Ans. (d) Lokmanya Tilak

2. Consider the following details.

Name	Details
Dadabhai Naoroji	Grand Old Man of India
Gopal Krishna Gokhale	Deccan Education Society
?	Civil Service Examination
W C Bonnerjee	First President of India

Fill the above blank with the help of suitable options below.

(a) Surendranath Bannerjee (b) M G Ranade
(c) R C Dutt (d) Rashbehari Ghosh

Ans. (a) Surendranath Bannerjee

3. Early nationalists wanted to make some demand, which among the following was not a demand made by them?

(a) Creation of Council
(b) Control over the public purse
(c) To reduce expenditures on the army
(d) Adequate representation of Indians in the Executive Council of the Viceroy and the Governors.

Ans. (a) Creation of Council

4. Identify the correct methods followed by Early Nationalists.

P. They held meetings and gave speeches for pressing their demands.

Q. They encouraged the policies of the government through the press.

R. A British Committee of the Indian National Congress was established at America in 1990 which published a weekly journal, India, to present India's case before the British public.

S. Dadabhai Naoroji spent a major part of his life to create awareness among the British people and parliamentarians about the plight of the Indians.

(a) P and Q (b) R and S (c) R and P (d) Q and R

Ans. (c) R and P

5. Read the following statements regarding Early Nationalists.

A. Lord Dufferin wanted the Congress to devote itself to social rather than political affairs.

B. To reduce the effectiveness of the Congress, the government followed the 'Policy of Divide and Rule' by encouraging Sayyid Ahmad Khan and Raja Shiv Prasad of Banaras to start an anti-Congress movement.

(a) B contradicts A
(b) B is the reason for A
(c) A is true, but B is false
(d) B and A are independent of each other

Ans. (d) B and A are independent of each other

6. Read the two statements given below and select the option that shows the correct relationship between (A) and (R).

Assertion (A) Dadabhai Naoroji and Gopal Krishna Gokhale were the early nationalists leaders.

Reason (R) They wanted to launch violent agitations against the British.

Codes

(a) A is true, but R is false (b) R is the reason for A
(c) Both A and R are false (d) Only R is true, A is false

Ans. (a) A is true, but R is false

7. The below personality founded Deccan Education society. Identify the personality.

(a) Justice Ranade (b) RC Dutt
(c) Gopal Krishna Gokhale
(d) Ishwar Chandra Vidyasagar

Ans. (a) Justice Ranade

8. Richa is searching about a personality who founded the Indian Association in 1876 to oppose the unjust policies of the British. He convened the Indian National Conference in 1883 at Kolkata to create an all India political organisation.
(a) RC Dutt
(b) Surendranath Banerjee
(c) Gopal Krishna Gokhale
(d) Dadabhai Naoroji

Ans. (b) Surendranath Banerjee

Case Based Question

1. Read the excerpt given below and answer the questions that follow.
Dadabhai Naoroji, a leader who served India and Britain. On the day Rishi Sunak rose to the prime ministership of Great Britain, a long-time Parsi resident of London, Rusi Dalal, mailed me to say this historic event happened in a year that rhymes with another Indo-United Kingdom (UK) landmark moment.

Source Hindustan Times, November 2022

(i) What was above Nationalist leader popularly known as? Which association was established by him?
(ii) Name the theory propounded by him.
(iii) Discuss his contribution of this personality to early nationalism.

Ans. (i) The above Nationalist is known as Grand Old Man of India. East India Association was established by him.
(ii) He propounded the theory of Drain of Wealth.
(iii) His contributions were as follows
- He brought important matters related to India to the notice of the House of Commons. The House of Commons passed the resolution of holding the Indian Civil Service Examinations in India and England simultaneously largely because of his efforts.
- He took an active part in the foundation of the Indian National Congress. The four resolutions of self-government, boycott, swadeshi and national education were passed by the Congress under his Presidentship.
- He did a pioneering work in exposing the root causes of the economic ills of India. He compiled a book titled Poverty and Un-British Rule in India in which he explained how Indian wealth was drained to England.

3. The Partition of Bengal & Formation of the Muslim League

Multiple Choice Questions

1. According to British, the main reason for partition of Bengal was administrative necessity. Which actual reason best describes the partition of Bengal?
(a) To create divide between Hindus and Muslims.
(b) To have better administration.
(c) To encourage trade.
(d) To make Bengal as capital of British Empire.

Ans. (a) To create divide between Hindus and Muslims.

2. Consider the following details.

Year	Details
1906	Muslim League
1875	Mohammedan Anglo Oriental College
1905	Partition of Bengal
?	Morley Minto Reforms

Fill the above blank with the help of suitable options below.
(a) 1919 (b) 1909 (c) 1912 (d) 1907

Ans. (b) 1909

3. Read the two statements given below and select the option that shows the correct relationship between (A) and (R).
Assertion (A) East Bengal was dominated by Bengali Hindus.
Reason (R) Capital of East Bengal was declared to be Calcutta.
Codes
(a) A is true, but R is false (b) R is the reason for A
(c) Both A and R are false (d) Only R is true, A is false

Ans. (c) Both A and R are false

4. Identify the personalities who were not the part of Swadeshi Movement.
P. Lokmanya Tilak Q. Lala Lajpat Rai
R. WC Bonnerjee S. RC Dutt
(a) P and Q (b) R and S
(c) P and S (d) Q and R

Ans. (b) R and S

5. Read the following statements regarding Partition of Bengal.
A. The British advocated that Bengal was divided to efficiently administer the province.
B. The British hoped that by dividing the province on communal lines, they would be able to stop the rising wave of nationalism.

(a) B contradicts A
(b) B is the reason for A
(c) A is true, but B is false
(d) A and B are independent of each other

Ans. (d) A and B are independent of each other

6. A revolutionary movement in a country created a rift between moderates and radicals similar to that of India. Which movement might that be?
(a) Quit India Movement (b) Swadeshi Movement
(c) Civil Disobedience Movement
(d) Non-Cooperation Movement

Ans. (b) Swadeshi Movement

7. Who was the Editor of below depicted newspaper?

केसरी.
वर्ष १. पुणें—मंगळवार तारीख ४ जानेवारी १८८१. अंक १.

(a) RC Dutt (b) Lala Lajpat Rai
(c) Lokmanya Tilak (d) Surendranath Bannerjee

Ans. (c) Lokmanya Tilak

8. Rekha is studying about a personality who helped the opening of many Swadeshi stores in Bengal during Swadeshi Movement. Whom is she referring to?
(a) Lokmanya Tilak (b) Sri Aurobindo
(c) Rabindranath Tagore (d) Raja Ram Mohan Roy

Ans. (c) Rabindranath Tagore

Case Based Questions

1. Read the excerpt given below and answer the questions that follow.

The Swadeshi Movement has been the core of the Independence movement as well and has contributed a lot to the development of Indian nationalism. This Swadeshi Movement has got much wider support from the masses since 1906 against the erstwhile Partition of Bengal and ultimately turned into a full-blown independence movement in the early 20th century till we attained Independence.

(i) Name the major cause of this movement. Give any two reasons for partition of Bengal.
(ii) Discuss any three programmes of this movement.
(iii) Mention any four impacts of Swadeshi Movement.

Ans. (i) Partition of Bengal was the major and immediate cause of this movement.

Two reasons for the partition of Bengal were

- Bengal was an important centre of Indian nationalism. The British hoped that by dividing the province on communal lines, they would be able to stop the rising wave of nationalism.
- The partition also aimed at curbing the influence of Bengal by reducing Bengalis in minority in their own home state.

(ii) The programmes of this movement were

- Boycotting of British-made cloth and imported sugar and salt.
- To give up government posts and seats in the Legislative Council.
- To promote Hindi and vernacular languages.

(iii) The impacts of Swadeshi Movement were

- The movement brought people belonging to different sections of society closer to each other. The movement saw the participation of students and women in large numbers.
- The movement gave huge impetus to the indigenous industries. Many industries ranging from textile mills, soap and match factories to large-scale enterprises were opened and there was an increase in production of indigenous goods.
- The Swadeshi Movement gave employment opportunities to many craftsmen and weavers working in handloom and handicraft industries.
- The movement saw the flowering of nationalist poetry, prose and journalism. Poets such as Tagore and Syed Abu Mohammed wrote many inspirational poets and songs.

4. The Lucknow Pact

Multiple Choice Questions

1. The Sultan was regarded as the 'Caliph' or the religious head of the Muslims. Most of the Muslim sacred places were situated within this Empire.

Which country correctly describes the above statement?
(a) Afghanistan (b) Turkey
(c) Iran (d) Persia

Ans. (b) Turkey

2. Read the two statements given below and select the option that shows the correct relationship between (A) and (R).

Assertion (A) The Lucknow Pact demanded that India Council of Secretary of State should be replaced by two permanent under secretaries out of which one should be Indian.

Reason (R) The Lucknow Pact was signed in 1930.

Codes

(a) A is true, but R is false (b) R is the reason for A

(c) Both A and R are false (d) Only R is true, A is false

Ans. (a) A is true, but R is false

3. Read the two statements regarding Lucknow Pact.

A. The unity between the Muslim League and the Congress due to Lucknow Pact strengthened the Indian National Movement.

B. Acceptance of the principle of separate electorate for Muslims by the Congress undermined the political unity of the country

(a) B contradicts A

(b) B is the reason for A

(c) A is true but, B is false

(d) A and B are independent of each other

Ans. (d) A and B are independent of each other

4. Signing of Lucknow Pact occurred due to which reasons?

(a) Annulment of Partition of Bengal.

(b) Release of Bal Gangadhar Tilak from jail.

(c) Arrest of prominent Muslim leaders under the Seditious Meeting Act.

(d) All of the above

Ans. (d) All of the above

5. Promita is doing a research about personalities who played an important role in signing of Lucknow Pact. Who is she referring to?

(a) Bal Gangadhar Tilak (b) Annie Besant

(c) WC Bonnerjee (d) Both (a) and (b)

Ans. (d) Both (a) and (b)

Case Based Question

1. Read the excerpt given below and answer the questions that follow.

Around the same time, in 1913, Jinnah had finally joined the Muslim League. Remarkably, he continued to be a member, simultaneously, of the Congress, which he had joined in 1906. He was held in high esteem in both Congress and Muslim League circles, and was popularly known as an "ambassador of Hindu-Muslim unity". Tilak and Jinnah had already worked together in the previous decade. Hence, a confluence of India's two main political streams led to the historic Lucknow Pact in 1916.

(i) Mention some national events that led to signing of Lucknow Pact.

(ii) Discuss any three features of Lucknow Pact.

(iii) Describe any two achievements and limitations of Lucknow Pact.

Ans. (i) National events that led to signing of Lucknow Pact were

- The annulment of the Partition of Bengal, release of Bal Gangadhar Tilak from jail
- Arrest of prominent Muslim leaders under the Seditious Meeting Act
- The spread of nationalist ideas by Muhammad Ali and Shaukat Ali brought the Muslim League and the Congress closer to each other.

(ii) The three features of Lucknow Pact were

- The Imperial Legislation of India should not control India's defence (including making war and signing treaties) and foreign affairs.
- Four-fifths of the members of the Provincial Legislature were to be directly elected and one-fifth should be nominated.
- Muslims were to be elected through a separate electorate. Minorities should be given adequate representation in elected bodies.

(iii) Two achievements of Lucknow Pact were

- It led to Hindu–Muslim unity. While Congress accepted the scheme of separate electorates for the Muslims, the Muslim League accepted the principle of election and majority rule.
- The signing of the Lucknow Pact also reunited the Early and Assertive Nationalists (both wings of the Congress were split in the 1907 Session at Surat).

Two limitations of Lucknow Pact were

- The Lucknow Pact did not involve the masses and was confined to only rich and educated Hindus and Muslims.
- Acceptance of the principle of separate electorate for Muslims by the Congress undermined the political unity of the country.

5. Mahatma Gandhi and the National Movement

Multiple Choice Questions

1. The Indigo planters of this region had to sell Indigo at fixed rates (which were extremely low) to European planters. The Indigo cultivators invited Gandhi to look into their miseries and take up their cause. Which region best describes the above cause?

(a) Champaran (b) Kheda

(c) Ahmedabad (d) Awadh

Ans. (a) Champaran

2. Consider the following details.

Year	Details
Champaran Satyagraha	1917
Kheda Satyagraha	1918
Jallianwala Bagh Massacre	?

Complete the above blank with the help of following details.

(a) 1920 (b) 1919 (c) 1921 (d) 1925

Ans. (b) 1919

3. The Congress in the Kolkata Session asked the government to either accept the Nehru Report or be prepared to face the mass agitations. The government did not accept the Report, hence the Congress declared an objective.

What was the objective?

(a) Complete Independence
(b) Majority in Legislative Assembly
(c) Increase in minimum age for Civil Services
(d) Quit India Movement

Ans. (a) Complete Independence

4 What were the recommendations of Simon Commission? Choose the correct ones from the below given options.

P. Abolish diarchy
Q. Complete Independence
R. Increase in the number of members in the Provincial Legislative Council
S. Increase in minimum age for Civil Services

(a) P and Q (b) R and S (c) P and R (d) Q and S

Ans. (c) P and R

5. Read the two statements regarding Non-Cooperation Movement.

A. At the Kolkata Session in 1920, the Congress passed the resolution of the Non-Cooperation Movement.
B. The Non-Cooperation Movement emphasised on the use of swadeshi and boycott programmes.

(a) B contradicts A
(b) B is the reason for A
(c) A is true, but B is false
(d) A and B are independent of each other

Ans. (d) A and B are independent of each other

6. Read the two statements given below and select the option that shows the correct relationship between (A) and (R).

Assertion (A) The causes of the failure of Quit India Movement were failure of Simon Commission and Rowlatt Act.

Reason (R) Quit India Movement was started in 1919.

Codes

(a) A is true, but R is false (b) R is the reason for A
(c) Both A and R are false (d) Only R is true, A is false

Ans. (c) Both A and R are false

7. Which of the following movement was launched after the incident held at below place?

(a) Civil Disobedience Movement
(b) Non-Cooperation Movement
(c) Kheda Satyagraha
(d) Quit India Movement

Ans. (b) Non-Cooperation Movement

8. Prerna is doing a project on a Satyagraha launched by Gandhiji to take up a cause of Textile mill workers. Which Satyagraha is she doing a project on?

(a) Kheda Satyagraha (b) Champaran Satyagraha
(c) Awadh Satyagraha (d) Ahmedabad Satyagraha

Ans. (a) Kheda Satyagraha

Case Based Question

1. Read the excerpt given below and answer the questions that follow.

After a book on the history of non-violent resistance in the Indian nationalist movement, historian David Hardiman's latest work takes his study forward to examine the culmination of the first surge of struggle from its launch in 1920 to its end with Mahatma Gandhi's arrest two years later.

The book, "Non-Cooperation in India: Non-Violent Strategy and Protest", was released on Monday. It is published by Westland Books.

The Non-Cooperation Movement by the Indian National Congress (INC), organised and led by Gandhi, was the first mass movement organised nationwide during India's struggle for freedom.

(i) Who was the Viceroy of India during this movement? Name any two causes of this movement.
(ii) Mention any three activities under this movement.
(iii) Analyse any four impacts of this movement

Ans. (i) Lord Chelmsford was the Viceroy of India during this movement.

The Non-Cooperation Movement has had two main causes

- Jallianwala Bagh Massacre and resultant Punjab disturbances.
- Khilafat Agitation

(ii) Three activities under this movement were

- To popularise the use of swadeshi and khadi clothes.
- To establish national schools and colleges in India as an alternative to government schools and colleges.
- To boycott government-run schools, colleges and courts.

(iii) Four impacts of this movement were

- It made the national movement a mass movement as people from every profession and walk of life participated in the movement.
- It generated the desire for freedom among the people and inspired them to challenge the colonial rule.
- It fostered Hindu Muslim unity.
- It also promoted social reforms.

6. The Forward Bloc, The INA, Independence and Partition of India

Multiple Choice Questions

1. Rash Behari Bose, an Indian revolutionary and an organiser of the Indian Independence League planned the Tokyo Conference. Which cause correctly describes this event?

(a) Attack on British in India
(b) Looting British treasury
(c) Participation in World War
(d) Meet the military officers of Japan.

Ans. (d) Meet the military officers of Japan.

2. Refer to the following details.

Year	Details
Bangkok Conference	1942
A women wing of the INA	?
Provisional Government of Free India	1943
Free India Centre	1941

(a) 1942 (b) 1956
(c) 1949 (d) 1950

Ans. (a) 1942

3. Read the two statements given below and select the option that shows the correct relationship between (A) and (R).

Assertion (A) Subhash Chandra Bose gave resign from the presidentship of the Congress.

Reason (R) Subhash Chandra Bose had different views from Gandhiji.

Codes

(a) A is true, but R is false (b) R is the reason for A
(c) Both A and R are false (d) Only R is true, A is false

Ans. (b) R is the reason for A

4. Identify the correct recommendations of Cabinet Mission Plan with the help of options given below.

P. Proposed the formation of the federal union of the British Provinces and Princely States in India.
Q. The British Provinces were to be divided into groups.
R. Making of Constituent Assembly
S. Complete Independence

(a) P and Q (b) R and S (c) P and S (d) Q and R

Ans. (a) P and Q

5. Read the following statements regarding INA.

A. The INA did not succeed in its mission to liberate India.
B. The INA inspired uprisings in the armed forces of the country.

(a) B contradicts A
(b) B is the reason for A
(c) A is true, but B is false
(d) A and B are independent of each other

Ans. (d) A and B are independent of each other

6. Two religious communities who are in conflict within a Country A have accepted a plan similar to that of Mountbatten Plan. What could have been the most important cause of accepting the plan?

(a) Partition of the country
(b) Making of new Constitution
(c) Reservation of seats
(d) Separate electorates

Ans. (a) Partition of the country

7.

The Provisional Government of Free India acquired its first territories when Japan handed over which region to India?

(a) Bengal (b) Andaman and Nicobar
(c) Rangoon (d) Burma

Ans. (b) Andaman and Nicobar

8. Prachi is doing a project on a personality who formed a new party the Forward Bloc in May 1939. Whom is she researching about?
(a) Bipin Chandra Pal (b) Rashbehari Ghosh
(c) Subhash Chandra Bose (d) Mohan Singh

Ans. (c) Subhash Chandra Bose

Case Based Question

1. Read the excerpt given below and answer the questions that follow.

The Indian National Army trials was a historic event that took place between November 1945 and May 1946 at Delhi's Red Fort. The trial was a court martial of a number of INA officers on the charges of torture, treason, murder and abetment to murder during the World War II, with all Indians cutting across their differences supporting the freedom fighters.

Virtually refreshing the memory of today's generation about this event was the play "Lal Quile Ka Aakhri Muqadma" staged by Pierrot's Troupe and directed by M. Sayeed Alam at New Delhi's LTG Auditorium recently. ***Source*** *India Narrative June 2023*

(i) Name any two conferences that led to the formation of above organisation. Name any two persons associated with this.
(ii) Mention the three objectives of above organisation.
(iii) Name any four achievements of this organisation.

Ans. (i) Tokyo Conference and Bangkok Conference led to the formation of above organisation.
Rashbehari Bose and Captain Mohan Singh are two personalities associated with this.

(ii) Three objectives of the organisation were
- To fight the British army with modern arms and weapons.
- To organise Indians living abroad and plan an armed revolution against the British Government.
- To organise the Provisional Government of Free India.

(iii) The achievements of this organisation were
- The INA gave tough fight to the British. It not only advanced up to the frontiers of India but also captured the strong military post of Klang Klang. It also captured Ukhral and Kohima.
- The INA inspired uprisings in the armed forces of the country.
- The Indian Naval ratings in Mumbai rose in revolt against the British. Similar uprisings took place at Kolkata, Chennai and Karachi.
- The heroic deeds and sacrifices of the soldiers of the INA led to the awakening of political consciousness among the Indians.

7. The First World War and the Rise of Dictatorships

Multiple Choice Questions

1. The assassination of Archduke Francis Ferdinand was planned by a Secret society. Which of the following society best matches the Secret society?
(a) Black Hand (b) Black Band
(c) Red Shirts (d) Red Suits

Ans. (a) Black Hand

2. Refer to the following details

Events	Year
Murder of Archduke Francis Ferdinand	1914
Entry of USA in War	1917
Treaty of Versailles	?

Fill the above blank with the help of appropriate options given below.
(a) 1919 (b) 1918 (c) 1916 (d) 1920

Ans. (a) 1919

3. Read the two statements given below and select the option that shows the correct relationship between (A) and (R).

Assertion (A) Hitler formed different groups in Italy namely 'Fascios' i.e. groups or bands.

Reason (R) A conference of the Fascist Party was held at Napies in October 1922.

Codes
(a) A is true, but R is false (b) R is the reason for A
(c) Both A and R are false (d) Only R is true, A is false

Ans. (d) Only R is true, A is false

4. Identify the correct statements from given below options.
P. Germany and the Soviet Union were not made the members of the League.
Q. USA also did not join the League.
R. The rise of dictatorship in Germany and Italy strengthened the League.
S. All nations were permitted to enter any secret treaties and alliances.
(a) P and Q (b) R and S (c) P and S (d) Q and R

Ans. (a) P and Q

5. Read the two statements regarding Nazism.
A. There was an absence of a strong opposition party in Germany which could challenge the ideologies and plans of the Nazis.
B. The Nazis did not encounter any effective resistance, Hitler became extremely popular with the people.
(a) B contradicts A
(b) B is the reason for A
(c) A is true, but B is false
(d) A and B are independent of each other

Ans. (d) A and B are independent of each other

6. A ruler formed different groups similar to what is known as Fascios, who organised violence against the socialists and the communists. Who does this ruler resemble to?
(a) Hitler (b) Mussolini
(c) Victor Emmanuel (d) Kemal Pasha

Ans. (b) Mussolini

7. The below book is said to be written by who amongst the following?

(a) Woodrow Wilson (b) Archeduke Ferdinand
(c) Mussolini (d) Hitler

Ans. (d) Hitler

8. Raman is doing research project on an ideology that believes in expansion of territories through ,military conquests. Which ideology is he studying about?
(a) Fascism (b) Nazism
(c) Marxism (d) Leninism

Ans. (b) Nazism

Case Based Question

1. Read the excerpt given below and answer the questions that follow.

On 6th April, 1917, the United States formally entered the conflict in Europe, declaring war against Germany to join on the side of Allied nations.

When the war first began in 1914, President Woodrow Wilson strove to maintain American neutrality, but over two million U.S. troops would eventually go on to serve in a war that permanently transformed the world and significantly shaped the course of the twentieth century, both at home and abroad.

The assassination of Archduke Francis Ferdinand of Austria and his wife Sofia in Sarajevo on 28th June, 1914, set off a chain of events that culminated in a world war. ***Source** USA Today*

(i) Name the immediate cause of the above war. Mention any two other causes of the above event.
(ii) Identify any three events of the above war.
(iii) Discuss any four impacts of the war.

Ans. (i) The assassination of Archduke Francis Ferdinand of Austria and his wife Sofia in Sarajevo on 28th June, 1914 was the immediate cause of above war.

Two other causes of above event were
- Race for Armament
- Aggressive and Militant Nationalism

(ii) Three events of the above war were
- War on the Western Front
- War against Turkey
- Entry of USA in the War

(iii) Four impacts of the war were
- The treaty of Versailles was signed at Versailles in France by the victorious nations and Germany was held guilty of aggression.
- The war marked the end of three ruling dynasties in Europe i.e. the Romanov in Russia, the Hohenzollern in Germany and Hapsburg in Austria-Hungary.
- The war marked the end of three ruling dynasties in Europe-the Romanov in Russia, the Hohenzollern in Germany and Hapsburg in Austria-Hungary.
- Many independent states emerged during the war. Some of these were Finland, Estonia, Latvia, Lithuania and Yugoslavia.

8. The Second World War

Multiple Choice Questions

1. Treaty of Versailles led to the dissatisfaction among countries, especially Germany and Italy. This treaty is best related to which of the following event?
(a) World War II (b) World War I
(c) Cold War (d) Disintegration of USSR

Ans. (b) World War I

2. Refer the following details.

Events	Year
Fascism	Mussolini
Nazism	Adolf Hitler
League of Nations	First World War
Pearl Harbour	?

Select the option that appropriately fill the above blank.

(a) USA (b) Poland
(c) Cuba (d) Japan

Ans. (a) USA

3. Read the two statements given below and select the option that shows the correct relationship between (A) and (R).

Assertion (A) Britain signed 'A Gentleman's Pact' with Italy in 1933.

Reason (R) Adolf Hitler came into power in 1929.

Codes

(a) A is true, but R is false (b) R is the reason for A
(c) Both A and R are false (d) Only R is true, A is false

Ans. (c) Both A and R are false

4. These cities were bombed during the Second World War by USA. This marked the entry of USA in the World War. Identify the cities.

P. Hiroshima Q. Nagasaki
R. Beijing S. Austria

(a) P and Q (b) R and S
(c) P and S (d) Q and S

Ans. (a) P and Q

5. Read the two statements regarding Second World War.

A. League of Nations was created after World War I to maintain peace in the world.

B. It suffered initial failure after USA did not join the League.

(a) B contradicts A
(b) B is the reason for A
(c) A is true, but B is false
(d) B and A are independent of each other

Ans. (d) B and A are independent of each other

6. USA and USSR were engaged in War like situation after World War II. It included economic warfare, conventional weapons and a concept known as

(a) Proxy Wars (b) Political Wars
(c) Nuclear Wars (d) Parallel Wars

Ans. (a) Proxy Wars

7. The below picture depicts Germany's invasion on a country that led to beginning of World War II. Name the country.

(a) Poland (b) Cuba
(c) Japan (d) China

Ans. (a) Poland

8. Siya is doing research about an organisation whose charter was adopted on 24th October, 1945. Which organisation is she researching about?

(a) UN (b) League of Nations
(c) World Bank (d) WTO

Ans. (a) UN

Case Based Question

1. Read the excerpt given below and answer the questions that follow.

D-Day marked a crucial turning point in World War II as the Allies launched a monumental effort to liberate France and Europe from Nazi Germany's grip. Through a massive deployment of land, sea and air forces, the Allies successfully gained a vital foothold in Western Europe. However, this triumph came at a tremendous cost, with the loss of thousands of lives. Every year, millions of people gather in Normandy, France, to participate in memorials, re-enactments and festivals honoring the Battle of Normandy and D-Day.

(i) When did the above event begin? Mention any two causes of this event.

(ii) Name any three impacts of this event.

(iii) Briefly discuss the organisation that was formed after this.

Ans. (i) The above movement began in 1939.

The causes of this event were

- Dissatisfaction with the Treaty of Versailles.
- Failure of the League of Nations.

(ii) The three impacts of this event were

- The axis powers (Germany, Italy and Japan) were defeated in the war.

- The United Nations was formed to maintain international peace and security and to prevent the occurrence of any future wars.
- USA and Soviet Union had fought together during the Second World War. But by the end of the war, ideological differences began to appear between both nations leading to cold war.

(iii) The organisation formed after this event was the United Nations. The United Nations was formed in 1945 to maintain international peace and security and to prevent the occurrence of any future wars. The heads of three powerful countries—President Roosevelt of America, Prime Minister Churchill of Britain and Stalin of Soviet Union, convened a conference of representatives of all nations at San Francisco and drew up the 'Charter of the United Nations'. This led to the establishment of the United Nations.

9. United Nations and its Major Agencies

Multiple Choice Questions

1. This organisation was formed after the First World War to establish peace in the world. However, it was not able to prevent the outbreak of the Second World War.
Which among the following correctly matches the above description?
(a) United Nations (b) League of Nations
(c) Group 20 (d) Forum of Nations

Ans. (b) League of Nations

2. Refer the following details.

Agency	Headquarters
UNICEF	New York
WHO	Switzerland
UNESCO	?

Fill the above blank with the help of following options.
(a) Paris (b) Washington DC
(c) Tokyo (d) Berlin

Ans. (a) Paris

3. It organises seminars and conferences of scientists. Courier is its official monthly magazine. Which Agency is being mentioned here?
(a) ECOSOC (b) WHO
(c) UNESCO (d) UNICEF

Ans. (c) UNESCO

4. Identify the organs of the UN from the information given below.
P. General Assembly Q. UNESCO
R. Trusteeship Council S. WHO
(a) P and Q (b) Q and R
(c) R and S (d) P and R

Ans. (d) P and R

5. Read the statements below regarding Security Council.
A. Security Council has five permanent members i.e. China, France, Russia, Britain and the United States of America.
B. Decision in the Security Council is taken after at least nine members vote in its favour including the permanent members.
(a) B contradicts A
(b) B is the reason for A
(c) A is true, but B is false
(d) A and B are independent of each other

Ans. (d) A and B are independent of each other

6. Read the two statements given below and select the option that shows the correct relationship between (A) and (R).
Assertion (A) United Nations was set-up on 24th October, 1945 at San Francisco.
Reason (R) The headquarters of United Nations is situated at Hague, Netherlands.
Codes
(a) A is true, but R is false (b) R is the reason for A
(c) Both A and R are false (d) Only R is true, A is false

Ans. (a) A is true, but R is false

7. The headquarters of the below depicted organ of UN is located in which city?

(a) Hague (b) New York
(c) Paris (d) London

Ans. (a) Hague

8. Shubham is studying about an organ of UN that is the main organ of the UN, and all members of the UN are its members. Which organ is he studying about?
(a) Security Council (b) General Assembly
(c) WHO (d) ICJ

Ans. (b) General Assembly

Case Based Question

1. Read the excerpt given below and answer the questions that follow.

The Netherlands and Canada filed a joint application to the International Court of Justice (ICJ), the UN Court based in The Hague said on Monday, asking it to prosecute the government of Syrian President Bashar Assad for crimes committed during the country's civil war. ***Source** The Wire: 13th June, 2023*

(i) What is the principal function of the above organ? Name any two powers of this organ.
(ii) What are the functions of this organ under compulsory jurisdiction?
(iii) What is the structure of the above organ?

Ans. (i) Principal function of the above organ is that it settles legal disputes and gives advisory opinions on legal questions.

The functions of this organ are

- It decides cases in accordance with international treaties and conventions in force, international customs, etc.
- It may also decide matters in the cases which are referred to it by member nations.

(ii) Under compulsory Jurisdiction, the court decides the following

- It decides cases when many treaties include the submission of disputes to the Court.
- It decides disputes related to the interpretation of international laws.
- It decides cases related to the reparation which is to be made for breaching any international obligations.

(iii) The International Court of Justice is composed of 15 judges elected to nine-year terms of office by the United Nations General Assembly and the Security Council. These organs vote simultaneously but separately. In order to be elected, a candidate must receive an absolute majority of the votes in both bodies. This sometimes makes it necessary for a number of rounds of voting to be held.

In order to ensure a degree of continuity, one third of the Court is elected every three years. Judges are eligible for re-election. Should a judge die or resign during his or her term of office, a special election is held as soon as possible to choose a judge to fill the unexpired part of the term.

10. Non-Aligned Movement

Multiple Choice Questions

1. Many Asian and African nations who had become independent after the Second World War refused to join either of the blocs. Which among the following best describes the result of the above statement?
(a) Declaring war
(b) Creation of NAM
(c) Economic Isolation
(d) Creation of non-support movement

Ans. (b) Creation of NAM

2. Refer the following details.

Leader	Country
Josip Broz Tito	?
Nasser	Egypt
Ho Chi Minh	Vietnam
Kwama Nkumrah	Ghana

Complete the above blank with the help of appropriate options.
(a) Africa (b) Yugoslavia (c) Burma (d) Malaysia

Ans. (b) Yugoslavia

3. He is considered the greatest spokesman for neutrality of Asian and African states in the era of Cold War. Whom does this statement essentially credit to?
(a) Nehru (b) Tito
(c) Ho Chi Minh (d) Nasser

Ans. (a) Nehru

4. Consider the following statements and choose the correct option.
P. NAM helped reduce the tension between two power blocs and played an important role in bringing the Cold War to an end.
Q. It supported the race of armaments which existed among various countries during the Cold War.
R. It supported and promoted international peace, justice and freedom.
S. It did not advocated a new international economic order.
(a) P and Q (b) P and S (c) R and P (d) R and Q

Ans. (c) R and P

5. Read the following statements regarding NAM.

A. India played an important role in NAM and world affairs during the Cold War.

B. It supported many countries in the efforts to attain independence

(a) B contradicts A

(b) B is the reason for A

(c) A is true, but B is false

(d) B and A are independent of each other

Ans. (d) B and A are independent of each other

6. Read the two statements given below and select the option that shows the correct relationship between (A) and (R).

Assertion (A) The two superpowers America and Russia tried to influence other weak nations.

Reason (R) Both wanted to show the world their respective dominance. They tried to attract them by aids and ideas.

Codes

(a) A is true, but R is false (b) R is the reason for A

(c) Both A and R are false (d) Only R is true, A is false

Ans. (b) R is the reason for A

7. The below movement was given a final shape in which conference?

(a) Badung (b) Bangkok

(c) Tokyo (d) Ghana

Ans. (a) Badung

8. Sakshi is doing a project on NAM. She enquires about the country that took the initiative to launch NAM. Choose the most appropriate country.

(a) India (b) Yugoslavia

(c) Ghana (d) Egypt

Ans. (a) India

Case Based Question

1. Read the given news carefully.

During the bipolar era of the Cold War, when most nations aligned themselves with either of the two superpowers, a few nations chose to pursue a different path and advocated for a non-aligned policy that upheld their sovereignty and independence. India and Egypt demonstrated that it was possible to exist in a bipolar world without joining any of the two power blocs. They were among the nations that defied the pressure to align with either of the superpowers.

***Source** The Quint*

(i) When was the above movement launched? Who were the members of the movement?

(ii) What were the objectives of the movement?

(iii) Give any four effects of this movement.

Ans. (i) The above movement was launched in 1961.

NAM was established by initiative of Yugoslavia President Josip Broz Tito, Indian Prime Minister Jawaharlal Nehru, Egyptian President Gamal Abdel Nasser, Ghanaian President Kwame Nkrumah, and Indonesian President Sukarno.

(ii) The objectives of NAM were

- Not to join any power bloc or any military alliance.
- To eliminate all those causes which may lead to a war.
- To oppose colonialism, imperialism and racial discrimination.

(iii) The effect of this movement were

- NAM helped reduce the tension between two power blocs and played an important role in bringing the Cold War to an end.
- It opposed the race of armaments which existed among various countries during the Cold War.
- It supported and promoted international peace, justice and freedom.
- It advocated a new international economic order which was based on greater economic cooperation and justice.

ICSE Fully Solved

SAMPLE PAPER 01

Time : 2 hrs
Marks : 80

History & Civics X

General Instructions

1. Answers to this Paper must be written on the paper provided separately.
2. You will not be allowed to write during the first 15 minutes. This time is to be spent in reading the question paper.
3. The time given at the head of this paper is the time allowed for writing the answers.
4. Attempt all questions from Part I (Compulsory). A total of 5 questions are to be attempted from Part II, 2 out of 3 questions from Section A and 3 out of 5 questions from Section B.
5. The intended marks for questions or parts of questions are given in brackets [ ].

Part - I [30 *Marks*]

Atttempt all questions from this part

1. Choose the correct option. **[16 × 1]**

(i) Question Hour is an important device of the members of the Parliament to seek information about matters of Public Importance.

Which among the following best describes Question Hour?

(a) First hour of every Parliamentary sitting
(b) Last hour of every Parliamentary sitting
(c) First session of Lok Sabha
(d) Joint session of Parliament

(ii) Given below are the details of few citizens.

Candidate	Age	Other details
A	45	Bankrupt
B	28	Votes regularly
C	27	Belongs to Russia
D	21	Have been in jail for theft

Choose the person who fulfills the eligibility to become member of Lok Sabha.

(a) A (b) B
(c) C (d) D

(iii) President feels that State X is misgoverned and wants to stabilise the rule.

Which of these emergencies will be declared?

(a) National Emergency (b) President's Rule
(c) Financial Emergency (d) Civil Emergency

(iv) Observe the given picture. If fewer than 10% of the total members are present in the Lok Sabha, what action can the Speaker take?

(a) Conduct voting regardless.
(b) Adjourn the house for lack of quorum.
(c) Invite the Rajya Sabha to participate.
(d) Nominate more members on the spot.

(v) Identify the Executive powers of the President.

P. All the executive actions are formally taken in his/her name.
Q. Appointment of members of UPSC.
R. Introduce annual budget in the Parliament.

S. Dismissing the Council of Ministers.

(a) P and Q (b) R and S
(c) P and S (d) Q and S

(vi) A High Court Judge addresses his letter of resignation to

(a) President (b) Chief Justice of India
(c) Governor (d) Chief Justice of State

(vii) Identify the odd one out from the following Moderates in the Indian National Movement.

(a) Gopal Krishna Gokhale
(b) Surendranath Banerjee
(c) Dadabhai Naoroji
(d) Bal Gangadhar Tilak

(viii) Country X that is under Colonial rule is demanding self-government. Which is the movement that was launched in India similar to the movement by Country X for self government?

(a) Home Rule Movement
(b) Civil Disobedience Movement
(c) Swadeshi Movement
(d) Non-cooperation Movement

(ix) Read the two statements given below and select the option that shows the correct relationship between (A) and (R).

Assertion (A) East Bengal was dominated by Bengali Hindus.

Reason (R) Capital of East Bengal was declared to be Calcutta.

Codes

(a) A is true, but R is false
(b) R is the reason for A
(c) Both A and R are false
(d) Only R is true, A is false

(x) The movement mentioned in the below picture emerged after which event?

(a) World War I (b) World war II
(c) Cold War (d) Disintegration of USSR

(xi) Who was the Viceroy of India at the time of Second Round Table Conference?

(a) Lord Irwin (b) Lord Wavell
(c) Lord Willington (d) Lord Reading

(xii) Riya is doing a research work on a prominent leader who gave a slogan' "Give me blood and I shall give you the freedom".

Who is she most likely talking about?

(a) Bal Gangadhar Tilak
(b) Lala Lajpat Rai
(c) Subhash Chandra Bose
(d) Bhagat Singh

(xiii) Identify the name of personality who gave the slogans 'Delhi Chalo' and 'Jai Hind'.

(a) Mahatma Gandhi (b) Jawaharlal Nehru
(c) Rash Behari Bose (d) Subhash Chandra Bose

(xiv) The Unification of Italy between 1860 and 1870 completed under ....

(a) Victor Emmanuel (b) Victor Emmanuel III
(c) Mussolini (d) Hitler

(xv) Which of the following is/are a common cause of Fascism and Nazism?

(a) Favoured totalitarian system against democratic rules
(b) Feared threat of Communism
(c) Both (a) and (b)
(d) None of the above

(xvi) Complete the given analogy.

London Declaration : 1941 :: Washington Declaration : ?

(a) 1940 (b) 1942
(c) 1943 (d) 1944

2. (i) **Headline** – Access to Internet is a Fundamental Right : SC

The court said access to internet becomes the part of right to education as well as right to privacy under Article 21 of the Constitution of India.

Source : *Hindustan Times. 11th January,* 2020

Imagine you are a victim of this incident and you approach Supreme Court. Through which instruments will it restore your fundamental rights? **[2]**

(ii) Discuss the main contributions of Surendranath Banerjee in Indian Freedom Struggle. **[2]**

(iii) Mention any two socio-religious causes of the First War of Independence in 1857. **[2]**

(iv) What were the objectives of 'The Servants of India Society'? Who founded it? **[2]**

(v) Analyse any two reasons for the indirect election of the President in India. **[2]**

(vi) State the two objectives of INA. **[2]**

(vii) Mention any two factors responsible for the development of the Non-Aligned Movement. **[2]**

Part - II [50 *Marks*]

Section A

*Attempt any **two** questions from this Section*

3. With reference to the Indian Parliament and governance, answer the following questions.
   (i) Mention any three qualifications required to become a member of the Lok Sabha. **[3]**
   (ii) Define the following terms. **[3]**
   (a) Adjournment (b) Speaker (c) Bill
   (iii) Explain any four legislative powers of the Indian Parliament. **[4]**

4. With reference to the Union Executive, answer the following questions.
   (i) Mention any three legislative powers of the President of India. **[3]**
   (ii) Mention any three situations in which the President can declare a National Emergency. **[3]**
   (iii) With reference to the powers of the President, explain. **[4]**
   (a) Any two Judicial Powers
   (b) Any two Discretionary Powers

5. (i) What is the role of High Court in India? State any two composition of the High Court. **[3]**
   (ii) Mention the three kinds of cases which come under the apellate jurisdiction of the High Court. **[3]**
   (iii) State any four cases under original jurisdiction of the High Court. **[4]**

Section B

*Attempt any **three** questions from this Section*

6. The establishment of the Indian National Congress was a significant event in the development of the National Movement in India. In this context
   (i) Explain the formation of the Indian National Congress. **[3]**
   (ii) The primary objective of the Indian National Congress (INC), established in 1885, was to foster a sense of national unity among Indians. Mention any four of its objectives to justify the statement. **[4]**
   (iii) Explain the sessions of the Congress. **[3]**

7.

   (i) Identify the event in the above picture and explain the causes of this event. **[3]**
   (ii) Mention any three impacts of the event. **[3]**
   (iii) Discuss the course of the event. **[4]**

8. Read the excerpt given below and answer the following questions.

   Yet Meerut's fame rests not on beads and terracotta cakes no matter how ancient, but on bullets and blood, more accurately cartridges with possibly cow and pig fat, and rifles with which began India's First War of Independence on 10th May, 1857. The British were well and truly in the saddle in the 19th century.

   A year after muskets were introduced in 1856, Lord Canning was planning to send back the 84th Regiment of the Army to Burma, when news came of a serious outbreak in Meerut which was, as G.W. Forrest writes in A History of the Indian Mutiny (published by William Blackwood), "situated 36 miles from the Imperial City of Delhi traversed by two main roads, the one from Ghaziabad to Roorkee, and the Mall, lined with a fine avenue of lofty trees. ***Source*** *The Hindu*

   (i) During which Governor's tenure Revolt of 1857 took place? Name any two causes of the Revolt of 1857. **[3]**
   (ii) Mention any three effects of this event. **[3]**
   (iii) Due to this event, many changes were made in the army. Mention any four changes. **[4]**

9. The rise of Fascism and Nazism in Italy and Germany respectively, contributed to the causes which led to the Second World War. In this context, explain:
   (i) Any three principles of Fascism. **[3]**
   (ii) Any three causes of rise of Nazism in Germany. **[3]**
   (iii) Rise of Mussolini in Italy **[4]**

10. The UN charter establishes the UN's six principal organs. With reference to the United Nations, explain the following

(i) Functions of the International Court of Justice. **[3]**

(ii) Composition of the General Assembly and its working. **[3]**

(iii) Explain any three roles of WHO in combating diseases. **[4]**

Answers

1. (i) (a) First hour of every Parliamentary sitting

(ii) (b) B

(iii) (b) President's Rule

(iv) (b) Adjourn the house for lack of quorum.

(v) (a) P and Q

(vi) (a) President

(vii) (d) Bal Gangadhar Tilak

(viii) (a) Home Rule Movement

(ix) (c) Both A and R are false

(x) (b) World War II

(xi) (c) Lord Willington

(xii) (c) Subhash Chandra Bose

(xiii) (d) Subhash Chandra Bose

(xiv) (a) Victor Emmanuel

(xv) (c) Both (a) and (b)

(xvi) (b) 1942

2. (i) Any citizen whose fundamental rights have been violated can directly approach the Supreme Court and the latter can issue writs such as Habeas Corpus, Mandamus, Quo Warranto, etc for the enforcement of fundamental rights.

The Supreme Court can declare any law made by the Government as null and void if it violates the fundamental rights of any individual.

(ii) The main achievements of Surendranath Banerjee were

- He advocated constitutional means for attaining his political goals. He advocated for the establishment of self-government in India. He also advocated the idea of boycotting foreign goods and using Swadeshi as methods of anti-colonial protest.
- He set up his own school that later called Ripon College.

(iii) Two socio-religious causes of the First War of Independence were as follows

(a) The reforms like the Abolition of Sati (1829), the introduction of the Widow Remarriage Act (1856) and the opening of Western education to girls were not welcomed by the masses.

(b) The British officers were rude and arrogant towards the Indians. Such acts of unjust discrimination alienated the British from the Indian masses.

(iv) The objectives of 'The Servants of India Society' were to cultivate love for their motherland among the Indians and to involve people to work for the welfare of the Indians. It was established by Gopal Krishna Gokhale.

(v) The President of India is indirectly elected to maintain balance and stability in the democratic system. Two reasons for the Indirect election of the President in India are

- **Federal Representation** Indirect election ensures equal representation of both the Union and States in choosing the President.
- **Neutrality** It maintains the President's neutrality, preventing party dominance and ensuring stability.

(vi) The two objectives of the Indian National Army are as follows

(a) To organise an armed revolution and to fight the British army of occupation with modern arms.

(b) To organise a provisional government of free India in order to mobilise all forces effectively.

(vii) Two factors responsible for the development of the Non-Aligned Movement were as follows

(a) Most of the newly independent countries of Asia and Africa realised that the division of the world into two power blocs was not in their larger interest and might endanger world peace.

(b) The newly independent nations opted for Non-alignment, because of some emotional and psychological constraints.

3. (i) Three qualifications required to become a member of the Lok Sabha are
 - Must be a citizen of India.
 - Must be at least 25 years old.
 - Must not hold an office of profit under the government.

 (ii) (a) **Adjournment** It refers to the suspension of the sitting of the House for a specific period.
 (b) **Speaker** The presiding officer of the Lok Sabha, elected from among its members.
 (c) **Bill** A proposal for a new law or a change in the existing law presented in Parliament.

 (iii) Four legislative powers of the Indian Parliament are
 - Parliament can make laws on subjects in the Union and Concurrent Lists.
 - It can make laws on State List subjects during emergencies.
 - It can pass laws for new Union Territories.
 - It can amend existing laws or repeal them.

4. (i) Three legislative powers of the President of India are
 - The President can summon and prorogue both Houses of Parliament.
 - He/She can dissolve the Lok Sabha and call for fresh elections.
 - No bill passed by Parliament can become law without the President's assent.

 (ii) Three situations in which the President can declare a National Emergency are
 - When there is a war or external aggression.
 - When there is armed rebellion within the country.
 - When there is an imminent threat to the security of India or any part of it.

 (iii) (a) **Judicial powers**
 - The President can grant pardon, reprieve, respite or remission of punishment.
 - He/She can suspend or commute sentences in certain cases, especially related to Union laws or military court punishments.

 (b) **Discretionary Powers**
 - Appointing a Prime Minister when no party has a clear majority.
 - Sending back a bill (except money bills) to Parliament for reconsideration.

5. (i) Each High Court consists of a Chief Justice and some other judges as the President of India may appoint from time to time. Besides, the President also has the power to appoint.
 (a) Additional judges for a temporary period not exceeding 2 years.
 (b) An acting judge, when a permanent judge is temporarily absent.

 (ii) The High Court's appellate jurisdiction is over the decision of the subordinate courts under its supervision and also over the decision of single judge bench of the High Court.

 The appellate jurisdiction of High Courts extends to both civil and criminal cases. The jurisdiction also extends to cases tried by courts of munsifs and district sub-judges. In criminal cases, it extends to cases decided by Session and Additional Session Judges. Thus, the jurisdiction of the High Courts extends to all cases under the state or federal laws in which the sentence of imprisonment exceeds 7 years or the death sentence.

 (iii) Original Jurisdiction means the power of a High Court to hear disputes in the first instance, not by way of appeal. These include the following
 - Will, divorce, marriage, company law, contempt of court.
 - Matters of admirality.
 - State revenue and its collection.
 - Enforcement of Fundamental Rights of citizens.

6. (i) **Formation of the Indian National Congress**

 There was need of an All India political association to make consensus on the political demands of the Indians and to draw the government's attention to the administrative drawbacks and suggest means to rectify them. AO Hume, a retired British member of the Indian Civil Service, helped in this direction.

 In 1884, Hume in consultation with the Indian leaders, laid the foundation of the Indian National Union. On the suggestion of Dadabhai Naoroji, the name of the union later was changed to the Indian National Congress.

 (ii) **Aims and Objectives of the Indian National Congress**

 The Indian National Congress (INC) aimed to promote unity and political awareness among Indians.

Four of its main objectives were

(a) To promote friendly relations between nationalist political workers from different parts of the country.

(b) To develop and consolidate the feelings of National unity irrespective of caste, religion or province.

(c) To formulate popular demands and present them before the government.

(d) To train and organise the public opinion in the country.

(iii) **Sessions of the Congress**

The Congress held its sessions every year in December to check out programmes to achieve its aims.

The First Session of the Congress was attended by 72 delegates from all parts of India including such eminent persons as Dadabhai Naoroji, W C Bonnerjee, K T Telang, Badruddin Tyabji etc.

The Second Session of the Congress was held at Kolkata under the Presidentship of Dadabhai Naoroji. Thereafter, the National Congress met every year in December in different parts of the country. The Surat Session of the Congress was held in 1907 under the Presidentship of Rash Behari Ghosh.

7. (i) The event in the given picture depicts the demonstration against the Simon Commission. In 1927, the British Government appointed the Indian Statuatory Commission, known as Simon Commission, to investigate the need for further Constitutional Reforms. It had no Indian members. This was seen as a violation of the principle of self-determination and a deliberate insult to the self-respect of the Indians.

(ii) The government used brutal suppression and police attacks to break the popular opposition. Lala Lajpat Rai was beaten up mercilessly and lost his life as a result of the lathi blows. After his death, the Extremists followed more aggressive paths. In spite of all the protests, the Simon Commission travelled to different parts of the country, met people and made their recommendations.

(iii) At the Madras Session of Congress in 1927, presided over by Dr Ansari, the National Congress decided to boycott the commission at every stage and in every form. The Muslim League and the Hindu Mahasabha decided to support the Congress decision on 3rd February. The day the commission reached Bombay, an All India Hartal was organised. Wherever the Commission went, it was greeted with Hartals and Black Flag demonstrations.

8. (i) Revolt of 1857 took place during the tenure of Lord Canning.

Two causes of the Revolt of 1857 were

- Exploitation of economic resources
- Policy of racial discrimination

(ii) The three effects of this event were

- End of the Company's Rule
- End of Mughals and Peshwaship
- The strength of European troops in India was increased.

(iii) The four changes brought in the army were

- European soldiers were posted in key strategic locations.
- Artillery was placed under British control.
- Discriminations on the basis of caste, region and religion were practiced in the recruitment of soldiers in the army to prevent another anti-British uprising.
- Newspapers, journals and nationalist publications were prevented from reaching the soldiers to avoid any kind of mutiny.

9. (i) Three principles of Fascism were as follows

(a) Fascism was a supporter of one party and one leader.

(b) Fascism believed that the interests of the state were superior to the rights of the people. The individual exists solely for the society of which he forms a part and that the state obliterates all individual rights.

(c) Fascism believed in enhancing the power and the prestige of the state, and stressed greatly on nationalism.

(ii) Three causes for the rise of Nazism in Germany were as follows

(a) A democratic republic, which was set-up after the abdication of Kaiser Wilhelm II could not face up to the many problems, which surmounted the country.

(b) After the First World War, there was an economic slump in Europe, which affected Germany also. The republic failed to solve this economic problem.

(c) Inspired by the Russian Revolution, the German Communists tried to bring about a revolution in Germany.

(iii) Mussolini formed different groups in Italy namely **Fascios** i.e. groups or bands. This group used to organise violence against socialists and communists. They wore a black uniform and were known as **Black-Shirts**. The 'fasces' (a bundle of rods with a projecting axe blade) was their symbol.

These volunteers believed in violence and took over factories, municipalities and police stations. Later this group was organised into the 'Fascist Party'. Then onwards, he became anti-socialist and advocated dictatorship.

10. (i) The functions of International Court of Justice are as follows

(a) It advises other organs of the UN.

(b) It settles disputes about International established conventions and interpretation of International Laws.

(c) It codifies International Laws.

(ii) The General Assembly consists of all the members of the United Nations. Each member shall have not more than 5 representatives in the General Assembly, but each has one vote. Important decisions regarding budgetary matters, admission of members etc. are taken by 2/3rd majority of the assembly.

The General Assembly meets every year on the 3rd Tuesday of September. Additional meetings can be called for by the Secretary General.

(iii) The WHO works for the health of the people to achieve its aim. The WHO helps countries strengthen their health system, promotes research in all health related aspects. The WHO also issues periodicals and health journals to inform about the latest developments in health care.

ICSE Unsolved

SAMPLE PAPER 02

History & Civics X

Time : 2 hrs
Marks : 80

General Instructions

1. Answers to this Paper must be written on the paper provided separately.
2. You will not be allowed to write during the first 15 minutes. This time is to be spent in reading the question paper.
3. The time given at the head of this paper is the time allowed for writing the answers.
4. Attempt all questions from Part I (Compulsory). A total of 5 questions are to be attempted from Part II, 2 out of 3 questions from Section A and 3 out of 5 questions from Section B.
5. The intended marks for questions or parts of questions are given in brackets [ ].

Part - I [30 *Marks*]

Attempt all questions from this part

1. Choose the correct option. **[16 × 1]**

(i) On the last allotted days at the appointed time, the Speaker puts every necessary question to dispose of all outstanding matters in connection with demand for grants.

Which among the following concept best describes the concept mentioned above?

(a) Zero Hour (b) Question Hour
(b) Cut Motion (d) Guillotine Motion

(ii) Given below are some details of few Indian citizens.

Candidate	Age	Other Details
A	45	Belongs to USA
B	67	Belongs to sound financial background
C	64	Advocate of High Court for 10 years
D	41	Been in jail for kidnapping

Select the person who fulfills the eligibility criteria to become the Judge of Supreme Court.

(a) A (b) B (c) C (d) D

(iii) Country Y's judiciary is single integrated judicial system similar to that of India.

Which of the following facts prove that Y has a single integrated judiciary?

(a) Supreme Court is at the head of the judicial system.
(b) Judges of the Courts are appointed by the President.
(c) Judiciary is independent from Legislature and Executive.
(d) Supreme Court of the country is located in its capital.

(iv) Observe the given picture. If a member changes political party after getting elected, what can happen under the Anti-defection Law?

(a) They are promoted to a ministerial post.
(b) They are given a warning only.
(c) They are disqualified from their seat.
(d) Nothing happens; switching parties is allowed.

(v) Identify the officers who are appointed by the President of India

A. Attorney General of India
B. Chairman of UPSC
C. State Election Commissioners
D. Chancellors of Universities

(a) A and B (b) B and C
(d) B and D (d) A and D

(vi) Complete the given analogy.

Judge of Supreme Court : 65 years :: Judge of High Court : ?

(a) 60 years (b) 62 years (c) 65 years (d) 63 years

(vii) Identify the odd one out among the following early Congress sessions Presidents.

(a) W.C. Bonnerjee
(b) Badruddin Tyabji
(c) Surendranath Banerjee
(d) Subhash Chandra Bose

(viii) Country A's province was divided by its colonialists on the basis of religious fragments. They decided to launch a movement similar to that India . What should have been major feature of this movement?

(a) Use of machine made goods
(b) Declaration of Independence
(c) Use of swadeshi goods
(d) Organising a revolt

(ix) Who among the following was the founder of the London Indian Society in collaboration with WC Bonnerjee in 1865?

(a) Dadabhai Naoroji (b) Gopal Krishna Gokhale
(c) Surendranath Banerjee (d) Pherozeshah Mehta

(x) The event depicted in the below succeeded which global event?

GALESBURG EVENING MAIL
PEACE TREATY SIGNED
"Peace is Just", Says President to American People
GERMANS SIGN PACT; WAR IS FORMALLY OVER

(a) Second World War (b) First World War
(c) Cold War (d) Fall of Berlin Wall

(xi) Read the two statements given below and select the option that shows the correct relationship between (A) and (R).

Assertion (A) The causes of the failure of Quit India Movement were failure of Simon Commission and Rowlatt Act.

Reason (R) Quit India Movement was started in 1919.

Codes

(a) A is true, but R is false
(b) R is the reason for A
(c) Both A and R are false
(d) Only R is true, A is false

(xii) Parimal is doing a project on revolutionaries. She researched about Father of Revolutionary Thought in India.

Who is she most likely talking about?

(a) Bal Gangadhar Tilak (b) Bipin Chandra Pal
(c) Lala Lajpat Rai (d) Dadabhai Naoroji

(xiii) The Indian National Planning Committee was set up by Subhash Chandra Bose in ....

(a) December, 1939 (b) January, 1938
(c) November, 1939 (d) December, 1938

(xiv) The Second World War began with the German invasion of .... on 1st September, 1939.

(a) Belgium (b) Poland
(c) Austria (d) Soviet Union

(xvi) The Treaty of Versailles was signed between the Allies and Germany on 28th June, 1919 at … .

(a) Paris (b) Moscow
(c) Tokyo (d) Rome

(xvi) Which of the following countries is not a permanent member of the UN Security Council?

(a) USA (b) Japan (c) France (d) Russia

2. (i) **Headline** – President dissolves Lok Sabha, Elections by the Year End, Charan Singh Caretaker PM

Source *Indian Express 23rd August, 1979*

State a condition in which President can dissolve Lok Sabha. **[2]**

(ii) State any two reasons for the rise of fascism. **[2]**

(iii) Explain different methods followed by the Early Nationalists. **[2]**

(iv) Write any two causes of the failure of the Swadeshi Movement. **[2]**

(v) Write any two clauses of the Mountbatten Plan in India. **[2]**

(vi) Mention any two causes of the failure of the Revolt of 1857. **[2]**

(vii) Briefly explain the factors responsible for Non-Aligned Movement. **[2]**

Part - II [50 *Marks*]

Section A

*Attempt any **two** questions from this Section*

3. With reference to the Indian Parliament, answer the following questions.

(i) Mention any three qualifications required to become a member of the Rajya Sabha. **[4]**

(ii) Explain the following terms. **[3]**

(a) Zero Hour

(b) Adjournment Motion
(c) Speaker

(iii) When can the Parliament pass a law without the approval of the Rajya Sabha? Mention any three reasons why the Lok Sabha is considered more powerful than the Rajya Sabha. [3]

4. The executive power of the country is vested in the President and Vice President. With reference to this, answer the following questions.

(i) Describe the procedure for electing the President of India. [3]

(ii) Mention any three differences between the powers of the President and the Prime Minister. [3]

(iii) With reference to the powers of the President, mention. [4]
(a) Any two legislative powers
(b) Any two financial powers

5. The Constitution of India provides for a High Court for each State. With reference to the jurisdiction and functions of the High Court, explain the following:

(i) Its Original Jurisdiction. [3]

(ii) Its Appellate Jurisdiction. [3]

(iii) Composition of High Court. [4]

Section B

*Attempt any **three** questions from this Section*

6. There were a number of Political Associations formed in the second half of the 19th century. In this context, answer the following questions:

(i) Contribution of Raja Ram Mohan in development of Political Associations in India. [3]

(ii) Who founded the Indian League? Mention its two objectives. [3]

(iii) Why was there a need for creation of All India Political Association? Give four reasons. [4]

7. Read the excerpt given below and answer the following questions.

Movement was the expression of the outrage triggered in Bengal by the partition of the province of Bengal in 1905. Though the colonial masters cited administrative reasons, the Bengalis were convinced that the Partition was a Machiavellian move to destroy the unity of the Bengali people, whose political activism the government had come to fear.

There was now an increasing sense of impatience among sections of Bengalis, including some politicians within the Congress, because they felt that the official Congress policy of pleading with and petitioning the government for reforms, which was rejected as 'mendicancy', had proven to be completely ineffective.

The Swadeshi movement, which swept up the people of Bengal, especially the educated and the politically conscious, in a tide of nationalist emotion, is today remembered as the first mass movement, a forerunner to Mahatma Gandhi's politics of mass involvement that altered the structure, form and tone of Indian nationalist politics.

(i) The above movement was launched during the tenure of which Governor General of India? State any two causes of this movement. [3]

(ii) Mention any three impacts of this movement. [3]

(iii) Discuss the event that led to launching of this movement. [4]

8.

(i) Who is the man in the above picture? Briefly mention about him. [3]

(ii) How did he influence the National Movement? [3]

(iii) Mention the contributions of the person in the freedom struggle. [4]

9. With reference to the Second World War, explain the following

(i) Consequences of Second World War with reference to Cold War [3]

(ii) Agressive Nationalism of Germany [3]

(iii) Four causes of Second World War [4]

10. In the Political scenario of 1939, important developments took place in India and abroad. In this context, answer the following questions.

(i) Who was the founder of the 'Forward Bloc'? Why was this organisation formed? [3]

(ii) Write about the main objectives of the Forward Bloc? [3]

(iii) How the Indian National League and Indian National Army were formed? [4]

Answers

1. (i) (d) Guillotine Motion
   (ii) (c) C
   (iii) (a) Supreme Court is at the head of the judicial system.
   (iv) (c) They are disqualified from their seat.
   (v) (a) A and B
   (vi) (b) 62 years
   (vii) (d) Subhash Chandra Bose
   (viii) (c) Use of swadeshi goods
   (ix) (a) Dadabhai Naoroji
   (x) (b) First World War
   (xi) (c) Both A and R are false
   (xii) (b) Bipin Chandra Pal
   (xiii) (d) December, 1938
   (xiv) (b) Poland
   (xv) (a) Paris
   (xvi) (b) Japan

ICSE Unsolved

SAMPLE PAPER 03

Time : 2 hrs
Marks : 80

History & Civics X

General Instructions

1. Answers to this Paper must be written on the paper provided separately.
2. You will not be allowed to write during the first 15 minutes. This time is to be spent in reading the question paper.
3. The time given at the head of this paper is the time allowed for writing the answers.
4. Attempt all questions from Part I (Compulsory). A total of 5 questions are to be attempted from Part II, 2 out of 3 questions from Section A and 3 out of 5 questions from Section B.
5. The intended marks for questions or parts of questions are given in brackets [ ].

Part - I

[30 *Marks*]

Attempt all questions from this part

1. Choose the correct option. **[16 × 1]**

(i) India is federal in form and unitary in spirit. Which among the following best describes the same?

(a) India has certain unitary features which limit the powers of the State governments.
(b) Constitution of India is both rigid and flexible.
(c) India has a federal form of Government.
(d) Both Union and State Governments draw their power and the authority from the Constitution.

(ii) Given below are the details of few citizens.

Candidate	Age	Details
A	31	Bankrupt
B	35	Belongs to rural areas
C	30	Actor
D	32	Member of Lok Sabha

Select the candidate who fulfills the criteria of becoming the Vice-President of India.

(a) A (b) B
(c) C (d) D

(iii) Indian State A and B are in conflict over sharing of river water. They approach Supreme Court for the resolution of their dispute. Such a dispute comes in which type of jurisdiction of Supreme Court?

(a) Appellate Jurisdiction
(b) Original Jurisdiction
(c) Writ Jurisdiction
(d) Advisory Jurisdiction

(iv) Who advises the President of India with regard to the appointment of important officials like the Attorney General of India, Comptroller and Auditor-General of India?

(a) Governor
(b) Chief Justice of India
(c) Home Minister
(d) Prime Minister

(v) A person is under a trial for theft. He will be tried in which court?

P. District court
Q. Sessions Court
R. Court of Chief Judicial Magistrate
S. Court of First Class Magistrate

(a) P and Q
(b) R and S
(c) P and S
(d) Q and R

(vi) Observe the given picture. What can the Speaker do if members walk into the well of the House and protest?

(a) Ignore the protest and continue.
(b) Ask security to remove all members.
(c) Adjourn the House until order is restored.
(d) Suspend the Constitution.

(vii) Choose the odd one out among the social reformers.
(a) Raja Ram Mohan Roy
(b) Ishwar Chandra Vidyasagar
(c) Swami Dayanand Saraswati
(d) Lala Lajpat Rai

(viii) Country A wants to gain independence and wants to use the methods similar to the ones used by Indian Assertive Nationalists.

Based on the above information, which methods would not fit the ones used by Country A?
(a) National Education (b) Swadeshi
(c) Prayers and Petition (d) Boycott

(ix) Identify the name of the greatest social and religious reformer of the 19th century who established the Brahmo Sabha in 1828.
(a) Radha Kanta Dev (b) Jyotiba Phule
(c) Debendranath Tagore (d) Raja Ram Mohan Roy

(x) Complete the given analogy.

Moderates leader : Gopal Krishna Gokhale :: Extremists leader : ?
(a) Bipin Chandra Pal
(b) Dadabhai Naoroji
(c) Surendranath Banerjee
(d) Womesh Chandra Bonnerjee

(xi) What was the immediate cause of the below incidence?

(a) Invasion of Poland by Hitler
(b) Bombing of Hiroshima and Nagasaki
(c) Murder of Archeduke of Austria
(d) None of the above

(xii) Siya, a school girl is doing a research on an Assertive Nationalist who said " Swaraj is my birthright and I shall have it." Who is Siya doing researching about?
(a) Bipin Chandra Pal (b) Lala Lajpat Rai
(c) Bal Gangadhar Tilak (d) Dadabhai Naoroji

(xiii) The .... marked the end of the British rule in India and the Dominions of India and Pakistan came into existence.
(a) Mountbatten Plan
(b) Regulating Act
(c) Indian Independence Act
(d) Pitt's India Act

(xiv) Which of the following is/are factors contributed to the rise of Fascism in Italy?
(a) Discontentment after the treaty of versailles
(b) Threat of socialism or communism
(c) Leadership provided by Mussolini
(d) All of the above

(xv) Read the two statements given below and select the option that shows the correct relationship between (A) and (R).

Assertion (A) United Nations was set-up on 24th October, 1945 at San Francisco.

Reason (R) The headquarters of United Nations is situated at Hague, Netherlands.

Codes
(a) A is true, but R is false
(b) R is the reason for A
(c) Both A and R are false
(d) Only R is true, A is false

(xvi) The first Non-Aligned Movement (NAM) Summit was held in September 1961 at ....
(a) Cairo (b) Belgrade
(c) Nairobi (d) Havana

2. (i) **Headline** Objection Milord : Four SC Judges publicly critique CJI

In an unprecedented and dramatic turn of events, four seniormost Supreme Court judges publicly critiqued the Chief Justice of India, Dipak Misra, saying "the administration of the court is not in order" and "efforts to persuade CJL to take remedial measures (have) failed." ***Source** Economic Times*

State any two qualifications for the appointment of Chief Justice of India. **(2)**

(ii) Write a note on powers and functions of United Nations General Assembly. **[2]**

(iii) Imagine you are student in British India, how would you support the freedom struggle in your own way? Give two examples **[2]**

(iv) What virtues did the Swadeshi Movement instill among the Indians? **[2]**

(v) Mention any two terms of the Gandhi-Irwin Pact. **[2]**

(vi) Write any two objectives of the Indian National Army. **[2]**

(vii) Give any two features of the policy of Non-Alignment. **[2]**

Part - II

[50 *Marks*]

Section A

*Attempt any **two** questions from this Section*

3. With reference to the Parliament of India, answer the following

(i) State the Legislative powers of the Parliament. **[3]**

(ii) State the Financial powers of the Parliament. **[3]**

(iii) How does the Parliament exercise control over the Cabinet? **[4]**

4. The executive authority of India lies in the President, Vice President, and Prime Minister. With reference to this, answer the following questions.

(i) What is the role of the President in the legislative process? Mention any three ways in which the President participates in the law-making process. **[3]**

(ii) Mention any three qualifications required for a person to be elected as the Vice President of India. **[3]**

(iii) With reference to the powers of the President, mention. **[4]**

(a) Any two Diplomatic Powers

(b) Any two Ordinance-making Powers

5. The High Court is the highest judicial authority at the state level in India. With reference to this, answer the following questions.

(i) What is meant by the term Appellate Jurisdiction of the High Court? Mention any two types of cases it can hear under this jurisdiction. **[3]**

(ii) Mention any two functions of a Nyaya Panchayat. How does it differ from a regular court in terms of its structure or procedure? **[3]**

(iii) Explain the following with reference to the powers of the High Court. **[4]**

(a) Power of Judicial Review

(b) Power to issue Writs

Section B

*Attempt any **three** questions from this Section*

6. In the context of the First War of Independence, explain the following

(i) The attitude of the British towards the people of India with regard to their religious customs. **[3]**

(ii) Factors causing dissatisfaction among the Indian soldiers. **[3]**

(iii) Decline of the landed aristocracy. **[4]**

7. In terms of the rise of Assertive Nationalism in the Congress, describe briefly

(i) The true nature of the British Rule. **[3]**

(ii) Role of the International events. **[3]**

(iii) Ill-treatment of the Indians. **[4]**

8. **[3]**

(i) Who is the man in the above picture? What was his main motives behind the Partition of Bengal?

(ii) Briefly explain the policies of this man. **[3]**

(iii) How did these policies affect the National Movement? **[4]**

9. Read the excerpt below and answer the following questions

The movement democratised India's freedom struggle and saw the participation of women, peasants, workers, students and people from all castes and religions. it energised the Congress leadership and base. The British were stunned. And then a violent incident in Chauri-Chaura saw Gandhi withdraw the movement on principle, much to the disappointment of even his colleagues. ***Source** : Hindustan Times*

(i) Which movement was combined with this movement? When was his movement started? [3]

(ii) Mention any three impacts of this movement. [3]

(iii) Describe any three programs undertaken in this movement. [4]

10. With reference to the United Nations, Explain

(i) The Security Council [3]

(ii) The International Court of Justice [3]

(iii) The World Health Organisation (WHO) [4]

Answers

1. (i) (a) India has certain unitary features which limit the powers of the state governments.

(ii) (b) B

(iii) (b) Original Jurisdiction

(iv) (d) Prime Minister

(v) (b) R and S

(vi) (c) Adjourn the House until order is restored.

(vii) (d) Lala Lajpat Rai

(viii) (c) Prayers and Petition

(ix) (d) Raja Ram Mohan Roy

(x) (a) Bipin Chandra Pal

(xi) (a) Invasion of Poland by Hitler

(xii) (c) Bal Gangadhar Tilak

(xiii) (c) Indian Independence Act

(xiv) (d) All of the above

(xv) (a) A is true, but R is false

(xvi) (b) Belgrade

ICSE Fully Solved

Latest Specimen Paper

History & Civics X

Time : 2 hrs
Marks : 80

General Instructions

1. Attempt all questions from Part I (Compulsory). A total of 5 questions are to be attempted from Part II, 2 out of 3 questions from Section A and 3 out of 5 questions from Section B.
2. The intended marks for questions or parts of questions are given in brackets ( ).

PART- I [30 Marks]

Attempt all questions from this Part.

1. Choose the correct answers to the questions from the given options. **(16)**

(i) On 19th May, 2023, the President of India exercised legislative power under Article 123 of the Constitution, during the period Parliament was in recess, to promulgate The Government of National Capital Territory of Delhi Ordinance, 2023.

–The Hindu, 26th May, 2023

What information about an ordinance can be obtain from the above passage? **(1)**

(a) The ordinance must be approved within six weeks.
(b) Only the Cabinet can prepare an ordinance.
(c) It is issued when the Parliament is not functioning.
(d) If the Parliament does not approve it within six weeks it becomes inoperative. **[Application]**

(ii) Given below are details of few Indian citizens.

Person	Age [In years]	Description
W	34	Is a Professor in the Government College
X	35	Has taken up the citizenship of the United States of America
Y	27	Is a reputed sportsperson
Z	36	Is a scientist

Select the person who fulfils the eligibility criteria to become the President of India. **[Understanding] (1)**

(a) W (b) X
(c) Y (d) Z

(iii) Who made the amendment which resulted in the below headline? **[Application] (1)**

THE TIMES OF INDIA
In Historic Move Within 100 Days Of Modi-2, Govt Bifurcates State Into 2 UTs, Defangs Article 370 & Scraps 35A
KASHMIR IS NOW UNION'S TERRITORY
J&K To Lose Special Status, Centre To Directly Rule Ladakh
INDIA'S NORTH POLE SHIFTS TO CENTRE
Why now? PM, Shah felt political tide and timing favoured action

(a) The Supreme Court (b) The President
(c) The Parliament (d) The Prime Minister

(iv) Residents of Jodhpur, X and Y got married in the year 2014 and after 4 months of wedlock, petty family issues and arguments resulted in their separation for 6 years. The matter was placed before the Bench of Lok Adalat Family Court, Jodhpur wherein all efforts were made to reunite the family again. With constant efforts of counselling parties agreed to live together and withdraw their Divorce Petition. *Case Study, Lok Adalat, District - Jodhpur.*

Which advantage of the Lok Adalat is highlighted in the above case? **[Application] (1)**

(a) Saves money
(b) Speedy justice
(c) Works on the spirit of compromise
(d) Reduces the burden on High Courts

(v) District Judge : Cases :: Sessions Judge : Criminal Cases **[Recall] (1)**

(a) Advisory (b) Civil
(c) Constitutional (d) Appellate

(vi) Identify the exclusive powers of the Rajya Sabha.

P : Can introduce a new All India Service

Q : Can impeach the President

R : Can never be dissolved as a whole

S : Can introduce a Money Bill **[Recall] (1)**

(a) P and Q (b) R and S
(c) P and R (d) Q and S

(vii) Read the two statements given below about the Civil Disobedience Movement and select the option that shows the correct relationship between (A) and (R).

Assertion (A) The Civil Disobedience Movement was renewed by Mahatma Gandhi.

Reason (R) The Second Round Table Conference was a failure. **[Analysis] (1)**

(a) R contradicts A
(b) R is the reason for A
(c) A is true but R is false
(d) A and R are independent of each other

(viii) The government of Country X has introduced a law similar to Ilbert Bill introduced in 1883. Who will be impacted by this Bill? **[Understanding] (1)**

(a) The Farmers (b) The Artisans
(c) The Soldiers (d) The Judges

(ix) The area in which Anand stays has had no water supply for three days in spite of repeated complaints. The residents have a meeting and discuss a few methods to resolve this problem. Being a follower of the beliefs and methods of the Early Nationalists, which of the following methods is Anand not likely to approve? **[Application] (1)**

(a) Peaceful procession by the residents
(b) Follow the method of boycott
(c) Write a petition to the government
(d) Write an article in the newspaper highlighting the problem.

(x) Which of the given policies is not aligned with the ideologies of the leader seen in the picture? **[Understanding] (1)**

(a) Prioritising military expansion
(b) Promoting racist policies
(c) Hosting an anti-communist seminar
(d) Holding pro-democracy rallies

(xi) Identify the odd one out of the following objectives of the Muslim League. **[Analysis] (1)**

(a) To promote among Muslims of India, support for the British.
(b) To promote cultural and socio-economic cooperation among Muslims.
(c) To protect and advance political rights and interests of the Muslims.
(d) To present the needs and demands of the Muslims to the government.

(xii) Your school has organised a poster making competition on the topic - Education empowerment for girls in India. Which of the following leaders would most likely be part of the poster? **[Understanding] (1)**

(a) Surendranath Banerjee
(b) Pherozeshah Mehta
(c) Dadabhai Naoroji
(d) Jyotiba Phule

(xiii) Read the description and identify the person–

He established the Forward Bloc and coined the slogan, 'Delhi Chalo'. **[Recall] (1)**

(a) Mahatma Gandhi (b) Subhash Chandra Bose
(c) Bal Gangadhar Tilak (d) Dadabhai Naoroji

(xiv) Which of the following countries will not be part of this cartoon? **[Application] (1)**

(a) China (b) Japan
(c) Russia (d) Britain

(xv) Identify the cities most affected by American action in World War II. **[Recall] (1)**
(a) Rome, Berlin (b) Tokyo, Berlin
(c) Hiroshima, Nagasaki (d) Tokyo, Rome

(xvi) Which of the following scenarios describes the Non-Alignment Policy (NAM)? **[Understanding] (1)**
(a) A country forms a military alliance only with the United States.
(b) A country maintains relations with both factions during the Cold War and does not take sides.
(c) A country is part of a religious movement advocating non-violence.
(d) A country aligns with Soviet Union and receives military aid.

2. Read the extract given below and answer the question which follows.

Congress member's adjournment motion disallowed. The notice, along with another moved demanding a discussion on China, was disallowed in the Lok Sabha.
The Times of India, 10th Feb, 2023

(i) Who can allow or disallow the above motion? What does this motion mean? **[Understanding] (2)**

(ii) Which category of power is being exercised by the President in the following. **[Recall] (2)**
(a) Approval of Bills
(b) Appointment of the Supreme Court judges

(iii) Imagine you were an artisan, in the year 1856. Mention any two ways in which the economic policies of the British would have affected you. **[Understanding] (2)**

(iv) Give two reasons for the acceptance of the Mountbatten Plan by the Congress. **[Recall] (2)**

(v) Mention any two leaders of the Assertive Nationalists. **[Recall] (2)**

(vi) Mention any two objectives of the League of Nations. **[Recall] (2)**

(vii) Name the two alliances formed in Europe before the beginning of the First World War. **[Recall] (2)**

PART II

[50 Marks]

Section A

*Attempt any **two** questions from this Section.*

3. The Union Legislature of India is not only the law-making body, but the center of all democratic political process. With reference to the Parliament, answer the following questions.

(i) The Lok Sabha is more powerful than the Rajya Sabha. Justify this by mentioning any three points. **[Analysis] (3)**

(ii) Rajya Sabha adjourned sine die, overall productivity at 79 percent. *–Deccan Herald, 21st December, 2023*
Who can adjourn the above session? Explain the composition of this house. **[Recall] (3)**

(iii) Mention any four legislative powers of the Parliament. **[Recall] (4)**

4. The President is the nominal head of the executive, the first citizen of the country, as well as the commander-in-chief of the Indian Armed Forces. With reference to this, answer the following questions.

(i) The President is the nominal head of the country and cannot act independently.
Mention any three legislative powers of the President which justifies the nominal position. **[Understanding] (3)**

(ii) Mention any three financial powers of the President. **[Recall] (3)**

(iii) Describe the procedure of impeachment of the President. **[Recall] (4)**

5. The Supreme Court of India is the supreme judicial authority and the highest court of the Republic of India. It is the final court of appeal for all civil and criminal cases. With reference to the Supreme Court, answer the following questions.

(i) Who appoints the judges of the Supreme Court?
Mention any two qualifications required for a person to be appointed as a judge of the Supreme Court. **[Recall] (3)**

(ii) Under Article 129, the Supreme Court of India is called a Court of Record.
Justify this statement with any three points. **[Analysis] (3)**

(iii) Explain the following terms.
(a) Revisory Jurisdiction
(b) Advisory Jurisdiction **[Recall] (4)**

Section B

*Attempt any **three** questions from this Section.*

6. The Indian Rebellion of 1857 was a major uprising against the rule of the British East India Company, which functioned as a sovereign power on behalf of the British Crown. With reference to this, answer the following questions.

(i) The British used many policies of expansion. Mention any three such policies. **[Recall] (3)**

(ii) How did the failure of this Revolt impact the Mughals and the Peshwas? **[Recall] (3)**

(iii) The India army was reorganised after 1858, to prevent the reoccurrence of another uprising. Analyse this statement by stating any four changes made in the army after the Revolt. **[Analysis] (4)**

7. Nationalism refers to the feeling of oneness that emerges when people consider themselves as one nation. With reference to
the growth of nationalism, answer the following.

(i) Name the first President of Congress. Mention any two of its objectives. **[Recall] (3)**

(ii) The press played an important role in the growth of Indian Nationalism. Thus, the British saw the need for curbs on the press. Mention any three points to analyse the role of the press in the growth of nationalism. **[Analysis] (3)**

(iii) Lord Lytton's repressive policies led to the growth of Nationalism. Mention any four policies enforced by him. **[Recall] (4)**

8. Read the excerpt given below and answer the questions that follow

The March, which took place in India, was led by Mohandas Gandhi to protest British rule in India. During the march, thousands of Indians followed Gandhi from his religious retreat near Ahmedabad to the Arabian Sea coast, a distance of some 240 miles. The march resulted in the arrest of nearly 60,000 people, including Gandhi himself.

–The Marion (Ohio) Star [Edited]

(i) Name the march being discussed above. Which movement did this march lead to? In which year was that movement launched? **[Recall] (3)**

(ii) The movement which began with this march made a considerable impact on the social and political surroundings of the country. Analyse this statement by mentioning any three impacts. **[Analysis] (3)**

(iii) Mention any four clauses of the Gandhi Irwin Pact. **[Recall] (4)**

9. Look at the picture given and answer the following questions. **[Recall] (3)**

(i) Describe the incident depicted in the cartoon.

(ii) Mention any three points to analyse how Europe was rearranged as a consequence of the war caused by this incident. Consequence of the war caused by this incident. **[Recall] (3)**

(iii) The Germans described the Treaty of Versailles as harsh and humiliating.

Give any four reasons that justify this statement. **[Analysis] (4)**

10. The United Nations Organisation aims to maintain international peace. With reference to its organs and agencies, answer the following.

(i) What is the composition of the International Court of Justice? **[Recall] (3)**

(ii) Mention any three functions of the General Assembly. **[Recall] (3)**

(iii) Gujarat's famed garba dance received the intangible heritage tag. Which agency of the United Nations is authorized to give this tag? Mention any three other contributions of that agency in the preservation of culture. **[Application & Recall] (4)**

Answers

1. (i) (c) It is issued when the Parliament is not functioning.
(ii) (d) Z
(iii) (c) The Parliament
(iv) (c) Works on the spirit of compromise
(v) (b) Civil
(vi) (c) P and R
(vii) (b) R is the reason for A
(viii) (d) The Judges
(ix) (b) Follow the method of boycott
(x) (d) Holding pro-democracy rallies
(xi) (a) To promote among Muslims of India, support for the British.
(xii) (d) Jyotiba Phule
(xiii) (b) Subhash Chandra Bose
(xiv) (b) Japan
(xv) (c) Hiroshima, Nagasaki
(xvi) (b) A country maintains relations with both factions during the Cold War and does not take sides.

2. (i) The Speaker of the Lok Sabha has the authority to allow or disallow an adjournment motion. This power is crucial for maintaining order and focusing the discussion in the house.
An adjournment motion is used to temporarily stop proceedings to discuss a matter of urgent public importance. The discussion must be specific and is intended to draw the government's attention to a particular issue that needs immediate attention.
(ii) (a) The President of India exercises legislative powers under Article 111 of the Constitution to approve bills passed by both houses of Parliament.
(b) The President exercises executive power to appoints judges to the Supreme Court of India under Article 124 of the Constitution.
(iii) An artisan in the year 1856 would have been affected by the British policies in the following ways
- **Reduced demand for local goods** As an artisan in 1856, British economic policies such as the promotion of British-made goods would have severely affected his/her livelihood by reducing the demand for locally made products.
- **Taxation and raw material supply** One would likely face heavy taxes imposed by the British, which would diminish their earnings. Additionally, the colonial focus on raw material exportation would limit his/her access to necessary resources, further impacting his/her ability to produce and sell.

(iv) Two reasons for the acceptance of the Mountbatten Plan by the Congress were
(a) **Immediate Transfer of Power** One of the primary reasons Congress accepted the Mountbatten Plan was the provision for immediate transfer of power from British to Indian hands, which promised a quicker end to British rule.
(b) **Avoidance of Civil War** The plan proposed the partition of India into two dominions, which, despite being a painful decision, was seen by Congress leaders as a necessary compromise to prevent a civil war between different communal groups.
(v) Two leaders of the Assertive Nationalists were
(a) **Bal Gangadhar Tilak** Often referred to as 'Lokmanya, Tilak' was a prominent leader of the Assertive Nationalists, advocating for Swaraj as a birthright of Indians. He initiated the Shivaji festival in 1896 to inspire nationalism in addition to the Ganesh festival.
(b) **Lala Lajpat Rai** He was also called 'Punjab Kesari' and 'Lion of Punjab' and was instrumental in the freedom struggle and was known for his advocacy of aggressive policies against British rule. Along with Bipin Chandra Pal and Bal Gangadhar Tilak, he formed the Lal-Bal-Pal trio of extremist leaders.
(vi) Following are the two main objectives of League of Nations.
(a) **Prevention of wars** The League of Nations aimed to maintain peace and prevent wars through collective security and disarmament and settling international disputes through negotiation and arbitration.
(b) **Promotion of international cooperation** The league of Nations aimed to foster cooperation among nations in solving international problems of an economic, social, or humanitarian nature and to achieve international peace and security.

(vii) Before the beginning of the First World War, two major alliances were formed in Europe. These were

(a) **The Triple Entente** This alliance, established in the early 20th century, included France, Russia and the United Kingdom. It was formed through a series of agreements that aimed to counterbalance the growing strength of the Triple Alliance and provide mutual support and cooperation among the member nations.

(b) **The Triple Alliance** This alliance was formed in 1882 and comprised and Germany, Austria-Hungary and Italy. It was intended primarily as a defensive pact, where each member promised to support the others in case of an attack by two or more powers, or in case of aggression by France against Germany or Italy.

3. (i) The Lok Sabha is more powerful than the Rajya Sabha because it has

- **Legislative Power over Money Bills** The Lok Sabha holds exclusive powers to introduce and make decisions on money bills.
  While the Rajya Sabha can suggest amendments, it cannot reject or indefinitely withhold its approval of money bills, which must be returned within 14 days.
- **Major Role in Government Formation** The Lok Sabha is directly involved in the formation of the government, as the Prime Minister and the majority of the cabinet ministers are typically from the Lok Sabha. This house reflects the direct choice of the electorate.
- **Motion of No-Confidence** Only the Lok Sabha has the power to move and pass a motion of no confidence against the sitting government.
  If such a motion passes, it necessitates the resignation of the entire cabinet, underscoring the greater political power of the Lok Sabha.

(ii) The session of the Rajya Sabha can be adjourned sine die by the Chairman of the Rajya Sabha, who is the Vice-President of India. This type of adjournment marks the end of a session without any definite date for resumption.

The Rajya Sabha, or the Upper House of Parliament, is composed of representatives from the states and union territories. 238 members are elected by the state legislative assemblies, and 12 members are nominated by the President of India.

The total membership is limited by the Constitution, which allocates seats based on the population of each state and territory.

(iii) The four legislative powers of the Parliament are as follows

(a) **Amendment of the Constitution** Parliament can amend the Constitution, subject to the provisions of Article 368.

(b) **Passing Laws** Parliament can legislate on subjects listed in the Union List and, under certain circumstances, on the Concurrent List shared with states.

(c) **National Emergency** During a national emergency, Parliament assumes the power to make laws on any subject, including those normally reserved for states.

(d) **Creation or Abolition of States** Parliament can pass laws changing the boundaries of states or creating new ones.

4. (i) The three legislative powers of the President that justify the nominal position are as follows

- **Bill Assent** The President has the power to give assent to bills passed by Parliament, which is required for a bill to become law. This role is largely ceremonial as refusal to assent is rare and usually done on the advice of the cabinet.
- **Ordinance Issuance** The President can issue ordinances under article 123, when Parliament or any of the two houses are not in session, which have the same force as laws passed by Parliament.
- **Summoning and Proroguing Parliament** The President summons and prorogues the sessions of Parliament, but these actions are typically performed on the advice of the Prime Minister and the cabinet.

(ii) The three financial powers of the President are as follows

(a) **Budget Presentation** The budget is presented in the Parliament with the President's prior recommendation, necessary for any proposals involving expenditure from the Consolidated Fund of India.

(b) **Financial Bills** No financial bills involving expenditure can be introduced in Parliament without the President's recommendation.

(c) **Contingency Fund** The President is the custodian of the Contingency Fund of India (Article 267(1) of the Indian Constitution), allowing him to make advances to meet unforeseen expenses.

(iii) Impeachment procedure of the President is discussed below

- **Initiation** The process can be initiated by either house of Parliament i.e Rajya Sabha or Lok Sabha. The motion to impeach must be supported by at least one-fourth of the total number of members of that house.
- **Investigation** The charges are investigated, and the President has the right to appear and to be represented at the investigation.
- **Decision** For the impeachment to succeed, it must be passed by a two-thirds majority of the total membership of each house of the Parliament.

This rigorous procedure emphasises the stability of the executive head and ensures that impeachment is a measure of last resort based on substantial misdeeds or incapacity.

5. (i) Appointment and Qualifications of Supreme Court Judges.

The Judges of the Supreme Court are appointed by the President of India after consulting the Chief Justice of the Supreme Court.

The qualifications required for being a Supreme Court Judge are

(a) **Experience in the Judiciary** A person must have been a judge of one or more high courts for at least five years, or an advocate there for at least ten years.

(b) **Distinguished Jurist** Alternatively, a person must be a distinguished jurist in the opinion of the President, recognised for their expertise and contributions to the legal field.

(ii) Under Article 129, the Supreme Court of India is called a Court of Record. This statement can be justified the rough the following points

(a) **Permanent Record Keeping** As a Court of Record, all judgments, proceedings, and acts of the Supreme Court are recorded for perpetual memory and testimony.
These records are recognised as legal precedents and authoritative references.

(b) **Power to Punish for Contempt** The Court of Record status grants the Supreme Court the authority to punish for contempt of itself. This power helps maintain the respect and authority of the court.

(c) **Precedential Value** Decisions made by the Supreme Court as a Court of Record are binding on all lower courts within the territory of India. This ensures consistency and predictability in the application of the law across the country.

(iii) (a) Revisory jurisdiction refers to the power of the Supreme Court to review, revisit and possibly overturn its own decisions or those of lower courts. This jurisdiction is exercised to correct errors or injustices in judgments and to ensure that justice is served in accordance with law and evolving legal standards.

(b) Under Article 143 of the Constitution, the President of India can seek the advice of the Supreme Court on any question of law or fact that is of public importance or that which involves interpretation of the Constitution. This is known as the Advisory Jurisdiction. While the advice provided by the Supreme Court is generally respected, it is not binding on the President. This jurisdiction helps in clarifying legal issues and aiding executive decisions with judicial insight.

6. (i) The three British Policies of expansion were as follows

(a) **Doctrine of Lapse** Introduced by Lord Dalhousie, this policy allowed the British to annex any princely state where the ruler died without a direct heir.

(b) **Subsidiary Alliance** This strategy, pioneered by Lord Wellesley, involved placing British forces in a princely state and making it a protectorate of the British Empire, effectively controlling its external affairs.

(c) **Direct Conquest** Several regions of India were directly conquered through military force, expanding British territorial holdings and control over resources.

(ii) The impacts of the failure of Revolt of 1857 on the Mughals and Peshwas were

- **End of the Mughal Empire** The failure of the Revolt marked the end of the Mughal Empire, with Emperor Bahadur Shah II being deposed and exiled. This effectively eliminated the Mughal Empire as a political entity and symbol of authority in India.

- **Decline of the Peshwas** The Peshwas, who were leaders of the Maratha Empire, also faced decline as their power had been waning through earlier defeats. After the Revolt, any remaining influence or claims to authority by the Peshwas were further diminished, consolidating British dominance.

(iii) The Indian army was reorganised after the Revolt of 1857 in the following ways

- **Reduction of Indian Troops** The proportion of Indian soldiers in the army was reduced, and the number of European troops was increased to prevent future revolts.
- **Strategic Placement of Troops** The artillery units, which were crucial in any military engagement, were placed under direct British control and Indians were largely removed from these key positions.
- **Enhanced Segregation** The troops were reorganised based on ethnicity and religion to divide and rule by fostering distrust among different groups.
- **Improved Communication** The British improved infrastructure, like roads and telegraphs, to facilitate faster movement and communication of their forces across the country.

7. (i) The first President of the Indian National Congress was Womesh Chunder Bonnerjee.

The Objectives of Congress were

(a) **Promote Political Education and Unity** One of the main objectives was to promote political education among Indians and to foster a sense of unity against colonial rule.

(b) **Formulate and Present Demands** The Congress aimed to provide a platform for all Indians to discuss public matters and to formulate demands for greater civil and political rights from the British administration.

(ii) The role of the Press in the Growth of Nationalism was

(a) **Educating the Masses** Newspapers and periodicals played a critical role in educating the masses about political ideas and the impacts of colonial policies.

(b) **Fostering Unity** The press helped in creating a shared sense of identity and purpose among diverse linguistic and cultural groups across India.

(c) **Exposing Injustices** The press was instrumental in exposing the injustices and exploitation under British rule, which galvanised support for nationalist movements.

(iii) The four policies enforced by Lord Lytton's were

(a) **Vernacular Press Act (1878)** This act aimed to curb the freedom of the Indian press, particularly vernacular newspapers, to prevent the spread of nationalist ideas.

(b) **Arms Act (1878)** This law prohibited Indians from possessing arms without a licence.

(c) **Reduction of Maximum Age for Civil Service Examinations** Lord Lytton reduced the maximum age for appearing in civil service exams, making it difficult for Indians to enter the service.

(d) **Imperial Assemblies** Lord Lytton hosted luxurious assemblies and durbar to reinforce the might of the British Empire, even during famines and hardships faced by Indians, showing a stark disconnect and fueling resentment.

8. (i) The Salt March, also known as the Dandi March, is one of the most iconic events in the history of India's struggle for independence.

This march was a key part of the Civil Disobedience Movement, where Indians were encouraged to disobey British laws non-violently to press for independence.

The Civil Disobedience Movement was officially launched in 1930 following the culmination of the Salt March. The march itself began on 12th March, 1930.

(ii) The impacts of the Civil Disobedience Movement were as follows

- **Increased National Unity** The Civil Disobedience Movement, sparked by the Salt March, played a crucial role in bringing together Indians from different backgrounds. It transcended regional, caste and religious boundaries, creating a widespread collective consciousness against British rule.
  This unity was pivotal in strengthening the national movement and making it a mass movement rather than being limited to the intellectuals and the elite.

- **Economic Impact** By boycotting British goods, refusing to pay taxes, and halting other economic activities that benefited the British economically, the movement delivered a blow to the British economy in India.
These boycotts were effective in reducing the revenue the British could extract from India.
- **International Attention** The non-violent nature of the protest drew widespread international attention, particularly from the Western world. Reports of British repression during the movement helped gain sympathy for the Indian cause, boosting support for Indian independence on an international level.

(iii) The four clauses of the Gandhi-Irwin Pact were

(a) **Release of Political Prisoners** A significant achievement of the pact was the release of thousands of political prisoners who were imprisoned for participating in the Civil Disobedience Movement. However, those convicted of violence were not included in this amnesty, which was a point of contention among some nationalists.

(b) **Salt Manufacture** The agreement allowed the collection and manufacture of salt by the coastal communities, which was crucial since the Salt March was specifically initiated against the salt tax imposed by the British.

(c) **Return of Confiscated Properties** Under the pact, the British agreed to return the confiscated lands and properties of the satyagrahis, although properties seized directly by the government were not returned. This clause aimed at alleviating some of the financial strains on the protesters who had sacrificed much in their fight against British laws.

(d) **Right to Peaceful Protests** The pact acknowledged the right of Indians to conduct peaceful protests. It also allowed Gandhi to represent the Indian National Congress at the Round Table Conference in London, marking a significant step toward negotiations for Indian self-rule.

9. (i) The cartoon likely illustrates the assassination of Archduke Franz Ferdinand of Austria in Sarajevo. This event occurred on 28th June, 1914, when the heir to the Austro-Hungarian throne was assassinated by Gavrilo Princip, a Bosnian Serb nationalist.
This assassination is widely acknowledged as the spark that ignited the First World War I, leading to the mobilisation of allied and central powers into one of the deadliest conflicts in human history.

(ii) Europe was rearranged as a consequence of the first world war in the following ways

(a) **New Nations Formed** The map of Europe was dramatically redrawn with several new nations emerging, such as Czechoslovakia, Poland and Yugoslavia, as multi-ethnic empires like Austro-Hungarian and Ottoman were dismantled.

(b) **Territorial Losses for Central Powers** Countries like Germany and Austria-Hungary lost significant territories to neighbouring states and new nations, altering the political landscape of Europe.

(c) **New Blocks Formed** There were formation of new blocks in Europe along with other non-European countries for example; UK sided with USA etc.

(iii) The Treaty of Versailles was viewed as Harsh and humiliating by Germans due to the following reasons

(a) **Territorial Losses** Germany lost significant territories, such as Alsace-Lorraine to France and parts of Prussia to the new Polish state, reducing its size and economic power.

(b) **War Guilt Clause** Article 231, known as the War Guilt Clause, forced Germany to accept sole responsibility for starting the war, a point of national humiliation.

(c) **Reparations** Germany was required to pay huge reparations, which strained its economy and contributed to severe economic hardships during the interwar period.

(d) **Military Restrictions** The treaty drastically limited the size and capability of the German military, undermining national defence and pride.

10. (i) The International Court of Justice (ICJ) is composed of 15 judges elected to nine-year terms by the United Nations General Assembly and the Security Council. These judges represent the principal legal systems of the world and no two judges may be from the same country, ensuring a diversity of legal traditions.

(ii) The three functions of the General Assembly are

(a) **Legislative Functions** The General Assembly passes resolutions that influence international law and practices.

(b) **Budgetary Functions** It approves the budget of the United Nations and determines the financial contributions of member states.

(c) **Electoral Functions** The General Assembly elects non-permanent members of the Security Council, judges of the International Court of Justice and other key officials within the UN system.

(iii) UNESCO (United Nations Educational, Scientific and Cultural Organisation) is authorised to give the intangible heritage tag.

The contributions of UNESCO in the preservation of culture are as follows

(a) **World Heritage Sites** It identifies and preserves cultural sites and natural wonders around the world that are of outstanding value to humanity.

(b) **Preserves Heritage** It aims at preserving the rich cultural heritage of the countries and focuses on preserving its significance.

(c) **Intangible Heritage** It also maintains a list of Intangible heritage for example, Garba, Vedic Chanting etc from India to preserve their cultural significance.

ICSE Fully Solved

Solved Paper 2024

History & Civics X

Time : 2 hrs
Marks : 80

General Instructions

1. Attempt all questions from Part I (Compulsory). A total of 5 questions are to be attempted from Part II, 2 out of 3 questions from Section A and 3 out of 5 questions from Section B.
2. The intended marks for questions or parts of questions are given in brackets [].

Part - I

[30 *Marks*]

Attempt all questions from this Part

1. Select the correct answers to the questions from the given options. **[16 ×1]**

(i) The salaries and allowances of the ministers are decided by the

(a) Parliament (b) Finance Minister
(c) President (d) Prime Minister

(ii) Civil Cases: Court of District Judge: : Criminal Cases:

(a) Revenue Court (b) Family Court
(c) Sessions Court (d) Commissioner's Court

(iii)

The Lok Adalat has many advantages. Which of the following statements about the advantages of the Lok Adalat is best described in the picture given above?

(a) It is inexpensive
(b) It is organised in various parts of the country
(c) It works on the spirit of compromise
(d) It reduces the burden of the higher courts

(iv) Given below are details of Indian citizens. Select the ones who are eligible for appointment as a High Court Judge.

Candidate	Age	Details
P	65	Is a distinguished jurist
Q	61	Has been a High Court Advocate for 10 years
R	67	Has been a High Court Advocate for 5 years
S	56	Has held a judicial office for at least 10 years

(a) P and R (b) Q and S
(c) R and P (d) Q and R

(v) The strength of the house is 550. On a particular day 50 members are present. The speaker decides to adjourn the house. Identify the most likely reason for the adjournment.

(a) Disorder in the house
(b) Lack of quorum
(c) Breach of privilege
(d) Contempt of the House

(vi) During a hung assembly when no party gets the majority, the President appoints the Prime Minister. What power is the President exercising?

(a) Legislative (b) Executive
(c) Discretionary (d) Judicial

(vii) Read the two statements given below and select the option that shows the correct relationship between (A) and (R)

Assertion (A) Forward Bloc had the objective of abolishing Zamindari System.

Reason (R) Subhash Chandra Bose wanted to establish a socialist state.

Codes

(a) A is true but R is false (b) R is the reason for A
(c) Both A and R are false
(d) Only R is true, A is false

(viii) The ...... aimed to introduce equality between British and Indian Judges.
(a) Vernacular Press Act
(b) Gagging Act
(c) Indian Universities Act
(d) Ilbert Bill

(ix) The Rowlatt Act was called the Black Act because the Indians
(a) could not possess any arms
(b) could not export any goods
(c) could be arrested without a warrant
(d) could be sent overseas on duty

(x) Who organised the Grand Delhi Durbar?
(a) Lord Curzon
(b) Lord Canning
(c) Lord Lytton
(d) Lord Dalhousie

(xi) Tina is inspired by the methods of the Early Nationalists and wants to follow them. She notices that the road leading to her school is damaged and has many potholes. Which of the following methods is she most likely to follow, to solve this problem?
(a) Boycott the civic authorities
(b) Gather a group of students and protest
(c) Write a petition to the authorities highlighting the problem
(d) Block the entrance to the road

(xii) Given below are the objectives of the Indian National Army. Identify the odd one out of the following.
(a) To organise a provisional government of Free India
(b) Total mobilisation of Indian manpower and money
(c) Unity, faith and sacrifice
(d) To train and organise public opinion in the country

(xiii) Tahir is preparing to give a speech about the Sati system in India. Which of the following Indian leader's contribution must he mentions in his speech?
(a) Raja Rammohan Roy
(b) WC Bonerjee
(c) Bipin Chandra Pal
(d) Jyotiba Phule

(xiv) Which of the following is not a consequence of the Second World War?
(a) Austria and Hungary became separate states
(b) Defeat of the Axis powers
(c) Beginning of the Cold War
(d) Formation of the United Nations

(xv) Identify the principle of Panchsheel.
(a) Mutual non-aggression
(b) Regulate armaments
(c) Take action against aggressor
(d) Recommend admission of members

(xvi)

Which incident depicted in the above cartoon led to the beginning of the Second World War?
(a) Hitler's policy of Imperialism
(b) Hitler's attack on Poland
(c) Hitler's annexation of Austria
(d) Hitler's attack on Czechoslovakia

2. (i) Mention any two writs issued by the High Court. **[2]**

(ii) Imagine you are an Indian ruler who has signed the Subsidiary Alliance. Mention any two conditions of this agreement which will affect you. **[2]**

(iii) Mention any two causes of the Quit India Movement. **[2]**

(iv) In which year did the *Surat Split* happen? What was the result of this split? **[2]**

(v) Mention any two common ideologies of Fascism and Nazism. **[2]**

(vi) Name the two cities of Japan which were bombed by America in the year 1945. **[2]**

(vii) Read the given news carefully and answer the question that follows.

Govt's power to promulgate, repromulgate Ordinances _ why and how

An Ordinance "shall have the same force and effect as an Act of Parliament". But the government is required to bring an Ordinance before Parliament for ratification - and failure to do so will lead to its lapsing "at the expiration of six weeks from the reassembly of Parliament".

The Indian Express - 25th May, 2023

Mention any two points regarding an ordinance that can be deduced from the above news. **[2]**

Part - II

Section A [20 *Marks*]

Attempt any two questions from this Section.

3. The Union Parliament is the supreme legislative body in the country. With reference to the Indian Parliament answer the following questions.

(i) The Rajya Sabha is called a Permanent House. Explain this statement. **[3]**

(ii) Explain the composition of the Rajya Sabha. **[3]**

(iii) Mention any two exclusive powers of the Lok Sabha and two powers exclusive to the Rajya Sabha. **[4]**

4. The Council of Ministers headed by the Prime Minister aids and advises the President. In this context, answer the following questions.

(i) Mention any three points to distinguish between the Council of Ministers and the Cabinet **[3]**

(ii) Who appoints the Cabinet Ministers? Mention any two administrative powers of the Cabinet. **[3]**

(iii) *The President is the nominal head of the Indian Union.* Mention any four functions of the Prime Minister with reference to the President. **[4]**

5. The judiciary is the system of courts that interprets and guards the Indian Constitution. With reference to the Supreme Court of India, answer the following:

(i) What is the composition of the Supreme Court? Why is it called the Court of Record? **[3]**

(ii) Explain the power of Judicial Review. **[3]**

(iii) What is meant by the term Original Jurisdiction? Mention any three cases which come under this jurisdiction. **[4]**

Section B [30 *Marks*]

Attempt any three questions from this Section.

6. The Revolt of 1857 was the beginning of the independence struggle against the colonial rule of the British. With reference to the consequences of the Revolt, answer the following.

(i) Mention any three changes made in the administration with the end of the Company's Rule. **[3]**

(ii) State any three policies promised to Indians in Queen Victoria's Proclamation. **[3]**

(iii) Mention any four changes made in the army after the Revolt. **[4]**

7. The Indian National Movement is divided into three phases. With reference to the Second Phase of the Indian National Movement, answer the following questions:

(i) Who partitioned Bengal? Mention any two points to explain the perspective of the Nationalists regarding the actual motive behind the decision of Partition. **[3]**

(ii) What was the objective of the Assertive Nationalists? Mention any two contributions of Bal Gangadhar Tilak. **[3]**

(iii) In which year was the Muslim League formed? Mention any three objectives of the Muslim League. **[4]**

8. Look at the picture given and answer the following questions.

The Times of India

WAY OUT OF INDIAN DEADLOCK

BRITAIN'S PLAN FOR SMOOTH TRANSFER OF POWER

Immediate Dominion Status Granted

PEOPLE ASKED TO DECIDE PARTITION QUESTION

Present Constituent Assembly Not Disturbed

Only Practical Method

Plan Commended To Commons

MR. NEHRU COMMENDS PLAN TO NATION

Mr. Jinnah Hopeful Of League's Acceptance

SARDAR BALDEV SINGH CALLS IT "SETTLEMENT"

"UNIFIED INDIA BEST SOLUTION"

Viceroy's Appeal

(i) Name the Viceroy who announced the plan for smooth transfer of power. Mention any two clauses of his plan with reference to the Princely States. **[3]**

(ii) Mention any three reasons for the acceptance of his plan by the Congress. **[3]**

(iii) Mention any four provisions of the Indian Independence Act of 1947. **[4]**

9. The final act of the long-drawn-out negotiations took place at Versailles on Saturday afternoon, and to-day Germany and the Allies - always with the exception of America - are at peace. Peace is a blessed word, and both the word and the fact are welcome to-day. So far as Germany is concerned there is for the present an end of strife, and at least a formal return to the decent relations of civilised states.

Editorial : Peace in force (12th January, 1920)

The Guardian

(i) Mention any three causes of the World War which ended with the signing of the treaty being discussed in the passage above. **[3]**

(ii) Name the organisation which was established in 1920 to maintain peace after this war. Mention any two of its objectives. **[3]**

(iii) Mention any four clauses of the Treaty which affected Germany. **[4]**

10. Both the United Nations Organisation and the Non-Aligned Movement aim to achieve international peace and security. In this context, answer the following

(i) Mention any three functions of the Security Council. **[3]**

(ii) Mention any three functions of the World Health Organisation. **[3]**

(iii) Name any two founders of the Non-Aligned Movement. Mention any two of its objectives. **[4]**

Answers

1. (i) (a) Parliament

(ii) (c) Sessions Court

(iii) (c) It works on the spirit of compromise

(iv) (b) Q and S

(v) (b) Lack of quorum

(vi) (c) Discretionary

(vii) (b) R is the reason for A

(viii) (d) Ilbert Bill

(ix) (c) could be arrested without a warrant

(x) (a) Lord Curzon

(xi) (c) Write a petition to the authorities highlighting the problem

(xii) (b) Total mobilisation of Indian manpower and money

(xiii) (a) Raja Rammohan Roy

(xiv) (a) Austria and Hungary became separate states

(xv) (a) Mutual non-aggression

(xvi) (b) Hitler's attack on Poland

2. (i) The writs issued by the High Court are Habeas Corpus, Mandamus, Certiorari, Prohibitions and Quo-Warranto.

(ii) As an Indian ruler who has signed the Subsidiary Alliance, two conditions of this agreement that would significantly affect me are

(a) Military control and presence

(b) Financial burden

(iii) The two causes of the Quit India Movement were

(a) Failure of Cripps Mission

(b) Hardships caused during World War II

(iv) The Surat split happened on December 26, 1907.

The result of this split was the division of the Indian National Congress into Moderates and Radicals (extremists).

(v) The two common ideologies of Fascism and Nazism are as follows

(a) Both Mussolini and Hitler aimed at restoring the status and dignity of their nations by making them strong powers.

(b) Both aimed at providing strong, stable and efficient Governments.

(vi) Hiroshima and Nagasaki were the cities of Japan which were bombed by America in 1945.

(vii) The two points regarding an ordinance that can be deduced from the given news are

- Ordinance are temporary in nature
- Parliamentary Approval is necessary for an ordinance to remain in effect.

3. (i) The Rajya Sabha is called a Permanent House as it is the upper house of the Indian Parliament. Since, it is a permanent assembly, it cannot be dissolved. The Lok Sabha is the only body that can be dissolved. One-third members of Rajya Sabha retire every two years.

(ii) The composition of Rajya Sabha at present includes 245 members. Out of which 233 members are elected from States and Union Territories of Delhi and Puducherry and 12 are nominated by the President. These 12 nominated members are distinguished people in the field of Literature, Science, Art and Social Sciences.

(iii) The two exclusive powers of the Lok Sabha are

(a) Only the Lok Sabha can vote on the demands for grants in the budget.

(b) The Council of Ministers is collectively responsible only to the Lok Sabha. Thus, the Lok Sabha alone can vote a minister out of office.

The two exclusive powers of Rajya Sabha are

(a) The Parliament can assume temporary power to legislate on State List subjects (Article 249) only if Rajya Sabha passes a resolution, which is supported by two-third (2/3rd) majority of its members present and voting.

(b) The All-India Services can be established only if the Rajya Sabha passes a resolution for it, which is supported by two-third (2/3rd) majority of its members present and voting.

4. (i) The three points to distinguish between the Councils of Ministers and the Cabinet are

	Council of Ministers	Cabinet Ministers
(a)	It is a wider body.	It is a smaller body.
(b)	It includes all three categories of ministers, Cabinet members, ministers of state and deputy ministers.	It includes the ministers holding important ministries.
(c)	It does not meet, as a body,to transact government business.It has no collective functions.	It meets as a body usually once a week to take decisions regarding the transactions of government business.

(ii) The Cabinet Ministers are appointed by the President on the advice of the Prime Minister.

The two administrative powers of the cabinet are

(a) **Policy Making** The Council of Ministers is mainly a policy formulating body. It formulates both external and domestic policies of the government on important matters.

(b) **Implementation of Policies** When the policy decision on any subject is taken by the Cabinet, then, the Minister of State and the Deputy Minister of the concerned ministry examine the policies.

(iii) The President is the nominal head of the Indian Union. The four functions of the Prime Ministers with reference to the President are as follows

(a) The Prime Minister is the principal advisor to the President.

(b) The Prime Minister chooses the ministers and on his advice the President appoints them.

(c) The Prime Minister acts as a link between the President and the Council of Ministers as it communicates all the decisions of the Council of Ministers to the President on administration of the Union.

(d) The Prime Minister advises the President with regard to the appointment of important officials, such as CAG, members of UPSC, ECs, etc.

5. (i) The Composition of the Supreme Court consists of 34 judges including 1 Chief Justice and 33 other Judges. Originally the strength was fixed at 8 (1 Chief Justice and 7 other Judges).

The Supreme Court is called the Court of Record because the judgments, proceedings and acts of the Supreme Court are recorded for perpetual memory and testimony. These records cannot be questioned when produced before any court.

(ii) Judicial Review is a power given to the courts of India to examine the actions of the legislatures, executive and administrative arms of the centre and state government. It is to ensure that such actions comply with the provisions of the Constitution.

If the enactments and orders are found to be violative of the Constitution, they can be declared as illegal, unconstitutional and invalid (null and void) by the judiciary.

(iii) The term Original Jurisdiction refers to the power to hear and determine a dispute in the first instance. It happens in those cases, which cannot be transferred in any court other than the Supreme Court.

Three cases which come under this jurisdiction include

(a) Centre-State or Inter-State Disputes

(b) Transfer of cases

(c) Protection of Fundamental Rights

6. (i) Three changes made in the administration with the end of the Company's Rule

(a) **Establishment of the British Raj** The British government took direct control over India, replacing the rule of the East India Company.

(b) **Centralisation of Power** Authority was concentrated in the hands of British administrators appointed by the Crown.

(c) **Implementation of British Policies** New policies were introduced to impose British dominance.

(ii) The three policies promised to Indians in Queen Victoria's Proclamation are as follows

(a) Treat all subjects i.e. Indians and Europeans as equal (education and ability would be the basis of all appointments).

(b) Follow a policy of non-intervention in social and religious matters of Indians.

(c) A general pardon was granted to all those who laid down arms by 2nd January, 1859, except those who were found guilty of murder of British subjects.

(iii) The four changes made in the army after the Revolt were

(a) The proportion of the Europeans to Indians in the army was raised.

(b) Artillery and other effective weapons of war were placed exclusively under the charge of the Europeans.

(c) To curb nationalism, Indian soldiers of different communities, castes and religions were all mixed up and they were kept away in remote places.

(d) Indian soldiers were not provided newspapers, journals and nationalist publications to keep them separated from the life of the rest of the population.

7. (i) Bengal was partitioned by the Viceroy Lord Curzon.

The two major points to explain the perspective of the Nationalists regarding the actual motive behind the decision of partition were as follows

(a) At that period, Bengal had become the main centre of the Indian politics and Indian nationalism. So, the British expected to regulate the rising tide of nationalism by the division of Bengal.

(b) Another reason of the Partition of Bengal was to destroy the political influence of the educated middle class, among whom the Bengali intellectuals was the most prominent.

(ii) The objectives of Assertive Nationalists were to achieve 'Swaraj' by self-reliant methods and sacrifices.

The major contributions of Bal Gangadhar Tilak were

(a) In 1880, he started the Poona New English School with a view to educate Indians by charging small fees.

(b) He started two newspapers i.e. Maratha (English) and Kesari (Marathi) in order to spread the idea of nationalism.

(iii) The Muslim League was formed on 1st October, 1906. The three objectives of the Muslim League were

(a) To promote the feelings of loyalty towards the British Government amongst the Indian Muslims.

(b) To remove any misconception regarding the intentions of the government in relation to the Indian Muslim.

(c) To protect and advance the political rights and other interests of the Muslims of India.

8. (i) Lord Mountbatten was the Viceroy who announced the plan for smooth transfer of power. The two clauses of his plan with reference to the Princely states were as follows

(a) India would be divided into two dominions, i.e. India and Pakistan.

(b) It was up to the two Dominions, i.e. India and Pakistan, to decide what relations they would have with the British Commonwealth and with each other.

(ii) The three reasons for the acceptance of his plan by the Congress were

(a) The Congress leaders realised that the large-scale communal riots and mass killing could be prevented only by accepting the Muslim League's demand for Pakistan.

(b) The Congress believed that it could not have the joint administration with the Muslim League as it had bitter experience in interim government of 1946.

(c) The Congress leaders realised that the extension of the British rule would be harmful to India. By applying the 'Divide and Rule Policy' the Britishers divided Hindu and Muslim community in India.

(iii) The four major provisions of Indian Independence Act of 1947 were

(a) India would be partitioned and two independent dominions i.e. India and Pakistan would be created from 15th August, 1947. The act provided the legislative supremacy of both the dominions.

(b) The territories of the two dominions were divided in such terms that Pakistan would comprise of Sindh, British Baluchistan, North-West Frontier Province, the West Punjab and East Bengal. The exact boundaries of the dominions would be determined by a Boundary Commission.

(c) For each of the two dominions, there would be a Governor-General who would be appointed by the British King and who would represent the king for the purposes of the government of the dominions.

(d) Each of the Dominions and all Provinces were to be governed in accordance with the Act of 1935 till the new Constitution was formed.

9. (i) The three main causes of the World War which ended with the signing of the treaty being discussed in the passage are

(a) **Military** The First World War was fought not only by the soldiers but also by the civilians. The use of arms and the spreading of new types of weapons by every nation made the situation unfavourable for peace. To protect their colonies the European powers developed their defence system in the colonies. This created an atmosphere of fear, insecurity and mutual hatred.

(b) **Alliance System** The war was fought between allied powers (Britain, France, Russia and their allies) and central powers (Germany, Austria and their allies). These alliances have their benefits for which they allied together and fought on different fronts.

(c) **Imperialism** Germany, Italy, Russia and Japan worked to increase their influence over the colonies in the least developed continents like Asia and Africa. Competition between European powers for colonies and resources around the world exacerbated tensions.

(ii) In 1920, the League of Nations was established. The main objectives of this organisation were

(a) To ensure disarmament, war prevention through collective security.

(b) It also focuses on international conflict resolution through conversation and diplomacy and global well-being.

(iii) The four clauses of the Treaty which affected Germany were

(a) **War Guilt Clause** This clause assigned full responsibility for the war and its damages to Germany and its allies.

(b) **Territorial Losses** The mineral-rich land of Ruhr was given to France, which further deteriorated the conditions for Germany.

(c) **Reparations** A huge sum of money was signed to give as the war guilt by the winning parties. It put an additional pressure on the economy of Germany.

(d) **Demilitarisation and Military Restrictions** Germany was demilitarised and only a small number of the police force was allowed to be formed. This condition was given to reduce the chance of war initiation by Germany.

10. (i) The three main functions of the Security Council are

(a) It maintains international peace and security in accordance with the principles and purposes of the United Nations.

(b) It investigates any dispute or situation which might lead to international friction.

(c) It recommends methods of adjusting such disputes or the terms of settlement.

(ii) The three main functions of World Health Organisation are as follows

(a) It helps countries to improve their health system by building up infrastructure.

(b) It gives important drugs needed for medical care.

(c) It launches programmes to immunise children against 6 major diseases such as measles, diphtheria, tetanus, tuberculosis, polio and whooping cough.

(iii) The two founders of the Non-Aligned Movement were Jawaharlal Nehru of India and Kwame Nkrumah of Ghana.

The two main objectives of Non-Aligned Movement are

(a) To remove all those factors and tendencies that could lead to war.

(b) To project the growing freedom of the newly independent Asian and African countries and help them to keep away from colonial domination.

ICSE Fully Solved

Solved Paper 2025

Time : 2 hrs
Marks : 80

History & Civics X

General Instructions

1. Attempt all questions from Part I (Compulsory). A total of 5 questions are to be attempted from Part II, 2 out of 3 questions from Section A and 3 out of 5 questions from Section B.
2. The intended marks for questions or parts of questions are given in brackets [].

Part - I [30 *Marks*]

Attempt all questions from this Part

1. Select the correct answers to the questions from the given options. **[1]**

(i) The Council of Ministers is collectively responsible to the............... .

(a) Lok Sabha (b) President
(c) Rajya Sabha (d) Prime Minister

(ii) Given below are details of a few Indian Citizens. **[1]**

Person	Age (In years)	Description
W	25	Is a famous journalist
X	45	Is an industrialist
Y	35	Has declared insolvency
Z	50	Has taken citizenship of another country

Select the one who is eligible to be a member of the Rajya Sabha.

(a) X (b) W
(c) Y (d) Z

(iii) With reference to the Supreme Court of India, complete the following **[1]**

Advisory Jurisdiction : Advice the President ::
Judicial Review : ....

(a) Review its own judgements.
(b) Review the judgements of the High Court.
(c) Review the laws passed by the Parliament.
(d) Review the administration of the Government.

(iv) Observe the given picture. In case of a similar unruly situation in the Lok Sabha, choose the action that may be taken by the Speaker. **[1]**

(a) Adjourn the House for lack of quorum.
(b) Dissolve the Lok Sabha.
(c) Adjourn the House for lack of discipline.
(d) Disqualify the members under Anti-defection law.

(v) If an Adjournment Motion is passed in the Lok Sabha .... **[1]**

(a) the Lok Sabha will be dissolved.
(b) the House will discuss a matter of urgent public importance.
(c) the President ends the session.
(d) the Government will fall.

(vi) Which emergency will be declared by the President if the security of the Nation is under threat? **[1]**

(a) General Emergency
(b) Financial Emergency
(c) Constitutional Emergency
(d) President's Rule

(vii) Read the statements given below and select the option that shows the correct relationship between (A) and (R). **[1]**

Assertion (A) Lord Curzon partitioned Bengal in 1905.

Reason (R) The Nationalists felt that the British wanted to divide the Hindus and the Muslims.

(a) (A) is true and (R) is false.
(b) (R) is true but (A) is false.
(c) Both (A) and (R) are independent of each other.
(d) (A) is the reason for (R).

(viii) Read the description and identify the person. **[1]**

He introduced the Subsidiary Alliance to expand the British control over India.

(a) Lord Dalhousie (b) Lord Canning
(c) Lord Wellesley (d) Lord Curzon

(ix) Identify the odd one out of the following Assertive Nationalists Leaders. **[1]**

(a) Bipin Chandra Pal (b) Lala Lajpat Rai
(c) Dadabhai Naoroji (d) Bal Gangadhar Tilak

(x) Who among the following is most associated with this picture? **[1]**

(a) Jyotiba Phule
(b) Raja Ram Mohan Roy
(c) Swami Dayanand Saraswati
(d) Aurobindo Ghosh

(xi) Identify the contributions of Subhash Chandra Bose **[1]**

P. Was the Supreme Commander of INA
Q. Signed the Lucknow Pact
R. Led the Quit India Movement
S. Founded the Forward Bloc

(a) P and Q (b) Q and R
(c) P and S (d) R and S

(xii) The market of a small industrial town *X* has been dominated by many products of foreign companies. The local residents decide to save the Indian industries by helping them increase their sales. Which method of the Assertive Nationalists must they follow to become self-reliant? **[1]**

(a) Passive Resistance (b) National Education
(c) Swadeshi (d) Revivalism

(xiii) Which of the following is not an objective of the United Nations Organisation? **[1]**

(a) Disarm (b) Disengage
(c) Decolonise (d) Develop

(xiv) Which agency of the United Nations Organisation is associated with this picture? **[1]**

(a) UNESCO (b) UNICEF
(c) WHO (d) ILO

(xv) Which of the following is a common cause for the rise of dictatorship? **[1]**

(a) Faith in Democracy (b) Economic Crisis
(c) Freedom of Press (d) Political Stability

(xvi) Which of the following causes of the First World War is connected to this headline? **[1]**

The Washington Times
SUNDAY EVENING EDITION
SERB STUDENT ASSASSINATES ARCHDUKE AND HIS DUCHESS

(a) Imperialism (b) Aggressive Nationalism
(c) Armament Race (d) Sarajevo Crisis

2. (i) Mention any two powers of the Prime Minister with reference to the Cabinet. **[2]**

(ii) Imagine you are an Early Nationalist leader. Mention any two methods you would follow to fight against the British. **[2]**

(iii) Mention any two factors that led to the formation of the Muslim League. **[2]**

(iv) Mention any two objectives of the Forward Bloc. **[2]**

(v) Mention any two ways in which the Treaty of Versailles affected the German Miliary Force. **[2]**

(vi) What is meant by the term Non-Alignment? **[2]**

(vii) When a judicial system is correctly calibrated, the law is applied by judges fearlessly, without favour or fear and with respect. That is why judicial security of tenure is so fundamental. It is also why judges must be properly paid without any interference from the Executive or Legislature.

-(The Need for Independent Judiciary) UNODC

From the passage, deduce and mention any two ways in which the Constitution ensures the independence of the Judiciary. **[2]**

Part - II

Section A [20 *Marks*]

Attempt any two questions from this Section.

3. The Parliament of India comprises the President and the two houses. With reference to the Indian Parliament, answer the following questions

(i) Mention any three circumstances under which the Parliament can make laws on subjects in the State List. **[3]**

(ii) Explain the following terms **[3]**

(a) Question Hour (b) Quorum

(c) No-confidence Motion

(iii) When can the term of the Lok Sabha be extended? **[4]**

Mention any three powers of the Lok Sabha which show its superiority over the Rajya Sabha.

4. The Executive Power of the country is in the President and Vice President. With reference to this, answer the following questions

(i) Explain the impeachment process through which the Parliament can remove the President from power. **[3]**

(ii) Mention any three powers of the Vice President in her/his role as the Chairman of the Rajya Sabha. **[3]**

(iii) With reference to the powers of President, mention **[4]**

(a) any two Financial Powers

(b) any two Executive Powers

5. The High Courts of India are the highest courts of appeal in each state. With reference to the High Courts of India, answer the following questions

(i) What is meant by the term Original Jurisdiction of the High Court? Mention any two cases which fall under this jurisdiction. **[3]**

(ii) Mention any two advantages of the Lok Adalat. Mention any one difference between the Sessions Court and the Court of the District Judge. **[3]**

(iii) Explain the following with reference to the High Court. **[4]**

(a) Revisory Jurisdiction (b) Court of Record

Section B [30 *Marks*]

Attempt any three questions from this Section.

6. The Revolt of 1857 was conscious beginning of the independence struggle against the British. With reference to this, answer the following questions

(i) What was the Doctrine of Lapse? Who introduced it? **[3]**

(ii) The British Government interfered in the social and religious matters of the Indians. Mention any three socio religious causes to justify this statement. **[3]**

(iii) Mention any four military causes which led to this revolt. **[4]**

7. The oppressive British colonial rule led to the growth of nationalism in India. With reference to this answer the following questions

(i) The repressive policies of Lord Lytton became a catalyst to the growth of nationalism. Mention any three of his repressive policies to justify this statement. **[3]**

(ii) Mention any three ways in which the Press promoted nationalism. **[3]**

(iii) Who presided over the second session of the Indian National Congress? Mention any three objectives of the Congress. **[4]**

8. Look at the given picture and answer the questions that follows.

Tears of Blood : When 1,650 Bullets Changed India Forever

—*The Times of India, April 2019*

(i) Identify the above incident. Which Gandhian movement did it lead to? Which incident led to the suspension of that movement? **[3]**

(ii) Mention any three repressive provisions of the Rowlatt Act. **[3]**

(iii) Mention the following. **[4]**

(a) Any two causes of the Quit India Movement.

(b) Any two causes of the Civil Disobedience Movement.

9. Read the passage given and answer the following questions.

In an effort to secure resources for its expanding industries, Japan invaded the Northern Chinese province of Manchuria. Although many Western nations protested the Japanese action, most members of the League of Nations, including Canada, opposed any form of military intervention to defend Chinese sovereignty. A League of Nations commission, headed by the British diplomat Lord Lytton, was dispatched to Manchuria to investigate.

—Loyal Edmonton Regiment Museum

(i) How did the incident being described above become a cause for the Second World War? [3]

(ii) Mention any three reasons for Hitler's attack on Poland. [3]

(iii) Mention any four reasons for the failure of the League of Nations. [4]

10. The organs and the agencies of the United Nation Organisation work towards the development of the world. With reference to this, answer the following questions.

(i) What is the composition of the General Assembly? [3]

(ii) Mention any three functions of the International Court of Justice. [3]

(iii) Give the full form of UNICEF. Mention any three of its functions. [4]

Answers

1.

(i) (a)	(ii) (a)	(iii) (c)
(iv) (c)	(v) (b)	(vi) (a)
(vii) (d)	(viii) (a)	(ix) (c)
(x) (a)	(xi) (c)	(xii) (c)
(xiii) (b)	(xiv) (a)	(xv) (b)
(xvi) (d)		

2. (i) Two powers of the Prime Minister with reference to the cabinet are

- **Appointment and Allocation of Portfolios** The Prime Minister selects ministers and assigns them specific departments.
- **Presiding Over Cabinet Meetings** The Prime Minister leads discussions and ensures decisions align with government policies.

(ii) Two methods I would follow to fight against the British are

- **Petitions and Appeals** I submit petitions and requests to the British government to demand reforms and justice.
- **Public Meetings and Speeches** I organise meetings to raise awareness and encourage Indians to demand their rights peacefully.

(iii) Two factors that led to the formation of the Muslim League are

- **British Policy of Divide and Rule** The British encouraged communal divisions to weaken the nationalist movement.
- **Muslim Fear of Hindu Domination** Some Muslim leaders felt that their political and economic interests needed separate representation.

(iv) Two objectives of the Forward Bloc were

- **Complete Independence** To achieve full and immediate independence from British rule.
- **Radical, Social and Economic Reforms** To work for the upliftment of the poor through socialist policies and economic equality.

(v) Two ways in which the Treaty of Versailles affected the German military force were

- **Reduction in Army Size** The German army was limited to 100,000 soldiers, with no conscription allowed.
- **Ban on Heavy Weapons** Germany was prohibited from having tanks, submarines and an air force, weakening its military strength.

(vi) Non-Alignment refers to the foreign policy adopted by countries that chose to remain independent and not align with any major power blocs (USA or USSR) during the Cold War. It aimed at peaceful coexistence, economic development, and protecting national sovereignty.

(vii) Two ways in which the Constitution ensures the independence of the Judiciary are

- **Security of Tenure** Judges cannot be removed arbitrarily; they can only be removed through impeachment on grounds of proven misconduct.
- **Financial Independence** Judges' salaries and allowances are charged on the Consolidated Fund of India, ensuring they are not controlled by the Executive or Legislature.

3. (i) Three circumstances under which Parliament can make laws on subjects in the State List are

- **During a National Emergency** Under Article 249, Parliament can legislate on State List subjects when an emergency is declared.
- **When Rajya Sabha Passes a Resolution** If the Rajya Sabha declares, by a two-thirds majority, that a subject in the State List is of national importance, Parliament can legislate on it.

- **When States Request Parliament** If two or more states pass resolutions requesting Parliament to make a law on a State List subject, Parliament can legislate on it.

(ii) (a) **Question Hour** The first hour of a Parliamentary sitting where members ask questions to ministers regarding government policies and decisions.

(b) **Quorum** The minimum number of members required to be present in either House for proceedings to take place. In Lok Sabha, it is 1/10th of total number of members.

(c) **No-confidence Motion** A motion moved in Lok Sabha to test if the government still has majority support. If passed, the government must resign.

(iii) The term of the Lok Sabha can be extended by one year at a time during a National Emergency under Article 352.

Three powers of Lok Sabha that show its superiority over Rajya Sabha are

- **Control Over the Executive** The Council of Ministers is responsible to the Lok Sabha and it can be removed through a No-confidence Motion.
- **Financial Supremacy** Money Bills can only be introduced in the Lok Sabha and the Rajya Sabha cannot amend or reject them.
- **Final Decision in Case of Disagreements** In case of a disagreement over an Ordinary Bill, a joint session is held, where the Lok Sabha's larger strength ensures its dominance.

4. (i) The President of India can be removed through impeachment under Article 61 for violating the Constitution. The process involves

- **A charge** is initiated in either House of Parliament with one-fourth of the members signing a notice.
- **Investigation** The charges are investigated and the President is given an opportunity to defend.
- **Two-thirds Majority Required** If both Houses pass the resolution with a two-thirds majority, the President is removed from office.

(ii) Three powers of the Vice President as Chairman of the Rajya Sabha are

- **Presiding Over Sessions** The Vice President conducts and maintains order in the Rajya Sabha.
- **Deciding on Points of Order** The Vice President interprets rules of procedure and ensures smooth functioning of debates.
- **Casting Vote in Case of a Tie** If there is a tie in voting, the Vice President (as Chairman) casts the deciding vote.

These powers make the Vice President an important figure in the parliamentary system, ensuring efficiency and impartiality.

(iii) (a) Two financial powers of the President are

- **Money Bills Require Presidential Recommendation** No Money Bill can be introduced in Parliament without the President's approval.
- **Control Over the Contingency Fund** The President authorises emergency expenditures from the Contingency Fund of India.

(b) Two executive powers of the President are

- **Appointment Powers** The President appoints the Prime Minister, Governors, Chief Justice, Judges and other key officials.
- **Administration of Union Territories** The President directly administers Union Territories through Lieutenant Governors or Administrators.

5. (i) The Original Jurisdiction of a High Court refers to cases that can be directly filed in the High Court, rather than coming through an appeal from lower courts.

Two cases under this jurisdiction are

- **Disputes involving Fundamental Rights** The High Court can issue writs under Article 226 to protect citizens' rights.
- **Cases involving State Government and Individuals** The High Court can hear cases between the state government and private parties.

(ii) Two advantages of Lok Adalat are

- **Speedy and Low-Cost Justice** Cases are resolved quickly without expensive court procedures.
- **Binding Decisions with No Appeal** The decision of Lok Adalat is final, preventing unnecessary delays.

The difference between Sessions Court and the Court of the District Judge can be seen as

Session Court	Court of the District Judge
It deals with criminal cases like murder, robbery and serious offenses.	It handles civil cases like property disputes and contracts.

(iii) (a) **Revisory Jurisdiction** The High Court has the power of Revisory Jurisdiction, which allows it to review and correct decisions made by lower courts if they contain legal errors. If a subordinate court exceeds its authority or fails to follow proper legal procedures, the High Court can call for records, examine the case and make necessary corrections. This ensures that justice is administered fairly and that lower courts function within their prescribed limits. However, the High Court does not re-examine evidence but only checks for procedural and legal correctness.

(b) **Court of Record** The High Court is a Court of Record, meaning its judgements, decisions and legal proceedings are permanently recorded and can be used as legal precedents in future cases. These records hold binding authority over lower courts. Additionally, as a Court of Record, the High Court has the power to punish for contempt of court if someone disrespects or disobeys its rulings, ensuring the dignity of the judiciary.

6. (i) The Doctrine of Lapse was a policy introduced by Lord Dalhousie, the Governor-General of India. According to this doctrine, if a ruling king died without a biological heir, his kingdom would automatically be annexed by the British East India Company. Adopted sons were not recognised as legitimate heirs. Using this policy, the British annexed several princely states, including Satara, Jhansi, Nagpur and Awadh. This caused widespread resentment among Indian rulers and was one of the major political causes of the Revolt of 1857.

(ii) The British government interfered in the social and religious matters of Indians, which led to widespread dissatisfaction. The three socio-religious causes to justify this statement are

- **Interference in Religious Practices** The British banned Sati (1829) and discouraged child marriage, which was seen as an attack on Hindu customs and traditions.
- **Promotion of Christian Missionaries** The British encouraged Christian conversions, making Indians fear that their religion and cultural practices were under threat.
- **Social Discrimination** Indians were treated as inferior to the British, facing racial discrimination in jobs and administration, which created resentment among the people.

(iii) Four military causes which led to this revolt were

- **Discontent Among Sepoys** Indian soldiers (sepoys) were paid less, treated unfairly and had fewer promotion opportunities compared to British soldiers.
- **General Service Enlistment Act (1856)** This act forced sepoys to serve overseas, which was against Hindu religious beliefs, as crossing the sea (Kala Pani) was considered impure.
- **Greased Cartridge Incident** The new Enfield rifle cartridges were rumored to be greased with cow and pig fat, offending both Hindus and Muslims. Sepoys who refused to use them were punished, increasing their anger.
- **Annexation of Awadh** Many sepoys were from Awadh, which was annexed under the Doctrine of Lapse, leading to resentment among soldiers who had family ties to the region.

7. (i) Lord Lytton's repressive policies fueled nationalist sentiments in India. The three policies that became a catalyst for the growth of nationalism are

- **Vernacular Press Act (1878)** This act restricted the Indian press from publishing material against British rule, suppressing freedom of speech and limiting nationalist expressions.

- **Arms Act (1878)** This law prohibited Indians from possessing weapons without British permission, while Europeans were exempted, creating a sense of discrimination and weakening Indian resistance.
- **Extravagant Expenditure on Delhi Durbar** (1877) Despite a severe famine, Lytton hosted a lavish Delhi Durbar to celebrate Queen Victoria's title as Empress of India, showing British insensitivity toward the suffering of Indians.

(ii) Three ways in which the Indian press promoted nationalism were

- **Exposing British Policies** Newspapers like Kesari and The Hindu criticised British exploitation and called for reforms.
- **Uniting Indians** The press spread awareness about freedom movements, inspiring people across India to fight for independence.
- **Encouraging Political Participation** Nationalist leaders used newspapers to mobilise public opinion and urge Indians to join protests, boycotts and the Swadeshi movement.

(iii) The second session of the Indian National Congress (INC) was presided over by Dadabhai Naoroji in 1886 in Calcutta.

The Indian National Congress (INC) was formed in 1885 by A.O. Hume with the goal of achieving political rights and self-governance for Indians. Its three key objectives were

- **Promoting National Unity** The INC aimed to bring together Indians from different regions, religions and communities to develop a common national identity.
- **Political Awareness and Representation** It worked to educate Indians about their rights and demanded greater representation in government through constitutional means.
- **Social and Economic Reforms** The Congress sought to address issues like poverty, taxation and economic exploitation caused by British rule while promoting Indian industries and education.

8. (i) The incident described is the Jallianwala Bagh Massacre on 13th April, 1919, when General Dyer ordered troops to fire on a peaceful gathering in Amritsar, killing thousands.

This incident led to nationwide outrage and was a major cause of the Non-Cooperation Movement (1920-1922) launched by Mahatma Gandhi.

The movement was later suspended due to the Chauri Chaura Incident (1922), where violent protesters burned a police station, killing policemen. Gandhiji, being a strong advocate of non-violence, called off the movement to prevent further bloodshed.

(ii) The Rowlatt Act was passed by the Imperial Legislative Council in March 1919 and was strongly opposed by Indian leaders. Three repressive provisions of the Rowlatt Act were

- **Arrest without Warrant** The government could arrest and detain any person suspected of anti-British activities without a trial for up to two years.
- **In Camera Trials** Trials could be conducted in secret (closed-door hearings) without allowing the accused to know the evidence against them.
- **Curb on Freedoms** The Act restricted freedom of speech, press, and movement and protests against the government were considered illegal.

(iii) (a) Two causes of the Quit India Movement were

- **Failure of the Cripps Mission** (1942) The British government sent the Cripps Mission to offer Dominion Status after World War II, but Congress rejected it as it did not promise full independence.
- **Japanese Threat** The Japanese Army was advancing towards India, increasing fears of an invasion. Indian leaders saw this as a chance to force the British to leave India immediately.

(b) Two causes of the Civil Disobedience Movement were

- **Simon Commission Boycott** (1927) The Simon Commission was sent to review India's political situation, but no Indian members were included. This angered Indian leaders, leading to widespread protests.
- **Declaration of Purna Swaraj** (1929) The Lahore Session of Congress (1929), under Jawaharlal Nehru's presidency, declared Complete Independence (Purna Swaraj) as India's goal, leading to mass protests against British rule.

9. (i) The Manchurian Incident (1931) exposed the weakness of the League of Nations, as it failed to take strong action against Japan. Despite investigations, no military intervention was made, encouraging aggressive expansionism. This emboldened other axis powers like Germany and Italy, showing that international bodies would not stop territorial invasions. Hitler and Mussolini saw this as a green light for their own ambitions, leading to further aggression in Europe and Africa. The failure of diplomacy and unchecked invasions ultimately escalated tensions, contributing to World War II.

(ii) Three reasons for Hitler's attack on Poland were

- **Reclaiming Lost Territory** Hitler wanted to take back Polish lands that Germany lost after World War I under the Treaty of Versailles.
- **Lebensraum** (Living Space) He aimed to expand German territory for its growing population.
- **Weak Western Response** Britain and France followed a policy of appeasement, making Hitler believe they would not intervene.

(iii) Four reasons for the failure of the League of Nations were

- **Lack of Cooperation Among Member Nations** Countries prioritised their own interests rather than supporting the League's principles of collective security. Even member nations ignored League decisions when it did not suit them.
- **Failure to Prevent Aggression** The League remained inactive when Poland seised Lithuania (1920) and Italy refused intervention in the Greece-Italy conflict (1923). This weakened its authority.
- **Ineffectiveness Against Expansionist Powers** The League failed to act when Italy annexed Abyssinia, Japan took Manchuria and Germany took Austria and Czechoslovakia. This encouraged further aggression.
- **Loss of Faith in the League** The League's inability to stop conflicts led nations to lose trust in it. Instead of maintaining peace, countries started preparing for war, leading to World War II.

10. (i) The General Assembly is the main deliberative body of the United Nations, where all member countries are represented. It consists of 193 member nations, with each nation having one vote, regardless of size or power. Every member country can send five representatives, but they still hold only one vote. The General Assembly meets annually and can hold special sessions in case of urgent matters. Important decisions, such as electing non-permanent members of the Security Council or approving the UN budget, require a two-thirds majority, while others are decided by a simple majority.

(ii) The International Court of Justice (ICJ) is the judicial organ of the UN, headquartered in The Hague, Netherlands. Its three main functions are

- **Settling Legal Disputes** It resolves disputes between member nations based on international law.
- **Advisory Opinions** It provides legal advice to the General Assembly, Security Council and UN agencies.
- **Interpreting International Treaties** The ICJ interprets treaties and agreements, ensuring their proper implementation.

(iii) The full form of UNICEF is United Nations International Children's Emergency Fund. Although its name later changed to United Nations Children's Fund, the acronym UNICEF remains the same.

Three major functions of UNICEF are

- **Child Healthcare and Immunisation** It provides vaccines to protect children against diseases like polio, measles and tuberculosis.
- **Education and Literacy Programs** It promotes education for underprivileged children, especially girls and disabled children.
- **Emergency Relief** UNICEF provides food, clean water and medical aid during natural disasters, wars and crises.